Assembly Programming and Computer Architecture for Software Engineers

Brian R. Hall
Champlain College, Burlington, VT

Kevin J. Slonka
Pennsylvania Highlands Community College, Johnstown, PA

Prospect Press

Founded in 2014, Prospect Press serves the academic disciplines of Computer and Information Systems by publishing innovative textbooks across the curriculum including introductory, emerging, and upper level courses. Prospect Press offers reasonable prices by selling directly to students. Prospect Press provides tight relationships between authors, publisher, and adopters that many larger publishers are unable to offer in today's publishing environment. Based in Burlington, Vermont, Prospect Press distributes titles worldwide. We welcome new authors to send proposals or inquiries to Beth.Golub@ProspectPressVT.com.

Editor: Beth Lang Golub
Production Management: Kathy Bond Borie
Cover Design: Annie Clark
Cover Illustration: Hanah Leo

eTextbook ISBN: 978-1-943153-31-2
  • Available from Redshelf.com and VitalSource.com

Printed Paperback ISBN: 978-1-943153-32-9
  • Available from Redshelf.com and CreateSpace.com

For more information, visit
http://prospectpressvt.com/titles/hall-assembly-programming/

About the cover
Why the mountains on the cover? Mountains are both beautiful and forbidding, much like the two foundational topics addressed throughout this book: Assembly Programming and Computer Architecture. They are the source of a challenging journey that opens your eyes to a heightened view of computing. Why the metallic waterfall on the cover? That is just a metaphor for the deep dive into the content that awaits.

Contents

Preface

Mission of the text

Assembly Programming and Computer Architecture for Software Engineers is an educational examination of Assembly programming and computer architecture. We approach these topics from a practical point of view, addressing *why* and *how* questions throughout the text. We begin by laying the foundation of computer language and computer architecture, and then we delve into Assembly programming as a mechanism for gaining a better understanding of computer architecture, and how Assembly can be used for software development.

Most of the existing books on computer architecture have one or more of the following disadvantages: (1) based on a non-mainstream architecture; (2) written for computer and electrical engineers as opposed to computer scientists and software engineers; (3) focused on a single platform-specific development environment; (4) over-priced; and (5) lacking in practical content. We wanted to give our students something better.

Audience

Assembly Programming and Computer Architecture for Software Engineers is primarily intended for undergraduate students in computer science and software engineering programs. Prerequisites for this book include introductory computing courses and a solid programming foundation up to and including data structures, preferably in C/C++. Working professionals are also likely to find this book helpful for independent learning and for writing both low-level and high-level code.

Book Development and Pedagogical Approach

The notion to write a book arises every so often in an academic career, with one driver for book ideas being the courses we teach. Both of us teach a course on computer architecture, which has been a staple of computer science and software engineering programs for decades. We also teach in programs where applied and practical skills are foremost.

During our doctoral studies, we made passing comments about writing a book together and at some point we decided that doing so was a real possibility. Writing a book takes a lot of effort, thus our collaboration was essential. So after several years teaching computer architecture and discussing ideas with our wonderful Prospect Press partner, Beth Golub, we arrived at a basic but unique concept. We would write a book for teachers, students, and professionals seeking educational content for computer architecture that overcomes the previously stated disadvantages. Our book is based on mainstream architecture(s), written for computer scientists and software engineers, written for multiple development environments, well priced, and loaded with practical content.

Many hours, days, and weeks have been poured into this text and, in particular, the programs. Writing Assembly code can be infuriating, compelling, and fun, as you are about to discover. Writing about such a complex topic in a clear and efficient manner was also a particular challenge, as was choosing what aspects to cover and when— a classic issue with computing content.

For many computing students, learning about computer architecture via Assembly programming is an advantageous approach. While learning about architecture, useful programming skills are fostered. We knew that a book based on such an approach would help in our courses and was likely to provide a much-needed resource for similar institutions, educators, and students. We did our best and we hope you enjoy learning about Assembly programming and computer architecture the way we enjoy teaching the topics.

Organization and Objectives

CHAPTERS 1 AND 2 discuss computer language and computer architecture fundamentals.
CHAPTERS 3 THROUGH 5 introduce x86 and x86_64 Assembly syntax and a variety of instructions.
CHAPTERS 6 THROUGH 8 cover the more complex topics of functions, structures, and floating-point operations.

CHAPTERS 9 AND 10 show advanced ways to use Assembly with high-level languages and system software, as well as introduce other advanced aspects of computer and system architecture.

CHAPTER 11 explores architectures other than x86

CHAPTER 12 introduces basic hardware principles and components.

Chapter Objectives

Chapter 1: Describe computer language translation
Chapter 2: Identify computer and processor components
Chapter 3: Distinguish between Assembly syntaxes
Chapter 4: Perform basic arithmetic
Chapter 5: Control program flow
Chapter 6: Follow function calling conventions
Chapter 7: Use strings and structures
Chapter 8: Execute floating-point operations
Chapter 9: Integrate low-level and high-level code
Chapter 10: Issue system calls
Chapter 11: Compare computer architectures
Chapter 12: Build simple circuits and devices

Supplements

Chapters 1 and 2, Chapter 6, Chapter 8, and Chapter 10 have additional supplements that provide programs and content for the respective chapters.

Appendices

The INTRODUCTION TO THE APPENDICES and APPENDICES A THROUGH I provide practical information such as resources, translating between Assembly syntaxes, development environment setup, disassembling, debugging, linking Assembly and C++, following calling conventions, using CPUID, performing Decimal and ASCII arithmetic, and using intrinsics.

Resources

- Book website: http://www.prospectpressvt.com/titles/hall-assembly-programming/
- Book repository: https://github.com/brianrhall/Assembly
- Instructor resources: http://prospectpressvt.com/titles/hall-assembly-programming/instructor-resources/
- Student resources: http://prospectpressvt.com/titles/hall-assembly-programming/student-resources/
- Brian's website: http://www.brianrhall.net
- Kevin's website: http://www.kevinslonka.com
- For content-specific resources see the APPENDICES (particularly the INTRODUCTION TO THE APPENDICES) and the WEB RESOURCES links at the beginning of each chapter.

Acknowledgements

We owe a debt of thanks to the people who have been supportive of our efforts in writing this book. Thank you to the *teachers* who have led us to where we are in our careers. Thank you to *Beth Golub* for giving us the opportunity to publish with Prospect Press and for her wonderful guidance throughout the writing process. Thank you to our *reviewers* for taking time to provide valuable feedback. They include:

John Doyle, Indiana University Southeast
Hai Jiang, Arkansas State University
Saad Khattak, University of Ontario Institute of Technology
Susan Lincke, University of Wisconsin - Parkside
Ray Toal, Loyola Marymount University

Thank you to our *colleagues* and *students* for putting up with us clamoring so much about the book over the past two years. And most of all, thank you to our *families* -- for Brian, *Narine* and *Aven*; for Kevin, his fiancé, *Kelli*. Without your tolerance and willingness to sacrifice precious time together, this work would have not been possible. Thank you.

Brian and Kevin

## CHAPTER 1

Language and Data Fundamentals

Objectives

- Distinguish between computing languages
- Identify uses of Assembly programming
- Convert values between number systems
- Solve basic arithmetic problems
- Describe character storage methods
- Evaluate Boolean expressions
- Explain the basics of computer operation

Outline

1. Web Resources
2. Welcome
3. Introduction
4. Computing Languages
   a. Language Relationships
   b. Translation Pipeline
   c. File and Utility Relationships
   d. Why Assembly?
5. Data Representation
   a. Number Systems
   b. Integer Storage
   c. Unsigned Integer Storage
   d. Signed Integer Storage
   e. Character Storage
6. Boolean Expressions
7. 3-bit Computer Example
8. Summary
9. Key Terms
10. Code Review
11. Questions
    a. Short Answer
    b. True/False
12. Assignments

Web Resources

Wikis

- https://en.wikibooks.org/wiki/X86_Assembly (Assembly Programming Overview)
- https://en.wikibooks.org/wiki/X86_Disassembly (Assembler and Disassembler Overview)

Developer

- http://www.unicode.org
- http://www.unicode.org/charts/PDF/U0000.pdf (ASCII)
- http://devimages.apple.com/llvm/videos/LLVM_Assembler_Infrastructure.mov (LLVM-MC Overview)

Videos

- Video 1.1: Welcome (https://youtu.be/HBwgXY88hyc)
- Video 1.2: Signing Integers (https://youtu.be/vHijiZMbj9E)
- Video 1.3: A 3-bit Computer Example (https://youtu.be/gYczcmDywag)

Welcome (Video 1.1: https://youtu.be/HBwgXY88hyc)

Welcome to *Assembly Programming and Computer Architecture for Software Engineers*! The purpose of this book is to provide an educational examination of Assembly programming and computer architecture. Our goal is to approach these topics from a practical point of view. We address questions of *why* and *how* throughout the text. The first two chapters lay the foundation of computer language and computer architecture. The rest of the book uses Assembly programming to help you gain a better understanding of computer architecture, and guides you in using Assembly for software development. What makes this book unique is our multifaceted approach.

- This book is based on a dominant architecture in the computing market—x86 and x86_64—and what you learn will be transferable to other architectures.
- The programming examples are unique in that we provide code for three common assemblers: GAS, MASM, and NASM. This allows for learning on any OS platform: Mac, Windows, and Linux. This approach also ensures code examples in both AT&T and Intel syntax.
- We provide context and examples in both 32 and 64-bit, both of which are useful for a programmer.
- The Appendices provide practical information to help you learn and use the technologies associated with Assembly and architecture.
- Chapter Supplements provide a deeper dive into topics as necessary.
- We provide links to wikis, developer resources, and videos to assist in further exploration of topics.
- We use Attention notes, Programming notes, and Learning notes throughout the text to guide the reader in beneficial ways.

| ⬡ ! ATTENTION | ▮ PROGRAMMING | 📖 LEARNING |

> ⬡ ! ATTENTION: The GNU Assembler (GAS) is primarily a Linux-based assembler used by the GNU project and has been developed since 1987. GAS is part of the GNU Binutils package and is used to assemble the Linux kernel amongst other software. The Netwide Assembler (NASM) is a Linux-based open-source assembler/disassembler for x86 and x86_64 that has been developed since 1996 by very small team of developers. The Microsoft Macro Assembler (MASM) is a proprietary assembler for Microsoft's operating systems, which is packaged with Visual Studio. MASM has been developed since 1981.

- For the sake of our students, we have focused on keeping this text educational, useful, and affordable.

We hope you enjoy this book and find it beneficial in your education and career. Happy learning and coding!

Brian

Kevin

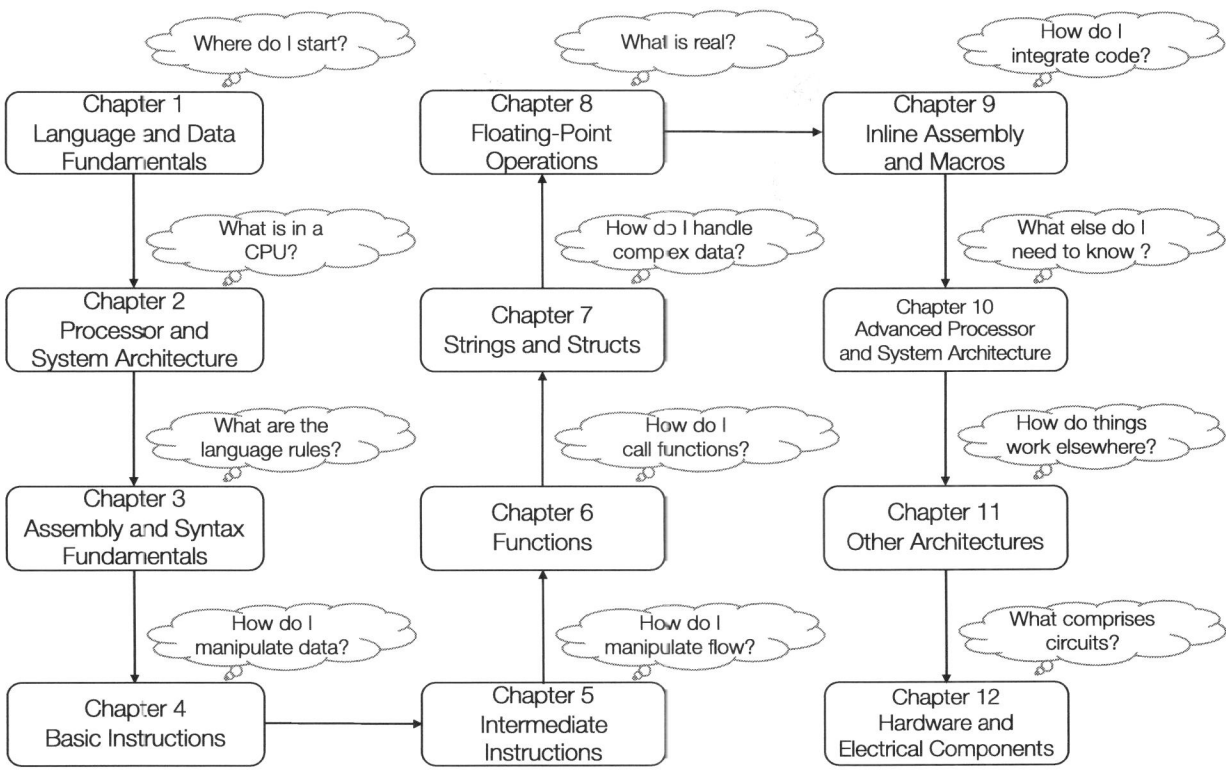

Figure 1.1 Chapter roadmap

Introduction

The purpose of this chapter is to introduce fundamental concepts of computer programs and computer architecture. We cover relationships between computing languages and Assembly language's place in the language hierarchy. We discuss the basics of data representation, number systems, and Boolean expressions. Additionally, we illustrate chapter concepts with a 3-bit computer system. This chapter will prepare you for a deeper dive into a specific architecture, x86/x86_64 in **CHAPTER 2**, and for understanding Assembly fundamentals beginning in **CHAPTER 3**.

Computing Languages

Language Relationships

As programmers, we live in a world of computer languages. Understanding where Assembly fits in the computer language hierarchy is important. Typically, we write code in a **high-level language**, which simply means that the statements are roughly English-like. Throughout this text we use the high-level language C++ in examples. An example of the English-likeness of a high-level language would be the if...else control structure.

Example 1.1 if...else control structure

English-likeness	C++

`if (this is true) {`
`    perform this series of actions`
`}`
`else {`
`    perform this series of actions`
`}`
	`if ( x == y ) {`
	`    cout << "X and Y are the same";`
	`}`
	`else {`
	`    cout  << "X and Y are different";`
	`}`

High-level languages and the abstraction they provide are great for humans, but the statements must be translated from high-level to **machine-level** for execution by a computer. Modern computer processors are made up of billions of transistors that switch between allowing (1) or not allowing (0) the flow of electrical current. A system based on two states is called a binary system. Processors must be fed instructions in numeric binary form; so how do we get from high-level to Assembly to machine-level?

Translation Pipeline

At this point, we want to illustrate the process of moving from high to low level. Using a practical approach, we accomplish this by thinking of the process as a **translation pipeline** (Figure 1.2).

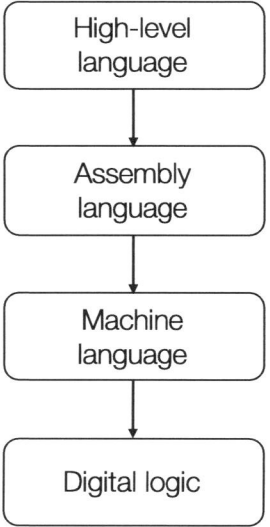

Figure 1.2 Translation pipeline

> ⬡ **!** ATTENTION: The "virtual machine" concept is a more abstract way of thinking about levels in machine organization and is used in classical examples. You may encounter the term in other texts and explanations of multilevel design. Virtual machines can be implemented in hardware or software.

A program written in a high-level language must be translated in order to run at a lower level. Translation has two forms: (1) **interpreting**, which is translating line-by-line as the program executes, and (2) **compiling**, which is translating all the code in a single step before execution. An example of a high-level interpreted language is Python. An example of a high-level compiled language is C++.

A high-level language statement such as `int x = y + 2;` has a one-to-many relationship with machine language; that is, each high-level statement corresponds to multiple Assembly and machine instructions.

Assembly is an intermediate form in the translation pipeline. A high-level program is translated into Assembly and the Assembly is further translated into machine language based on a processor's instruction set architecture. The process of Assembly code being translated into machine language is often called encoding. The inverse process of machine language being translated into Assembly is often called decoding.

Assembly language statements have a one-to-one relationship with machine language; that is, each Assembly language instruction corresponds to a single machine language instruction. Machine language instructions are typically represented in an intermediate numeric form such as hexadecimal, which is then translated and implemented physically as binary on the hardware, what we call digital logic.

PROGRAMMING: Some compilers, such as Microsoft's C compiler, translate high-level code directly to machine language, and creating Assembly is an option. Other compilers, such as GCC, translate to Assembly first, then the Assembly code is translated to machine code.

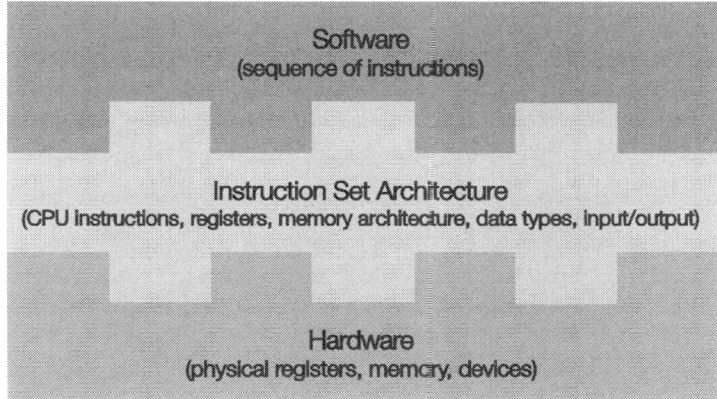

Figure 1.3 Instruction set architecture

An **instruction set architecture (ISA)** is the programming-related aspect of **computer architecture**. The ISA specifies the instructions, registers, memory architecture, data types, and other attributes native to a particular processor that are available to a programmer. Think of an ISA as the language a computer speaks. As shown in Figure 1.3, an ISA facilitates communication between software and hardware.

We can think of instruction set architectures as complex or reduced. **Complex instruction set computing (CISC)** architectures have instructions that are of varying length (in bytes) and are complex in the sense that a single instruction may perform more than one task (e.g., access a memory location and perform arithmetic). An alternative ISA design is **reduced instruction set computing (RISC)** in which all instructions are the same length and perform only one task (e.g., access a memory location).

x86 and x86_64 are CISC architectures, while the majority of other ISAs are RISC architectures. CISC attributes of x86 will be shown when instructions are discussed in more detail in **CHAPTERS 4 AND 5**. Also, when **disassembly** examples are provided, such as in **CHAPTERS 6** and **11**, the varying length and complexity of instructions will be evident. You can also see variable length instructions in the **CHAPTER 1 PAGE 7** PROGRAMMING note on relocatable machine language.

 PROGRAMMING: Disassembly is the Assembly code output produced by a disassembler after decoding an object file containing machine language (i.e., decoding machine language bit sequences into Assembly instructions). Most assemblers, compilers, debuggers, and development environments, such as NASM (ndisasm), GDB, LLVM, Xcode, and Visual Studio provide disassembly options. Independent disassemblers are also available such as Capstone, IDA, objdump, and otool. To learn how to disassemble object files, see **APPENDIX C: DISASSEMBLY**.

Common 32-bit x86 ISA names	Common 64-bit x86 ISA names
x86	x64
IA-32	x86_64
i386	Intel: IA-32e (past), Intel 64 (current)
	AMD: AMD64

> ⚠ ATTENTION: The 32-bit version of the x86 instruction set is commonly known as IA-32 (Intel Architecture 32-bit). IA-32 is synonymous with i386. The 64-bit version of the x86 instruction set is commonly known as x64 or x86_64, but other names are used depending on manufacturer. The 64-bit version of x86 should not be confused with the 64-bit Intel Architecture (IA-64) used in the Itanium line of processors as it is a completely different instruction set architecture. IA-32 and x64 are not compatible with IA-64.

Table 1.1 provides an example of the translation process. The high-level C++ statement `sum = 5;` assumes that an integer called sum exists. In Table 1.1, the statement is translated into Assembly using the GNU Assembler (GAS), which uses AT&T syntax. The statement is further encoded into machine language based on the instruction set architecture for an Intel 32-bit (IA-32) processor. The machine language instruction is in hexadecimal form, which is digitally (physically) implemented in binary.

Table 1.1 The translation process

Level	Language	Code
High-level language	C++	`sum = 5;`
Assembly language	GNU Assembler, AT&T syntax	`movl $0x5, -0x8(%ebp)`
Machine language	IA-32	`C745F805000000`
Digital logic	Binary (physical implementation)	`1100 0111 0100 0101 1111 1000 0000` `0101 0000 0000 0000 0000 0000 0000`

Next, we reinforce the translation process by presenting three encoded Assembly instructions in Example 1.2. Here, the specifics are not the focus, but rather the concept. **CHAPTERS 4** and **5** discuss instructions in further detail.

Assume we have the 32-bit Assembly instruction: `MOV eax, 5`. If abstracted to a higher-level statement, this is similar to saying something like `variable = 5;` but more specifically we are saying to move (copy) the immediate value 5 to the *eax* register in Intel Assembly syntax. The MOV instruction is an opcode and *eax* is a register, both of which are specified as part of the IA-32 instruction set architecture. The operation of moving an immediate value to the *eax* register has a specific machine language counterpart, which encoded in hexadecimal is B8. The immediate value operand becomes part of the instruction.

Example 1.2 Assembly instructions encoded into Intel 32-bit machine language

Assembly language	Machine language
`MOV eax, 5`	`B8 05 00 00 00`
`MOV eax, 32555`	`B8 2B 7F 00 00`
`MOV ebx, 5     ;a different register`	`BB 05 00 00 00`

Machine language is numeric, so it is helpful to understand number systems, specifically hexadecimal and binary. Machine language is also specific to a processor. Processor families understand a common machine language, so code written for x86 or x86_64 processors will run on any processor that is part of that family.

> PROGRAMMING: Assembly code is not portable across processor families. For example, code written for the x86 processor family will not run on processors such as SUN Sparc, IBM 370, and ARM Cortex.

The x86/x86_64 processor family includes Intel processors such as Pentium, Core-Duo, and Core i7, and AMD processors such as Athlon, Phenom, and Opteron. Both Intel and AMD implement the x86 instruction set as part of their processor design, but the processor design techniques used to implement the instruction set, also known as the **microarchitecture**, are very different.

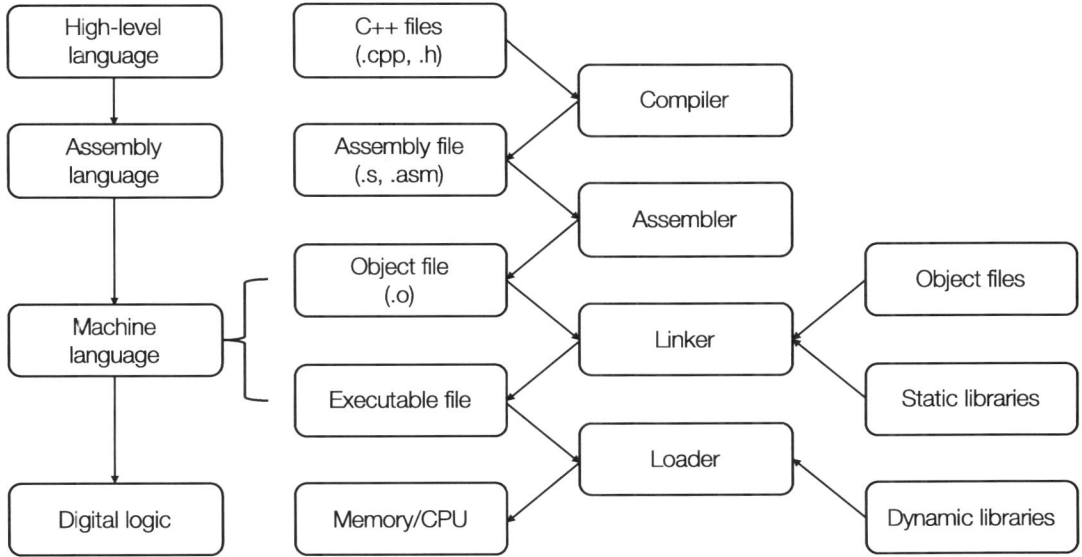

Figure 1.4 File and utility relationships

File and Utility Relationships

Considering file and utility relationships in relation to the translation pipeline is also helpful. Figure 1.4 illustrates the language levels in relation to files, and also the role of computer utilities that translate one language into another.

The role of a **compiler** is to translate high-level source code into the intermediate form of Assembly based on the processor's instruction set. The role of the **assembler** is to encode Assembly code into **object code**, which is relocatable machine language formatted for a specific operating system (OS) platform. Table 1.2 lists common object file formats by OS platform. The role of the **linker** is to combine multiple object files and static libraries into a single executable file. The role of the **loader** is to take the executable instructions contained in the executable file produced by the linker, along with dynamic libraries, and load the machine code into memory for execution by the central processing unit (CPU).

> PROGRAMMING: What do we mean by "relocatable" machine language? When Assembly code is assembled into object code, the code is in a generic form with the first instruction starting at address 0x0h and subsequent instruction addresses are offsets based on the preceding instructions' sizes in bytes. When the program is actually loaded into memory, the first instruction will have a legitimate address, with the subsequent instruction addresses based on the offsets.

Relocatable machine language				Running machine language			
main:				nain:			
00000000	b80a000000	movl	$0xa, %eax	0x1fac <+0>:	movl	$0xa, %eax
00000005	48	decl	%eax	0x1fb1 <+5>:	decl	%eax
00000006	bb05000000	movl	$0x5, %ebx	0x1fb2 <+6>:	movl	$0x5, %ebx
0000000b	c3	retl		0x1fb7 <+11>:	retl	

Table 1.2 Common object file formats by OS platform

Windows	macOS	Linux
COFF, PE, Win32, Win64	Mach-o	ELF, a.out (deprecated)

Why Assembly?

An important and reasonable question that we must ask and answer is "Why learn Assembly?" What is the benefit of knowing low-level details if we can write code in high-level languages? The answer to these questions is multifaceted.

- Learning Assembly will enhance your understanding of computer operation. Assembly is a mechanism by which a programmer can learn details of computer hardware, CPU components, memory organization, and the interactions among these elements of computer architecture.
- Programmers make extensive use of a **debugger**, a utility for troubleshooting code, when writing programs. Debuggers provide Assembly, disassembly, register, and memory information so that the programmer can step through programs at a low level. Understanding Assembly language and computer architecture will help with identifying and fixing code bugs.
- Knowledge of Assembly and computer operation helps a programmer make informed decisions about implementation at high and low levels. A programmer can take advantage of the hardware and optimize for efficiency.
- Knowledge of Assembly removes layers of abstraction from tasks such as bit manipulation and function (procedure) calls.
- Some areas of software development rely on intimate knowledge of Assembly, such as programming for embedded devices, programming device drivers, and system (OS) programming.

Learning Assembly will give you a fuller understanding of how computers operate and how code executes, which you can use to your advantage. Additionally, from the vantage point of an engineer there is nothing quite as satisfying as talking directly to the processor.

 LEARNING: Refer to the BUBBLE SORT EXAMPLE at the end of the chapter to consider differences in file sizes and memory footprint for comparable programs written in Assembly and C++.

Data Representation

Number Systems

Most computers operate physically in binary form. For example, a memory cell is either charged or not charged, a location on disk is magnetized or not magnetized, a transistor in a CPU is either allowing current flow or not allowing current flow. Therefore, binary (1s and 0s) is used to represent data at the lowest level. However, binary is typically difficult for humans to interpret quickly, so other number systems serve as shorthand representations of binary.

 LEARNING: Fundamentally, binary is the only number system a computer understands with regard to execution of machine language. So why is binary the number system of computing?
Answer: The reliability of binary representation and bi-stable environments.
Physical characteristics of binary hardware components:

- The component has two stable energy states, representing 0 and 1. Examples: full on/full off, fully charged/fully discharged, positively charged/negatively charged, magnetized/non-magnetized, reflects light/does not reflect light;
- The two states are separated by an energy barrier (they cannot become each other or be confused);
- Possible to sense the state of the component;
- Possible to switch between the states.

Imagine the complexity of storing a value in a computer based on the decimal or hexadecimal system. A component would have to be able to represent 10 or 16 different states. Using two states makes it much easier to represent physical properties, which in a typical computer are electrical.

Reading and writing low-level code requires programmers to be adept at number systems and formats. The most common formats are binary, octal, decimal, and hexadecimal. Each number system has a base, which indicates the number of symbols available for a digit. Table 1.3 shows details of common number systems. Decimal and hexadecimal are the most common number system formats used in Assembly code.

Table 1.3 Number systems

Number System	Base	Digits
Binary	2	0 1
Octal	8	0 1 2 3 4 5 6 7
Decimal	10	0 1 2 3 4 5 6 7 8 9
Hexadecimal	16	0 1 2 3 4 5 6 7 8 9 A B C D E F

Integer Storage

To programmers, the binary number system means 0/1 or false/true. A binary digit is a **bit**. Bits are combined into **bytes** to store data like integer (whole number) values. Table 1.4 presents the bits, bytes, terms, and ranges associated with **unsigned** and **signed** integer storage. Unsigned means only positive integers are represented, while signed means positive and negative integers are represented.

Table 1.4 Integer storage sizes

Bits	Bytes	Term	Unsigned range	Signed range
8 bits	1 byte	byte	0 to $2^8 - 1$	-2^7 to $2^7 - 1$
16 bits	2 bytes	word	0 to $2^{16} - 1$	-2^{15} to $2^{15} - 1$
32 bits	4 bytes	doubleword	0 to $2^{32} - 1$	-2^{31} to $2^{31} - 1$
64 bits	8 bytes	quadword	0 to $2^{64} - 1$	-2^{63} to $2^{63} - 1$
80 bits	10 bytes	tenbyte	0 to $2^{80} - 1$	-2^{79} to $2^{79} - 1$
128 bits	16 bytes	double quadword	0 to $2^{128} - 1$	-2^{127} to $2^{127} - 1$

When multiple bits are combined, the leftmost bit is the most significant bit (MSB) and the rightmost bit is the least significant bit (LSB). In the 1-byte example below, if the LSB (bit 0) is changed the value is only altered by 1, but if the MSB (bit 7) is changed the value is altered by 128.

MSB							LSB
0	1	1	0	1	0	0	1
7				bit			0

Unsigned Integer Storage

Two useful skills when dealing with number systems is the ability to convert between systems and the ability to perform basic arithmetic like addition. Table 1.5 shows unsigned integer equivalents in decimal, binary, and hexadecimal.

Table 1.5 Number system unsigned equivalents

Decimal	Hex	Binary
0	0	0000
1	1	0001
2	2	0010
3	3	0011
4	4	0100
5	5	0101
6	6	0110
7	7	0111
8	8	1000
9	9	1001
10	A	1010
11	B	1011
12	C	1100
13	D	1101
14	E	1110
15	F	1111

The following nine examples demonstrate ways to perform a variety of unsigned conversions and additions:

1. Binary ↔ decimal: using a scale of 2^n, where n = *bits* -1
2. Binary → decimal: using positional notation
3. Decimal → binary: using division
4. Calculating number of bits for a decimal value
5. Binary addition
6. Hexadecimal ↔ binary ↔ decimal
7. Hexadecimal → decimal: using positional notation
8. Decimal → hexadecimal: using division
9. Hexadecimal addition

 ATTENTION: Decimal values can be converted to any other base in one of the following ways:
- Scale of *base^n* (see Examples 1.3 and 1.8)
- Positional notation: $decimal = (D_{(n-1)} \times B^{(n-1)}) + (D_{(n-2)} \times B^{(n-2)}) + \ldots + (D_1 \times B^1) + (D_0 \times B^0)$ where B = *base*, D = *digit*, and n = *number of digits* (see Examples 1.4 and 1.9)
- Division (see Examples 1.5 and 1.10)

In Example 1.3, we show how to convert an 8-bit value between binary and decimal using a Base 2 scale. The conversion is $00010111_2 = 23_{10}$. Essentially, you add up the decimal values based on the scale where a 1 exists in the binary sequence.

Example 1.3 Binary ↔ decimal (scale 2^n)

	MSB							LSB
Bits	0	0	0	1	0	1	1	1
Base 2 scale	2^7	2^6	2^5	2^4	2^3	2^2	2^1	2^0
Decimal values	128	64	32	16	8	4	2	1
Add values				16+		4+	2+	1
Decimal total								23

In Example 1.4, we show how to convert from binary to decimal using positional notation. The conversion is $00010111_2 = 23_{10}$.

Example 1.4 Binary → decimal (positional notation)

$$decimal = (D_{(n-1)} \times 2^{(n-1)}) + (D_{(n-2)} \times 2^{(n-2)}) + \dots + (D_1 \times 2^1) + (D_0 \times 2^0)$$
$$decimal = (D_7 \times 2^7) + (D_6 \times 2^6) + (D_5 \times 2^5) + (D_4 \times 2^4) + (D_3 \times 2^3) + (D_2 \times 2^2) + (D_1 \times 2^1) + (D_0 \times 2^0)$$
$$decimal = (0 \times 2^7) + (0 \times 2^6) + (0 \times 2^5) + (1 \times 2^4) + (0 \times 2^3) + (1 \times 2^2) + (1 \times 2^1) + (1 \times 2^0)$$
$$decimal = (1 \times 2^4) + (1 \times 2^2) + (1 \times 2^1) + (1 \times 2^0)$$
$$decimal = (16) + (4) + (2) + (1)$$
$$decimal = 23$$

In Example 1.5, we show how to convert from decimal to binary using division. The conversion is $42_{10} = 101010_2$. First, divide the decimal number (42) by the base (2), which results in a quotient of 21 and a remainder of 0. Place the remainder (0) out to the right. The first remainder is the LSB. Then, keep dividing the quotient by the base until nothing is left, placing the remainder to the right after every division. The quotient of the final division (which will be a 0 or 1) is the MSB. The binary sequence is constructed by concatenating the values in reverse order starting with the final quotient as the MSB and the first remainder as the LSB.

Example 1.5 Decimal → binary (division)

Division	Quotient	Remainder	
42 / 2	21	**0**	LSB
21 / 2	10	**1**	
10 / 2	5	**0**	
5 / 2	2	**1**	
2 / 2	1	**0**	↑

→
MSB $binary = 101010$

In Example 1.6, we show how to calculate the number of bits needed to store a given decimal value. For example, the value 42_{10} needs 6 bits of storage.

Example 1.6 Calculating bits for a decimal value

$$bits = floor(\log_2 n) + 1$$
$$bits = floor(\log_2 42) + 1$$
$$bits = floor(5.392317) + 1$$
$$bits = 6$$

📖 **LEARNING:** When calculating the number of bits needed to store a decimal value, you may be tempted to use $bits = ceiling(\log_2 n)$, which would work for most values (like Example 1.6). However, ceiling will result in an incorrect value when n is a power of 2, like the value 32_{10}. So, $ceiling(\log_2 32) = 5$ *bits*, which is incorrect. We would need 6 bits to store 32_{10}, which is 100000_2.

In Example 1.7, we show binary addition. The rules are simple.

0 + 0 = 0	0 + 1 or 1 + 0 = 1	1 + 1 = 0, carry the 1	1 + 1 + 1 = 1, carry the 1

Example 1.7 Binary addition

carry						1	1		
	0	0	0	1	0	1	1	1	23_{10}
+	0	1	0	0	0	1	1	0	70_{10}
	0	1	0	1	1	1	0	1	93_{10}

In Example 1.8, we show how to convert between hexadecimal, binary, and decimal. Hexadecimal to binary is based on the rule that each hexadecimal digit is comprised of four bits. The hexadecimal to decimal conversion can be accomplished using a Base 16 scale of 16^n (like Example 1.3). The conversion is $0001101010110111_2 = 6839_{10} = 1AB7_{16}$.

Example 1.8 Hex ↔ binary ↔ decimal

	Decimal equivalent of hexadecimal digit	1				10				11				7			
Convert between hex and binary	Hexadecimal	1				A				B				7			
	Bits	0	0	0	1	1	0	1	0	1	0	1	1	0	1	1	1
Convert between hex and decimal	Base 16 scale	16^3				16^2				16^1				16^0			
	Decimal values	4096				256				16				1			
	Add values	(1 x 4096) +				(10 x 256) +				(11 x 16) +				(7 x 1)			
	Decimal total													6839_{10}			

In Example 1.9, we show how to convert from hexadecimal to decimal using positional notation. The conversion is $1AB7_{16} = 6839_{10}$.

Example 1.9 Hexadecimal decimal (positional notation)

$$decimal = (D_{(n-1)} \times 16^{(n-1)}) + (D_{(n-2)} \times 16^{(n-2)}) + ... + (D_1 \times 16) + (D_0 \times 16^0)$$
$$decimal = (D_3 \times 16^3) + (D_2 \times 16^2) + (D_1 \times 16^1) + (D_0 \times 16^0)$$
$$decimal = (1 \times 16^3) + (A \times 16^2) + (B \times 16^1) + (7 \times 16^0)$$
$$decimal = (1 \times 4096) + (10 \times 256) + (11 \times 16) + (7 \times 1)$$
$$decimal = (4096) + (2560) + (176) + (7)$$
$$decimal = 6839$$

In Example 1.10, we show how to convert from decimal to hexadecimal using division. The conversion is $8039_{10} = 01F67_{16}$. The process is exactly the same as in Example 1.5, except we divide by 16.

Example 1.10 Decimal → hexadecimal

Division	Quotient	Remainder	
8,039 / 16	502	**7**	LSB
502 / 16	31	**6**	
31 / 16	1	**15**	F
1 / 16	**0**	**1**	↑

→
MSB   *hexadecimal* = 01F67

In Example 1.11, we show hexadecimal addition using the following formula, which applies to any base.

$$\text{if } x_i + y_i \geq base(b), \text{ then } z_i = (z_i \, MOD \, b) \text{ and carry } 1$$

The addition is $4B2_{16} + 6A4_{16} = B56_{16}$. We have denoted x_i, y_i, and z_i in the left column.

Example 1.11 Hexadecimal addition

carry		1			
x_i		4	**B**	2	1202_{10}
y_i	+	6	**A**	4	1700_{10}
z_i		B	**5**	5	2902_{10}

$z_i = z_i MOD b$
$z_i = (B + A) \, MOD \, 16$
$z_i = (11 + 10) \, MOD \, 16$
$z_i = 21 \, MOD \, 16$
$z_i = 5$

Signed Integer Storage

! ATTENTION: One of the reasons for signing integers is for the purpose of subtraction. Addition circuits are straightforward and easy to implement from an electrical engineering perspective. Three of the basic arithmetic operations are forms of addition: (1) addition, (2) subtraction (adding a negative value), and (3) multiplication (repetitive addition). Therefore, many CPU circuits are addition circuits.

Integers can be signed several ways in a system. Some examples are sign (magnitude) notation, **one's complement**, and **two's complement**. In all three methods, the MSB indicates positive (0) or negative (1). Many modern architectures, such as x86 and x86_64, use two's complement for signing integers. Example 1.12 shows two cases of signed binary values and their decimal equivalents.

Example 1.12 Signed binary

	MSB							LSB	
positive	**0**	0	0	1	0	1	1	1	$+23_{10}$
negative	**1**	0	0	1	0	1	1	1	-105_{10}

 LEARNING: Refer to Video 1.2: Signing Integers (https://youtu.be/vHijiZMbj9E) for a comparison of the three signing methods mentioned.

Sign notation and one's complement are problematic because both systems have a two zero problem; that is, two forms of zero exist (non-negative and negative), and the methods are more difficult to implement in hardware. Two's complement solves the two zero problem and is based on the additive inverse principle: if you add a number to its additive inverse the sum is zero.

Two's complement is a two-step process: (step 1) flip the bits, and (step 2) add 1. Examples 1.13 and 1.14 are two examples of using two's complement to represent positive and negative integer values in binary.

Example 1.13 Two's complement of $+23_{10}$

original value	0	0	0	1	0	1	1	1	$+23_{10}$
carry									
step 1 (flip bits)	1	1	1	0	1	0	0	0	1's complement
step 2 (add 1)	+							1	
	1	1	1	0	1	0	0	1	-23_{10} (2's complement)

If we were to perform two's complement on the binary value for -23_{10}, we would arrive back at $+23_{10}$.

Example 1.14 Two's complement of -105_{10}

original value	1	0	0	1	0	1	1	1	-105_{10}
carry									
step 1 (flip bits)	0	1	1	0	1	0	0	0	1's complement
step 2 (add 1)	+							1	
	0	1	1	0	1	0	0	1	$+105_{10}$ (2's complement)

 PROGRAMMING: Understanding signed binary is useful, but even more useful is understanding signed hexadecimal, which is what a programmer will typically see in registers and memory when debugging programs.

Signed hexadecimal values using two's complement follows a similar two-step process to that of signing binary values: (step 1) reverse the digits by subtracting each digit from 15 and (step 2) add 1. The quick way to tell if a hexadecimal value is positive or negative is according to the following rule:

If Most Significant Digit (MSD) ≤ 7, then value is positive; if MSD ≥ 8, then value is negative.

Example 1.15 shows the process of calculating the two's complement of $+1AB7_{16}$.

Example 1.15 Two's complement of $+1AB7_{16}$

	↓	if MSD ≤ 7, then value is positive			
	1	A	B	7	$+6839_{10}$
step 1 (reverse digits)	15 − 1	15 − 10	15 − 11	15 − 7	
1's complement	14 (E)	5	4	8	
step 2 (add 1)			+	1	
2's complement	**E**	5	4	9	-6839_{10}
	↑	if MSD ≥ 8, then value is negative			

Here are some other processes for converting signed values between number systems:

- Signed decimal → binary: (1) convert absolute decimal value to binary, and (2) if signed decimal was negative, then calculate two's complement.
- Signed decimal → hexadecimal: (1) convert absolute value to hex, and (2) if signed decimal was negative, then calculate two's complement.
- Signed hexadecimal → decimal: (1) if hexadecimal value is negative calculate two's complement, (2) convert to decimal, and (3) if original hexadecimal value was negative, then append the negative sign.

When subtracting hexadecimal values, it is much easier to reverse the sign of the value being subtracted by calculating its two's complement and then add the two values.

Character Storage

Characters such as 'A' and '$' are logical symbols that have to be represented in a numeric way for low-level uses. The guidelines for mapping between characters and their integer representations are defined by **character sets,** also called character maps or code maps. We will briefly review several of the most common character sets and their relationships to each other.

One of the oldest and most common character sets is the **American Standard Code for Information Interchange (ASCII).** ASCII is 7-bit (2^7), which means it can be used to represent 128 unique characters. Much of the ASCII map represents the English alphabet. ASCII is the default character map for high-level languages such as C++. The complete ASCII map can be found on many websites, such as https://en.wikipedia.org/wiki/ASCII.

Table 1.6 ASCII character ranges

ASCII Range	Characters
0 – 31	Non-printable control characters
32 – 126	Printable characters
127	Delete (control character)

A code map such as ASCII is what facilitates the translation from character to integer. For example, look at the ASCII translation from 'A' and '$' to their binary equivalents in Example 1.16.

Example 1.16 ASCII character translation

ASCII	Decimal	Hexadecimal	Binary
A	65	41	0100 0001
$	36	24	0010 0100

ASCII has been extended in several ways to allow for other Latin-based alphabets and symbols. One of the most common standardized character sets developed by the International Organization for Standardization (ISO) and the International Electrotechnical Commission was called ISO/IEC 8859. ISO-8859 extended ASCII by using the eighth bit, which meant 256 (2^8) characters. Other examples of extending ASCII to eight bits were IBM Code page 437, Windows-1252, and Mac OS Roman. In all of these character maps the standard ASCII range is the same, but they have different encodings for symbols 128-255.

Eventually, around 2008, mapping schemes such as ISO/IEC 10646 and **Unicode** became more common character sets. These more complex map schemes support more symbols and are backward compatible with standard ASCII. The Unicode character set can be encoded any number of ways. One of the most common encodings is the Unicode Transformation Format (UTF) called UTF-8, which dominates **character encoding** for the World Wide Web. UTF-8 encodes 1,112,064 characters using one to four octets (a group of 8 bits; a byte). Other Unicode character encodings are UTF-16, which maps characters with one or two 16-bit words, and UTF-32, which maps characters with one 32-bit value.

> **(!)** ATTENTION: A character set such as Unicode defines a list of characters (symbols) with unique numbers, sometimes called "code points" (e.g., A = U+0041). A character encoding, such as UTF-8, is an algorithmic translation for characters to a binary sequence (e.g., U+0041 = 01000001).

The Unicode character set maps a unique logical symbol to a code point comprised of the letter U plus a hexadecimal value as seen in Example 1.17. The UTF encoding then transforms the Unicode character into a binary sequence. The encodings can be expressed using any number system. Notice in Example 1.17 that when using UTF-8, the copyright symbol requires two bytes, which is different than the number sequences in UTF-16 and UTF-32. The example illustrates just how different character encodings (UTFs) can be even when based on the same character set (Unicode).

Example 1.17 Unicode and UTF character translation

Symbol	Unicode	UTF-8 (binary)	UTF-8 (hex)	UTF-16 (hex)	UTF-32 (decimal)	C++
T	U+0054	01010100	0x54	0x0054	84	"\u0054"
©	U+00A9	11000010:10101001	0xC2 0xA9	0x00A9	169	"\u00A9"

Standard 7-bit ASCII can be thought of as a subset of ISO-8859 and UTF encodings. For example, ASCII encodings are valid UTF-8 when prefixed with a zero in the seventh bit (assuming 0-bit numbering). The first 128 characters of UTF-8 correspond one-to-one with ASCII.

Strings are typically presented as a sequence of characters, which can be based on ASCII or Unicode. For example, the ASCII string "ABC123" is the hexadecimal ASCII sequence 41h, 42h, 43h, 31h, 32h, 33h, 0h. The 0h at the end is the NULL character indicating the end of the string. Keep in mind that when programming and debugging, characters and character sequences will typically be shown as their hexadecimal equivalents. We will discuss strings further in **CHAPTERS** 3 and 7.

Boolean Expressions

Boolean logic is a foundational topic in computing and programming. Understanding Boolean fundamentals is important for content in later chapters. Boolean expressions allow a programmer to write specific tests for decision structures and provide ways to perform bitwise operations. Boolean expressions define operations on the values 0/1 or false/true. We cover the four Boolean expressions NOT, AND, OR, and XOR. Different symbols can be used to denote Boolean expressions (Table 1.7), but for our purposes, we will simply use the terms.

Table 1.7 Boolean symbols

Expression	AND	OR	NOT	XOR
Math	∧ · &	∨ + |	¬ ' ~ !	⊕
C++	& (bitwise), && (logical)	| (bitwise), || (logical)	~ (bitwise), ! (logical)	∧ (bitwise)
Assembly	AND	OR	NOT	XOR

Boolean expressions operate as follows.
- NOT: reverses (negates) a value
- AND: only *true* if both (all) values are *true*, else *false*
- OR: only *false* if both (all) values are *false*, else *true*
- XOR: *true* if one or the other are *true*, *false* if both are *true* or *false*

Table 1.8 NOT Boolean expression

x	NOT x
F	T
T	F

Table 1.9 AND Boolean expression

x	y	x AND y
F	F	F
F	T	F
T	F	F
T	T	T

Table 1.10 OR Boolean expression

x	y	x OR y
F	F	F
F	T	T
T	F	T
T	T	T

Table 1.11 XOR Boolean expression

x	y	x XOR y
F	F	F
F	T	T
T	F	T
T	T	F

In binary, 0 is false and 1 is true. Example 1.18 provides some examples of Boolean operations on binary values.

Example 1.18 Boolean binary expressions

Given

x	1110 1101
y	0110 1010

Result

NOT (x)	0001 0010
AND (x AND y)	0110 1000
OR (x OR y)	1110 1111
XOR (x XOR y)	1000 0111

Each of the Boolean expressions are useful in terms of Assembly programming, as we will see in later chapters. Some examples we cover include using NOT to compute one's complement; AND to align stack and to change letters from uppercase to lowercase; OR to determine if a number is greater than, less than, or equal to zero; and XOR to clear values and determine parity.

Also, AND can be used to turn bits off (0) and OR can be used to turn bits on (1) by using a **mask**. A mask is a value used to manipulate a bit field in a desired way. Example 1.19 shows three ways to use a mask. The first shows how to turn all bits on in a value by using OR. The second example shows how to turn all bits off using AND. The third is a more practical use of a mask in which we want to query if bit 2 is set (assuming 0-bit numbering); we AND all the bits with 0 except for the bit(s) we want to test.

Example 1.19 Masking

Mask-on using OR	Mask-off using AND	Mask-query using AND
1001 value OR 1111 mask	1001 value AND 0000 mask	1101 value AND 0100 mask
= 1111 value	= 0000 value	= 0100 value bit 2 is set

3-bit Computer Example

LEARNING: Refer to Video 1.3: A 3-bit Computer Example (https://youtu.be/gYczcmDywag) for a demonstration of this section's content.

Programmers mostly work in a world of 32-bit and 64-bit systems, but visualizing a system with less bits can be helpful in understanding computing. Therefore, we provide an example of a 3-bit computer system.

Table 1.12 3-bit computer

Binary	Sign/Magnitude	One's Complement	Two's Complement
000	0	0	0
001	+1	+1	+1
010	+2	+2	+2
011	+3	+3	+3
100	-0	-3	-4
101	-1	-2	-3
110	-2	-1	-2
111	-3	-0	-1

leading 0's always positive

leading 1's always negative

Some general rules apply no matter how many bits are in a two's complement system.

- 0 is always all zeros
- -1 is always all ones
- The smallest negative number is always 1 with trailing zeros
- The largest positive number is always 0 with trailing ones

We can examine how computation works in our 3-bit computer with the two's complement representation of integers. The following examples illustrate different scenarios.

Example 1.20 3-bit computation examples

	#1		#2		#3		#4		#5
2	010	3	011	2	010	3	**0**11	-4	**1**00
+ 1	+ 001	- 1	+ 111	- 4	+ 100	+ 2	+ **0**10	-3	+ **1**01
3	011	2	**1**010	-2	110	5	**1**01	-7	**1**001

In #1, we add two positive numbers and achieve the expected result. In #2, we perform a subtraction by adding a negative. The arithmetic in #2 results in a carry that is dropped because it exceeds the capacity of a 3-bit integer in our 3-bit computer, leaving the expected result. In #3, we subtract again to achieve a negative result within the bounds of the system. In #4, we add two numbers that exist in our 3-bit system but result in a value beyond the bounds of the system. We can detect the overflow scenario by noticing that two positive values result in a negative value (see the leading bits). An overflow scenario causes the overflow bit to be set in the CPU's status register (which will be introduced in CHAPTER 2). In #5, we subtract two negatives that exist in the system but again result in overflow as indicated by two negative values with a positive result. We discuss how overflow conditions are handled beginning in CHAPTER 4.

> **PROGRAMMING:** How does a CPU know an integer is signed or unsigned? Answer: The CPU does not know! The CPU uses Boolean logic to set status flags after arithmetic operations regardless of the scenario. The programmer must decide what flags to interpret or ignore based on the operation. Status flags and related topics are covered further in future chapters, particularly in **CHAPTERS 2** and **4**.

Summary

In this chapter we presented the basics of computing via an exploration of computing languages, data representation, Boolean expressions, and a 3-bit computer example. Computing languages form a hierarchy, which we illustrated as a translation pipeline. Assembly language is an intermediate language that allows us to better understand and explore low-level details in computer operations. We also presented methods of data representation for integers and characters using number systems and character sets, respectively. We discussed Boolean expressions, which are a building block for more complex tasks. Lastly, we showed how binary two's complement computation works within a 3-bit computer system. These foundational concepts will prepare you for more advanced topics presented throughout this book.

Key Terms

American Standard Code for Information Interchange (ASCII)
assembler
bit
byte
character encoding
character set
compiler
compiling
complex instruction set computing (CISC)
computer architecture
debugger
disassembly
high-level language
instruction set architecture (ISA)

interpreting
linker
loader
machine-level
mask
microarchitecture
object code
one's complement
reduced instruction set computing (RISC)
signed
translation pipeline
two's complement
Unicode
unsigned

Code Review

The reason for this Bubble Sort Example and comparison is twofold: (1) to show that Assembly is not as daunting a language as might be initially thought, and (2) to show that well-written Assembly can provide some size and performance gains (keep in mind this is a very simple example).

Bubble sort example – comparison

	Memory footprint	.s file	.cpp file	.o file	executable file
Assembly	348kb	346b	N/A	1kb	9kb
C++	424kb	21kb	410b	3kb	9kb

Notice the size difference between the Assembly .s file and the .s file produced by the C++ compiler. The executable code in the C++ compiler's .s file is about 3kb of the 21kb total, which translates to the sizes seen in the .o file comparison. However, the resulting executable files are comparable, with the Assembly version's memory footprint being slightly smaller.

Bubble sort example – code

```
# Assembly Bubble Sort
.data
array: .long 3, 2, 6, 4, 1
count: .long 5

.text
.globl _main
_main:

mov count, %ecx
dec %ecx

outerLoop:
push %ecx
lea array, %esi

innerLoop:
mov (%esi), %eax
cmp %eax, 4(%esi)
jg nextStep
xchg 4(%esi), %eax
mov %eax, (%esi)

nextStep:
add $4, %esi
loop innerLoop
pop %ecx
loop outerLoop

push $0
sub $4, %esp
mov $1, %eax
int $0x80
.end
```

```
// C++ Bubble Sort
int main(){

    int  size = 5;
    int  value[5] = {3, 2, 6, 4, 1};
    int  i, tmp;
    bool swapped;

    do
    {
        swapped = false;
        for (i = 0; i < size - 1; i++){
            if (value[i + 1] < value[i])
            {
                tmp = value[i];
                value[i] = value[i + 1];
                value[i + 1] = tmp;
                swapped = true;
            }
        }
    } while (swapped);

    return 0;
}
```

Questions

Short Answer

1. x86 and IBM 370 are examples of processor _____.
2. Assembly language statements have a one-to-_____ relationship with machine language statements.
3. A high-level language statement has a one-to- _____ relationship with machine language statements.
4. Translating between language layers has two forms: _____ and _____.
5. x86 and x86_64 are examples of _____ instruction set architecture.
6. A "word" is _____ bits, in terms of x86 architecture.
7. _____ is the fundamental number system of computing due to its reliability.
8. _____ is the formula for calculating the number of bits needed to store a given decimal value.
9. _____ to _____ is the numeric range for an unsigned byte.
10. When converting from hexadecimal to binary, each hexadecimal digit is represented by _____ bits.
11. On x86 processors, a most significant bit of 1 indicates that the number is _____.
12. In a two's complement system, a hexadecimal value with a leading 7 would indicate the value is _____.
13. _____ to _____ is the numeric range for a signed byte.
14. Character storage is achieved via the use of _____.
15. _____ is the Boolean expression that results in a false if both inputs are true.
16. An _____ condition is when a computed result goes beyond what can be stored given the computer's architecture.

True/False

1. Assembly is portable across processor families. (T/F)
2. Two's complement has the problem of two zeros. (T/F)
3. The x86_64 architecture is not synonymous with IA-64. (T/F)
4. An assembler encodes high-level statements into object code. (T/F)
5. A CPU inherently understands whether an integer is positive or negative. (T/F)

Assignments

1.1   Explain one practical reason for learning Assembly programming.

1.2   Two's complement is based on what mathematical principle and what does the principle mean?

1.3   Complete the CHAPTER 1 ACTIVITY SUPPLEMENT.

1.4   **Challenge Assignment**: Disassemble an object file from a high-level language. You may use an object file from an existing C++ project. Use your chosen platform and disassembler. Review APPENDIX C: DISASSEMBLY for help. Examine the output. What are the shortest and longest instructions in bytes?

Processor and System Architecture

Objectives

- Recognize components of computer architecture
- Distinguish between memory types and location
- Identify CPU sub-components
- Describe CPU register use in Assembly programming
- Evaluate various Input and Output methods.

Outline

Web Resources

Wiki

- https://en.wikipedia.org/wiki/X86
- https://en.wikipedia.org/wiki/X86-64

Developer

- http://www.intel.com/content/www/us/en/processors/architectures-software-developer-manuals.html
- http://developer.amd.com/resources/documentation-articles/developer-guides-manuals/

Introduction

This chapter provides a general overview of the x86 and x86_64 architectures. To become an efficient Assembly programmer, you must have a solid understanding of the hardware on which your programs run. Even more crucial is your understanding of the processor and how it handles data at each step of the execution cycle. As was introduced in CHAPTER 1 and as you will learn in future chapters, Assembly instructions map directly to specific operations implemented in a processor, thus writing Assembly programs requires an understanding of architecture. Although the bulk of CHAPTER 2 is dedicated to the processor, we also cover other major components to ensure that you understand the flow of data from input to processing to output.

By the end of this chapter you will have a firm grasp on the underlying hardware that executes the Assembly programs you will be learning and writing throughout future chapters.

ATTENTION: Although many different processor architectures exist (x86, x86_64, IA-64, ARM, Alpha, Sparc, PowerPC, etc.), this book focuses on the x86 and x86_64 architectures as they are common platforms for the computing market and Assembly programmers.

Architecture Overview

By looking at a computing system from a high level, we can see the major components that comprise a typical computer. Though the **central processing unit (CPU)** is the brain of the computer, it could not function without other components such as the motherboard, memory, and various Input/Output (I/O) devices. Figure 2.1 depicts the general layout of common components.

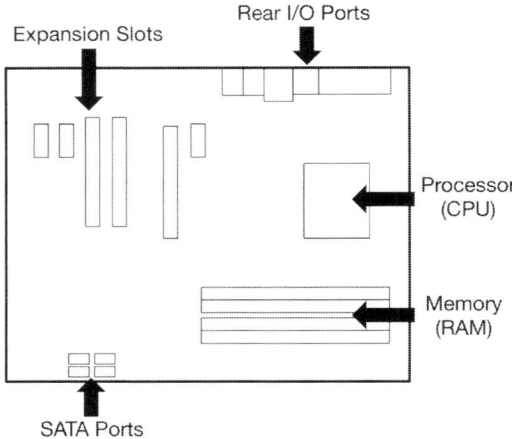

Figure 2.1 Motherboard components

The **motherboard** is the ground that connects the primary components that comprise a computer; the motherboard is the highway system for data travelling from component to component. The motherboard is comprised of a series of connections for computing components: slots for main memory, a socket for the CPU, connections for hard drives and optical drives, slots for expansion cards, as well as external connections for the keyboard, mouse, and other various I/O devices. In order for any components to communicate, they must send their data across the communication channels (buses) of the motherboard.

Figure 2.2 Underside of a motherboard

A **bus** is a group of wires, or conductive channels on a motherboard, that is used to transfer data from one component to another. We can see buses by examining the underside of a motherboard, as shown in Figure 2.2, where the conductive channels appear as a lighter color due to the presence of copper between the layers of fiberglass.

The main bus in a computer, shown in Figure 2.3, is the **system bus**, which is actually a collection of three separate buses: the data bus, the address bus, and the control bus. The system bus is how the CPU communicates with memory and other I/O devices in a computer. Such components connect to each of the three buses so proper communication can occur. The **data bus** is the bus that transfers instructions (such as load from memory, store in memory, read from the optical drive, etc.) and data between components. In order for information to be transferred, the correct memory address of the instructions and/or data must also be sent. Communication of addresses is the purpose of the **address bus**. The **control bus** has an equally important role in the communication of system components; it transfers signals between components to ensure that they are synchronized for appropriately timed communication (e.g., one component does not try to read from a device that is busy).

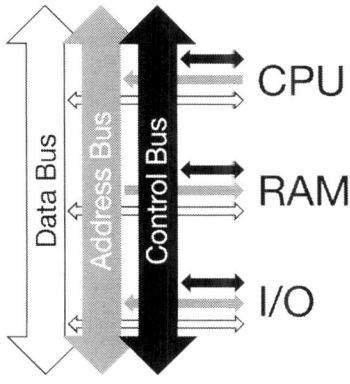

Figure 2.3 System bus

In addition to the system bus, component communication requires another puzzle piece. Without a component acting as an operational metronome (a metronome is a device that helps musicians keep a consistent rhythm while performing by "ticking" the beat), components could send data across the buses at random intervals whether or not the component on the other end is ready or able to communicate. The **system clock**, a motherboard component, solves the communication problem by pulsing at a constant rate, essentially keeping time for computer components.

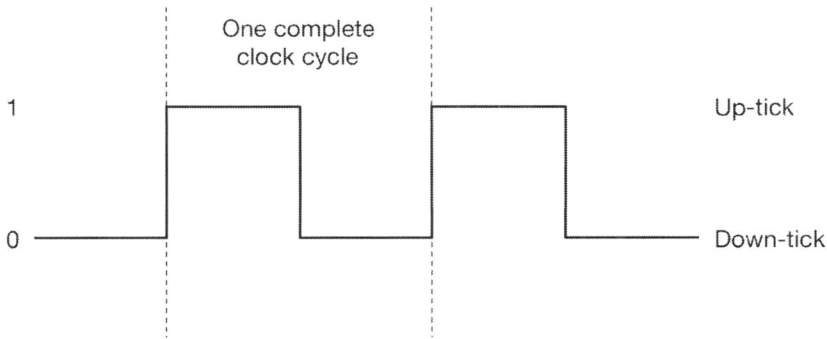

Figure 2.4 Clock cycle

The base unit for the system clock is a **clock cycle**, which consists of an up-tick (the first half of the cycle, where the voltage goes from low to high, or in binary 0 to 1) and a down-tick (the second half of the cycle, where the voltage goes from high to low, or in binary 1 to 0). Figure 2.4 shows a clock cycle.

Data transfer operations raise the issue of data and instruction storage. In order to store data and instructions, a computer must have **memory**. When discussing memory, we must be clear about which type of memory is under consideration. We can think of the different kinds of memory in a computer as a hierarchy, as depicted in Figure 2.5.

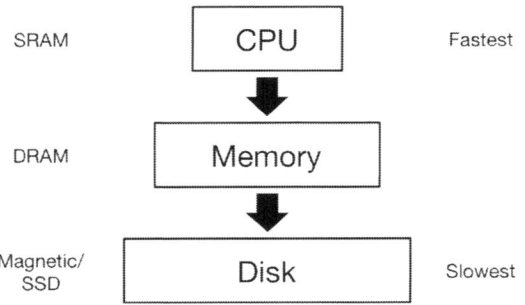

Figure 2.5 Memory hierarchy

At the top of the hierarchy is the memory physically closest to the arithmetic circuits of the CPU (usually residing on the CPU itself), while the bottom of the hierarchy is the memory physically farthest from the CPU. As memory is located farther from the CPU, the size grows, the cost shrinks, and the speed drastically slows. Consequently, memory types closer to the CPU are smaller in size and more expensive, but much faster. The relationship of speed, size, and cost is due to the type of memory in use at each location.

> **PROGRAMMING:** Due to memory speed decreasing with distance from the CPU, we encourage programmers to be conscious of memory use in Assembly programs. If a program can be written so that the amount of data used is small enough to not exceed the size of cache, then the program will execute faster than if data must overflow into RAM. Likewise, writing to disk should be avoided unless absolutely necessary, due to the amount of time needed to read and write to disk.

Closest to the CPU (on the chip itself) is **static random access memory** (SRAM). As we will discuss in the next section, SRAM is commonly referred to as cache. SRAM is the fastest of the memory types. Next is **dynamic RAM** (DRAM). DRAM is the memory found on "sticks" that plug into the motherboard near the CPU. When someone speaks about a computer's main memory, typically they are referring to the DRAM (or RAM for short). The slowest form of memory, which falls into the category of storage more so than memory, is a magnetic or solid-state **disk**. Disk memory, commonly referred to as a hard drive and discussed in a later section, is used for long-term storage as opposed to temporary storage like cache and RAM. Just like transferring data to/from the CPU, data accesses to any type of memory must abide by the ticking of the system clock.

The process of accessing main memory (DRAM) is typically four steps. Each step takes at least one clock cycle (sometimes more), so the total time in clock cycles will be four clock cycles at a minimum.

1. Place the address of the data to be read onto the address bus.
2. Change the value of the processor's Read (RD) pin, which is an assertion. Instruction execution will halt if the RD pin value is not properly changed.
3. Wait for the memory controller to respond (minimum one clock cycle).
4. Copy the data from the data bus to the destination location.

When interacting with memory, a programmer must be aware of the storage method. Computers typically store data in memory in architecture-specific chunks (32 and 64 bits for x86 and x86_64, respectively), with values being composed of bytes. If we were to store the 32-bit hexadecimal value `12345678h` into a computer's memory, the 32-bit value is split into byte-sized chunks, as shown in Table 2.1. Remember, each hexadecimal digit is four bits, so two hexadecimal digits are one byte.

Table 2.1 32-bit value split into bytes

Value			
Byte 1	**Byte 2**	**Byte 3**	**Byte 4**
12	34	56	78

To store the value, we have to find the next available memory location. For the sake of clarity, let us assume that the next available memory location is `0x00000000h`. Most likely you would place the data into memory as demonstrated in Table 2.2, with the values read from top to bottom in order (i.e., lowest memory address to highest memory address).

Table 2.2 Big-Endian byte order

Memory Address	Data
0x00000000	12
0x00000008	34
0x00000010	56
0x00000018	78

As the memory addresses increase by 8-bits (1 byte), the data is stored in left-to-right order in the way most people are used to writing values. However, instead of thinking of the data being in left-to-right order we should think of the data in terms of byte order. In Table 2.2, the most significant byte of data is stored first, at the lowest memory address, which is known as **Big-Endian** byte order: the "big end" is stored first. Some computing systems do the reverse and store the least significant byte, or "little end", first. **Little-Endian** byte order for the value `12345678h` is demonstrated in Table 2.3.

Table 2.3 Little-Endian byte order

Memory Address	Data
0x00000000	78
0x00000008	56
0x00000010	34
0x00000018	12

> PROGRAMMING: When accessing data stored in memory using typical methods (i.e., basic variables), you do not need to be concerned with whether your computer architecture uses Big-Endian or Little-Endian byte ordering. However, when you access or view memory locations by using memory addresses, you need to be aware of your architecture's byte ordering so that you access the correct data in the correct location.

Architectures such as Intel's x86 and x86_64 use Little-Endian ordering. Motorola's 68XX[X] series processors, along with IBM's Z series, use Big-Endian ordering. Some processors can use either, coined bi-endian, such as the Sun SPARC, ARM, and PowerPC.

Processors

Think of the CPU, or processor, as the brain of the computer. The CPU is the system component that handles the main arithmetic and logical operations. At a high level, as shown in Figure 2.6, the CPU has four major components: the arithmetic logic unit (ALU), the control unit (CU), the CPU clock, and memory (cache and registers).

The **ALU** is the mathematical sub-component of the CPU. The ALU performs arithmetic and logical operations on **integer** operands. (Integer operands is a key distinction, since a different component is responsible for operations on **floating-point** operands.) The **CU** is responsible for directing the flow of data within the CPU, ensuring that all other CPU sub-components receive the correct data at the correct time and act accordingly. CPU instructions, which rely on many sub-tasks in order to properly execute, follow the Instruction Execution Cycle as orchestrated by the CU. The **CPU clock**, different from the system clock, is a clock on the CPU itself that keeps time for CPU operations.

Another word for the speed of the CPU clock is **frequency**, which is measured in Hertz. Keeping the math simple, if a processor has a frequency of 1 Hertz (Hz), this means that the clock ticks one time per second. The ticking, as previously shown in Figure 2.4, is a full oscillation (an up-tick and down-tick). Modern processors are measured

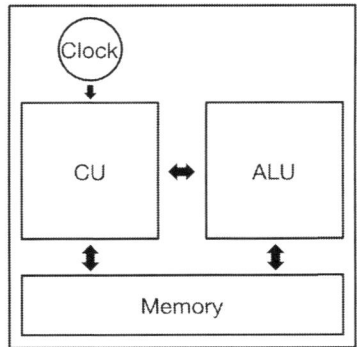

Figure 2.6 CPU components

in megahertz (MHz) or gigahertz (GHz), which indicate 1 million ticks per second and 1 billion ticks per second, respectively. To express speed in terms of the clock cycle rate rather than the processor frequency, we take the reciprocal of the frequency. So, if the frequency is 1 GHz (1 billion ticks per second), each clock cycle would be 1 billionth of a second in duration. An important note is that the speed at which the CPU clock ticks is a multiple of the system clock speed, which is determined by the **multiplier**. For example, if a system clock is running at 800MHz and the multiplier is 4, then the frequency of the CPU will be 3.2GHz. The CPU clock is running four times faster than the system clock and can perform four times the number of operations in the same amount of time.

Cache and Registers

As a processor is performing operations on data, a place must exist for the processor to store operands, results, and addresses. We previously explained that in the memory hierarchy, the farther away from the ALU the memory exists, the slower data access becomes. In order for the CPU to execute operations as quickly as possible, it has to be able to access and store instructions and data as quickly as possible. Thus, the location of instructions and data needs to be as close to the ALU and CU as possible. Close proximity memory, which is actually on the CPU die along with the logic circuits, is known as **cache**. While cache can be viewed in terms of the aforementioned memory hierarchy, cache also has a hierarchy of its own.

In modern processors, cache typically is divided into three tiers: level 1 (L1), level 2 (L2), and level 3 (L3). The cache hierarchy follows the same principles as the memory hierarchy: The farther from the ALU, the slower, larger, and cheaper it becomes. Both L1 and L2 cache are very close to the ALU, with L2 being slightly farther away and larger in capacity. L3 cache has become typical on multi-core processors. L1 and L2 cache are present for each core, while the L3 cache is shared amongst all cores, as shown in Figure 2.7. L3 cache provides the last layer of static memory before data must be sent to RAM for storage.

One example of the cache hierarchy is the Intel Core i7 processor. The Core i7 has an L1 cache of 64kb per core (32kb for instructions and 32kb for data). The L2 cache is 256kb per core. The L3 cache ranges from 4mb to 24mb shared amongst the cores, depending on how much you want to pay.

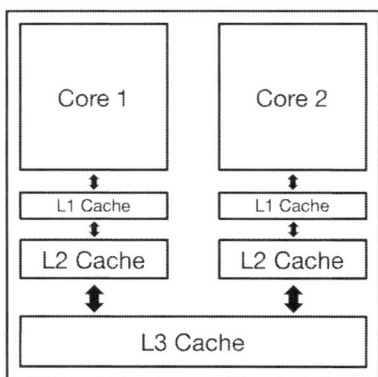

Figure 2.7 CPU cache

Usually, programmers do not access or manipulate cache with code in a non-automatic way, though some cache instructions do exist. Cache accesses are abstracted from programmers because the caches are managed by complex algorithms that ensure the data we need is available as quickly as possible. For example, if our code references a certain variable multiple times, the processor will likely assume that piece of data is important. The data is likely to be pre-fetched and kept in cache for quick retrieval by future operations. Such behavior happens dynamically throughout the execution of a program.

However, memory locations do exist on the processor that we can easily access in code. The locations are known as **registers,** and they are the fastest memory locations on a processor. Registers are the top of the memory hierarchy, even smaller and faster than cache. Registers are small storage areas closest to the ALU that are used for holding operands, addresses, and results during the execution of instructions.

 ATTENTION: Just as each processor core has separate caches, each core has its own set of registers. When writing Assembly code, we do not have to specify the core to which a register belongs. We simply reference the register name, as presented in Table 2.4, and the processor handles the execution.

Table 2.4 x86 and x86_64 registers

	64-bit	32-bit	16-bit			64-bit	32-bit	16-bit
	RAX	EAX	AX				CS	CS
	RBX	EBX	BX				DS	DS
	RCX	ECX	CX		**Segment registers**	N/A	ES	ES
General purpose registers	RDX	EDX	DX				SS	SS
	RSI	ESI	SI				FS	
	RDI	EDI	DI				GS	
	RBP	EBP	BP		**Instruction pointer**	RIP	EIP	IP
	RSP	ESP	SP		**Flags register**	RFLAGS	EFLAGS	FLAGS
	R8 – R15							

The registers presented in Table 2.4 can be grouped into four distinct categories: general purpose, segment, flags, and instruction pointer. Most register use in Assembly programs revolves around the general purpose registers, of which there are eight in 32-bit and sixteen in 64-bit. General purpose registers are used for tasks such as calculations and data movement. Because 64-bit processors were built upon the preceding 32-bit design, and 32-bit processors were built upon the preceding 16-bit design, not only can you use the 64-bit registers, but you can also use the 32-bit and 16-bit registers. Additionally, if you only need to use eight bits for data or a calculation, you can address a 16-bit register as two 8-bit registers. Figure 2.8 takes the 64-bit *rax* register and shows the addressing available from 8-bit up to 64-bit.

One issue register overlapping raises is how it affects stored data. For example, if you store a 32-bit value into *eax* and then store a 16-bit value in *ax*, is the original 32-bit value maintained or overwritten? Figure 2.9 provides the

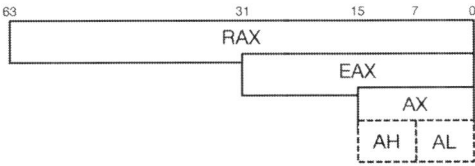

Figure 2.8 Register addressing

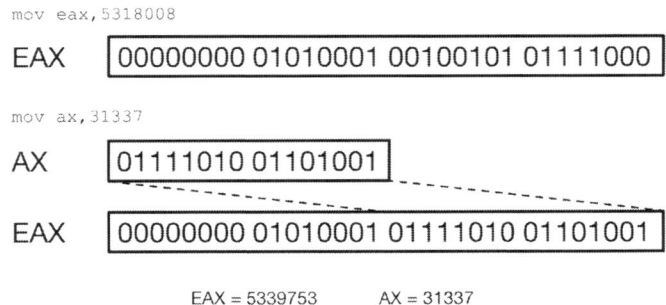

Figure 2.9 Writing AX destroys EAX

answer; each bit-variant of a register is comprised of the same bits. The *rax* register only occupies 64 bits of space in total, not 128 bits as if you added the sizes of *rax*, *eax*, *ax*, *ah*, and *al* (64+32+16+8+8). So, when a value is stored in *ax*, the existing value in *eax* is irrecoverably overwritten because *ax* occupies the lower bits of *eax*. The same is true for any register that shares space with smaller-sized registers.

In Figure 2.9 you see that when a value was copied to *ax*, the lower 16 bits of *eax* were overwritten, destroying the original value in *eax*. Again, the two registers share memory space. Not all registers share space with sub-registers, and even the ones that do may share a different amount of space. The four general purpose 64-bit registers *rax-rdx* have a sharing relationship with their 32-bit, 16-bit, and 8-bit counterparts as shown in Table 2.5. Table 2.6 lists the remaining general purpose registers, *rsi*, *rdi*, *rbp*, and *rsp*, which only have a sharing relationship with their 32-bit and 16-bit counterparts.

Table 2.5 Register overlapping for RAX, RBX, RCX, and RDX

	Register name			
64-bit	RAX	RBX	RCX	RDX
32-bit	EAX	EBX	ECX	EDX
16-bit	AX	BX	CX	DX
8-bit High/Low	AH/AL	BH/BL	CH/CL	DH/DL

Table 2.6 Register overlapping for RSI, RDI, RBP, and RSP

	Register name			
64-bit	RSI	RDI	RBP	RSP
32-bit	ESI	EDI	EBP	ESP
16-bit	SI	DI	BP	SP

Although you are able to use all of the aforementioned registers in your programs, some of the registers have special purposes of note. You can store data in a register such as *rax*/*eax* only to have it overwritten (perhaps unknowingly) after the next operation. Here we list some of the special uses of 64-bit and 32-bit registers so you can avoid errors when programming.

- *rax*/*eax* is commonly used as the default accumulator register. Operations such as multiplication will automatically place part of the result in *rax*/*eax*. Function calls use *rax*/*eax* for the return value. Do not use *rax*/*eax* for data storage when performing such operations.
- *rcx*/*ecx* is used to hold the loop counter value for executing loops. So, avoid using *rcx*/*ecx* to hold data inside of loops.
- *rbp*/*ebp* is used as the frame pointer for stack frames, which will be discussed in **CHAPTER 6**. The register is used to reference data on the stack. We recommend only using *rbp*/*ebp* for its intended purpose.
- *rsp*/*esp*, the stack pointer register, is also used for stack management and typically points to the top of the active stack frame. Again, it is best to use *rsp*/*esp* for its intended purpose.

- *rsi/esi* and *rdi/edi* are index registers used with string operations such as STOSB, MOVSB, and SCASB to store, load, and scan large amounts of data. Such operations essentially put the CPU into an automatic loop mode that is more efficient than having the programmer write a loop.
- *rip/eip* is the extended instruction pointer register. The register is used to point to the memory address containing the next instruction to be fetched, decoded, and executed in a program and is adjusted automatically. Do not modify this register programmatically.
- *rflags/eflags*, discussed in more detail next, is the status and control register. Special instructions such as LAHF and SAHF can be used to load and store the CPU flags from and to the *ah* register. Do not modify *rflags/eflags* directly. Bits in the *rflags/eflags* register are set automatically according to a set of Boolean rules after each arithmetic operation. Although *rflags* is 64-bits, only the lower 32-bits are utilized. Status flags are the same for both x86 and x86_64 processors.

CPU **flags** are individual bits that either control CPU operations in some way or reflect the status of CPU operations. The eight flags listed in Table 2.7 are usually viewable in most development environments. Some flags can be edited by the programmer using the LAHF and SAHF instructions, which are listed in Table 2.8. Set means the bit is 1 and clear means the bit is 0.

Table 2.7 Viewable flags

Flag	Symbol	Bit	Description
Carry	CF	0	Set as a result of unsigned carry or borrow out of the most significant bit. For example, the result of an operation is too large for the destination (e.g., 255 + 5 using 3-bit registers would yield a carry into a 9th bit).
Parity	PF	2	Set if the number of set bits in the result is even. Used in error correction operations.
Auxiliary carry or adjust	AF	4	Used primarily for binary-coded decimal (BCD) arithmetic. The flag indicates when a carry or borrow occurs out of the low nibble (4 least significant bits).
Zero	ZF	6	Set if the result of the operation is zero.
Sign	SF	7	Set if the result of an operation is negative (i.e., the most significant bit is set in Two's complement notation).
Interrupt	IF	9	Enables the processor to handle maskable hardware interrupts, also known as interrupt requests (IRQ).
Direction	DF	10	When clear, strings are processed left-to-right by the incrementing of the string index registers *rsi/esi* and *rdi/edi* after each string operation (e.g., MOVS). When set, strings are processed right-to-left and the registers are decremented after each string operation.
Overflow	OF	11	Set if a Two's complement result will not fit into the number of bits used for the operation. Unlike the Carry flag, the Overflow flag is for signed integers and would be set when the result's sign is different from the operands' signs (e.g., 127+127 using 8-bits results in a Two's complement result that is negative because the high-order bit is 1).

 PROGRAMMING: In Table 2.8, bits 1, 3, and 5 are marked as 'U', which means the bits are unused/reserved. The bits will always be 0 and should not be set to 1 when using SAHF to save the flags back into the *flags* register.

Table 2.8 Editable flags in bit order for LAHF/SAHF

7	6	5	4	3	2	1	0
SF	ZF	U	AF	U	PF	U	CF

64-bit Processors

Although some specifics of 64-bit processors have already been discussed, a few more important details need to be covered. The x86_64 instruction set is an extension of the x86 (32-bit) instruction set. So, 32-bit operations are possible on x86_64 processors. While the 64-bit nature of an x86_64 processor means that data and addresses can be stored with 64 bits, current x86_64 processors only utilize the lower 48 bits for addresses. The result is that x86_64 processors address 2^{48} bytes of memory instead of the theoretical 2^{64} bytes. The 48-bit physical address space allows the processor to address up to 256TB of RAM, a huge improvement over the 4GB maximum of a 32-bit processor. In addition to being able to address more RAM, x86_64 processors also have eight more general purpose registers, *r8* through *r15*.

Instruction Execution

In order for an instruction to be executed (e.g., ADD), a sequence of steps known as the **instruction execution cycle** is followed. Although the ADD instruction is only one instruction and might seem like a one-step process to a programmer, many smaller sub-tasks, or stages, comprise instruction execution. The number of stages can vary from as few as three stages at an abstract level (Figure 2.10) to upwards of 20 or more stages in modern high-end processors.

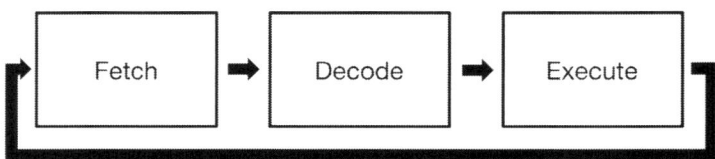

Figure 2.10 3-Stage instruction execution cycle

So, when a programmer writes the ADD instruction to compute the sum of two values, 20 steps may occur behind the scenes to proceed through the execution cycle in order to produce the sum.

A common high-level view of the cycle is seen as three steps: Fetch, Decode, and Execute. During the **Fetch** stage the CPU retrieves the next instruction to be executed (i.e., where *rip/eip* is pointing in memory). In the **Decode** stage, the CPU determines what the instruction is and on what data it operates. During the Decode stage, the CPU looks at the bits of the instruction (0s and 1s) and is able to determine the type of operation (e.g., ADD, SUB, MOV) and whether or not the operation includes operands. If the operation includes operands, the CPU may need to fetch those as well. Once all necessary data is fetched and decoded, the CPU can **Execute** the instruction. Should the operation produce a result, as with the ADD and SUB instructions, the CPU will store the result in the appropriate place (e.g., register, memory).

Pipelining

In modern processors, each part of the 3-stage cycle can contain sub-steps. Processor architects have found over the years that overlapping the stages of the cycle results in better performance because the processor can work on fetching a second instruction when moving onto decoding the first instruction and so on. The overlapping design is known as **pipelining** as depicted in Figure 2.11.

A common analogy for better understanding pipelining is washing clothes. The typical process of washing clothes is to gather the clothes, wash them in a washing machine, dry them in a dryer, and then put them away. Is it more efficient to wait until you have completed all four stages for a single load of laundry before starting the next load? Or is it more efficient to gather the second load while the first load is washing, wash the second load while the first load is drying, and so on? Clearly, the second method is the best use of your time. The laundry example illustrates the concept of pipelining. A CPU with separate Fetch, Decode, and Execute units may not be able to perform three fetches at the same time, but it can perform a Fetch, a Decode, and an Execute simultaneously. Doing so is a better use of a processor's time and results in better performance.

> **!** ATTENTION: Modern processors actually contain multiple Fetch, Decode, and Execute units to maximize throughput of instruction execution.

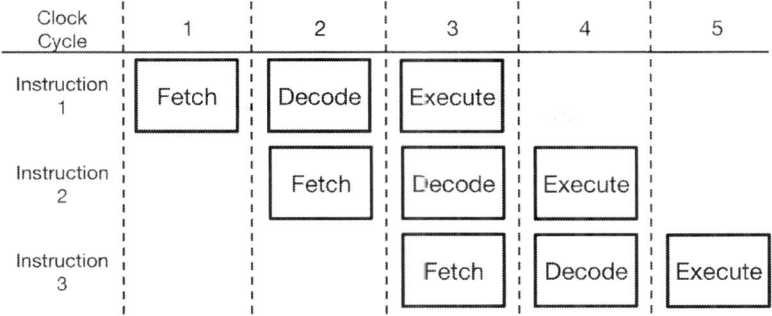

Figure 2.11 Pipelined instruction execution cycle

As previously mentioned, a pipeline could have upwards of 20 stages, which is known as a **superpipeline**. A CPU could be working on 20 different steps simultaneously, with instructions in different stages. The more pipeline stages the CPU uses, the more work can be performed by the CPU in a specific time frame. With a 20-stage Instruction Execution Cycle in a non-pipelined processor, a minimum of 200 clock cycles would be needed to complete 10 operations because each instruction would have to wait for all 20 stages of the previous instruction to finish. With a 20-stage pipelined processor, such as in Figure 2.12, the number of required clock cycles is reduced to 29, a 690% improvement. The improvement percentage grows as the number of operations performed increases.

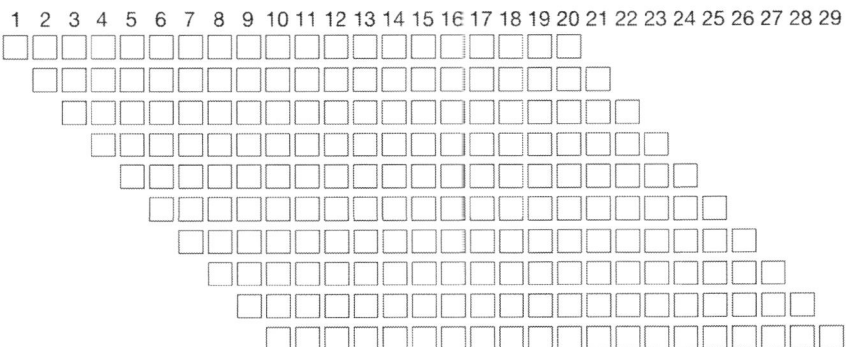

Figure 2.12 20-stage superpipeline

Input and Output

Up to this point we have discussed the processor in some detail and how it communicates with other major components located on the motherboard. But how does the processor communicate with external devices? External devices such as keyboards, monitors, and network adapters connect to the computer via an **input/output (I/O) module**. I/O modules connect to the system bus so that external devices can communicate with components in the computer, such as the CPU. In addition to providing a means of buffered communication between the processor and the I/O device, an I/O module also handles some critical actions, such as data transfer, command decoding, and device status interrogation.

Just as the processor needs a control unit to act as a traffic control agent that ensures instructions execute exactly when they should without interfering with other operations, an I/O module must coordinate communication between the computer's internal components and the external device connected to the module. As previously explained, the farther away that components are located from the CPU, the slower they become. External devices are the farthest away; they are the slowest devices in a computing ecosystem. Due to speed differences, an I/O module needs to act as a data buffer to ensure that neither the processor is slowed down nor the external device is overrun with too much data. Different external devices operate at different speeds (e.g., compare saving data to a CDRW versus a USB thumb drive). So each I/O module needs to be aware of the attached device's data rate and adjust accordingly.

LEARNING: Many error detection and correction algorithms exist. Search the Web for different methods such as checksums, Cyclic Redundancy Checks (CRC), Hamming Code, and parity bits to learn more.

Another critical action I/O modules perform is error detection. Ensuring that the data sent to an external device is the same data received by the external device is crucial. Various methods of error detection may be used, but the goal is always the same: to ensure integrity of the data.

When discussing methods by which processors execute I/O operations, generally four methods exist: programmed I/O (PIO), interrupt-driven I/O, direct memory access (DMA), and I/O channels. **Programmed I/O (PIO)**, depicted in Figure 2.13, is the simplest of the four techniques to implement, but it creates the most overhead, thus making it the most inefficient of the choices. When a processor executes an I/O operation in PIO mode, the CPU sends a command to the specified I/O module and waits. The I/O module is responsible for executing the command and setting the appropriate bits in the I/O status register to signify the completion of the command. The processor must periodically check the I/O status register to see if the I/O module has completed the operation. Overhead is caused by the periodic checking, especially in the case of very long I/O operations where the processor must check multiple times.

The processor could be much more efficient if, after sending a command to an I/O module, it could continue with

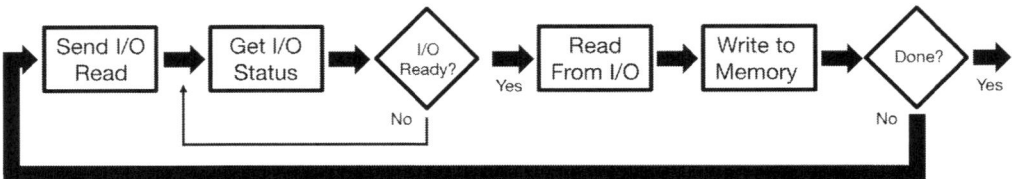

Figure 2.13 Programmed I/O

other operations instead of waiting for the I/O command to finish. Such is the concept of **interrupt-driven I/O**, depicted in Figure 2.14. Once the processor has delivered a command to an I/O module, it moves on to other instructions and only returns to the external operation when the I/O module sends an interrupt. The interrupt pauses other operations so that the processor can finish the I/O operation at hand. The processor checks for interrupts at the end of every instruction cycle, so the I/O module will never have to wait longer than one full instruction cycle after delivering an interrupt message for the transaction to complete. Although it seems like the processor is completely hands-off during the I/O module's execution of a command, the processor still has to be used each time data is moved to/from main memory (RAM).

Both Programmed I/O and interrupt-driven I/O require constant involvement of the processor. Since many I/O operations are straightforward data transfers between external devices and RAM, the processor is wasting clock cycles on mundane tasks. Such overhead needs a remedy to further increase the efficiency of the processor and **direct memory access (DMA)**, depicted in Figure 2.15, is the answer. Using DMA requires an additional module on the motherboard strictly for DMA operations. When the processor needs to execute an I/O operation, the CPU sends the information to the DMA module instead of directly to the device's I/O m. In a sense, the DMA module emulates the processor

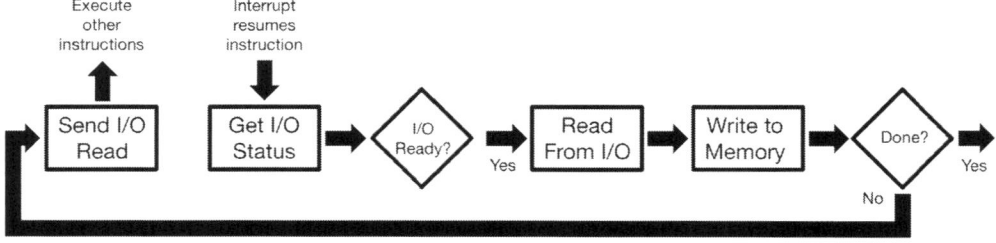

Figure 2.14 Interrupt-driven I/O

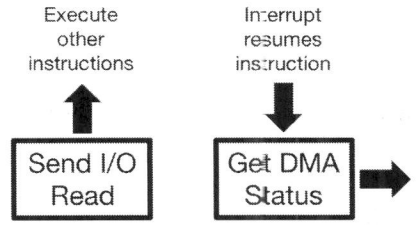

Figure 2.15 Direct memory access

by taking control of the I/O operation by pausing the processor for one cycle at a time so the DMA module can gain unfettered access to the system bus (a process called cycle stealing). When the DMA module has completed the I/O operation, it sends an interrupt to the processor to signify completion. The processor is only responsible for non-data transfer instructions related to the I/O operation, which saves clock cycles and makes the computer's usage of the processor more efficient.

Although DMA appears to solve the problem of the CPU dealing with I/O operations, the DMA module itself is not a complete processor; it must steal cycles from the CPU to accomplish DMA tasks. Thus, the CPU is still doing more work than is optimal. A solution to the cycle-stealing problem is to have a module dedicated to I/O operations that is, in fact, a real processor. Such a technique eliminates the need for a module to steal cycles from the CPU. The solution is an **I/O channel**. Different I/O channels exist; some handle I/O with one device at a time, and others can multiplex (i.e., handle I/O with multiple devices at a time). When I/O channels are present, the CPU is relieved of every I/O instruction except the very first instruction that tells the I/O channel to perform a task. After the first instruction, the I/O channel takes over and controls the I/O module, completing the I/O operation without using any more CPU cycles.

Summary

Now that you have finished this chapter, you should have a basic understanding of processor and system architecture. We have covered important aspects of architecture that are necessary for learning of Assembly programming, including the CPU, memory, instruction execution, and I/O. Although no Assembly code was discussed in this chapter, all of the concepts are crucial for what you will learn in subsequent chapters. You will find yourself referring to this chapter, specifically the sections on memory and CPU registers, as you read future chapters and write your first Assembly programs.

Key Terms

address bus
arithmetic logic unit (ALU)
Big-Endian
bus
cache
central processing unit (CPU)
clock cycle
control bus
control unit (CU)
CPU Clock
data bus
Decode

direct memory access (DMA)
disk
dynamic RAM (DRAM)
Execute
Fetch
flags
frequency
I/O channel
input/output (I/O) module
instruction execution cycle
interrupt-driven I/O

Little-Endian
memory
motherboard
multiplier
pipelining
programmed I/O (PIO)
registers
static random access memory (SRAM)
superpipeline
system bus
system clock

Questions

Short Answer

1. The processor is more commonly known by the abbreviation _____.
2. A group of wires that connects components allowing them to communicate is known as a _____.
3. The _____ bus transmits signals that enable components to know where in memory instructions and data exist.
4. The up-tick of the system clock is when the voltage changes from _____ to _____.
5. As memory gets physically closer to the CPU it can be accessed _____.
6. _____ byte ordering is when the hexadecimal number "1984" would appear sequentially in memory as "8419."
7. The _____ is responsible for directing the flow of data in the CPU.
8. The speed of a CPU is determined by two factors: the _____ and the _____.
9. _____ cache is the slowest form of CPU cache.
10. The lower 8 bits of the *RCX* register is the _____ register.
11. The _____ register is the 32-bit stack pointer register.
12. The Instruction Execution Cycle's _____ stage is when the CPU determines the operation denoted by the instruction/opcode.
13. A _____ processor is able to perform multiple operations at the same time as long as each operation is in a different execution stage.
14. _____ will take the processor away from its current sequence of operations in order to attend to another matter.
15. The I/O method with the least amount of CPU overhead is _____.

True/False

1. The motherboard has connections for RAM, expansion cards, and external I/O devices.
2. Moving a value into the *edx* register will overwrite the *ds* register.
3. A value of 1 in the SF bit of the *rflags* register indicates a positive value resulted from the previous operation.
4. PIO is the fastest of the I/O methods.
5. I/O channels require a minimum of two CPU cycles to complete an I/O operation.

Assignments

2.1 Memory

Given the equation: `taxableIncome = salary - exempts - percent401k / 100 * salary`
and the variables: `salary = 50000, exempts = 7000, percent401k = 4.5`

Show how the value in `taxableIncome` will be stored in memory (in hexadecimal format) on a system with an Intel Core i7 processor if the next available memory address is `0x013A32A8h`.

2.2 Instruction Execution

A program contains a total of 220 instructions. Calculate the number of clock cycles it would take to complete execution on systems with the following processors:

- Non-pipelined 3-stage processor
- 3-stage pipelined processor
- 15-stage superpipelined processor

2.3 Input/Output (Challenge Assignment)

When performing a long listing (`ls -la`) in the `/dev/` directory of a Linux system, you will see the special files for all connected devices and important information about each. Use the Web to research the different classes of I/O devices and how they are represented in the long listing.

More Architecture Details

Program Loading

As discussed in **CHAPTER 1**, programs are loaded by a utility called the program loader. After a program is loaded, the CPU (*eip/rip*) points to the program's entry point (e.g., main, start). Here we generally describe the steps of starting a program; what happens when we open a program (e.g., double-click).

1. The OS retrieves program information such as file size and physical location on disk.
2. The OS determines an appropriate location in memory, allocates the space, and places necessary information in a descriptor table (descriptors are discussed in **CHAPTER 10**).
3. The OS begins execution of the first instruction (entry point), thus becoming a process, which is assigned an ID.
4. The process runs independently, and the OS responds to the process's requests for resources.
5. When the process ends, the memory is relinquished.

Memory Access Improvements

As discussed in **CHAPTER 2**, reading from main memory (RAM) is slower than reading from registers due to proximity to the ALU and the process required to read values from memory. Over time, improvements have been made in instruction and data access.

- **Cache** memory helps relieve the speed of memory accesses. If the instruction or data being fetched is found in cache, a cache hit occurs. If not found, a cache miss occurs. Instructions can also be moved in bulk to and from cache.
- **Prefetching** algorithms examine memory access patterns with the intent to fill cache and prefetch buffers with instructions and data likely to be needed soon. Most modern CPUs also have predecoding as part of the pipeline.
- **Integrated memory controllers** eliminate CPU to RAM hops via the front side bus (Northbridge) by integrating the memory controller onto the CPU die.
- **Multi-core/multi-processor** systems allow the workload of executing instructions to be distributed.

Support Processors

A computer system has many processors and components that support the work of the CPU by performing special tasks. Here are a few worth mentioning.

- **Floating-point unit (FPU)** — typically integrated with the CPU (**CHAPTER 6**).
- **Clock generator** — the CPU clock
- **Programmable interrupt controllers (PICs)** — handles interrupts from keyboards, hard drives, and other hardware devices (**CHAPTER 10**)
- **Programmable interval timer** — interrupts the system 18.2 times/sec, updates the system time and clock, and controls the system speaker; responsible for refreshing main memory (RAM)
- **Graphical processing unit (GPU)** — a specially designed processor that efficiently processes matrices and vectors and displays visual data to screens

Pipelining and Multi-unit Processing

As discussed in CHAPTER 2, pipelining is the overlapping of instruction processing to increase speed of execution. CPUs generally contain the following units: fetch unit, decode unit, execution control, addressing unit, memory controller, multiplier, bit shifter, ALU, FPU, etc. Modern CPUs typically have multiples of some units per processor and core. So, given the hardware environment, pipelining can take on many forms.

Scalar processing is when only one datum, an instruction in this case, is processed at a time. Thus average instruction execution is approximately equal to the clock speed.

Superscalar processing is when multiple instructions are fetched and dispatched to separate functional units in a single processor in parallel to achieve a higher throughput than the clock speed.

Consider the following examples of multi-unit processors. The examples are just a sampling of the thousands of variations, past, present, and future.

- Example 1: The PowerPC 970 has two ALUs, two FPUs, two load/store units, two SIMD units, with varying pipelines between ten and sixteen stages, depending on the unit.
- Example 2: The Pentium 3 has three ALUs, while the Pentium 4 has two ALUs (but each runs at twice the clock rate of the P3 ALUs), and both have one FPU.
- Example 3: The AMD Athlon has three ALUs, three AGUs (address-generation units), and one FPU.
- Example 4: An Intel Core i7 (Haswell) with four cores supports **HyperThreading**, meaning two logical processors per core. Each execution unit has eight "ports" for eight micro-ops per clock tick and four ALUs.

Input/Output System

A deeper knowledge of hardware and devices can allow a programmer to take advantage of features and optimize code. Generally, I/O is available at three levels.

- **Application level**: High-level libraries and application programming interfaces (APIs)
- **System level**: System calls using Assembly instructions
- **UEFI level**: Unified Extensible Firmware Interface (UEFI) is low-level software that communicates directly with hardware and provides boot and runtime services; UEFI is the modern and more sophisticated replacement of basic input/output system (BIOS).

Device Drivers contain routines that allow the OS to communicate directly with hardware.

To illustrate an I/O hierarchy exchange consider the following example.

1. A high-level statement in a C++ program calls on a library function to write a string to standard output (e.g., `cout << "This is string";`)
2. The library function calls a system routine (OS) function and passes relevant parameters such as the address of the string and the size.
3. The system call uses a loop to call a Driver or UEFI subroutine, passing the ASCII/Unicode value and color of each character.
   a. The Driver or UEFI subroutine receives a character, maps it to a font, and sends the character to a hardware port attached to a video controller.
   b. The video controller prints the character by using timed hardware signals to the screen that control the displaying of pixels.
   c. The system calls another Driver or UEFI subroutine to advance the cursor.

Assembly programs have the power and flexibility to access all I/O levels. At the application level, a programmer can call on library functions to perform console and file-based I/O. At the OS level, a programmer can call on the kernel to perform console and file-based I/O. At the UEFI/Driver level, a programmer can call on functions to control device-specific features. When coding, a programmer should consider tradeoffs between the I/O levels concerning efficiency, results, and *portability*. This topic is discussed further in **CHAPTER 10**, along with application-level and system-level calls.

## CHAPTER 3

Assembly and Syntax Fundamentals

Objectives

- Distinguish differences in Assembly syntaxes
- Identify sections of Assembly code and explain the use of each
- Construct semantically correct data definitions
- Create working Assembly programs

Outline

Web Resources

- https://sourceware.org/binutils/docs/as/ (GAS Reference)
- https://msdn.microsoft.com/en-us/library/afzk3475.aspx (MASM Reference)
- http://www.nasm.us/doc/nasmdoc0.html (NASM Reference)

Introduction

This chapter introduces x86 and x86_64 Assembly language. Because software engineers often work in various operating systems depending on the type of problem needing solved, this chapter and subsequent chapters examine Assembly language using three prominent assemblers—GAS, MASM, and NASM. The approach offers examples and preparedness for common operating systems (Mac, Windows, and Linux) and development environments. Development environments you might use to write Assembly include Apple Xcode, Microsoft Visual Studio, and command-line assembling within Linux.

We take great care to show the differences in assembler syntaxes, when such differences exist, by denoting code snippets with a border and a title of the assembler for which the code is written. In some instances, the purpose of a code snippet is not to teach syntax specifics but rather to explain a concept. Such code snippets do not have a border or a title. Because different assemblers can use different Assembly syntaxes, we use the convention detailed in Table 3.1.

Table 3.1 Syntax conventions

Assembler	Syntax	Development environment
GAS	AT&T	Apple Xcode
MASM	Intel	Microsoft Visual Studio
NASM	Intel	Command-line in Linux

> ⚠ **ATTENTION:** Xcode does not use the standard GNU Assembler (GAS). Instead, Xcode uses an integrated assembler with Clang as the front end and LLVM as the back end. While minor differences exist between GAS and the Clang/LLVM integrated assembler, Clang was designed to be a replacement for the GNU toolchain. Thus, Assembly code written in Xcode will also assemble with current versions of GAS (2.27 as of this writing). The version of GAS that ships with macOS (1.38 as of this writing) should be avoided. All GAS code in this book has been tested in Xcode on macOS and GAS 2.x on Linux to ensure compatibility. For consistency, we refer to the assembler as GAS throughout the text.

By the end of this chapter, you will be familiar with the basic structure and syntax of x86 and x86_64 Assembly programs. A solid understanding of Assembly syntax fundamentals is necessary for the remainder of the book.

Basic Elements

Unlike higher-level programming languages, Assembly language operates at a level where each line of code performs a single operation. Assembly cannot be written without knowledge of the computer's architecture, such as CPU registers, flags, floating-point capabilities, etc. Low-level details and coding can be daunting for the novice programmer and the experienced programmer alike, but knowledge of low-level details allows a programmer to write code with control and efficiency unmatched by high-level languages. As you master Assembly language, you will likely find that your programs written in higher-level languages benefit in design.

Pillars of Assembly Code

In order to begin the journey of Assembly programming, five pillars found in Assembly programs are important to discuss: reserved words, identifiers, directives, sections (segments), and instructions. A clear understanding of the five pillars is paramount for your ability to follow future sections of this chapter and book. Let us examine a simple Assembly program in which we will identify the five pillars. Program 3.1 defines a 32-bit variable, adds two numbers, and saves the result in the aforementioned variable.

Reserved words, as in any programming language, are words that can only be used for their defined purpose. For example, MOV is a reserved word because it is an instruction. MOV cannot be used as a variable name or in any other way except to execute the MOV instruction. In Assembly language, reserved words are case-insensitive. Examples of reserved words include instructions (e.g., MOV), directives (e.g., PROC), registers (e.g., *eax*), and attributes (e.g., FLAT for the .MODEL directive).

Table 3.2 shows the sample program with the reserved words appearing in black. Notice that most of the program consists of reserved words. Some of the reserved words are also other pillars, such as directives and code sections.

Program 3.1 *Sample Assembly program*

GAS	MASM	NASM
| ```
.data
sum: .long 0

.text
.globl _main
_main:
movl $25, %eax
movl $50, %ebx
addl %ebx, %eax
movl %eax, sum

pushl $0
subl $4, %esp
movl $1, %eax
int $0x80
.end
``` | ```
.386
.MODEL FLAT, stdcall
.STACK 4096
ExitProcess PROTC,
dwExitCode:DWORD

.data
sum DWORD 0

.code
_main PROC
mov eax, 25
mov ebx, 50
add eax, ebx
mov sum, eax

INVOKE ExitProcess, 0
_main ENDP
END
``` | ```
SECTION .data
sum: DD 0

SECTION .text
global _main
_main:
mov eax, 25
mov ebx, 50
add eax, ebx
mov DWORD [sum], eax

mov eax, 1
mov ebx, 0
int 80h
``` |

Table 3.2 Sample reserved words

GAS	MASM	NASM
| ```
.data
sum: .long 0

.text
.globl _main
_main:
movl $25, %eax
movl $50, %ebx
addl %ebx, %eax
movl %eax, sum

pushl $0
subl $4, %esp
movl $1, %eax
int $0x80
.end
``` | ```
.386
.MODEL FLAT, stdcall
.STACK 4096
ExitProcess PROTO,
dwExitCode:DWORD

.data
sum DWORD 0

.code
_main PROC
mov eax, 25
mov ebx, 50
add eax, ebx
mov sum, eax

INVOKE ExitProcess, 0
_main ENDP
END
``` | ```
SECTION .data
sum: DD 0

SECTION .text
global _main
_main:
mov eax, 25
mov ebx, 50
add eax, ebx
mov DWORD [sum], eax

mov eax, 1
mov ebx, 0
int 80h
``` |

Identifiers are programmer-defined names given to items such as variables, constants, and procedures. The length of identifiers is limited to 247 characters and cannot begin with a number. Also, in order to be a valid identifier the name must begin with a letter (A-Z, a-z), underscore (_), question mark (?), at-symbol (@), or dollar sign ($), though we do not recommend using ?, @, or $ as part of standard identifiers. Numbers may be used in identifiers as any character after the first character. The following list shows valid identifiers using characters we recommend.

- userInputValue
- sum_of_values
- weight1

Table 3.3 highlights the identifiers in the sample program.

Table 3.3 Sample identifiers

GAS	MASM	NASM
| ```
.data
sum: .long 0

.text
.globl _main
_main:
movl $25, %eax
movl $50, %ebx
addl %ebx, %eax
movl %eax, sum

pushl $0
subl $4, %esp
movl $1, %eax
int $0x80
.end
``` | ```
.386
.MODEL FLAT, stdcall
.STACK 4096

ExitProcess PROTO,
dwExitCode:DWORD

.data
sum DWORD 0

.code
_main PROC
mov eax, 25
mov ebx, 50
add eax, ebx
mov sum, eax

INVOKE ExitProcess, 0
_main ENDP
END
``` | ```
SECTION .data
sum: DD 0

SECTION .text
global _main
_main:
mov eax, 25
mov ebx, 50
add eax, ebx
mov DWORD [sum], eax

mov eax, 1
mov ebx, 0
int 80h
``` |

Directives are assembler-specific commands not related to the instruction set that allow you to define variables, indicate memory segments, and many other things. Directives direct the assembler to do something. For example, in the following code snippet the directive DWORD tells the assembler to reserve 32 bits of memory (a doubleword), which we initialize with a value of 42, and assign the name "answer" to that specific memory block for future programmer use.

```
answer DWORD 42          ; DWORD is the directive
```

Table 3.4 shows the sample program with the directives highlighted.

Table 3.4 Sample directives

GAS	MASM	NASM
| ```
.data
sum: .long 0

.text
.globl _main
_main:
movl $25, %eax
movl $50, %ebx
addl %ebx, %eax
movl %eax, sum

pushl $0
subl $4, %esp
movl $1, %eax
int $0x80
.end
``` | ```
.386
.MODEL FLAT, stdcall
.STACK 4096

ExitProcess PROTO,
dwExitCode:DWORD

.data
sum DWORD 0

.code
_main PROC
mov eax, 25
mov ebx, 50
add eax, ebx
mov sum, eax

INVOKE ExitProcess, 0
_main ENDP
END
``` | ```
SECTION .data
sum: DD 0

SECTION .text
global _main
_main:
mov eax, 25
mov ebx, 50
add eax, ebx
mov DWORD [sum], eax

mov eax, 1
mov ebx, 0
int 80h
``` |

At this point we need to discuss some major differences with MASM directives. You may have noticed that the beginning of the MASM sample program has a few lines of code that GAS and NASM do not have, before the data section. The MASM directives used are necessary for 32-bit programs; they configure specific environment settings for the program. Table 3.5 lists and describes the MASM-specific directives.

Table 3.5 32-bit MASM-specific directives

Directive	Description
.386	Enables the 80386 processor instructions and disables newer instructions. Other valid settings to enable additional instructions are .486, .586, .686, .MMX, and .XMM, among others.
.MODEL	Sets the memory model. The only valid parameter for 32-bit programs is FLAT (protected mode). The .MODEL directive also takes a second parameter to set the function-calling convention, which is discussed in **CHAPTER 6**.
.STACK	Sets the size of the stack memory segment for the program. The directive cannot be used without the .MODEL directive. While the default value is 1024, we recommend using 4096 to make stack the same size as a memory page in 32-bit Windows.

The directives in Table 3.5 are not used in 64-bit MASM programs. The beginning of a 64-bit MASM program starts similarly to GAS and NASM programs with the data section.

Program sections, also called segments, are denoted with directives that specify the segment for the assembler. Segments are special sections pre-defined by the assembler. Table 3.6 lists the common Assembly sections for use in programs.

Table 3.6 Assembler-specific program sections

GAS	MASM	NASM	Description
.bss	.data	SECTION .bss	Uninitialized variables
.data		SECTION .data	Initialized variables
.text	.code	SECTION .text	Executable code/instructions

Table 3.7 shows the sample program with the section directives highlighted.

Table 3.7 Sample program sections

GAS	MASM	NASM

`.data`
`sum: .long 0`
 	
`.text`
`.globl _main`
`_main:`
`movl $25, %eax`
`movl $50, %ebx`
`addl %ebx, %eax`
`movl %eax, sum`
 	
`pushl $0`
`subl $4, %esp`
`movl $1, %eax`
`int $0x80`
`.end`
	`.386`
	`.MODEL FLAT, stdcall`
	`.STACK 4096`
	`ExitProcess PROTO,`
	`dwExitCode:DWORD`
	
	`.data`
	`sum DWORD 0`
	
	`.code`
	`_main PROC`
	`mov eax, 25`
	`mov ebx, 50`
	`add eax, ebx`
	`mov sum, eax`
	
	`INVOKE ExitProcess, 0`
	`_main ENDP`
	`END`
		`SECTION .data`
		`sum: DD 0`
		
		`SECTION .text`
		`global _main`
		`_main:`
		`mov eax, 25`
		`mov ebx, 50`
		`add eax, ebx`
		`mov DWORD [sum], eax`
		
		`mov eax, 1`
		`mov ebx, 0`
		`int 80h`

The section on Data Definition later in this chapter further explains how program segments are used and what information they contain.

Instructions are the executable statements in a program that we begin covering in detail in **CHAPTER 4**; however, a preliminary explanation is warranted here. Instructions are comprised of two basic parts defined by the following syntax.

```
mnemonic [operands]
```

The **mnemonic** is the instruction name a programmer uses to refer to a particular instruction in the architecture's instruction set. A mnemonic is an abbreviation or acronym that identifies the action of the instruction and in reality is an English-like representation of a numeric opcode (as shown in **CHAPTER 1**). Table 3.8 highlights the instructions in the sample program.

Table 3.8 Sample instructions

GAS	MASM	NASM
.data sum: .long 0 .text .globl _main _main: **movl** $25, %eax **movl** $50, %ebx **addl** %ebx, %eax **movl** %eax, sum **pushl** $0 **subl** $4, %esp **movl** $1, %eax **int** $0x80 .end	.386 .MODEL FLAT, stdcall .STACK 4096 ExitProcess PROTO, dwExitCode:DWORD .data sum DWORD 0 .code _main PROC **mov** eax, 25 **mov** ebx, 50 **add** eax, ebx **mov** sum, eax INVOKE ExitProcess, 0 _main ENDP END	SECTION .data sum: DD 0 SECTION .text global _main _main: **mov** eax, 25 **mov** ebx, 50 **add** eax, ebx **mov** DWORD [sum], eax **mov** eax, 1 **mov** ebx, 0 **int** 80h

Some instructions do not require any operands, some require one, some two, and some three. The following lines of code are examples of instructions that require a different number of operands.

```
stc                 ; no operands, sets the carry flag
inc eax             ; 1 operand, increments eax by 1
mov eax, 5          ; 2 operands, moves literal value 5 into eax
imul eax, ebx, 5    ; 3 operands, multiplies literal value 5 and the
                    ; value in ebx and stores the result in eax
```

LEARNING: At this point it will be helpful to use Appendices B and D to write, execute, and debug Program 3.1 to ensure that you have a working programming environment and get a feel for the basics. Before continuing through the chapter, make sure the sample program assembles, and use a breakpoint to watch register values change as you step through the program line by line. Then, you can modify the program as you learn new concepts throughout the chapter and reinforce your understanding of each concept.

Literals

Literal values, often called **immediates**, are explicit values specified by the programmer, such as integers, real numbers, characters, and strings. For example, the following line of code would add the literal value 5 to the current contents of the 32-bit register *eax*.

```
add eax, 5
```

> **PROGRAMMING:** Immediates are used in cases where the programmer knows the exact value to be used in an instruction. Many programs rely on user input for data, but in other cases constant values are useful. For example, consider a simple program that converts a person's weight from pounds to kilograms. The program would expect one piece of data from the user (weight in pounds) and would multiply pounds by a conversion factor (2.2) in order to convert the weight to kilograms. The conversion factor is a constant value that can be specified as a literal value.

By default, **integer literals** are whole-number decimal (base-10) values. In some situations, using a different base for literal values is useful or even necessary. In MASM and NASM, writing numbers in other bases can be done by appending a radix (numeric base) character to the literal value, as shown in Table 3.9.

Table 3.9 MASM/NASM integer radix characters

Radix	Base
b	Binary (base-2)
d	Decimal (base-10)
h	Hexadecimal (base-16)
q, o	Octal (base-8)

The following examples show how to encode the base-10 value 31 in each of the supported bases with MASM and NASM.

MASM/NASM
```
00011111b   ; b is the radix character for binary
31          ; decimal values do not need radix characters
31d         ; but you can specify d for decimal
1Fh         ; h is the radix character for hexadecimal
37o         ; o is the radix character for octal
```

A case worth noting is when a hexadecimal value begins with a character, such as memory addresses. When a literal value begins with a character, the assembler interprets it as an identifier instead of a value. The conflict can be overcome by prefixing the hexadecimal value with a zero.

MASM/NASM
```
0FFFF0342h   ; the actual value is FFFF0342 in hexadecimal
```

GAS takes a different approach to integer literals depending on the program section (sections were discussed in Pillars of Assembly Code). As shown in Table 3.10, literal values in the *.data* section must be prefixed with radix characters to delineate the base, while literal values in the *.text* section must be prefixed with the dollar sign ($) in addition to the radix characters. Base-10 numbers are the exception, which are written without radix characters.

Table 3.10 GAS prefix and radix characters

.*data* Prefix	.*text* Prefix	Base
0b	$0b	Binary (base-2)
n/a	$	Decimal (base-10)
0x	$0x	Hexadecimal (base-16)
0	$0	Octal (base-8)

The following examples show how to encode the base-10 value 31 in both the .*data* and .*text* sections using GAS syntax.

GAS

```
.data              .text
0b00011111         $0b00011111
31                 $31
0x1F               $0x1F
037                $037
```

Real numbers (floating-point values) are much more complex than integers and so we cover real numbers in **Chapter 8**.

Character literals are single character values that, like integer literals, are explicit values specified by the programmer. Single quotes or double quotes can be used to enclose a character literal in MASM and NASM, thus making the following two values equivalent.

MASM/NASM

```
"A"
'A'
```

In GAS, character literals are specified differently depending on the section. In the .*data* section, characters are surrounded by single quotes while in the .*text* section characters are also prefixed with the dollar sign ($).

GAS

```
.data              .text
'A'                $'A'
```

 ATTENTION: As described in **Chapter 1**, characters are stored in memory as ASCII-encoded values (integers). For example, the letter 'A' is stored in memory as 65 decimal (41 hexadecimal).

String literals are multiple character literals grouped together, typically forming a word or phrase. Like characters, strings can be enclosed in either single or double quotes in MASM and NASM, but GAS requires double quotes. Sometimes you may want quotes to be part of a string. In MASM and NASM, you must use the opposite type of quotes to enclose the string. With GAS, you must escape the inner quote(s) with a backslash (\) so the string is not prematurely ended.

GAS

```
"This string \"contains\" double quotes!"
```

MASM/NASM

```
"I don't understand contractions."          ; strings that have one
'"Good job," said the father to his son.'    ; type of quotes on the
                                             ; outside and a different
                                             ; type on the inside
```

Strings are usually stored as a byte array, with each byte containing an ASCII-encoded value of an individual character in the string. The following example shows a string literal and the individual array elements stored in memory as ASCII decimal values.

String Characters	D	a	i	s	y	,		d	a	i	s	y
ASCII Decimal Values	68	97	105	115	121	44	32	100	97	105	115	121

Labels and Comments

Labels give you the ability to partition code for programmatic or design purposes. Labels not only allow for greater clarity when reading code, but more importantly they facilitate jumping or looping to different parts of a program when necessary. Labels are created by using an identifier followed by a colon.

```
identifier:
```

Labels can be created on their own line or on the same line as an instruction. Depending on the assembler, labels are either case-sensitive and used in the *.text* section (GAS and NASM), or case-insensitive and used in the equivalent *.code* section (MASM).

```
userLoop:
            inc counter

otherLoop: inc counter2
```

CHAPTER 5 discusses using labels to implement loops in Assembly language.

Comments are an integral part of every program. Comments allow you to explain the *why* and *how* of the code (as opposed to the *what*, which is usually more obvious). Comments are very important with Assembly code since more abstract objectives are not always easily comprehendible when reading a sequence of primitive instructions.

Two types of comments exist in Assembly: single-line comments and multi-line comments. **Single-line comments** begin with a hash (#) in GAS or a semi-colon (;) in MASM and NASM. A comment can be on its own line or be appended to any existing line of code.

GAS

```
# Moves the counter value into eax
movl counter, %eax
```

MASM/NASM

```
mov eax, counter ; Moves the counter value into eax
```

Multi-line comments can only be used in GAS and MASM. In GAS, multi-line comments are identical to C-style multi-line comments, beginning with /* and ending with */ and they can appear anywhere in the code. In MASM, multi-line comments must be separate from other lines of code and they consist of four parts: the word COMMENT, a beginning character, the comment text, and an ending character, which must be the same as the beginning character. One caveat to MASM multi-line comments is that the character used to begin and end the comment cannot be found within the comment text. Traditionally, the exclamation point (!) is used for multi-line comments in MASM.

GAS

```
mov $10, %eax        /* This is a multi-line comment that is
                        partially on the same line as
                        an instruction and partially on
                        separate lines */
```

MASM

```
COMMENT !
     This is the section of the code where
     employee salaries are calculated. Note
     how the exclamation point is not in the
     text of the comment.
!
```

Data Definition

Data types in Assembly language are indicative of their size (8 bits, 16 bits, 32 bits, etc.) rather than their contents (integer, double, string, etc.) as in high-level programming languages. Data, no matter the contents, is defined using a default set of data types. Table 3.11 lists the data type naming conventions by assembler.

Table 3.11 Default data type directives

Directive			Description
GAS	MASM	NASM	
.byte, .ascii	DB, BYTE	DB	1 byte (8-bit) integer
	SBYTE		1 byte (8-bit) signed integer
.word	DW, WORD	DW	2 byte (16-bit) integer
	SWORD		2 byte (16-bit) signed integer
.long	DD, DWORD	DD	4 byte (32-bit) integer
	SDWORD		4 byte (32-bit) signed integer
.quad	DQ, QWORD	DQ	8 byte (64-bit) integer
	DT, TBYTE	DT	10 byte (80-bit) integer
.octa			16 byte (128-bit) integer

Table 3.11 appears to suggest that MASM can work with more data types than GAS or NASM, but that is not the case. MASM performs many of its operations by assuming the data type from context, whereas GAS and NASM do not make assumptions. You can work with all of the same data in all three assemblers. However, as you will learn in future chapters, in GAS and NASM you must explicitly tell the assembler what data types (size) are being used when executing an instruction.

> **PROGRAMMING:** Choosing the correct size for variables is important. A programmer should anticipate the possible values that will be stored in a variable to avoid semantic errors. Semantic (logic) errors will not halt the assembling or execution of a program, but they can produce incorrect results when the program runs. For example, if you create two 8-bit variables and ask the user to enter two values to be multiplied together, the result of the multiplication could be larger than 8 bits. So, you would need at least a 16-bit variable for the result. Using variables that are too small for their intended use could result in the loss of data, and thus an incorrect result.

A **variable** definition has the following syntax.

GAS/NASM

```
[identifier:] directive initializer [,initializer]...
```

MASM

```
[identifier]  directive initializer [,initializer]...
```

All variables defined in the *.data* section (for all assemblers) must be initialized (given an initial value). The following examples show valid variable definitions.

GAS

```
val1:        .byte 17
valArray:    .long 0xFFFFFF, 0xFFFFFE, 0xFFFFD
```

MASM

```
charInput    BYTE 'A'
myArray      DWORD 41h, 75, 0C4h, 01010101b
```

NASM

```
counter:     DB 0
wageArray:   DD 75, 100, 125
```

Notice the examples that use multiple initializers separated by commas. Using multiple initializers for an identifier is the method for creating an **array**. An array is a sequence of same-size values referenced by a single name that identifies the first location/value in the sequence. Instead of creating four separate identifiers, we created one identifier that represents the start of a four-value sequence, each one doubleword (32 bits) in size. Each array identifier is actually the memory reference of the first value. We address methods of accessing values in an array in **CHAPTER 4**.

Sometimes **uninitialized variables** are necessary in a program. Uninitialized variables are variables that are not given an initial value; they simply reserve a certain amount of memory for programmer use. Different assemblers accomplish uninitialized memory allocation in very different ways. MASM offers the question mark (?) as an initializer so that uninitialized variables can be created in the *.data* section, which is only meant for initialized variables in GAS and NASM.

MASM

```
.data
num DWORD   6                 ; defines an initialized identifier
sum SDWORD  ?                 ; defines an uninitialized identifier
myArray    BYTE 10 DUP (1)    ; defines an array of initialized bytes
myUArray   BYTE 10 DUP (?)    ; defines an array of uninitialized bytes
```

The **DUP** directive can be used in MASM to create duplicate values of a specified size and initializer in sequence. Any valid initializer can be used, including the question mark. In the MASM example, `myArray` is an array of 10 byte values each initialized to 1, and in `myUArray` each is initialized to ? (uninitialized).

GAS and NASM require that all uninitialized variables be created in the *.bss* (Block Started by Symbol) program segment. Both GAS and NASM require you to use data type directives specifically for uninitialized data, which are listed in Table 3.12.

Table 3.12 Uninitialized data type directives

Directive		Description
GAS	NASM	
.lcomm	RESB	Reserve a byte (8 bits)
	RESW	Reserve a word (16 bits)
	RESD	Reserve a double word (32 bits)
	RESQ	Reserve a quad word (64 bits)
	REST	Reserve a ten-byte (80 bits)

The following examples show valid uninitialized variable definitions in GAS and NASM. Note how defining uninitialized variables in GAS differs from the syntax rule of [identifier: directive initializer]. Instead, the format is [directive identifier, reserved_bytes]. You can use the uninitialized data type directives in GAS and NASM to reserve memory for a single variable or an array. For example, in the NASM code we create a 64-byte buffer, which can be used as an array containing 64 values.

GAS

```
.bss
.lcomm sum, 2          # Reserve 2 bytes
.lcomm answer, 4       # Reserves 4 bytes
```

NASM

```
SECTION .bss
memAddr: RESD 1        ; Reserves 1 DWORD (4 bytes)
buffer:  RESB 64       ; Reserves 64 bytes
```

As previously explained, **strings** are stored as BYTE arrays. Strings need to be null-terminated, which means that the last byte must be ASCII-zero. Null-terminating a string is achieved differently depending on the assembler. GAS uses the \0 sequence to add the null terminator to the end of a string, while MASM and NASM just use the literal value 0 as the last byte. GAS also has an .ASCIZ directive that automatically adds a zero byte to the end of a string.

Line breaks are also an important aspect of strings. Inserting line breaks is different depending on the assembler. In GAS, the escape sequence \n will insert a newline (line-feed) character. In MASM, the CR/LF (carriage-return / line-feed) hexadecimal codes 0Dh and 0Ah need to be inserted where a line break is desired. In NASM, only the LF (line-feed) hexadecimal code 0Ah needs to be inserted.

GAS

```
# The \n in the middle of the string adds a newline
motd: .ascii "The only way to win\nis not to play\0"
motd: .asciz "The only way to win\nis not to play"
```

MASM

```
; motd contains a single-line string
motd  BYTE "Welcome to Earth...",0

; motd2 contains a multi-line string with a newline at the end
motd2 BYTE "Thank you for using our system.",0Dh,0Ah
      BYTE "All of your activity will be monitored"
      BYTE "by our system administrators",0Dh,0Ah,0
```

NASM

```
; The 0Ah in the middle of the string adds a newline
motd: DB "How about a nice",0Ah,"game of chess",0
```

Symbolic constants can be used in MASM in lieu of variables when you have certain values in a program that never change as a result of the program's execution. Symbolic constants hold 32-bit integers in x86 and 64-bit integers in x86_64 and are defined with the equal sign (=). Symbolic constants are for integer-based data.

MASM

```
identifier = value
```

Symbolic constants have some advantages. If you are going to use a value multiple times throughout a program, such as an employee's hourly wage, assigning the value to a regular identifier has two distinct advantages: (1) use of a name, such as HOURLY_WAGE, throughout a program makes the code more readable, and (2) having the numeric value in a single place makes changes easier should the hourly wage go up or down. Symbolic constants in MASM provide the same two advantages plus one more: symbolic constants do not use any memory. At assembly time, MASM replaces all instances of a symbolic constant with the programmer-defined value.

MASM

```
.data
HOURLY_WAGE = 75
.code
mov eax, HOURLY_WAGE
```

When assembled, the above code will be transformed automatically and instances of the symbolic constant will be replaced with the literal value.

```
mov eax, 75    ; MASM automatically replaces the symbol with the value
```

The symbolic constant example using the equal sign only works with the MASM assembler. Symbolic constants can also hold string values in MASM.

All assemblers can make use of symbolic constants when they hold expressions. In order to define a symbol that holds an expression, the **EQU** directive must be used. Unlike the previously explained methods of defining variables, symbols can be created with EQU in both the data and code segments (i.e., *.data* and *.text* for GAS, *.data* and *.code* for MASM, and *SECTION .data* and *SECTION .text* for NASM). The assemblers will replace every occurrence of a symbol with the expression at assembly time.

GAS

```
.equ identifier, expression    # numeric operations
.equ identifier, value         # a single value (constant)
.equ identifier, "symbol"      # another existing symbol
```

MASM

```
identifier EQU expression    ; numeric operations
identifier EQU symbol        ; another existing symbol
identifier EQU <text>        ; useful for non-integer data (float, string)
```

NASM

```
identifier: EQU expression    ; numeric operations
identifier: EQU value         ; a single value (constant)
identifier: EQU "text"        ; text can be four characters max (32-bit)
```

As demonstrated in the examples, symbolic constant syntax and behavior is very different in the assemblers. We recommend limiting the use of EQU to numeric expressions.

```
.equ test, (2 * 6 / 3)    # GAS
test EQU (2 * 6 / 3)      ; MASM
test: EQU (2 * 6 / 3)     ; NASM
```

EQU can also be useful for creating a constant symbol for the length of an identifier's memory space. The GAS and NASM examples below show how to use an expression to get the size of a string in bytes. The **current location counter**, the period (.) in GAS and the dollar sign ($) in MASM and NASM, represents the memory address of where the counter symbol exists in code. The current location counter can be used to subtract the starting memory address of the previous string from the current location, resulting in the size of the string in bytes. In MASM, the equal sign (=) can be used with the current location counter.

GAS

```
motd: .byte "Are you in the matrix?\0"
.equ len, (. - motd)
```

MASM

```
motd  BYTE "Are you in the matrix?",0
len = ($ - motd)
```

NASM

```
motd: DB "I'm in the matrix?",0
len:  EQU ($ - motd)
```

Another feature MASM offers is a way to create a symbol that is dynamic, called a text macro. The **TEXTEQU** directive is used to create such symbols, which can be expressions using other symbols and even instructions.

MASM

```
identifier TEXTEQU %(expression)
identifier TEXTEQU textmacro
identifier TEXTEQU <text>
```

Note how the instructions in the following example are not enclosed in quotes but are enclosed in angled brackets, since instructions are non-integer expressions.

MASM

```
MULTIPLIER = 2
freq    TEXTEQU %(400 * MULTIPLIER)
movFreq TEXTEQU <mov eax, freq>
```

With the `movFreq` text macro created, you could use it at any point in your code to execute the instruction (`mov eax, freq`).

MASM

```
.code
movFreq
```

Working Examples

The basic information explained in this chapter is crucial to comprehending subsequent chapters. Although CHAPTERS 4 AND 5 cover instructions in detail, it is important to see this chapter's content used in the context of a working Assembly program. The Program 3.2 examples are the same Assembly program written for the three assemblers. For brevity, the GAS version is fully commented, while the MASM and NASM programs are shown with just the code. Fully commented versions for all three assemblers are available for download (https://github.com/brianrhall/Assembly).

> LEARNING: Using your preferred development environment, write and execute one of the following code examples and ensure you have a working program. Then, purposefully create syntax errors in the program to see how those errors are described by the system. Errors such as mistyping variable names, using mismatched sizes with variables and registers, and forgetting a colon with program sections are typical errors that a programmer might make. Knowing what you did to cause an error and seeing the error message can help you decipher error messages you encounter in the future.

Program 3.2 *Working example*

GAS

```
.data                                   # Section for variable definitions

decimalLiteral:     .byte 31            # Variable storing 31
hexLiteral:         .long 0xF           # Variable storing F (15 in decimal)
charLiteral:        .byte 'A'           # Variable storing 65 in decimal

# Variable containing a string that has a line break and is null-terminated
stringLiteral:      .ascii "This string has\na line break in it.\0"

# Variable that calculates the value of an expression to determine the
# length, in bytes, of the variable "stringLiteral" by subtracting the
# starting memory address of the variable from the current memory address
.equ lenString, (. - stringLiteral)

.bss                                    # Section for uninitialized variables
.lcomm unInitVariable, 4                # Uninitialized, 4-byte variable

.text                                   # Section for instructions
.globl _main                           # Make the label "_main"
                                        # available to the linker as an
                                        # entry point for the program
_main:                                  # Label for program entry

# Label and instruction on
# the same line below
partOne: movl $10, %eax                 # Assign 10 to the eax register
addl hexLiteral, %eax                   # Add the value in hexLiteral to
                                        # the contents of the eax register
                                        # and store the result in eax

partTwo:                                # Label on its own line
inc %eax                                # Increment the value in eax

pushl $0                                # Push the return value on the stack
subl $4, %esp                           # Pad the stack for INT requirement
movl $1, %eax                           # Set the system call to 1 for exit
int $0x80                               # Issue the kernel interrupt
.end                                    # End assembling
```

MASM	NASM

<pre>.386
.MODEL FLAT, stdcall
.STACK 4096
 	
ExitProcess PROTO, dwExitCode:DWORD
 	
.data
decimalLiteral BYTE 31
hexLiteral   DWORD 0Fh
charLiteral   BYTE 'A'
unInitVariable DWORD ?
 	
stringLiteral
  BYTE "This is a stringthat",0dh,0ah
  BYTE "has a line break in it.",0
lenString   EQU ($ - stringLiteral)
 	
.code
_main PROC
 	
partOne: mov eax, 10
add eax, hexLiteral
 	
partTwo:
inc eax
 	
INVOKE ExitProcess, 0
_main ENDP
END</pre>
	<pre>SECTION .data
	
	decimalLiteral: DB 31
	hexLiteral: DD 0Fh
	charLiteral: DB 'A'
	
	stringLiteral:
	  DB "This is a string that",0ah
	  DB "has a line break in it.",0
	lenString: EQU ($ - stringLiteral)
	
	SECTION .bss
	unInitVariable: RESD 1
	
	SECTION .text
	global _main
	
	_main:
	
	partOne: mov eax, 10
	add eax, hexLiteral
	
	partTwo:
	inc eax
	
	mov eax, 1
	mov ebx, 0
	int 80h</pre>

PROGRAMMING: Program 3.2 demonstrates how to properly terminate (exit) an assembly program for the given environments (i.e., 32-bit Mac, Windows, and Linux) via system calls. Other exit routines are necessary in different environments (e.g., GAS on Linux, 64-bit, etc.). **APPENDIX A** includes 32-bit and 64-bit exit routines for GAS, NASM, and MASM, while system calls are covered in **CHAPTER 10**.

Summary

In this chapter we covered the basic elements of Assembly programs. You should now understand Assembly structure and program sections. You should also be able to define and initialize data in an Assembly program. We discussed important differences between the assembler syntaxes, from creating variables to making comments. The two working programs for each assembler in this chapter helped you get started with writing and assembling code. The programs can serve as templates for future programs.

Key Terms

array

character literals

comments

current location counter

directives

DUP

EQU

identifiers

immediate

instructions

integer literals

labels

mnemonic

multi-line comments

program sections

real numbers

reserved words

single-line comments

string literals

strings

symbolic constants

TEXTEQU

uninitialized variables

variable

Code Review

.ASCIZ	GAS data directive that automatically adds a zero byte to the end of a string
ADD	Instruction that adds the value in one register/variable to another register/variable
ADDL	GAS instruction that adds the value in one register/variable to another register/variable (long integer)
DUP	MASM directive to create duplicate values of a specified size and initializer in sequence
EQU, .equ	Directive to create a new symbol containing the result of an expression
INC	Instruction that increments the value in a register/variable
MOV	Instruction that copies the value in one register/variable to another register/variable
MOVL	GAS instruction that copies the value in one register/variable to another register/variable (long integer)
STC	Instruction that sets the processor's carry flag
TEXTEQU	MASM directive that creates a new symbol containing the resulting value of a text substitution

Questions

Short Answer

1. A _____ value is a value directly specified by the programmer rather than the result of an expression.
2. By default, integer literals are in base _____.
3. In order to use the base-10 value 50 as a hexadecimal value in NASM, you would specify it as _____.
4. In order to use the hexadecimal value 0x34 as a binary value in GAS, you would specify it as _____.
5. Character literals are stored as _____ in memory.
6. This book recommends only using the following characters in identifier names: _____, _____, and _____.
7. _____ are assembler-specific commands that allow you to do many things, such as define variables, indicate memory segments, and so on.
8. Labels must be followed by a _____.
9. _____ and _____ are the only assemblers that make use of multi-line comments.
10. The _____ character signifies a single-line comment in MASM.

11. The _____ directive is used to declare a 32-bit signed integer variable in MASM.
12. The _____ directive is used to reserve 64-bits of uninitialized memory in NASM.
13. In MASM, a newline in a string is represented by the _____ hexadecimal value(s). In NASM, a newline in a string is represented by the _____ hexadecimal value(s).
14. The EQU directive can be used with the _____ to determine the length of a string.
15. An abbreviated version of a longer word or words that explains the action of an instruction is a(n) _____.

True/False

1. The semicolon represents a single-line comment in GAS.
2. Instructions may not use any operands.
3. The current location symbol in NASM is the dollar sign.
4. The *.octa* directive is used to declare an 80-bit variable in GAS.
5. Uninitialized variables are declared in the *.bss* section of a program in MASM.

Assignments

Assignments 1 and 2 require you to use a specific assembler. Since one of the purposes of this chapter is to introduce you to differences in assemblers, we ask you to demonstrate what you have learned. Assignment 3 does not have any specific assembler requirement; solve the problem using the assembler with which you are most comfortable.

3.1 Defining variables

Create a program for GAS that contains the following items:

- A sum variable of the appropriate size to hold the initializer 0x10000
- A message variable that holds the text (preserving line breaks):
    ```
    Welcome to Assembly programming.
    Your grade will be randomly assigned
    by the Intel 8086 processor!
    ```
- An input variable that does not contain an initial value and is able to hold the values 0-255
- An instruction to assign the base-10 value 200 to the input variable as a binary literal

3.2 Using expressions with symbols

Create a program for NASM that contains the following items:

- A message variable that holds the text (preserving line breaks):
    ```
    You already know what the next
    variable will be, don't you?
    ```
- A length variable that holds the size of the message variable
- A length5 variable (also in the data section) that holds the result of adding 5 to length (use EQU)
- A one-operand instruction that adds 1 to the value in the length5 variable (think outside the box for this requirement)

3.3 Syntax translation

Translate the following GAS program into either MASM or NASM. Refer to APPENDIX A.

```
# Syntax translation - GAS
.data

.bss
.lcomm letter, 1
.lcomm r, 4
.lcomm s, 4
.lcomm t, 4
.lcomm x, 2
.lcomm y, 2
.lcomm z, 2

.text
.globl _main
_main:

movb $0x77, letter
movl $0x5, r
movl $0x2, s
movw $0xa, x
movw $0x4, y

movw x, %ax
addw y, %ax
movw %ax, z

movw x, %ax
subw y, %ax
movw %ax, z

movl $0x0, %edx
movl r, %eax
movl s, %ecx
divl %ecx
movl %eax, t

movl $0x0, %edx
movl r, %eax
movl s, %ecx
divl %ecx
movl %edx, t

pushl $0
subl $4, %esp
movl $1, %eax
int $0x80
.end
```

3.4 Order of operations (Challenge Assignment)

Create a program that calculates the following expression: `answer = (A + B) - (C + D)`

- The answer must be stored in a variable of the correct data type given your data
  (`A, B, C, D`).
- The values for your data (`A, B, C, D`) must be stored in registers (e.g., *eax*, *ebx*), not variables.
- You must supply the initial values for the data (`A, B, C, D`).
- Create a string that *could* accompany the answer in an output statement
  (e.g., `"The answer is:"`). You do not have to output the string.
- Comment each line of code, as demonstrated in the Working Examples Section Program 3.2 for GAS, to briefly describe each line's meaning.

CHAPTER 4

Basic Instructions

Objectives

- Perform integer arithmetic
- Manipulate data at the bit level
- Explain different addressing modes
- Construct arrays
- Convert data to different data sizes and types

Outline

Web Resources

Assembler References

- https://sourceware.org/binutils/docs/as/ (GAS Reference)
- https://msdn.microsoft.com/en-us/library/afzk3475.aspx (MASM Reference)
- http://www.nasm.us/doc/nasmdoc0.html (NASM Reference)

x86 Instruction Set Listings

- http://www.intel.com/content/www/us/en/processors/architectures-software-developer-manuals.html (Volume 1, Chapter 5 Instruction Set Summary, Section 5.1)
- http://www.felixcloutier.com/x86/
- http://x86.renejeschke.de
- https://en.wikipedia.org/wiki/X86_instruction_listings
- http://www.nasm.us/doc/nasmdocb.html

Introduction

Chapter 4 covers basic Assembly instructions that will enable you to begin writing simple programs. Since arithmetic is a foundational component of any piece of software, we begin by explaining basic arithmetic instructions. After covering some arithmetic, we break down instructions to explain exactly how data is used in operations: how data can be referenced and transferred. We address topics such as manually accessing memory locations based on byte offsets, creating and using arrays, and working with pointers.

> ⚠ ATTENTION: The x86 and x86_64 instruction sets are fairly complex. Throughout this chapter and book, we present an overview. We do not present and explain every single instruction. We do provide enough instruction information to cover important concepts, facilitate learning, and prepare you for programming in x86 Assembly. We expect that you will explore the instruction set further as necessary.

Due to the fact that not all instructions can accept every type of operand, we provide a naming convention that will be used in the syntax definitions throughout this chapter and subsequent chapters. Table 4.1 defines three different operand types and assigns shorthand notation for each.

Table 4.1 Operand definitions

Operand	Description
L	A literal (immediate) value (e.g., 42).
M	A memory (variable) operand (e.g., numOfStudents).
R	A register (e.g., eax).

Some instructions accept multiple types of operands. In such cases the operand list will have multiple operands from Table 4.1 separated by slashes (e.g., M/R). In addition to accepting multiple types of operands, some instructions are limited by the size of the operands they can accept. In such cases you will see the operand appended with a number denoting the size, in bits, of the operand (e.g., L8, M16, M32/R32).

> ▣ PROGRAMMING: In many cases MASM, and sometimes NASM, infers from context the data types of the operands used with an instruction. GAS does not assume data types. Consequently, GAS instructions are usually appended with a letter indicating the size of the operand(s) being used. The letter appended is the first letter of the data types detailed in **CHAPTER 3, TABLE 3.11** (e.g., ADDB for byte, ADDL for long, etc.).
>
> For NASM, dereferenced variables require the size to be specified when used as the destination operand. In such cases you must specify the size before the variable using a size directive (e.g., BYTE for byte, WORD for word, DWORD for doubleword, etc.). An example is mov DWORD [test], eax.

By the end of this chapter you will understand and be able to perform basic Assembly arithmetic, data addressing, and data transfer operations.

Data Movement and Arithmetic

CHAPTER 3 introduced you to the concept of one line of code being one operation, as opposed to high-level languages where more complex statements translate into multiple low-level operations. The C++ code result = (var1 + 5) / (var2 - 4); looks like a single operation to a programmer since it is a single line of code. In reality, the processor performs at least three distinct operations (addition, subtraction, and division) to arrive at the result. Storing the value in result is a fourth operation. When programming in Assembly you must be aware of the difference and write code accordingly.

A common mistake for a novice Assembly programmer is writing an incorrect order of operations. High-level languages typically perform arithmetic operations in the proper order automatically. Assembly language requires the programmer to write the instructions in the proper order to arrive at the correct result.

Data Movement

In order to complete most sequences of instructions, data must be copied from one location to another location. For example, the C++ code above needs to copy the result of the equation into the `result` variable. But first, values would have been copied into the `var1` and `var2` variables. Moving data between registers and memory is an important part of Assembly programming. Most data movement is accomplished via the **MOV** instruction. MOV copies data from the source location to the destination location. In our GAS examples, the italic `'S'`, as in MOV*S*, should be replaced with the letter representing the operand size.

GAS

```
MOVS $L/M/%R, M/%R          # MOVL $10, sum
```

MASM

```
MOV M/R, L/M/R              ; MOV eax, sum
```

NASM

```
MOV SIZE [M]/R, L/[M]/R     ; MOV DWORD [sum], edx
```

The MOV instruction has some specific rules:

- Both operands must be the same size (although this is flexible via directives as we will see later);
- Both operands cannot be memory operands (must use a register as an in-between);
- The instruction pointer register (*ip/eip/rip*) cannot be a destination operand.

A unique situation arises when data in two locations needs to be swapped. A data swap can be accomplished using the MOV instruction, but a swap requires an in-between step to save data to a temporary location. For example, swapping the data in *eax* with the data in *ebx* requires three steps: (1) temporarily copying the data in *ebx* to another location, such as *edx*; (2) copying the data in *eax* to *ebx*; and (3) copying the data temporarily moved to *edx* into *eax*. Such an approach requires three instructions to properly swap data between *eax* and *ebx*. A simpler approach is using the **XCHG** instruction, which performs a swap in a single instruction.

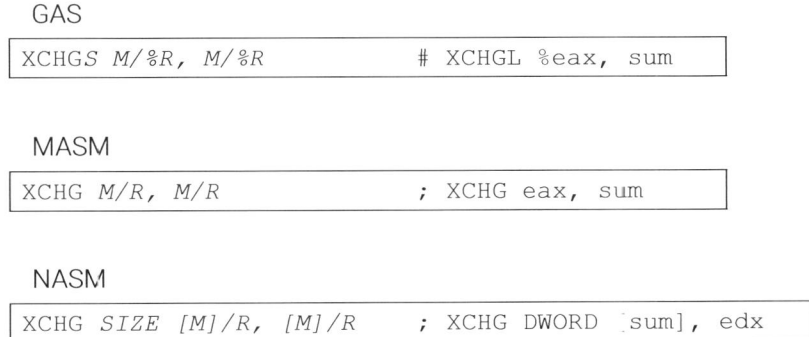

GAS

```
XCHGS M/%R, M/%R            # XCHGL %eax, sum
```

MASM

```
XCHG M/R, M/R              ; XCHG eax, sum
```

NASM

```
XCHG SIZE [M]/R, [M]/R     ; XCHG DWORD [sum], edx
```

As with MOV, the XCHG instruction cannot be executed with two memory operands.

More instructions exist for moving data that are for specific types of data moves. Such instructions are for more advanced scenarios and they will be covered later in this chapter.

 LEARNING: Write a program that attempts to copy data into each register discussed in **CHAPTER 2**. Beware of the registers not allowed as either the source or destination operand with the MOV instruction.

Addition and Subtraction

Before jumping into addition and subtraction with literals and variables, we will start with the simplest forms: adding one and subtracting one. Anyone who has written software knows that adding and subtracting one are important operations due to their varied use (e.g., loop counters, keeping track of user input, and array referencing). Just as high-level languages have operators to increment and decrement variables, Assembly language has increment and decrement instructions.

The **INC** and **DEC** instructions can be used on any memory (variable) or register operand. INC and DEC have a singular purpose: adding or subtracting one.

GAS

```
INCS M/%R          #  INCL sum
DECS M/%R          #  DECL %eax
```

MASM

```
INC M/R            ;  INC sum
DEC M/R            ;  DEC eax
```

NASM

```
INC SIZE [M]/R     ;  INC DWORD [sum]
DEC SIZE [M]/R     ;  DEC eax
```

> **PROGRAMMING:** NASM treats variables similar to the way pointers are treated in C++. Just using the identifier results in a memory address. If you want to refer to the data stored in the memory address, which is aliased by the identifier, you need to dereference the variable with brackets (e.g., [sum]), similar to using the asterisk in C++.

The **ADD** and **SUB** instructions allow you to perform addition and subtraction using literal values as well as values that exist in memory or registers.

GAS

```
# src, dest
ADDS $L/M/%R, M/%R      # ADDW $50, sum
SUBS $L/M/%R, M/%R      # SUBL val, %eax
```

MASM

```
; dest, src
ADD M/R, L/M/R         ; ADD sum, 50
SUB M/R, L/M/R         ; SUB eax, val
```

NASM

```
; dest, src
ADD SIZE [M]/R, L/[M]/R    ; ADD WORD [sum], 50
SUB SIZE [M]/R, L/[M]/R    ; SUB eax, [val]
```

> ▢ PROGRAMMING: A key difference between AT&T syntax (used by GAS and Clang) and the Intel syntax (used by MASM and NASM) is that the source and destination operands are switched. GAS always uses the first operand as the source, while MASM and NASM always use the first operand as the destination.

Another useful instruction is the **NEG** instruction, which gives you the ability to reverse the sign of a value, thus converting the value into its Two's Complement representation, which was discussed in **CHAPTER 1**.

GAS

```
NEGS M/%R            # NEGL %eax
```

MASM

```
NEG M/R              ; NEG sum
```

NASM

```
NEG SIZE [M]/R       ; NEG BYTE [sum]
```

Program 4.1 is a program that uses the INC, DEC, ADD, SUB, and NEG instructions. The program begins by creating two 32-bit variables—sum and val—and assigning each an initial value. The *eax* register is initialized to 0 and is immediately incremented by 1. Next, the literal decimal value 200 is added to the current value in *eax* and the result is stored back into *eax*. Then, the value stored in another variable val is subtracted from the value in *eax* and the result is stored back into *eax*. The value in *eax* is then stored in the sum variable, which is then decremented by 1. The final value in the sum variable at the end of Program 4.1 is -175 (11111111111111111111111101010001 in 32-bit binary Two's Complement).

Program 4.1 Addition and subtraction

GAS	MASM	NASM
.data	.386	SECTION .data
sum: .long 0	.MODEL FLAT, stdcall	sum: DD 0
val: .long 25	.STACK 4096	val: DD 25
	ExitProcess PROTO,	
.text	dwExitCode:DWORD	SECTION .text
.globl _main		global _main
_main:	.data	_main:
	sum DWORD 0	
movl $0, %eax	val DWORD 25	mov eax, 0
incl %eax		inc eax
addl $200, %eax	.code	add eax, 200
subl val, %eax	_main PROC	sub eax, [val]
movl %eax, sum		mov [sum], eax
decl sum	mov eax, 0	dec DWORD [sum]
negl sum	inc eax	neg DWORD [sum]
	add eax, 200	
pushl $0	sub eax, val	mov eax, 1
subl $4, %esp	mov sum, eax	mov ebx, 0
movl $1, %eax	dec sum	int 80h
int $0x80	neg sum	
.end		
	INVOKE ExitProcess, 0	
	_main ENDP	
	END	

Multiplication and Division

Performing multiplication and division is slightly more complicated than addition and subtraction. You might assume that the multiplication and division instructions would accept two operands and calculate the result, but that is not necessarily the case in x86 Assembly. The number of operands depends on whether the instruction is for unsigned or signed data. Unique multiplication and division instructions exist for unsigned and signed data. We examine the unsigned version first and the signed version second, since signed is more complex.

The **MUL** instruction performs *unsigned* integer multiplication. MUL accepts a single operand, the multiplier; but what about the multiplicand and the result? The multiplicand is a value that is stored in the accumulator register based on the multiplier size (8, 16, 32, and 64-bit), as shown in Table 4.2. Also, because MUL only accepts a single operand, the programmer does not specify the result destination, it is implicit.

Table 4.2 Unsigned multiplication operands

Multiplier	Multiplicand	Product
M8/R8	*al*	*ax*
M16/R16	*ax*	*dx:ax*
M32/R32	*eax*	*edx:eax*
M64/R64	*rax*	*rdx:rax*

Both the multiplicand and product locations are implied based on the multiplier size. Consider the example of multiplying 8096 by 64 (Example 4.1). The largest value is 8096, which uses 13 bits of storage; so we are forced to store the value in at least a 16-bit location. A good chance exists that the product of two 16-bit values could exceed 16 bits of storage. Consequently, the product of a 16-bit multiplication will be stored in a 32-bit destination: *dx:ax* (the high 16 bits of the product in *dx* and the low 16 bits of the product in *ax*). The product of 8096 * 64 is 518144, which requires 19 bits of storage. The result fits in *dx:ax*, but would have overflowed a 16-bit destination.

Example 4.1 Unsigned 16-bit multiplication

```
mov ax, 64      ; Store the multiplicand for 16-bit multiplication
mov bx, 8096    ; Store the multiplier in a 16-bit register so when
                ; we multiply, AX is used as the multiplicand and
                ; a 32-bit result is produced
mul bx          ; bx * ax = 518144
                ;         = 00000000000001111110100000000000
                ;     dx = 0000000000000111, ax = 1110100000000000
```

> **PROGRAMMING:** Check the status of the CPU flags after a multiplication. After unsigned multiplication, the Carry Flag (CF) will be set if the product has carried into the high bits. After signed multiplication, CF will be set unless all the high bits are just the sign extension of the most significant bit of the low bits.

GAS
```
MULS M/%R          # MULW %ax
```

MASM
```
MUL M/R            ; MUL ax
```

NASM
```
MUL SIZE [M]/R     ; MUL DWORD [sum]
```

To perform *signed* multiplication, use the **IMUL** instruction. IMUL allows the same one-operand format as MUL and in such cases uses the same locations shown in Table 4.2. The main difference between IMUL and MUL is that IMUL also has two-operand and three-operand formats. With the two-operand format, IMUL operates much like ADD and SUB, where both operands serve as sources and one is also the destination. So just like ADD and SUB, the value in the destination operand gets overwritten with the result of IMUL.

If you do not want operands to be overwritten, you can use the three-operand format of IMUL, which allows you to specify the multiplier, multiplicand, and product. In the following examples, pay particular attention to the sequence of possible operands given the assembler when using the two-operand and three-operand formats. Both formats store the product in a single register, and the three-operand format requires the use of a literal (immediate) value.

GAS

```
# One-operand - follows Table 4.2
IMULS M/%R                              # IMULL %ebx


# Two-operand - src, dst
IMULS $L/M/%R, %R                       # IMULW val, %ax


# Three-operand - imm, src, dst
IMULS $L, M/%R, %R                      # IMULL $10, val, %eax
```

MASM

```
# One-operand - follows Table 4.2
IMUL M/R                                ; IMUL ebx


# Two-operand - dst, src
IMUL R, L/M/R                           ; IMUL ax, val


# Three-operand - dst, src, imm
IMUL R, M/R, L                          ; IMUL eax, val, 10
```

NASM

```
# One-operand - follows Table 4.2
IMUL SIZE [M]/R                         ; IMUL DWORD [sum]


# Two-operand - dst, src
IMUL R, L/[M]/R                         ; IMUL ax, [val]


# Three-operand - dst, src, imm
IMUL R, [M]/R, L                        ; IMUL eax, [val], 10
```

 PROGRAMMING: Ensure that you choose the proper size registers for both multiplication and division. Choosing small registers to conserve space may result in carry or overflow if the product or quotient is too big for the destination register(s).

Similar to MUL, division has both unsigned and signed versions. The **DIV** instruction performs *unsigned* integer division and produces a two-part result: the quotient and the remainder.

Table 4.3 Unsigned division operands

Divisor	Dividend	Quotient	Remainder
M8/R8	*ax*	*al*	*ah*
M16/R16	*dx:ax*	*ax*	*dx*
M32/R32	*edx:eax*	*eax*	*edx*
M64/R64	*rdx:rax*	*rax*	*rdx*

When using DIV, the programmer only specifies the divisor (bottom number in standard division notation). The dividend (top number) must be pre-loaded into the correct register based on the size of the divisor, as shown in Table 4.3. Also, the sign of the dividend value must extend into the high-bit register. For example, when performing signed division, storing a negative value in *dx:ax* requires the sign bit (1) to be extended from *ax* through *dx*, so that the value retains the sign. Sign extension is discussed later in this chapter.

Let us examine how 32-bit unsigned division might work to solve the problem 32 / 3 (Example 4.2). We must pre-load the dividend into *edx:eax*, but because the positive value 32 does not extend past the 32 bits of *eax*, we need to ensure that *edx* contains 0. In other words, we need to extend the sign bit (0) for positive. Next, we choose a 32-bit register, *ecx*, to hold the divisor. After performing the division, *eax* contains the quotient 10 and *edx* contains the remainder of 2.

Example 4.2 Unsigned 32-bit division

```
        mov edx, 0      ; Load EDX:EAX with the dividend, 32
        mov eax, 32
        mov ecx, 3      ; Load ECX with the divisor, 3
        div ecx         ; 32 / 3 = 10r2
                        ; eax = 0000000Ah, edx = 00000002h
```

GAS
```
DIVS M/%R       # DIVW %ax
```

MASM
```
DIV M/R         ; DIV ax
```

NASM
```
DIV SIZE [M]/R      ; DIV DWORD [sum]
```

Signed division requires the use of the **IDIV** instruction. Unlike the IMUL instruction, IDIV does not have two-operand and three-operand formats. You still only provide one operand to the IDIV instruction, the divisor.

 ATTENTION: Division overflow is an event where the quotient of a division operation is too large for the destination. Division overflow causes a processor exception and halts the program. To account for all possible results, ensure that appropriately sized operands are used.

GAS
```
IDIVS M/%R      # IDIVW %ax
```

MASM
```
IDIV M/R        ; IDIV ax
```

NASM

```
IDIV SIZE [M]/R      ; IDIV DWORD [sum]
```

 PROGRAMMING: Unlike the multiplication instructions, neither of the division instructions set any status flags to indicate information about the result (the flags are undefined).

Program 4.2 is an example program that uses the MUL, IMUL, DIV, and IDIV instructions. The program performs the multiplication of 664751 and 8 using the MUL instruction and all three forms of the IMUL instruction. The program then performs both unsigned and signed division using 5318008 as the dividend and 8 as the divisor.

Program 4.2 *Multiplication and division*

GAS	MASM	NASM

`.data`
`mval: .long 664751`
`dval: .long 8`
`.text`
`.globl _main`
`_main:`
`# MUL 1-op`
`movl mval, %eax`
`movl $8, %ebx`
`mull %ebx`
`# IMUL 1-op`
`movl mval, %eax`
`movl $8, %ebx`
`imull %ebx`
`# IMUL 2-op`
`movl $8, %eax`
`imull mval, %eax`
`# IMUL 3-op`
`imull $8, mval, %eax`
`# DIV 1-op`
`movl $0, %edx`
`movl $5318008, %eax`
`movl dval, %ecx`
`divl %ecx`
`# IDIV 1-op`
`movl $0, %edx`
`movl $5318008, %eax`
`movl dval, %ecx`
`idivl %ecx`
`pushl $0`
`subl $4, %esp`
`movl $1, %eax`
`int $0x80`
`.end`
	`.386`
	`.MODEL FLAT, stdcall`
	`.STACK 4096`
	`ExitProcess PROTO,`
	`dwExitCode:DWORD`
	`.data`
	`mval DWORD 664751`
	`dval DWORD 8`
	`.code`
	`_main PROC`
	`; MUL 1-op`
	`mov eax, mval`
	`mov ebx, 8`
	`mul ebx`
	`; IMUL 1-op`
	`mov eax, mval`
	`mov ebx, 8`
	`imul ebx`
	`; IMUL 2-op`
	`mov eax, 8`
	`imul eax, mval`
	`; IMUL 3-op`
	`imul eax, mval, 8`
	`; DIV 1-op`
	`mov edx, 0`
	`mov eax, 5318008`
	`mov ecx, dval`
	`div ecx`
	`; IDIV 1-op`
	`mov edx, 0`
	`mov eax, 5318008`
	`mov ecx, dval`
	`idiv ecx`
	`INVOKE ExitProcess, 0`
	`_main ENDP`
	`END`
		`SECTION .data`
		`mval: DD 664751`
		`dval: DD 8`
		`SECTION .text`
		`global _main`
		`_main:`
		`; MUL 1-op`
		`mov eax, [mval]`
		`mov ebx, 8`
		`mul ebx`
		`; IMUL 1-op`
		`mov eax, [mval]`
		`mov ebx, 8`
		`imul ebx`
		`; IMUL 2-op`
		`mov eax, 8`
		`imul eax, [mval]`
		`; IMUL 3-op`
		`imul eax, [mval], 8`
		`; DIV 1-op`
		`mov edx, 0`
		`mov eax, 5318008`
		`mov ecx, [dval]`
		`div ecx`
		`; IDIV 1-op`
		`mov edx, 0`
		`mov eax, 5318008`
		`mov ecx, [dval]`
		`idiv ecx`
		`mov eax, 1`
		`mov ebx, 0`
		`int 80h`

Bit Shifting

Even though dedicated multiplication and division instructions exist, a programmer should know that alternative and historically faster methods exist to perform such operations. Understanding that the processor manipulates values as a sequence of bits can direct us to manipulate data in our programs as a sequence of bits. For example, multiplication and division can be performed without the use of the MUL or DIV instructions via bit manipulation.

Assume that we have a variable `val` with the value `20`.

```
val BYTE 20
```

If we examined `val` at the bit-level, we would see the representation in Example 4.3.

Example 4.3 Bit representation of the value `20`

0	0	0	1	0	1	0	0

If we were to shift the bits in Example 4.3 one digit to the left, our value would change from `20` to `40`. If we were to shift the bits two digits to the left, the value would change from `20` to `80`. The result of each left shift is multiplication by two. Shifting bits left is multiplication by powers of two, as shown in Table 4.4.

Table 4.4 Multiplier values for shifting left

Bits shifted left	Multiplier
1	2
2	4
3	8
4	16

Based on Example 4.3, shifting the value `20` left two bits performs a multiplication by four, producing a result of `80` (Example 4.4).

Example 4.4 Shift left

Before left shift of 2	0	0	0	1	0	1	0	0	20
After left shift of 2	0	1	0	1	0	0	0	0	80

Notice how each bit has been moved left two places, with new bits being zero. Example 4.4 works. But what would happen if we tried to shift the value `64` left two bits?

Example 4.5 Incorrect shift result

Before left shift of 2	0	1	0	0	0	0	0	0	64
After left shift of 2	0	0	0	0	0	0	0	0	0

What is the product of `64 * 4`? Will the product fit into our 8-bit variable? The answers are `256` and no, respectively. The maximum unsigned value that an 8-bit location can hold is `255` (i.e., every bit set to 1). The value `256` would "overflow" into the 9th bit, leaving our variable with a result of `0`. We have essentially lost the two bits that were shifted outside of our memory location.

Yet, all is not lost. Every time a shift is performed, a minimum of one bit is lost. In Example 4.5, we lost the most significant (left-most) bit on the first shift, which was `0`, so `1` became the most significant bit. On the second shift, we again lost the most significant bit, the `1`. The *last* bit that is "lost" as a result of each shift is actually saved in the

Carry Flag (CF). The first shift moved the leading 0 to CF and the second shift set CF to 1. We always have one bit of protection with CF when performing shifts, although you are responsible for ensuring that no data is lost when performing arithmetic.

While shifting left performs multiplication in powers of two, shifting right performs division in powers of two. The same rules apply, plus one more rule: right-shift division of an *odd* number will always lose data. Odd numbers always have the least significant bit set to 1. Performing a shift right of any number of bits will lose the least significant bit and result in an incorrect calculation.

Shift left and shift right instructions, **SHL** and **SHR**, can shift a memory operand or register by a literal number of bits.

GAS

```
SHLS $L, M/%R       # SHLL $2, val
SHRS $L, M/%R       # SHRL $1, %ebx
```

MASM

```
SHL M/R, L          ; SHL val, 2
SHR M/R, L          ; SHR ebx, 1
```

NASM

```
SHL SIZE [M]/R, L       ; SHL DWORD [val], 2
SHR SIZE [M]/R, L       ; SHR ebx, 1
```

 LEARNING: CHAPTER 5 covers branching, the ability of programs to follow different paths, such as executing certain instructions based on the state of the Carry Flag or the result of a mathematical operation.

The method of bit shifting shown in the preceding examples is known as **logical bit shifting**. As explained, bits are lost when shifted outside the bounds of the storage location, and the new bits are filled with zeros. Logical bit shifting generally works for unsigned data but damages signed data. Imagine the scenario where a negative value is shifted to the right, changing the sign bit from a 1 to a 0 and thus changing the value.

In order to perform multiplication or division on signed integers using bit shifting, we must use **arithmetic bit shifting**, which preserves the sign. The arithmetic shift instructions are **SAL** (Shift Arithmetic Left) and **SAR** (Shift Arithmetic Right). Example 4.6 illustrates the results of both arithmetic shift instructions on an 8-bit variable val containing the value -32 (11100000b) in NASM.

Example 4.6 Arithmetic shifts in NASM

Instruction	Binary result	Decimal result
SAL WORD [val], 2	10000000	-128
SAR WORD [val], 2	11111000	-8

 PROGRAMMING: SAL and SHL are identical (synonyms). Because of the way negative numbers use the most significant bits to denote the sign, shifting to the left will implicitly preserve the sign bit.

The syntax for SAL and SAR is similar to the logical shift instructions. A memory operand or register is shifted left or right a literal number of bits.

GAS

```
SALS $L, M/%R       # SALL $2, val
SARS $L, M/%R       # SARL $1, %ebx
```

MASM

```
SAL M/R, L          ; SAL val, 2
SAR M/R, L          ; SAR ebx, 1
```

NASM

```
SAL SIZE [M]/R, L       ; SAL DWORD [val], 2
SAR SIZE [M]/R, L       ; SAR ebx, 1
```

Working with Negative Values

Now that we have covered some basic arithmetic in both unsigned and signed formats, we will focus on signed values. An Assembly programmer needs to ensure that they have the correct values with the correct signs in the correct registers before executing any arithmetic instructions.

All assemblers allow you to store negative values in registers and variables without much effort, as shown in Example 4.7. The assembler automatically stores values in their Two's Complement representation.

Example 4.7 – Simple negative value usage

GAS	MASM	NASM

`.data`
`val: .long -5`
 	
`.text`
`movl $-10, %eax`
	`.data`
	`val DWORD -5`
	
	`.code`
	`mov eax, -10`
		`SECTION .data`
		`val: DD -5`
		
		`SECTION .text`
		`mov eax, -10`

One challenge of working with negative values arises when pre-loading specific registers with negative values before executing the IDIV instruction. Assuming we want to perform a 32-bit signed division, the dividend is a 64-bit value split across *edx* and *eax*, as shown in Table 4.3. If our goal is to perform the division of -534 by 15, we need to convert -534 into a 64-bit Two's Complement value with the high 32 bits in *edx* and the low 32 bits in *eax*. We can easily store -534 into *eax*, but how do we extend the sign (binary 1 in this case) into the upper bits so that *edx* contains all binary 1s?

Table 4.5 lists four instructions available to perform sign extension: **CBW** (Convert BYTE to WORD), **CWD** (Convert WORD to DWORD), **CDQ** (Convert DWORD to QWORD), and **CQO** (Convert QWORD to OCTA).

Table 4.5 Sign extension instructions

Instruction	From		To	
	Register	Size	Register	Size
CBW	*al*	8	*ax*	16
CWD	*ax*	16	*dx:ax*	32
CDQ	*eax*	32	*edx:eax*	64
CQO	*rax*	64	*rdx:rax*	128

Let us look at a simple example of using 8-bit (byte) to 16-bit (word) sign extension before we apply the concept to the problem of -534 divided by 15.

Example 4.8 CBW sign extension

GAS	MASM/NASM	
movw $0, %ax	mov ax, 0	; ax = 0000000000000000
movb $-5, %al	mov al, -5	; ax = 0000000011111011
cbw	cbw	; ax = 1111111111111011

In Example 4.8, we first move 0 to the 16-bit *ax* register to ensure a blank slate. Next, we store the value -5 into the 8-bit *al* register. Notice how the lower 8 bits of *ax*, the *al* register, contain the Two's Complement representation of -5. If we were to perform signed division at this point, the IDIV instruction would use *ax* as the dividend. But because the upper 8 bits of *ax* are zeros, the value would be interpreted as 251 (the highest bit of *ax* is 0, thus positive). To overcome this problem, we must sign extend *al* into *ax*. Sign extension fills the bits of *ax* with the leading bit of *al*, which in this case is 1 (negative), resulting in a 16-bit Two's Complement value of -5.

Now back to the division of -534 / 15. Program 4.3 presents the Assembly code. Once -534 has been moved into *eax*, the sign must be extended into *edx*. The CDQ instruction converts a doubleword to a quadword, extending the sign of *eax* into *edx*. The divisor is then set using *ebx* and the division is performed. After execution of the IDIV instruction, the results are stored in *eax* (quotient) and *edx* (remainder) with *eax* containing FFFFFFDDh (-35), and *edx* containing FFFFFFF7h (-9).

Program 4.3 *Negative division*

GAS	MASM	NASM
.text	.386	SECTION .text
.globl _main	.MODEL FLAT, stdcall	global _main
_main:	.STACK 4096	_main:
	ExitProcess PROTO,	
movl $-534, %eax	dwExitCode:DWORD	mov eax, -534
cdq		cdq
movl $15, %ebx	.code	mov ebx, 15
idivl %ebx	_main PROC	idiv ebx
pushl $0	mov eax, -534	mov eax, 1
subl $4, %esp	cdq	mov ebx, 0
movl $1, %eax	mov ebx, 15	int 80h
int $0x80	idiv ebx	
.end		
	INVOKE ExitProcess, 0	
	_main ENDP	
	END	

Data Addressing and Transfer

Data Alignment

One of the benefits of writing Assembly code is that you can ensure programs are operating in an efficient manner. An important aspect of efficiency is memory accesses. CPUs are much faster at accessing data stored at even-numbered addresses than odd-numbered addresses. For example, memory accesses in a 32-bit system are much simpler operations if data is in 32-bit slots and structures are on 16-byte boundaries. So storing program data at even-numbered addresses is beneficial.

GAS

```
.balign alignment      # .balign 2
```

MASM

```
ALIGN alignment        ; ALIGN 2
```

NASM

```
SECTION .data                          SECTION .bss
ALIGN alignment        ; ALIGN 2       ALIGNB alignment  ; ALIGNB 2
```

Each assembler has one or more directives that alter the location counter. GAS uses the **.balign** directive, MASM uses the **ALIGN** directive, and NASM uses the **ALIGN** or **ALIGNB** directive, depending on the program section. In each case, the alignment parameter is an integer that is a power of two. The alignment directive advances the location counter until the address is a multiple of the integer provided. As previously suggested, a useful example is making sure that data exists at even-numbered memory locations.

Example 4.9 Data alignment in MASM

```
; Assume the starting memory address is 0x00000000h
var BYTE 31        ; The next variable would start at 0x00000001h, which is odd
ALIGN 2            ; Ensure the next memory location is even
var2 WORD 1337     ; var2 starts at 0x00000002h
```

Manual alignment using align directives or automatic alignment using assembler or compiler commands is not particularly necessary or required for the programs in this book until we get to **CHAPTERS 6 AND 8,** when we deal with function calls and vector data.

> PROGRAMMING: GAS has different variants of the alignment directive. The standard .align directive works exactly like the .balign directive on x86 and x86_64 architectures. But when writing code for other architectures, such as ARM or PPC, the .align directive has a different behavior. So we recommend using .balign for more consistent behavior across target architectures.

Data Addressing

Having wandered into the territory of memory addresses, we need to discuss how to use addresses as operands. All of the variable use we have demonstrated in code so far is considered **direct addressing**, meaning directly accessing a value stored at a memory location, which is aliased by an identifier. But sometimes we need to work with memory addresses the way we work with pointers in high-level languages like C++. **Indirect addressing** is when we use a memory address to point to another address that contains a value. Figure 4.1 depicts the difference between direct and indirect addressing.

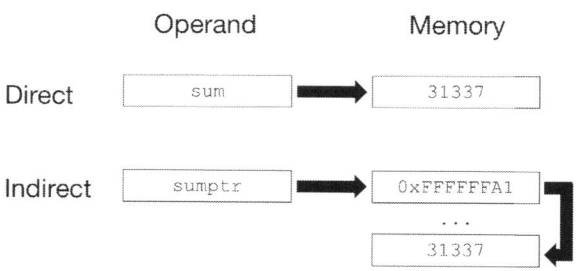

Figure 4.1 Direct and indirect addressing

While Figure 4.1 uses main memory for simplicity, direct and indirect addressing also applies to registers. A register operand can either directly reference a value stored in a register or it can indirectly reference a value stored in main memory via the address stored in a register. In either case, the principle illustrated in Figure 4.1 applies: one access for a direct value and multiple accesses for an indirect value.

With addressing methods in mind, we can start working with memory addresses. One important step is determining the memory address of a variable in relation to the beginning of the data segment in an Assembly program. In NASM, a variable name directly refers to the memory address, not the value stored in the address (to refer to the value use brackets, such as [sum]). To get the address of an operand in MASM, you can use the **OFFSET** directive along with the MOV instruction. In GAS, prefix a variable with the dollar sign ($) to refer to the address of the variable rather than the value.

The following code snippets in the template comments store the memory address of a 32-bit variable sum into the *esi* register for GAS and MASM and into a different variable for NASM.

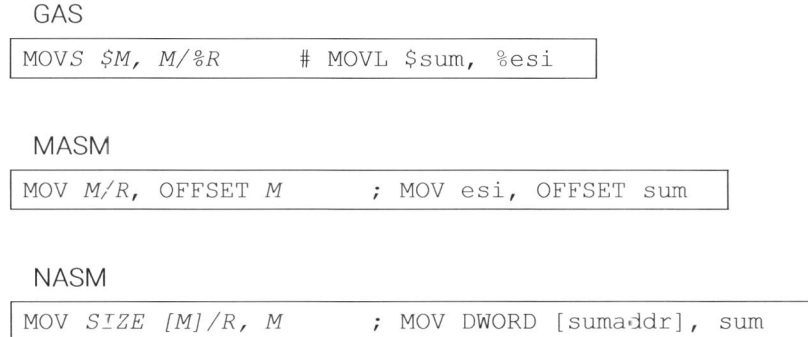

GAS
```
MOVS $M, M/%R       # MOVL $sum, %esi
```

MASM
```
MOV M/R, OFFSET M        ; MOV esi, OFFSET sum
```

NASM
```
MOV SIZE [M]/R, M        ; MOV DWORD [sumaddr], sum
```

> ▣ PROGRAMMING: If you refer to a memory address in GAS when using the MOV instruction, the size character must match the destination operand, which in 32-bit mode is a long data type (MOVL). The variable could be anything (e.g., byte, word, long), but if the code is assembled in 32-bit mode, the variable would be stored at a 32-bit memory address. If coding in 64-bit mode, use the MOVQ instruction since all addresses are quadwords (64-bits).

The **LEA** (Load Effective Address) instruction in 32-bit and 64-bit modes loads an operand address into the destination. LEA must be used for all runtime operations since actual addresses are not known until runtime.

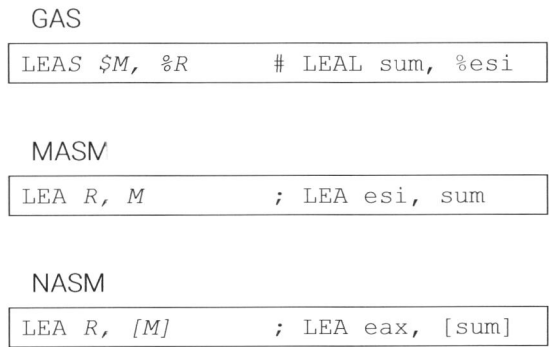

GAS
```
LEAS $M, %R       # LEAL sum, %esi
```

MASM
```
LEA R, M          ; LEA esi, sum
```

NASM
```
LEA R, [M]        ; LEA eax, [sum]
```

The key difference between the MOV and LEA instructions regarding addresses is that the destination operand of the LEA instruction must be a register.

Arrays

The usefulness of storing a memory address becomes particularly evident in more advanced scenarios. A common scenario for using indirect addressing is array manipulation. An **array**, as in high-level languages, is a collection of data spaced equally at memory addresses based on the data type, and is aliased to the first element. Assume we have created two arrays: the first is an array of bytes and the second is an array of doublewords.

Example 4.10 Arrays in MASM

```
arrayA BYTE 2, 4, 6, 8
arrayB DWORD 0FFFFFh, 0FFFFEh, 0FFFFDh, 0FFFFCh
```

Each array contains four items, but accessing either `arrayA` or `arrayB` will only give us the first item in each array. How do we access the subsequent items? The answer is by using a combination of instructions previously introduced. When working with arrays in high-level languages, we use an index to access elements starting at index 0 (e.g., `arrayA[0]`, `arrayA[1]`, etc.). The compiler does the difficult work of determining the size of array items and moving the location counter the appropriate number of bytes for each index. In Assembly, you are responsible for determining element size and performing index calculations.

In order to access array data, we must understand how to calculate the address of each element. Recall from **CHAPTER 2** that memory is addressed per byte. Figure 4.2 depicts a segment of main memory and the memory addresses of each element in our two arrays (`arrayA` and `arrayB`).

arrayA		arrayB	
Address	**Value**	**Address**	**Value**
0x00000000	2	0x00000000	FFFFF
0x00000001	4	0x00000004	FFFFE
0x00000002	6	0x00000008	FFFFD
0x00000003	8	0x0000000C	FFFFC

Figure 4.2 Array addressing

Since `arrayA` is a BYTE array, each value is located one byte away from the previous value. However, `arrayB` is a DWORD array (DWORDs are four bytes), which means each value in `arrayB` is four bytes away from the previous value.

> PROGRAMMING: When accessing array elements, be sure to calculate the proper byte offset. No automatic bounds checking exists in Assembly. The assembler will not produce an error if you add three bytes instead of four to access the next element of a DWORD array. You would access data that is not what you expect.

Recall calculating the size of a string (an array of characters) from **CHAPTER 3**. The size of any array, which is measured in bytes, can be calculated by using the *current location counter*.

GAS

```
arrayA: .long 2, 4, 6, 8
.equ len, (. - arrayA)        # len = 16
```

MASM

```
arrayA DWORD 2, 4, 6, 8
len EQU ($ - arrayA)          ; len = 16
```

NASM

```
arrayA: DD 2, 4, 6, 8
len: EQU ($ - arrayA)         ; len = 16
```

Now we revisit the LEA and MOV instructions, taking into account the need to load memory addresses at specific byte offsets. An offset is specified by using a byte constant. The following code examples show how to access elements [1] and [3] in both arrays and how to use the array elements as both a source and destination operand.

GAS

```
                                    # Store item 1 from arrayA in ebx
LEAS M, %R                          # LEAL arrayA, %eax
MOVS CONSTANT(%R), M/%R             # MOVL 1(%eax), %ebx
                                    # %ebx = 4

                                    # Store 10 into element 3 of arrayB
LEAS M, %R                          # LEAL arrayB, %eax
MOVS $L/%R, CONSTANT %R             # MOVL $10, 8(%eax)
                                    # arrayB = 0xFFFFF,0xFFFFE,0xA,0xFFFFC
```

MASM

```
                                    ; Store item 1 from arrayA in eax
MOV R, [M+CONSTANT]                 ; MOV eax, [arrayA + 1]
                                    ; eax = 4

                                    ; Store 10 into item 3 of arrayB
MOV [M+CONSTANT], R                 ; MOV [arrayB + 8], 10
                                    ; arrayB = 0xFFFFF,0xFFFFE,0xA,0xFFFFC
```

NASM

```
                                    ; Store item 1 from arrayA in eax
MOV R, [M+CONSTANT]                 ; MOV eax, [arrayA + 1]
                                    ; eax = 4

                                    ; Store 10 into item 3 of arrayB
MOV SIZE [M+CONSTANT], L/R          ; MOV DWORD [arrayB + 8], 10
                                    ; arrayB = 0xFFFFF,0xFFFFE,0xA,0xFFFFC
```

 PROGRAMMING: As with the MOV instruction in GAS when dealing with memory addresses, the LEA instruction's appended size character (e.g., leal for 32-bit, leaq for 64-bit) is the size of what the LEA instruction returns (a memory address). The character is not indicative of the size of the array elements.

 LEARNING: In your preferred development environment, define differently sized arrays and practice calculating byte offsets to access elements. Use a debugger to examine the results of correct and incorrect byte offsets.

Some programmers might prefer to keep array notation as similar to high-level languages as possible, which means using an index number in the instructions rather than using a constant to calculate a byte offset. You can modify the previous examples to accommodate index numbers. In the following examples we show how to access the last element (index 3) of arrayB. If using GAS, first load the starting address of the array, as in previous examples. Then store the index you wish to access into a register. Finally, use the MOV instruction and specify the size of the array elements in bytes (1, 2, 4, or 8) along with the array address and index number.

GAS

```
LEAS M, %R                       # LEAL arrayB, %eax
MOVS L, %R                       # MOVL $3, %edx
MOVS (%R, %R, L), %R             # MOVL (%eax, %edx, 4), %ebx
```

MASM/NASM

```
MOV R, L                         ; MOV edx, 3
MOV R, [M+R*L]                   ; MOV eax, [arrayB + edx * 4]
```

The cost of making Assembly code feel similar to high-level languages by using array indices is an additional instruction. You can decide which approach is most appropriate for your programs.

Lastly, for arrays, we introduce some MASM-specific directives that may be of use when working with arrays. We have covered combinable instructions for determining the size (in bytes) of each element in an array, the number of elements in an array, and the total size (in bytes) of an array. However, three MASM directives exist that assist in dynamically determining array (or variable) characteristics. The **TYPE** directive returns the number of bytes a variable occupies; the **LENGTHOF** directive returns the number of elements in an array; and the **SIZEOF** directive returns the total number of bytes an array occupies (equivalent to multiplying the results of the TYPE and LENGTHOF directives).

MASM

```
MOV eax, TYPE arrayA             ; eax = 1
MOV ebx, LENGTHOF arrayA         ; ebx = 4
MOV ecx, SIZEOF arrayA           ; ecx = 4

MOV eax, TYPE arrayB             ; eax = 4
MOV ebx, LENGTHOF arrayB         ; ebx = 4
MOV ecx, SIZEOF arrayB           ; ecx = 16
```

Program 4.4 creates an array with four values, reads two of the values, and overwrites the other two values.

Program 4.4 Array

GAS	MASM	NASM

`.data`
`array: .long 1, 2, 3, 4`
 	
`.text`
`.globl _main`
`_main:`
 	
`# Load using`
`# byte offsets`
`leal array, %esi`
`movl (%esi), %eax`
`movl 4(%esi), %ebx`
 	
`# Save using indices`
`movl $2, %edx`
`movl $10, (%esi, %edx, 4)`
`movl $3, %edx`
`movl $20, (%esi, %edx, 4)`
 	
`pushl $0`
`subl $4, %esp`
`movl $1, %eax`
`int $0x80`
`.end`
	`.386`
	`.MODEL FLAT, stdcall`
	`.STACK 4096`
	`ExitProcess PROTO,`
	`dwExitCode:DWORD`
	
	`.data`
	`array DWORD 1, 2, 3, 4`
	
	`.code`
	`_main PROC`
	
	`; Load using`
	`; byte offsets`
	`mov eax, array`
	`mov ebx, [array + 4]`
	
	`; Save using indices`
	`mov edx, 2`
	`mov [array+edx*4], 10`
	`mov edx, 3`
	`mov [array+edx*4], 20`
	
	`INVOKE ExitProcess, 0`
	`_main ENDP`
	`END`
		`SECTION .data`
		`array: DD 1, 2, 3, 4`
		
		`SECTION .text`
		`global _main`
		`_main:`
		
		`; Load using`
		`; byte offsets`
		`mov eax, array`
		`mov ebx, [array + 4]`
		
		`; Save using indices`
		`mov edx, 2`
		`mov DWORD [array+edx*4], 10`
		`mov edx, 3`
		`mov DWORD [array+edx*4], 20`
		
		`mov eax, 1`
		`mov ebx, 0`
		`int 80h`

Changing Data Sizes and Types

Sometimes, moving data from one location to another when memory sizes are different is necessary or optimal. For example, you may have a value in a 32-bit variable named val but wish to copy the lower 16 bits into a 16-bit register, such as *ax*, as we do in the examples below. Most instructions error (the program will not assemble) when source and destination operands are different sizes, so we need a solution. GAS handles size changes particularly easily since all MOV instructions are appended with the size of the data being copied. In the GAS example, we simply use the MOVW instruction because the destination is a WORD (16 bits). Using NASM is also relatively easy because you can specify the size of the source operand, similar to the way we have been specifying the size of the destination operand. MASM requires the use of a new directive, **PTR**, which allows us to override the defined size and treat a variable as a pointer of a specific size.

GAS
```
MOVS M, %R        # MOVW val, %ax
```

MASM
```
MOV R, SIZE PTR M        ; MOV ax, WORD PTR val
```

NASM
```
MOV R, SIZE [M]        ; MOV ax, WORD [val]
```

Taking data from a larger location and storing it in a smaller location is efficient, but sometimes the opposite is necessary. We presented something similar with *convert* instructions (CBW, CWD, CDQ, CQO), but they are only for use with the accumulator register (*al*, *ax*, *eax*, *rax*). When storing data into the low bits of a register (e.g., the *ax* portion of *eax*), the high bits may contain data from previous operations. If pre-existing data is not taken into account, using the whole register (e.g., *eax*) can lead to incorrect results.

Two instructions, **MOVZ/MOVZX** (move with zero extend) and **MOVS/MOVSX** (move with sign extend), are able to copy a value into the low bits of a register and simultaneously extend zeros or the sign into the high bits of the register, respectively. In the following examples we use both instructions to assign the value of a 16-bit variable (sum) to a 32-bit register (*eax*).

GAS
```
MOVZSS M/%R, %R        # MOVZWL sum, %eax
MOVSSS M/%R, %R        # MOVSWL sum, %eax
```

MASM
```
MOVZX R, M/R        ; MOVZX eax, sum
MOVSX R, M/R        ; MOVSX eax, sum
```

NASM
```
MOVZX R, SIZE [M]/R        ; MOVZX eax, WORD [sum]
MOVSX R, SIZE [M]/R        ; MOVSX eax, WORD [sum]
```

While the usage of MOVS and MOVZ needs little explanation, the GAS version may cause some confusion. Notice that the GAS instructions have two size suffixes. MASM assumes sizes based on the register(s) used and a variable's definition (e.g., sum defined as a WORD is being moved to a 32-bit register *eax*). NASM determines sizes based on the register(s) used and the use of a size directive with a variable (e.g., WORD [sum]). GAS needs both sizes specified as part of the instruction. The first suffix is the size of the source (left) operand and the second suffix is the size of the destination (right) operand. For example, the MOVZWL instruction copies a value from a 16-bit (WORD) location to a 32-bit (LONG) location and extends zeros into the high bits.

The *extension* instructions are also one of the few times in x86 Assembly when an instruction mnemonic is different, depending on the syntax. GAS uses AT&T syntax, which uses MOVZ and MOVS plus the size suffixes to zero or sign extend a value. MASM and NASM use Intel syntax, which uses MOVZX and MOVSX.

Summary

The big-picture topic of this chapter is how to manipulate data. We covered basic arithmetic instructions with examples in both unsigned and signed formats. We provided comparisons of data accesses using direct and indirect addressing, the latter being important when working with arrays. We explored examples that demonstrated shifting data and moving data between differently sized locations. At this point, you should be able to write Assembly programs that complete basic tasks such as temperature conversion, square footage calculations, or even emulating a basic classroom gradebook.

Key Terms

.balign	DIV	NEG
ADD	IDIV	OFFSET
ALIGN	IMUL	PTR
ALIGNB	INC	SAL
arithmetic bit shifting	indirect addressing	SAR
array	LEA	SHL
CBW	LENGTHOF	SHR
CDQ	logical bit shifting	SIZEOF
CQO	MOV	SUB
CWD	MOVS/MOVSX	TYPE
DEC	MOVZ/MOVZX	XCHG
direct addressing	MUL	

Code Review

.balign	GAS directive that moves the instruction counter to the next memory address that is a multiple of the given parameter
ADD	Performs addition of two operands
ALIGN	MASM and NASM directive that moves the instruction counter to the next memory address that is a multiple of the given parameter
ALIGNB	Same as ALIGN, but for NASM's .bss section
CBW	Converts the value in *al* to *ax*
CDQ	Converts the value in *eax* into *edx:eax*
CQO	Converts the value in *rax* into *rdx:rax*
CWD	Converts the value in *ax* into *dx:ax*
DEC	Decrements the operand by 1
DIV	Performs unsigned division producing a quotient and a remainder
IDIV	Performs signed division producing a quotient and a remainder
IMUL	Performs signed multiplication
INC	Increments the operand by 1
LEA	Loads the effective address of a variable into a register

LENGTHOF	MASM directive that returns the number of elements in an array
MOVS/MOVSX	Copies a value from one location to another and sign extends
MOVZ/MOVZX	Copies a value from one location to another and zero extends
MUL	Performs unsigned multiplication
NEG	Negates an operand (Two's Complement representation)
OFFSET	MASM directive that returns the memory location of a variable relative to the data program section
PTR	MASM directive that treats the operand as a pointer so it can be accessed as a different size
SAL	Bit shift arithmetic left for signed integers
SAR	Bit shift arithmetic right for signed integers
SHL	Bit shift left for unsigned integers
SHR	Bit shift right for unsigned integers
SIZEOF	MASM directive that returns the total number of bytes used by an array
SUB	Performs subtraction on two operands
TYPE	MASM directive that returns the number of bytes used by a variable

Questions

Short Answer

1. The INC instruction takes a maximum of _____ operands.
2. Finish the instruction to decrement 1 from a 16-bit val variable using NASM: DEC _____.
3. When using GAS, the first operand is the _____ operand.
4. When using MASM, the first operand is the _____ operand.
5. The NEG instruction changes a value from positive to negative by converting it into its _____ representation.
6. When using a QWORD value as an operand for the MUL instruction, the result will be stored in _____.
7. The IMUL instruction can accept _____ operand(s).
8. Performing division with DIV using a 32-bit dividend implies that the dividend must be stored in _____.
9. When using the DIV instruction and a 64-bit divisor, the quotient is stored in _____ and the remainder in _____.
10. The IDIV instruction can accept _____ operand(s).
11. CBW, CWD, CDQ, and CQO will allow you to _____ extend the _____ register.
12. Aligning data to _____ memory addresses can help the processor access data faster.
13. A variable that contains a memory address is an example of _____ addressing.
14. Storing the address of a variable in GAS is accomplished using the _____ instruction.
15. The _____ instruction copies a value and extends the sign, while the _____ instruction copies a value and extends zeros.

True/False

1. IDIV can accept 1, 2, or 3 operands.
2. Specifying the data size of a variable in NASM is only necessary when the variable is a source operand.
3. A value stored in the *ebx* register can be sign extended into *edx:ebx* with the CDQ instruction.
4. The ALIGNB directive can only be used in the .bss section of NASM code.
5. When using an extension instruction in GAS, you must append two characters to indicate the sizes of the source and destination operands.

Assignments

4.1 Will my breaker trip?

Write a program that determines the amperage that would be pulled from a standard 120-volt wall outlet by a computer with a 1200-watt power supply running at maximum power. Use the standard equation W=VA (Watts = Volts * Amperage).

4.2 Passing the class

Write a program that computes the final percentage grade of a student in a Computer Architecture class based on the following scores. The result should be a whole number (e.g., 75 to represent 75%).
The student took four exams (points earned/points possible).

- 25/30
- 89/100
- 49/50
- 80/150

4.3 Differently sized arrays (Challenge Assignment)

Write a program that multiplies each element of a WORD array by 8 and stores the new value in the same element of a DWORD array.

- The initial array should contain the values 5, 10, 15, and 20.
- The result array should contain 40, 80, 120, and 160.

Intermediate Instructions

Objectives

- Identify efficient uses of bitwise Boolean instructions
- Create control and decision structures for branching
- Create repeatable code blocks

Outline

Web Resources

Assembler References

- https://sourceware.org/binutils/docs/as/ (GAS Reference)
- https://msdn.microsoft.com/en-us/library/afzk3475.aspx (MASM Reference)
- http://www.nasm.us/doc/nasmdoc0.html (NASM Reference)

x86 Instruction Set Listings

- http://www.intel.com/content/www/us/en/processors/architectures-software-developer-manuals.html (Volume 1, Chapter 5 Instruction Set Summary, Section 5.1)
- http://www.felixcloutier.com/x86/
- http://x86.renejeschke.de
- https://en.wikipedia.org/wiki/X86_instruction_listings
- http://www.nasm.us/doc/nasmdocb.html

Introduction

Chapter 5 presents concepts and Assembly instructions that enable a programmer to manipulate the flow of programs. We revisit the Boolean expressions covered in **CHAPTER 1** and introduce you to using Boolean algebra in Assembly code. We present various methods of constructing conditional statements and loops in Assembly. The combination of Chapter 5 knowledge with content learned in previous chapters will give you a solid foundation for writing low-level solutions for computing tasks.

Boolean Bitwise Operations

Recall the Boolean expressions from **CHAPTER 1**: NOT, AND, OR, and XOR. We have already covered the concepts of Boolean logic, but Assembly programmers must understand how to use the expressions in the context of a program. Although we typically deal with numbers in decimal (base 10) or hexadecimal (base 16) form in Assembly, we can also operate at the binary (base 2) level by performing **Boolean *bitwise* operations** on individual bits that comprise a value. Bit-level instructions have many uses in Assembly such as encryption, updating values (e.g., clearing a register), masking (e.g., CPU and FPU control, network protocols), and controlling hardware peripherals.

The first bitwise operation we will cover is **NOT**, which simply inverts the bits in a given operand. Effectively, NOT computes a value's One's Complement. The Boolean NOT operation is reviewed in Table 5.1.

Table 5.1 NOT binary operation

x	NOT x
0 (F)	1 (T)
1 (T)	0 (F)

The Assembly instruction is also NOT and takes a single operand, which means that the operand value is overwritten with the One's Complement value.

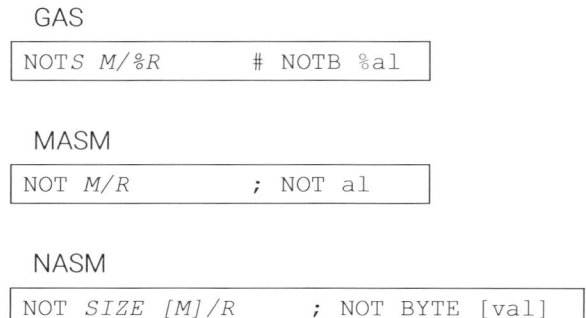

```
GAS
NOTS M/%R        # NOTB %al
```

```
MASM
NOT M/R          ; NOT al
```

```
NASM
NOT SIZE [M]/R        ; NOT BYTE [val]
```

Next, review the truth table (Table 5.2) for the **AND** instruction, which performs the Boolean AND on each pair of bits in two operands.

Table 5.2 AND truth table

x	y	x AND y
F	F	F
F	T	F
T	F	F
T	T	T

We can rewrite the truth table using binary values (0/1) instead of Boolean values (F/T) so the effect at the bit level is more apparent, as shown in Table 5.3.

Table 5.3 AND binary operations

x	y	x AND y
0	0	0
0	1	0
1	0	0
1	1	1

Understanding how the AND operation works with two single-bit operands (x and y) is a great start, however the benefits become more clear when the operands are numeric values you might see in a program. A relatively common use of AND is detecting if a value is even or odd. We can detect even or odd by verifying if the Least Significant Bit (LSB) is zero or one.

```
                ↓
40 = 00101000 Even
47 = 00101111 Odd
```

Visually, even or odd is obvious. A code-based approach could be more complex, like writing an IF statement to determine if the LSB is 1 or if a remainder exists after dividing by 2. Referring to the AND tables, we can see that the only way to get a result of True (1) is if both operands are True (1). If we are looking for a 1 in the LSB of a value, we can AND the bit with a 1 in the LSB of a second operand to determine the result. But what about the rest of the value?

We are dealing with 8-bit values in our example. For an odd number, the goal is for the result to have a 1 in the LSB and zeros in the remaining bits. Again, referring to the AND tables we see that having a 0 anywhere in the second operand will result in a 0, regardless of the value in the first operand. So we can write a Boolean statement to determine if the decimal value 47 is odd.

```
        47              00101111
AND     1       AND     00000001
------              -----------
        1              00000001
```

By using the AND operation with a 1 in the proper location and 0s in the others, we have verified that the value is odd.

Another scenario where the AND operation is an efficient solution is changing the case of an ASCII character. Performing a case change in high-level languages typically involves using functions that understand character case. But upon close examination of the bits that comprise a single character, a pattern emerges: the fifth bit (zero-bit indexing) controls character case and all other bits are the same, as shown in Table 5.4 regarding the letter a/A.

Table 5.4 Character cases

Character	Hex value	Binary value
a	61h	01100001
A	41h	01000001

```
                ↑
```

Using the AND operation, we can mask the bits we want left unchanged with 1, and mask the fifth bit with 0 so it becomes a 0. Changing cases can also be achieved using OR and XOR, with XOR working both directions.

```
        01100001 = a
AND     11011111 = mask
        ------------
        01000001 = A

        01000001 = A
XOR     00100000 = mask
        ------------
        01100001 = a
```

Bit masking is more efficient than testing to determine if the numeric value of the ASCII character is in the specific range of ASCII values that represents the alphabet and then either adding or subtracting 32, depending on which case is desired.

To execute the Boolean AND in Assembly, we use the AND instruction. The following examples perform the AND operation of a decimal value stored in the *al* register with 1. The result will be stored in the *al* register. In the examples, we use three different representations of the literal 1 (i.e., decimal, binary, and hexadecimal).

GAS

```
ANDS $L/M/%R, M/%R        # ANDB $1, %al
```

MASM

```
AND M/R, L/M/R            ; AND al, 00000001b
```

NASM

```
AND SIZE [M]/R, L/[M]/R        ; AND al, 0x1
```

When we want to do the logical opposite of AND (e.g., to set bits as opposed to clear bits), we can use the **OR** instruction, which performs the Boolean OR operation on each pair of bits in two operands. Before exploring applications of the OR instruction, review the table of binary OR operations (Table 5.5).

Table 5.5 OR binary operations

x	y	x OR y
0	0	0
0	1	1
1	0	1
1	1	1

From Table 5.5 we can see that as long as one of the operands in an OR operation is True (1) the result will be True (1). OR is useful when setting individual control bits or flags. Consider a simple application that allows a user to order a pizza with specific toppings. If we want to allow a choice of four toppings, we might consider using four separate 8-bit variables, which is 32 bits in total. But we could also use a single 8-bit variable and set individual bits in the variable as yes/no (1/0) to store topping choices.

```
      |----Onion
      ||---Green Pepper
      |||--Sausage
      ||||-Pepperoni
      ↓↓↓↓
00000000 Toppings
```

Beginning with the TOPPINGS variable clear (0s) indicating a cheese pizza, we can use OR to set bits based on the toppings a customer prefers. Assume that a customer wants pepperoni and onion. The topping options correspond to 1 (00000001b) and 8 (00001000b), respectively. One at a time, we can OR the topping values (e.g., PEPPERONI = 00000001b) with the TOPPINGS variable to end with an 8-bit variable that contains all toppings requested by the customer. Such an approach saves 24 bits of storage space compared to the four 8-bit variable approach.

```
      00000000 TOPPINGS              00000001 TOPPINGS
   OR 00000001 PEPPERONI         OR 00001000 ONION
      ----------                    ----------
      00000001 TOPPINGS              00001001 TOPPINGS
```

After both OR operations, TOPPINGS has the zero and third bits set, indicating that the customer requested both pepperoni and onion.

 LEARNING: Using the information in this chapter, write an algorithm that can parse a TOPPINGS variable to determine toppings requested by a customer.

The following templates and examples show the OR instruction in x86/x86_64 Assembly.

GAS

```
ORS $L/M/%R, M/%R        # ORB $8, %al
```

MASM

```
OR M/R, L/M/R        ; OR al, 00001000b
```

NASM

```
OR SIZE [M]/R, L/[M]/R        ; OR al, 0x8
```

A second scenario where OR is efficient is determining if a value is positive, negative, or zero. ORing a number with itself allows a programmer to test for all three conditions. Testing for positive, negative, or zero is possible because both the OR and AND instructions set various processor flags (e.g., CF, OF, PF, SF, and ZF). The following code ORs a variable (var) with itself and lists processor flags a programmer could test (assume var = 13).

```
or var, var        ; SF = 0 (positive), ZF = 0 (non-zero)
```

A similar instruction to OR is the exclusive OR (**XOR**) instruction, which performs a Boolean XOR operation between each pair of bits in two operands. But a key distinction exists between OR and XOR. Reviewing the XOR Boolean operations shown in Table 5.6, we see that the result of an XOR operation is True (1) if *one* of the operands is True (1), but the result is False (0) when *both* operands are True (1) or False (0).

Table 5.6 XOR binary operations

x	y	x XOR y
0	0	0
0	1	1
1	0	1
1	1	0

The XOR operation is a key component of many symmetric encryption and data storage algorithms due to its reversible nature. XORing an original value with a different value (key) twice will produce the original value.

```
    01101011  ORIGINAL              01111010  "ENCRYPTED"
XOR 00010001  KEY              XOR 00010001  KEY
    -----------                   -----------
    01111010  "ENCRYPTED"           01101011  ORIGINAL
```

A second scenario for the XOR operation is hard drive technology, specifically RAID (i.e., Redundant Array of Independent Disks). RAID is a technique whereby a system has multiple hard drives joined together into a RAID set, of which varying types exist (e.g., RAID0, RAID1, RAID5, etc.). The major benefit of RAID is data redundancy. A drive can fail and the system can still continue operation by rebuilding the lost data. Data recovery can be accomplished by using XOR.

Assume a system has five hard drives. Four drives are used to store data and one drive is used to store parity information, similar to how RAID3 functions. Bits on the parity drive are calculated by XORing corresponding bits on the four data drives (i.e., all bit [0]s, all bit [1]s, etc.). Once parity data exists on the fifth drive, the system can suffer the loss of any of the data drives without losing data. Assume the loss of drive1. The remaining data drives 0, 2, and 3 will have their corresponding bits XORed with the parity drive. The result is the same sequence of bits lost on drive1, and thus the data is rebuilt.

```
          ORIGINAL                          REBUILD
     drive0 = 00000000             drive0 = 00000000
     drive1 = 01010101  XOR        drive2 = 11110000  XOR
     drive2 = 11110000   ↓         drive3 = 11111111   ↓
     drive3 = 11111111             parity = 01011010
     ----------------              ----------------
     parity = 01011010             drive1 = 01010101
```

The following templates and examples show the XOR instruction in x86/x86_64 Assembly.

GAS

```
XORS $L/M/%R, M/%R          # XORB $8, %al
```

MASM

```
XOR M/R, L/M/R           ; XOR al, 00001000b
```

NASM

```
XOR SIZE [M]/R, L/[M]/R    ; XOR al, 0x8
```

Branching

The concept of **branching** is that a program can follow different code paths, even skip instructions, based on a programmer's implementation. Execution can either unconditionally follow a code path or can follow a code path based on the result of a conditional test. Before discussing conditional branching, we must first examine unconditional branching.

Unconditional Jumps

In **CHAPTER 3**, we introduced labels and the ability to segment code into blocks.

```
computePay:
            instruction
            instruction
addToList:
            instruction
            instruction
```

The above code contains four instructions and two labels. Recall that labels are simply ways to mark locations in our code without using any additional memory. Two instructions are found after the computePay label and two instructions are found after the addToList label.

One reason labels are useful is because of the **JMP** instruction in Assembly, which allows us to jump to a label at any given time.

```
top:
        mov al, 3
        add al, 5
        jmp bottom
middle:
        add al, 32
bottom:
        add al, 2
```

In the above code, the instructions would not be executed in consecutive top-down fashion. After adding 5 to the *al* register (add al, 5), the program unconditionally jumps to the "bottom" label, skipping the "middle" section. The value 32 is never added to the register, so *al* contains 10 at the end of the program.

The unconditional jump instruction behaves the same in all three assemblers.

GAS/MASM/NASM

```
JMP LABEL      ; JMP doTheMath
```

Conditional Jumps

Now we can proceed to learning about jumping to code blocks based on conditional testing. First, we will discuss methods of executing a conditional test, and then we will discuss methods of branching based on the result of the conditional test.

In Assembly, we have multiple ways to perform conditional tests. One method is using the **TEST** instruction. The TEST instruction performs an *implied* AND operation on two operands without modifying either operand. But the processor flags (e.g., PF, SF, ZF) are modified to denote the would-be result. PF is set if the number of set (1) bits in the result is even, SF reflects the most significant bit of the result, and ZF is set if the result is zero.

 ATTENTION: CF and OF are also modified by the TEST instruction, but they are always cleared (0).

GAS

```
TESTS $L/M/%R, M/%R      # TESTB $32, %al
```

MASM

```
TEST M/R, L/M/R          ; TEST al, val
```

NASM

```
TEST SIZE [M]/R, L/[M]/R    ; TEST BYTE [val], ah
```

A second method of performing a conditional test on two operands is by using the compare (**CMP**) instruction. CMP allows us to implement conditional tests similar to those we implement in high-level languages (e.g., equality, greater than, less than or equal to, etc.). In high-level languages, one example of a decision structure that uses a conditional test is the `if` statement.

```
if (condition is true)
    Do this sequence of instructions
else
    Do this sequence of instructions
```

Assembly requires at least two distinct instructions for a conditional jump: one instruction to perform the comparison of operands, and one or more instructions to act on the result of the comparison. Basic conditional tests in Assembly begin with CMP, which performs an *implicit* subtraction of the source operand from the destination operand and modifies the CPU flags accordingly.

 ATTENTION: As with the TEST instruction, the CMP instruction does not modify either operand.

GAS

```
CMPS $L/M/%R, M/%R        # CMPB $32, %al
```

MASM

```
CMP M/R, L/M/R           ; CMP al, val
```

NASM

```
CMP SIZE [M]/R, L/[M]/R    ; CMP BYTE [val], ah
```

Once we have compared two operands, many options exist for condition tests. As previously mentioned, the TEST and CMP instructions set various CPU flags. Almost all of the conditional jump instructions operate by testing one or more of the CPU flags. A few instructions operate based on the *cx/ecx/rcx* registers. Table 5.7 lists common conditional jump instructions, the CPU flags tested with each, and whether or not the instruction operates on signed or unsigned operands.

Table 5.7 Conditional jump instructions

Sign	Flag	Instruction	Description
Signed and unsigned	OF = 1	JO	Jump if overflow
	OF = 0	JNO	Jump if not overflow
	PF = 1	JP	Jump if parity
	PF = 0	JNP	Jump if not parity
	SF = 1	JS	Jump if sign
	SF = 0	JNS	Jump if not sign
	ZF = 1	JE	Jump if equal
		JZ	Jump if zero
	ZF = 0	JNE	Jump if not equal
		JNZ	Jump if not zero
	CX = 0	JCXZ	Jump if *CX* register is zero
	ECX = 0	JECXZ	Jump if *ECX* register is zero
	RCX = 0	JRCXZ	Jump if *RCX* register is zero
Signed	SF != OF	JL	Jump if less
		JNGE	Jump if not greater or equal
	SF = OF	JGE	Jump if greater or equal
		JNL	Jump if not less
	ZF = 1 or SF != OF	JLE	Jump if less or equal
		JNG	Jump if not greater
	ZF = 0 and SF = OF	JG	Jump if greater
		JNLE	Jump if not less or equal
Unsigned	CF = 1	JB	Jump if below
		JC	Jump if carry
		JNAE	Jump if not above or equal
	CF = 0	JAE	Jump if above or equal
		JNB	Jump if not below
		JNC	Jump if not carry
	CF = 1 or ZF = 1	JBE	Jump if below or equal
		JNA	Jump if not above
	CF = 0 and ZF = 0	JA	Jump if above
		JNBE	Jump if not below or equal

 PROGRAMMING: When choosing a conditional jump instruction, be certain to select the appropriate instruction for testing based on the signage of the operands. For example, selecting JA instead of JG when working with signed operands can result in an incorrect sequence of instructions being executed.

Consider the following `if` statement translated from a high-level language to Assembly using the correct conditional jump statements.

```
if (wages >= 50000)
    taxes = 5000
else
    taxes = 2000
```

Program 5.1 shows one of the possible translations of the high-level code into Assembly for each assembler.

Program 5.1 *Conditional jump (32-bit)*

GAS	MASM	NASM

`.data`
`wages: .long 46000`
 	
`.bss`
`.lcomm taxes, 4`
 	
`.text`
`.globl _main`
`_main:`
 	
`  movl $50000, %eax`
`  cmpl %eax, wages`
`  jae higher`
`  movl $2000, taxes`
`  jmp done`
 	
`higher:`
`  movl $4000, taxes`
 	
`done:`
`pushl $0`
`subl $4, %esp`
`movl $1, %eax`
`int $0x80`
`.end`
	`.386`
	`.MODEL FLAT, stdcall`
	`.STACK 4096`
	`ExitProcess PROTO,`
	`dwExitCode:DWORD`
	
	`.data`
	`wages DWORD 46000`
	`taxes DWORD ?`
	
	`.code`
	`_main PROC`
	
	`  mov eax, 50000`
	`  cmp wages, eax`
	`  jae higher`
	`  mov taxes, 2000`
	`  jmp done`
	
	`higher:`
	`  mov taxes, 4000`
	
	`done:`
	`INVOKE ExitProcess, 0`
	`_main ENDP`
	`END`
		`SECTION .data`
		`wages: DD 46000`
		
		`SECTION .bss`
		`taxes: RESD 1`
		
		`SECTION .text`
		`global _main`
		`_main:`
		
		`  mov eax, 50000`
		`  cmp DWORD [wages], eax`
		`  jae higher`
		`  mov DWORD [taxes], 2000`
		`  jmp done`
		
		`higher:`
		`  mov DWORD [taxes], 4000`
		
		`done:`
		`mov eax, 1`
		`mov ebx, 0`
		`int 80h`

Notice in Program 5.1 that we did not use multiple conditional jumps since doing so would be more processor-intensive than necessary by requiring a second check of processor flags. Instead, we arranged the instructions so the logic of the `else` statement follows the conditional jump to `higher` if `wages` is above or equal to $50000. After the compare, we perform the conditional test for the `if`. Should the test fail, which is the case in Program 5.1, execution simply moves to the next instruction, the logic for the `else` section. Then, we unconditionally jump to the `done` section, skipping the logic in the `if` section. We could have written the code in such a way that we check both cases: using JAE to check for higher taxes and JB to check for lower taxes. But the "below" check was unnecessary because of some clever instruction organization.

Compound Conditionals

Having discussed conditionals, we can perform slightly more complex logic by using compound conditionals. In C++, compound conditionals use **Boolean *logical* expressions**: the && (logical AND) and || (logical OR) operators.

```
if ( a > b && b > c)            if ( a > b || b > c)
    x = 1;                          x = 1;
```

The C++ code demonstrates an `if` statement that performs a logical AND operation and another `if` statement that performs a logical OR operation. Performing compound conditionals in Assembly can be achieved via the **short-circuit evaluation** method (also used in C++) as shown in Example 5.1. This method only tests the second conditional if the first conditional is not sufficient to determine the outcome of the entire compound Boolean expression.

Example 5.1 Compound conditionals (Intel syntax)

&& (Logical AND)	|| (Logical OR)
| ```
cmp ax, bx   ; first expression
jbe next     ; quit if false
cmp bx, cx   ; second expression
jbe next     ; quit if false
mov x, 1     ; both are true
next:
``` | ```
cmp ax, bx   ; first expression
ja L1        ; if true skip to L1
cmp bx, cx   ; second expression
jbe next     ; false: skip to next
L1: mov x, 1 ; true result
next:
``` |

For the logical AND example, both conditionals must evaluate to True for the entire compound expression to be True (recall the Boolean AND tables). So if the value in *ax* is below or equal to the value in *bx*, the initial expression (a > b) fails. Since both expressions must be True, if the first expression fails, we skip the rest of the conditional code and jump to the next label. The second expression is only checked if the value in *ax* is above the value in *bx*.

The code for the logical OR is slightly different. Instead of testing for a False expression as we did with the logical AND, we check for a True expression. The approach allows our program to jump to the L1 label, which sets x = 1, if the first expression is True. If a condition in an OR expression is True, then the entire expression is True and we do not need to spend time testing any other conditions. In both the logical OR and logical AND scenarios, the instructions are arranged as efficiently as possible such that the minimal number of instructions are executed to accomplish the goal.

Repetition

The concept of **repetition**, or looping, is to write a sequence of instructions once but have the instructions execute a given number of times in succession. The number of times a sequence of instructions repeats is usually controlled by either a counter variable or a conditional test. For example, in high-level languages, we know repetitive control structures as `for` loops and `while` loops.

```
for (int x = 0; x < 5; x++)          while (answer == "yes")
    Sequence of instructions             Sequence of instructions
```

While such constructs (directives) do not consistently exist in Assembly language, we can achieve the same control using only x86 instructions.

Using CX/ECX/RCX

The concept of a counter-controlled loop is easily implemented in Assembly with the **LOOP** instruction, which uses the value in the "*C*" register as a decrementing **counter**. Each iteration of the loop will decrement the *cx/ecx/rcx* counter by 1. When the counter reaches 0, the loop stops and execution continues with the first instruction after the loop.

 PROGRAMMING: In 16-bit mode the loop counter is the *cx* register. In 32-bit mode the counter is the *ecx* register. In 64-bit mode the counter is the *rcx* register.

The LOOP instruction is consistent across assemblers, with the instruction followed by a label.

GAS/MASM/NASM

```
LOOP LABEL      ; LOOP sumLoop
```

Consider Program 5.2, a 64-bit program that implements a high-level `for` loop in Assembly. First, note that we use the bitwise XOR instruction to clear *rax*, so its value is 0 (XOR is a common method for clearing values in Assembly). Upon reaching the LOOP instruction, some implicit operations happen: (1) *rcx* is decremented by 1; (2) *rcx* is tested to determine if it is greater than zero; (3) if *rcx* is greater than zero the program jumps to the specified label, otherwise execution continues to the next instruction. Program 5.2 loops five times and adds 1 to *rax* in each iteration. The final value in *rax* is 5.

Program 5.2 Looping (64-bit)

GAS	MASM	NASM

``
.text
.globl _main
_main:
 	
xorq %rax, %rax
movq $5, %rcx
 	
myLoop:
    incq %rax
    loop myLoop
 	
movq $0x2000001, %rax
movq $0, %rdi
syscall
.end
``
	``
	extrn ExitProcess : proc
	
	.code
	_main PROC
	
	xor rax, rax
	mov rcx, 5
	
	myLoop:
	    inc rax
	    loop myLoop
	
	mov rcx, 0
	call ExitProcess
	_main ENDP
	END
	``
		``
		SECTION .text
		global _main
		_main:
		
		xor rax, rax
		mov rcx, 5
		
		myLoop:
		    inc rax
		    loop myLoop
		
		mov rax, 60
		xor rdi, rdi
		syscall
		``

 LEARNING: Watching an Assembly loop execute step-by-step is a great way to learn how LOOP operates. In your preferred programming environment, set a breakpoint prior to the XOR instruction in Program 5.2 and step through the program while watching the contents of *rax* and *rcx*. Refer to **APPENDICES B AND D** for debugging help.

Writing a single loop is simple enough, but great care must be taken when writing a nested loop (a loop inside a loop). Each time a LOOP instruction executes, the "*C*" register is decremented, which means the translation of the C++ loop to Assembly shown in Example 5.2 will produce incorrect results.

Example 5.2 Incorrect loop translation

C++	GAS	MASM/NASM

``
int value = 0;
for (int x = 0; x < 2; x++)
   for (int y = 0; y < 3; y++)
      value++;
``
	``
	movl $0, value
	movl $2, %ecx
	outer:
	    movl $3, %ecx
	    inner:
	        incl value
	        loop inner
	    loop outer
	``
		``
		mov value, 0
		mov ecx, 2
		outer:
		    mov ecx, 3
		    inner:
		        inc value
		        loop inner
		    loop outer
		``

After executing the C++ code, the `value` variable contains 6. The Assembly code behavior is very different due to two issues. First, the `outer` loop needs a counter of 2, but we immediately overwrite the *ecx* register with 3 for the inner loop counter. Second, after the `inner` loop runs three times, `value` will be 3 and *ecx* will be 0. Consequently, the `loop inner` test if *ecx* is greater than zero fails, ending the inner loop. The next instruction is `loop outer`, which subtracts 1 from *ecx*, causing the value to roll over from 0x0h to 0xFFFFFFFFh, then checks if *ecx* is greater than zero and loops back to the `outer` label. The Assembly code is an infinite loop (and a nasty bug that has caused problems before).

 LEARNING: When subtractions happen on low values such as 0, nothing prevents a rollover to -1. As we learned in **CHAPTER 1**, -1 is all 1's in binary (or 0xFh), which if interpreted as an unsigned integer is the maximum number possible. One prominent example of this bug is Gandhi in the classic game *Civilization*, where Gandhi has the propensity to become very aggressive and bomb cities with nukes. Read more about the bug (or feature) here: http://civilization.wikia.com/wiki/Mohandas_Gandhi_(Civ1).

To fix the Assembly code in Example 5.2, we need to save the value of *ecx* once we reach the inner loop. Then we can overwrite *ecx* with the inner loop counter without worrying about losing the outer loop's state. At the end of the inner loop we can restore the outer loop's counter value so it can proceed as desired. Example 5.3 shows the correct translation of the C++ nested loop. The Assembly code assumes a `counter` variable has been defined in the *data* segment.

Example 5.3 Correct loop translation

C++	GAS	MASM/NASM

for (int x = 0; x < 2; x++)
  for (int y = 0; y < 3; y++)
    value++;
	`movl $2, %ecx`
	`outer:`
	`    movl %ecx, counter`
	`    movl $3, %ecx`
	`inner:`
	`    incl value`
	`    loop inner`
	`    movl counter, %ecx`
	`loop outer`
		`mov ecx, 2`
		`outer:`
		`    mov counter, ecx`
		`    mov ecx, 3`
		`inner:`
		`    inc value`
		`    loop inner`
		`    mov ecx, counter`
		`loop outer`

The loop translation examples demonstrate that care needs to be taken when using the LOOP instruction. In addition to issues with nested loops and implicit LOOP operations, other issues can arise when using instructions inside a loop that automatically store results in the "*C*" register, or if you need to use the counter register for another purpose within the logic of a loop. An alternative approach is to write loops using a counter of your choosing and the CMP instruction.

Using Programmer-defined Counters

Another way to translate the C++ `for` loop in Example 5.3 into Assembly without using the LOOP instruction is shown in Example 5.4. We use programmer-defined counter variables (x and y) and the CMP instruction to test whether to continue or discontinue iteration of each loop. The Assembly code in Example 5.4 assumes the existence of the variables x, y, and `value`. Within each loop iteration we decrement the proper counter variable (y for the inner loop and x for the outer loop) and eventually the counters will become 0, ending each loop due to the JNE (Jump if Not Equal) conditional instructions.

Example 5.4 Loop translation using CMP

C++	GAS	MASM/NASM

for (int x = 0; x < 2; x++)
  for (int y = 0; y < 3; y++)
    value++;
	`movl $2, x`
	`outer:`
	`    movl $3, y`
	`inner:`
	`    incl value`
	`    decl y`
	`    cmpl $0, y`
	`    jne inner`
	`decl x`
	`cmpl $0, x`
	`jne outer`
		`mov x, 2`
		`outer:`
		`    mov y, 3`
		`inner:`
		`    inc value`
		`    dec y`
		`    cmp y, 0`
		`    jne inner`
		`dec x`
		`cmp x, 0`
		`jne outer`

Two specific items in Example 5.4 deserve clarification. The first item is that the Assembly and C++ code act on the counters in an opposite manner. While the C++ code increments the counters, the Assembly code decrements the counters. The code can be written various ways depending on programmer preferences.

The second item is the use of variables as counters. One of the major benefits of programming in Assembly is that processor registers are available to store data instead of wasting memory by creating variables. Using processor registers instead of memory variables can also speed up the execution of programs; recall from **Chapter 2** that accessing data stored in memory requires more clock cycles. Although compilers and CPU algorithms may automatically perform optimizations behind the scenes, you should not assume optimizations. Programming in Assembly gives a programmer the ability to ensure effective optimizations.

Example 5.5 shows the same Assembly code as Example 5.4 with the optimization of replacing variables with registers.

Example 5.5 Optimized loop translation

GAS	MASM/NASM

```xorl %eax, %eax```
```movl $2, %ebx```
```outer:```
```   movl $3, %ecx```
```   inner:```
```   incl %eax```
```   decl %ecx```
```   cmpl $0, %ecx```
```   jne inner```
```   decl %ebx```
```   cmpl $0, %ebx```
```   jne outer```
	```xor eax, eax```
	```mov ebx, 2```
	```outer:```
	``` mov ecx, 3```
	``` inner:```
	``` inc eax```
	``` dec ecx```
	``` cmp ecx, 0```
	``` jne inner```
	``` dec ebx```
	``` cmp ebx, 0```
	``` jne outer```

After executing the Assembly code in Example 5.5, the *eax* register will contain the result of 6 as opposed to the `value` variable in Example 5.4.

> 📖 LEARNING: Another method of temporarily saving values is to use the stack via the PUSH and POP instructions, which is covered in **CHAPTER 6**.

Another high-level loop we can implement is the `while` loop. Example 5.6 presents two Assembly examples that show how the C++ `while` loop might be implemented with multiple jump instructions.

Example 5.6 `while` loop translations

C++	GAS v1	NASM/MASM v1	GAS v2	NASM/MASM v2

```x = 30;```
```while (x < 50)```
```   x++;```
	```movl $30, %eax```
	```while_loop:```
	``` cmpl $50, %eax```
	``` jae done```
	``` incl %eax```
	``` jmp while_loop```
	```done:```
		```mov eax, 30```
		```while_loop:```
		``` cmp eax, 50```
		``` jae done```
		``` inc eax```
		``` jmp while_loop```
		```done:```
			```movl $30, %eax```
			```while_loop:```
			``` cmpl $50, %eax```
			``` jb addone```
			``` jae done```
			```addone:```
			``` incl %eax```
			``` jmp while_loop```
			```done:```
				```mov eax, 30```
				```while_loop:```
				``` cmp eax, 50```
				``` jb addone```
				``` jae done```
				```addone:```
				``` inc eax```
				``` jmp while_loop```
				```done:```

Version 1 (v1) is not a synonymous translation of the C++ code. Instead of doing a less-than comparison we do the inverse, an above-or-equal comparison. Doing so results in a more efficient loop. Version 2 (v2) is synonymous, using a below (less-than) comparison. But using JB required a second comparison for the inverse condition (i.e., JAE) due to the sequential flow of instructions, which results in slightly longer code.

Since the Assembly code in Examples 5.3–5.6 was just partial code (and written for 32-bit), Program 5.3 presents a nested `for` loop and Program 5.4 presents a `while` loop for each of the assemblers in 64-bit. In Program 5.3, the final value in *rax* is 6 and in Program 5.4 the final value in *rax* is 50 (before the exit routines).

Program 5.3 – Nested `for` *loop (64-bit)*

GAS	MASM	NASM
| ```
.text
.globl _main
_main:

xorq %rax, %rax
movq $2, %rbx
outer:
  movq $3, %rcx
  inner:
    incq %rax
    decq %rcx
    cmpq $0, %rcx
    jne inner
  decq %rbx
  cmpq $0, %rbx
  jne outer

movq $0x2000001, %rax
movq $0, %rdi
syscall
.end
``` | ```
extrn ExitProcess : proc

.code
_main PROC

xor rax, rax
mov rbx, 2
outer:
  mov rcx, 3
  inner:
    inc rax
    dec rcx
    cmp rcx, 0
    jne inner
  dec rbx
  cmp rbx, 0
  jne outer

mov rcx, 0
call ExitProcess
_main ENDP
END
``` | ```
SECTION .text
global _main
_main:

xor rax, rax
mov rbx, 2
outer:
  mov rcx, 3
  inner:
    inc rax
    dec rcx
    cmp rcx, 0
    jne inner
  dec rbx
  cmp rbx, 0
  jne outer

mov rax, 60
xor rdi, rdi
syscall
``` |

Program 5.4 `while` *loop (64-bit)*

GAS	MASM	NASM
| ```
.text
.globl _main
_main:

movq $30, %rax
while_loop:
  cmpq $50, %rax
  jae done
  incq %rax
  jmp while_loop
done:

movq $0x2000001, %rax
movq $0, %rdi
syscall
.end
``` | ```
extrn ExitProcess : proc

.code
_main PROC

mov rax, 30
while_loop:
  cmp rax, 50
  jae done
  inc rax
  jmp while_loop
done:

mov rcx, 0
call ExitProcess
_main ENDP
END
``` | ```
SECTION .text
global _main
_main:

mov rax, 30
while_loop:
  cmp rax, 50
  jae done
  inc rax
  jmp while_loop
done:

mov rax, 60
xor rdi, rdi
syscall
``` |

As is always the case with programming, cleverly organizing instructions leads to finished code that is concise and optimized.

Summary

In this chapter we discussed how to manipulate data at the bit level using Boolean instructions. We also examined different ways of adding more complex logic to programs, such as executing different sequences of instructions based on conditions. Many programming tasks can be accomplished by combining conditional logic with repeating sequences of instructions. We demonstrated various implementation methods to manipulate program flow with jump instructions. You should now have the knowledge necessary to write moderately complex Assembly programs. In future chapters, we tackle more complex topics and techniques that require a strong understanding of CHAPTERS 1–5.

Key Terms

AND	LOOP
Boolean bitwise operations	NOT
Boolean logical expressions	OR
branching	repetition (looping)
CMP	short-circuit evaluation
counter	TEST
JMP	XOR

Code Review

AND	Bitwise AND operation
CMP	Performs an *implicit* subtraction of the source operand from the destination operand
JA	Jump if above (unsigned)
JAE	Jump if above or equal (unsigned)
JB	Jump if below (unsigned)
JBE	Jump if below or equal (unsigned)
JC	Jump if carry (unsigned)
JCXZ	Jump if CX register is zero
JE	Jump if equal
JECXZ	Jump if ECX register is zero
JG	Jump if greater (signed)
JGE	Jump if greater or equal (signed)
JL	Jump if less (signed)
JLE	Jump if less or equal (signed)
JMP	Unconditional jump
JNA	Jump if not above (unsigned)
JNAE	Jump if not above or equal (unsigned)
JNB	Jump if not below (unsigned)
JNBE	Jump if not below or equal (unsigned)
JNC	Jump if not carry (unsigned)
JNE	Jump if not equal
JNG	Jump if greater (signed)
JNGE	Jump if not greater or equal (signed)
JNL	Jump if not less (signed)
JNLE	Jump of not less or equal (signed)
JNO	Jump if not overflow
JNP	Jump if not parity
JNS	Jump if not sign
JNZ	Jump if not zero
JO	Jump if overflow
JP	Jump if parity
JRCXZ	Jump if RCX register is zero
JS	Jump if sign
JZ	Jump if zero

LOOP	Loop using CX/ECX/RCX as counter
NOT	Bitwise NOT operation
OR	Bitwise OR operation
TEST	Performs an *implied* AND operation on two operands
XOR	Bitwise XOR operation

Questions

Short Answer

1. Using the bitwise AND operation, the result of 1 AND 0 is _____.
2. 10100100 _____ 11010101 = 01110001.
3. A common way to detect whether a value is even or odd is to use the _____ operation to test if the least significant bit is set.
4. Combining multiple flags into a single variable can be accomplished via the _____ operation.
5. In order to implement branching in an Assembly program, you must use _____ to identify blocks of code.
6. The _____ instruction will move execution to a different section of code regardless of any conditions.
7. Before any conditional tests can be executed, two operands must be compared using the _____ instruction.
8. A comparison operation sets processor flags based on an implied _____ of two operands.
9. The JNGE instruction means to jump to a label if the first operand is _____ the second operand.
10. Only _____ operands should be used when executing the JNA instruction.
11. In order to jump if the Sign Flag is set to 0 after a compare instruction, use the _____ instruction.
12. Counter-based loops can be quickly written using the LOOP instruction, which uses _____ as the counter.
13. In 32-bit mode, the LOOP instruction automatically _____ *ecx* when executed.
14. Programmers can use a combination of the _____ instruction and a _____ instruction to create their own counter-controlled loops.
15. Using _____ instead of _____ to store data can help a program execute faster.

True/False

1. The AND bitwise operation is commonly used for setting bits in a value.
2. The JMP instruction does not require any specific processor flags to be set.
3. The JNZ instruction can be used with signed operands.
4. The LOOP instruction preserves the counter value automatically so the programmer is free to use the counter register (*cx/ecx/rcx*) within the loop.
5. In Assembly, you must always use two conditional jump instructions to test both the `if` case and the `else` case.

Assignments

5.1 Fibonacci's revenge

Write a program that calculates the sum of all odd numbers in the Fibonacci sequence between 0 and 1,000,000.

5.2 Letter frequency

Write a program that counts the number of times the letter "a" (lowercase or uppercase) appears in the following sentence: `Assembly is the best programming language!`

5.3 Prepare for output! (Challenge Assignment)

Write a program that takes a normal 32-bit numeric value (e.g., `0xFFFFh`) and converts it to a byte array such that it can be printed to the screen using a system call method. A loop is necessary for converting the numeric value to ASCII for output. Again, use a system call (e.g., `int 80h`) to print the value to the console (see CHAPTER 10). Calling external functions (e.g., `printf`) is not allowed for this assignment.

## CHAPTER 6

Functions

Objectives

- Deconstruct function implementations
- Compare function calling conventions
- Manipulate stack memory
- Create functions in Assembly

Outline

1. Web Resources
2. Introduction
3. Stack Memory Primer
4. x86 and x86_64 Calling Conventions
   a. cdecl (32-bit) – Function Overview
   b. stdcall (32-bit)
   c. x86_64 (64-bit)
   c. Some Useful Details
5. Implementations
6. Summary
7. Key Terms
8. Key Registers
9. Code Review
10. Platform Specific Notes
11. Questions
    a. Short Answer
    b. True/False
12. Assignments

Web Resources

Wikis

- http://en.wikipedia.org/wiki/Calling_convention
- http://en.wikipedia.org/wiki/X86_calling_conventions
- http://en.wikibooks.org/wiki/X86_Disassembly/Calling_Conventions
- http://wiki.osdev.org/Calling_Conventions

Developer

- https://developer.apple.com/library/mac/documentation/DeveloperTools/Conceptual/LowLevel ABI/000-Introduction/introduction.html (OS X ABI Function Call Guide)
- https://msdn.microsoft.com/en-us/library/k2b2ssfy.aspx (x86 Calling Conventions)
- https://msdn.microsoft.com/en-us/library/ms235286.aspx (x64 Calling Convention)
- http://refspecs.linuxfoundation.org/elf/x86-64-abi-0.99.pdf (AMD64 ABI)
- http://www.agner.org/optimize/calling_conventions.pdf (Calling Conventions)

Introduction

The purpose of this chapter is to introduce you to the implementation details of functions. We illustrate how registers and memory are used in the execution of procedures. This exploration provides a significant peek "under the hood" for a software developer seeking to better understand how functions—a foundational building block of modern programming languages—are implemented at a low level. Although many technical details exist that we could spend hundreds of pages covering, we will generally discuss the most common calling conventions and provide learning examples. This chapter will help you better understand how functions work, how to program functions in Assembly, and the implications of high-level programming decisions.

 ATTENTION: The terms **procedures** and **functions** are sometimes used interchangeably. Some texts may indicate a difference in that a procedure does not return a value, but a function does return a value.

Stack Memory Primer

Prior to learning function calling conventions, you need a basic understanding of **stack memory**. To review what you likely learned in fundamental programming courses, stack memory is an area of memory used for automatic variables (i.e., local, non-dynamic). When a function is called, the stack is used to store variables local to the function. When a function ends, the local variables (now out of scope) are dereferenced and the memory locations become available for other uses. A significant feature of high-level languages is that stack memory (sometimes called the run-time stack) is managed for you; such is not the case in Assembly.

When diving into low-level Assembly programming you will be actively involved in managing stack memory. Also, understanding the instructions that manipulate stack memory can help you when debugging programs. The following list suggests important points to remember about stack memory.

- The stack grows and shrinks as functions are called and return.
- The stack grows and shrinks as local variables are created (pushed) and dereferenced (popped).
- The stack has an OS-dependent size limit per process/thread (e.g., Linux/Mac default is 8MB, Windows default is 1MB).
- Every function call, including `main()` and recursive calls, has a **stack frame** (an area of stack memory that is supplied as a result of each function call).
- A stack frame is used to store a function's local variables.
- Stack memory grows down, with addresses descending.
- Every memory slot holds 4 bytes in 32-bit mode or 8 bytes in 64-bit mode.
- Values are stored by default in **Little-Endian** form. (See **CHAPTER 2** for details on Endianness.) The least significant byte is stored at the start of the address (higher) and the most significant byte is stored at the end (lower). For example, if we store the 32-bit hex value `0x9BFB3701` in memory, the value is stored as `01 37 FB 9B`.
- In x86_64, all functions must be 16-byte aligned (all platforms).

In the next section, we discuss the finer details of stack and further explain the aforementioned points within the context of calling conventions and a working Assembly program example.

x86 and x86_64 Calling Conventions

Calling conventions, sometimes called protocols, define the process of how a function call is implemented at a low level. A convention defines how parameters are passed, how stack memory is managed, and how values are returned. As we discuss calling conventions, we will use the terms **caller** and **callee**. The caller is the calling function and the callee is the called function. In the C++ Example 6.1, `main()` is the caller and `sum()` is the callee.

Example 6.1 Sum program in C++

```
int sum(int, int);                      // sum function prototype

int main() {                            // main function is caller
    int num1 = 2, num2 = 4, answer;
    answer = sum(num1, num2);           // sum function is callee
    return 0;
}

int sum(int num1, int num2){
    return num1 + num2;
}
```

cdecl (32-bit) – Function Overview

 ATTENTION: We use a 32-bit example to provide a detailed overview of function calls. Doing so allows us to examine differences between different 32-bit calling conventions and changes made in 64-bit. Since both architectures are widely used, coverage of both is beneficial and important.

The **cdecl** (C declaration) calling convention is the most common across 32-bit platforms because it is based on the C standard. Cdecl is typically the default convention in compilers such as GCC, Clang, and Visual Studio's C compiler. Some development environments, such as Visual Studio, allow you to set the default convention in a project's properties, as seen in Figure 6.1. Cdecl has four primary characteristics.

- Parameters are passed in reverse order (from right to left) via the stack.
- *eax, ecx,* and *edx* are caller-saved (volatile), while the rest of the general purpose registers are callee-saved (non-volatile). Consequently, if you want to save *eax, ecx,* and *edx,* you need to do so in the calling function because they will likely be overwritten during function execution.
- *eax* is used as the return register in most cases. *st(0)* is used for a floating-point return.
- The caller is responsible for cleaning up the stack.

C supports variadic/varargs functions (variable argument lists), which means the callee does not know how many arguments it has received. Therefore, the caller must clean up the stack and cleanup code is necessary every time a function is called. A prime example of a variadic C function is `printf()`.

Program 6.1 demonstrates the cdecl calling convention in x86. The program is an Assembly implementation of the C++ Sum program in Example 6.1. We use the GAS version to discuss cdecl in greater detail.

The Sum program pseudocode is as follows.

1. Declare and initialize variables (`num1` and `num2`)
2. Simulate computational activity pre function call
3. Call the `sum` function, which adds `num1` and `num2`
4. Simulate computational activity post function call

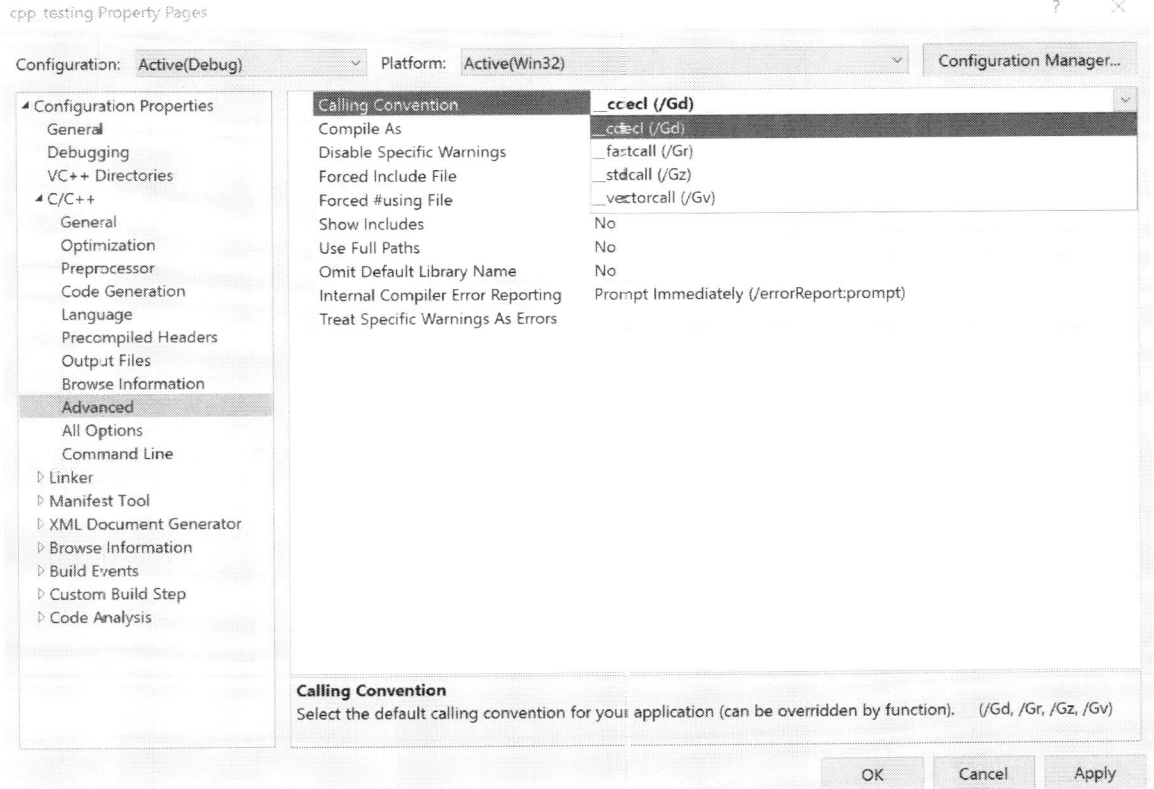

Figure 6.1 Set calling convention in Visual Studio

> PROGRAMMING: Understanding function implementations at a low level is important for code optimization and debugging. When using x86, you may independently chose calling conventions for functions. When using x86 or x86_64, you can better choose when implementing a function is appropriate and when repetitive operations are appropriate. Low-level function details highlight the pros and cons of recursive, inline, static, and template functions. Most development environments present disassembled code when debugging, so understanding what is happening and when helps in finding and fixing bugs.

Program 6.1 *Sum program x86 implementations*

GAS	MASM	NASM
| ```
.data
num1: .long 2
num2: .long 4

.text
.globl _main, _sum
_main:

movl $10, %eax
decl %eax
movl $5, %ebx

pushl num2
pushl num1
calll _sum
addl $8, %esp

addl %ebx, %eax
decl %eax

pushl $0
subl $4, %esp
movl $1, %eax
int $0x80

_sum:
pushl %ebp
movl %esp, %ebp
pushl %ebx
movl 8(%ebp), %ebx
movl 12(%ebp), %eax
addl %ebx, %eax
popl %ebx
popl %ebp
retl

.end
``` | ```
.386
.MODEL FLAT, C
ExitProcess PROTO stdcall,
dwExitCode:DWORD

.data
num1 DWORD 2
num2 DWORD 4

.code
_main PROC

mov eax, 10
dec eax
mov ebx, 5

push num2
push num1
call _sum
add esp, 8

add eax, ebx
dec eax

INVOKE ExitProcess, 0
_main ENDP

_sum PROC
push ebp
mov ebp, esp
push ebx
mov ebx, [ebp + 8]
mov eax, [ebp + 12]
add eax, ebx
pop ebx
pop ebp
ret
_sum ENDP

END _main
``` | ```
section .data
num1: dd 2
num2: dd 4

section .text
global _main, _sum
_main:

mov eax, 10
dec eax
mov ebx, 5

push DWORD[num2]
push DWORD[num1]
call _sum
add esp, 8

add eax, ebx
dec eax

mov eax, 1
mov ebx, 0
int 80h

_sum:
push ebp
mov ebp, esp
push ebx
mov ebx, [ebp + 8]
mov eax, [ebp + 12]
add eax, ebx
pop ebx
pop ebp
ret
``` |

 LEARNING: One way to explore this chapter is to code Program 6.1; and as you write each code section, refer to the following breakdown to explain the reasoning and behavior of the code.
```

```
.data
num1: .long 2
num2: .long 4

.text
.globl _main, _sum
```

The first section of the GAS code, the `.data` segment, defines two variables: `num1` with a value of 2 and `num2` with a value of 4, both 32-bits. Next is the `.text` segment, which contains the executable instructions for the program. Two global functions are declared: `_main` and `_sum`, with `_main` being the entry point of the program.

```
movl $10, %eax
decl %eax
movl $5, %ebx
```

The next three lines are meant to simulate other activities going on in the program and to set up a register-saving scenario. We move the value 10 to *eax*, decrease *eax* by 1, and move the value 5 to *ebx*. The status of the registers is *eax* = 9 and *ebx* = 5. If we wanted to save the value in *eax* (a caller-saved register), we would need to push *eax* to the stack prior to the function call so the value could be restored upon returning to `_main`. We do want to save *ebx* (a callee-saved register), so we will push *ebx* to the stack once we are inside the `_sum` function.

```
pushl num2
pushl num1
calll _sum
addl $8, %esp
```

Next is the function call. Remember, cdecl parameters are passed in reverse order (from right to left) via the stack. Given the function call
`answer = sum(num1, num2);`
`num2` will be pushed first and `num1` pushed second. For pass-by-value, push the value. For pass-by-reference, push the address of the value (see Example 6.2). The `call` is then made to `_sum`. After the `_sum` function has completed, the stack needs to be cleaned up in `_main`. Since two 4-byte values were pushed on the stack, 8 bytes is added to *esp* to "remove" the values.

Example 6.2 32-bit pass-by-reference

GAS	MASM	NASM

`.data`
`num1: .long 2`
 	
`.text`
`pushl $num1`
	`.data`
	`num1 DWORD 2`
	
	`.code`
	`push OFFSET num1`
		`section .data`
		`num1: dd 2`
		
		`section .text`
		`push num1`

 LEARNING: Refer to the **CODE REVIEW** section at the end of the chapter for details on new instructions introduced in this chapter (PUSH, POP, CALL, RET, and NOP). The chapter programs and code examples provide syntax specifics and we discuss operational details as we go along.

At this point, it will be helpful to take a look at the disassembly, stack, registers, and instructions with corresponding memory locations of Program 6.1 when running. The memory addresses will vary when running the program, but the process is consistent. Also, remember that stack grows down with addresses descending.

Figure 6.2 illustrates the state of the Sum Program before the parameters are pushed to stack. Notice that *eip* holds the address `0x1f86`, which is the next instruction to be executed (`pushl 0x2004`). When we step forward and execute the instruction, several things will happen.

1. *eip* will be incremented to `0x1f8c`, the next instruction to be fetched and executed.
2. The value contained in address `0x2004` will be pushed to the stack. If we were to look in memory location `0x2004`, we would find the value `04 00 00 00`, which is `num2`.
3. *esp* will be decremented 4 bytes to account for the 32-bit value pushed on the stack.

Figure 6.3 illustrates the state of the program after the two parameters have been pushed to the stack.

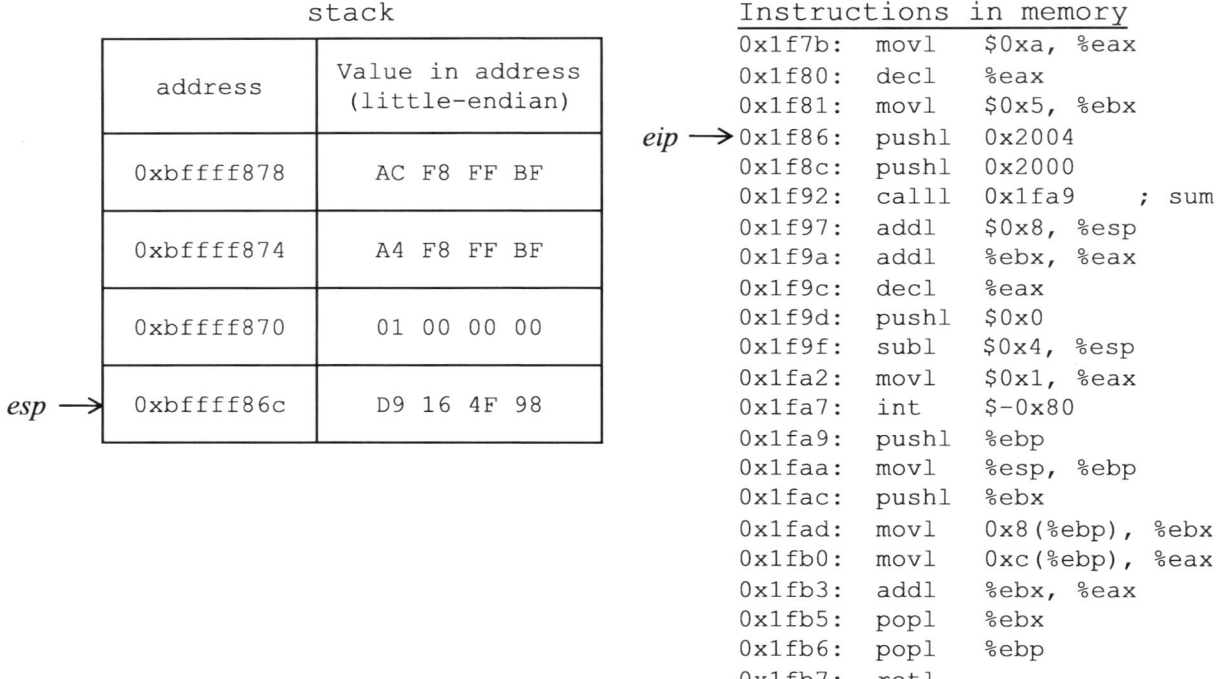

Figure 6.2 Before parameters pushed

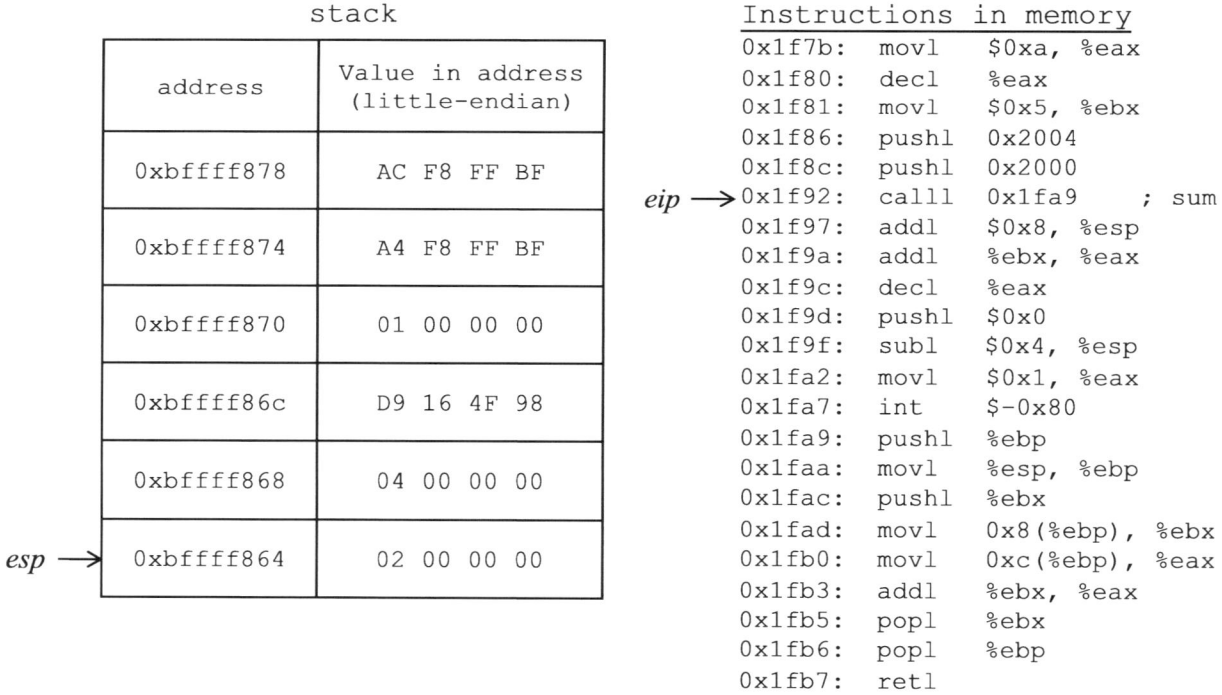

Figure 6.3 After parameters pushed

The next instruction to execute (see *eip* in Figure 6.3) is stored in `0x1f92` and is `calll 0x1fa9`. The CALL instruction will do several things.

1. Push the location of the next instruction on the stack. Upon completing the _sum function, we need to pick up where we left off in _main, which means saving the address of the first instruction after the `calll`. In this example that means the value (address) `0x1f97` is pushed on the stack.
2. Execution then transfers to the address called, in this case `0x1fa9`.
3. *eip* and *esp* are updated accordingly.

Figure 6.4 illustrates the state of the program after the CALL instruction has been executed.

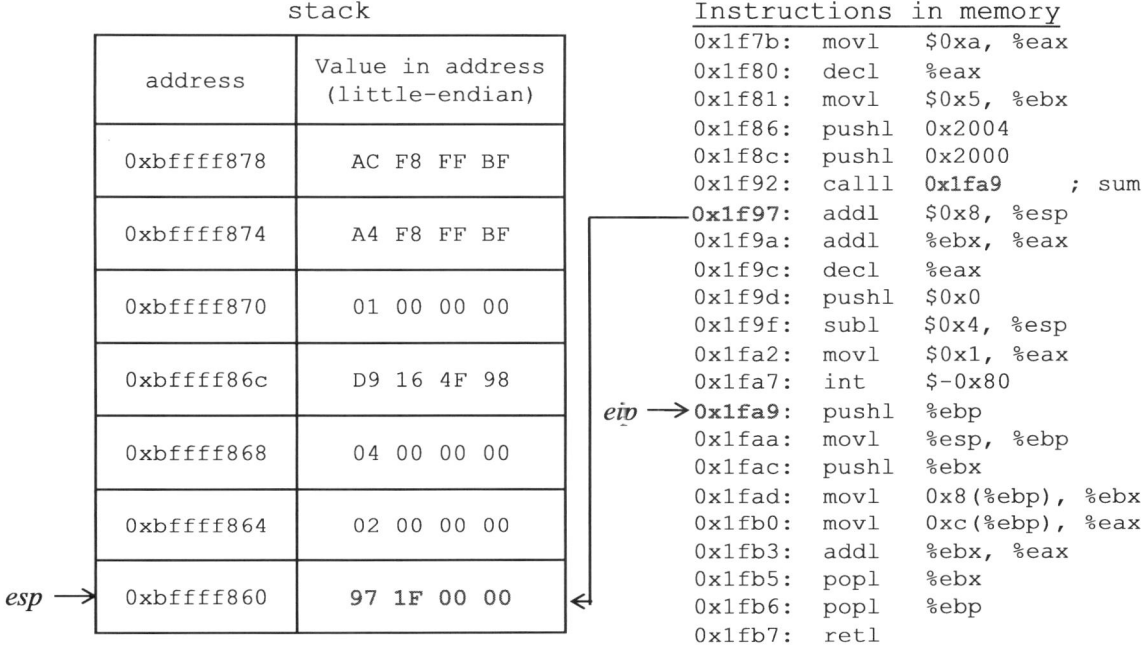

Figure 6.4 After CALL instruction

Upon entering the _sum function, the stack frame for _sum needs to be established. As previously stated, a stack frame is where local variables for a function are located, and the *ebp* register points to the beginning of the currently executing stack frame. The role of *ebp* is important because it provides a point of reference for the parameters passed and for local variables; *ebp* is how we will access values in the function. In x86, avoid using *esp* to reference parameters because its purpose is to always be pointing to the top of the stack and *esp* will change as values are pushed and popped. *ebp* gives us a constant reference point and it should not be changed throughout a function.

> **PROGRAMMING:** The way local variables are referenced varies from 32-bit to 64-bit. In 32-bit, *ebp* typically serves as the constant point of reference for accessing parameters. In 64-bit, *ebp* referencing is less common for several reasons: (1) registers are used more often than stack for passing parameters, (2) *rip*-relative addressing is available (see **APPENDIX F** and **CHAPTER 6 SUPPLEMENT**), and (3) default allocation of scratch space in stack memory enables use of *rsp* for referencing local variables. We discuss 64-bit implementations later in this chapter.

```
_sum:
pushl %ebp
movl %esp, %ebp
pushl %ebx
movl 8(%ebp), %ebx
movl 12(%ebp), %eax
addl %ebx, %eax
popl %ebx
popl %ebp
retl
```

The first two lines of the _sum function are the function **prologue**, which is entry code that exists for every function call. The frame pointer for the calling function (_main) needs saved so it can be restored later, therefore *ebp* is pushed to the stack (pushl %ebp). Then, *ebp* is set to the same value as the current top of the stack (movl %esp, %ebp). In effect, the two lines setup the new stack frame.

In our example, we want to use *ebx*, a callee-saved register, for the calculation in _sum so we save its current value (to be restored later) by pushing *ebx* on the stack.

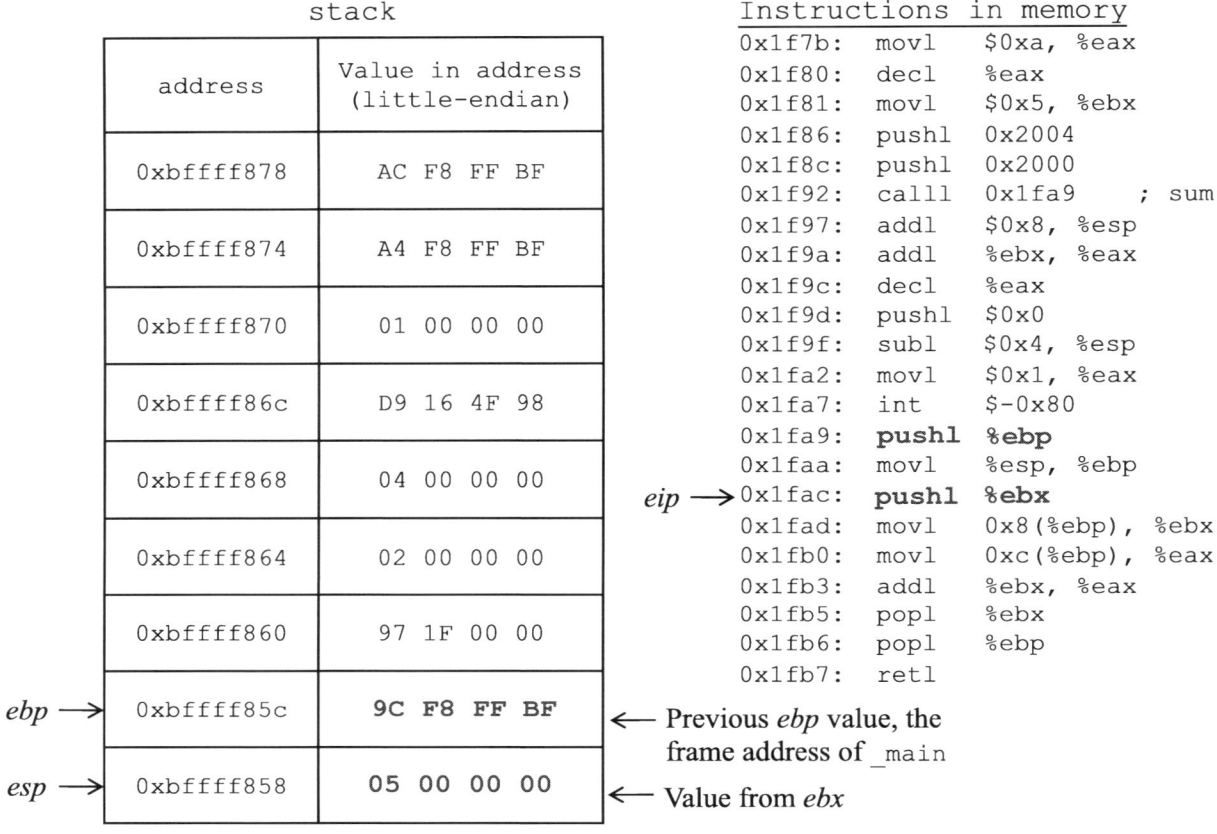

Figure 6.5 After establishing frame and saving *ebx*

Figure 6.5 illustrates the state of the program after setting up the stack frame and saving *ebx*.

```
movl 8(%ebp), %ebx
movl 12(%ebp), %eax
addl %ebx, %eax

; ebx = 2
; eax = 4
; eax = 6
```

Now the calculation can happen, which can be accomplished in many ways. In our example, we copy the two values from their memory locations within the stack frame to registers and then add the registers. Remember, *ebp* is our point of reference for the stack frame. The two parameters were pushed in reverse order prior to the CALL, and the CALL implicitly pushes the next address on the stack. Then, *ebp* was realigned for the stack frame.

Therefore, if we add 4 bytes to *ebp*, we will get the memory address of the instruction after the CALL. The first parameter is 8 bytes back up the stack and the second parameter 12 bytes back. In our case, we save the result in *eax* since it is the return register for integers. Consult **APPENDIX F** and the **WEB RESOURCES** for more complex return types.

```
popl %ebx
popl %ebp
retl
```

Next, we prepare for the return to _main. Having previously saved *ebx* to the stack, we perform a POP to restore 5 to *ebx*. Then comes what is often called the function **epilogue**, which is code always written upon exiting a function. Since we are returning to _main, we must restore the frame pointer for _main to *ebp*. The two POPs, in effect, remove the items off the stack and add a total of 8 bytes (4 bytes each) back to *esp*.

Then we arrive at the RET instruction. RET implicitly pops a value from the top of the stack into *eip*, which should be the address of the instruction that was pushed on the stack by the related CALL instruction. So, retl pops 0x1f97 off the stack and into *eip*, which will be the next instruction executed by the CPU.

Figure 6.6 illustrates the state of the program after the RET instruction. Meanwhile, *eax* = 6, the sum of the two values, and *ebx* = 5, its value prior to the function call.

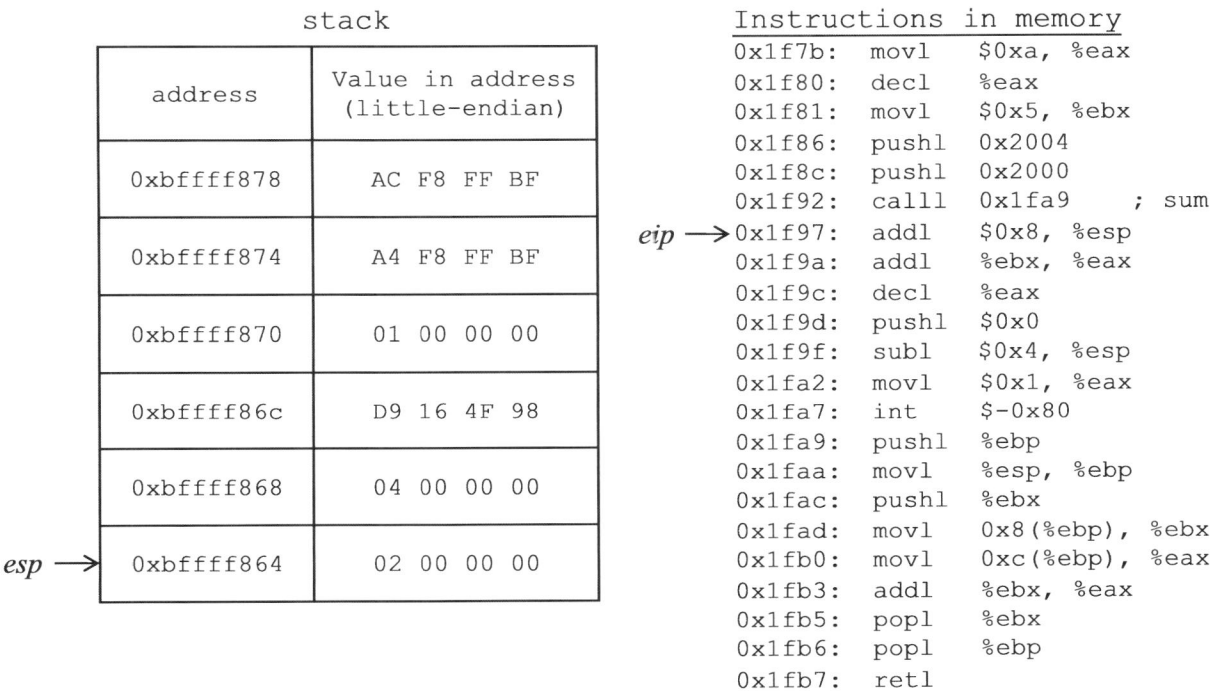

Figure 6.6 After RET instruction

```
addl $8, %esp
```

The cdecl convention requires the calling function (_main) to clean up the stack, which means dereferencing the parameters previously pushed in _main for the _sum procedure. We pushed two 4-byte parameters on the stack, so to clean up we must add 8 bytes to *esp*. Pushing values on the stack moves *esp* in descending memory (like subtracting), so adding to *esp* does the opposite by ascending and effectively removing (dereferencing) values off the stack.

```
addl %ebx, %eax
decl %eax

pushl $0
subl $4, %esp
movl $1, %eax
int $0x80
```

The last few lines continue more instructions in _main. *ebx* is added to *eax* and then *eax* is decremented by 1, for a final value of 10.

We conclude the GAS version of the program by pushing the exit parameter on the stack, padding the stack an extra 4 bytes, placing the exit system code in *eax*, and issuing an interrupt to the kernel. For more information on exit routines see **CHAPTER 10**.

stdcall (32-bit)

Another common calling convention is **stdcall**, which is best known for its use by the Windows API. Generally, stdcall follows the same rules as cdecl, with one difference (the last bullet point).

*   Parameters are passed in reverse order (from right to left) via the stack.
*   *eax, ecx,* and *edx* are caller-saved, while the rest of the general purpose registers are callee-saved.
*   *eax* is used as the return register in most cases. *st(0)* is used for a floating-point return.
*   **The callee is responsible for cleaning up stack.**

The advantage of stdcall is that the called function can perform stack cleanup as part of the return instruction, which means fewer lines of code in calling functions. Cleanup code is written once in the callee instead of every time a particular function is called. Callee cleanup is possible because stdcall does not allow variadic functions, so the callee can know how many parameters it received, and thus can perform the cleanup.

Stdcall uses an alternative form of the RET instruction that includes the number of bytes to be removed from stack. If we were to re-write Program 6.1 in MASM to use stdcall, two changes would be necessary.

1. Remove the line "add esp, 8" in _main
2. Modify the return in _sum to "ret 8"

We discussed function implementation in detail using cdecl because cdecl is the default calling convention for most C/C++ compilers. The advantage of cdecl is the availability of variadic functions. Though stdcall's use beyond the Windows API is uncommon, stdcall can be used on other platforms by defining a function as __stdcall (syntax varies by platform) as illustrated in Example 6.11 later in this chapter.

x86_64 (64-bit)

With the advent of 64-bit architecture, calling conventions have become more standardized, with one convention in two flavors: **Microsoft x64** and **System V AMD64 (AMD64)**. The x86_64 conventions attempt to increase the speed of function execution by passing some parameters in registers instead of on the stack (similar to **fastcall** in 32-bit mode). Table 6.1 shows the characteristics of the two 64-bit calling conventions.

 ATTENTION: Fastcall (see Example 6.11) is another 32-bit calling convention that attempts to pass values in registers if possible, as opposed to using the stack. Further information about fastcall can be found in the **WEB RESOURCES**.

Table 6.1 x86_64 Calling conventions

Convention	Parameter registers	Caller-saved registers	Callee-saved registers	Attributes
Microsoft x64	rcx/zmm0 rdx/zmm1 r8/zmm2 r9/zmm3	rax, rcx, rdx, r8 – r11, st(0) – st(7), k0 – k7, xmm0 – xmm5, All ymm regs, All zmm regs except lower 128 bits (xmm0 – xmm5)	rbx, rsi, rdi, rbp, r12 – r15, xmm6 – xmm15, and only the lower 128 bits of zmm regs	Stack aligned by 16 bytes. 32 bytes of shadow space reserved on the stack following the return address and preceding local variables. 4 parameters can be sent in parameter registers.
System V AMD64 (Linux, BSD, Mac, Gnu)	rdi rsi rdx rcx r8 r9 zmm0-7	rax, rcx, rdx, rsi, rdi, r8 – r11, st(0) – st(7), k0 – k7, xmm0 – xmm15, ymm0 – ymm15, zmm0 – zmm31	rbx, rbp, r12 – r15	Stack aligned by 16 bytes. 128-byte red zone reserved on the stack following the return address. 14 parameters can be sent in parameter registers.

In Windows 64-bit, a maximum of four parameters can be sent via registers in the order indicated in Table 6.1. If a function call has three parameters in the order of (int, float, int), the values will be passed in *rcx, zmm1*, and *r8*. In systems using AMD64, a maximum of 14 parameters can be sent via registers. Note that the order of parameter registers differs between the two conventions.

In both cases, if more parameters exist than parameter registers, the remaining parameters are passed via the stack in right-to-left order. Consider Example 6.3 given the Microsoft x64 convention.

Example 6.3 Parameter passing in Microsoft x64

```
int someFunction(int, int, float, float, char, char);  // prototype
x = someFunction(num1, num2, num3, num4, letter1, letter2);  // call
```

Parameter	Passed via
int num1	rcx
int num2	rdx
float num3	zmm2
float num4	zmm3

Parameter	Passed via
char letter2	stack – pushed first
char letter1	stack – pushed second

Functions in 64-bit mode must be 16-byte aligned. x86_64 supports **Streaming SIMD Extensions (SSE)**, the instructions behind parallel processing. SSE operations are typically 128 bits, which when divided by 8 bytes (the instruction length in x86_64) is 16, meaning use of such operations necessitates 16-byte alignment. To make sure any functions using SSE do not have stack alignment errors, all stack frames should be 16-byte aligned. Also, the CALL instruction pushes an 8-byte address on the stack, so in many cases the stack will need to be realigned by another 8 bytes.

> **!** **ATTENTION:** A good reference for understanding optimization and alignment is the *Intel 64 and IA-32 Architectures Optimization Reference Manual* (http://www.intel.com/content/dam/www/public/us/en/documents/manuals/64-ia-32-architectures-optimization-manual.pdf). Section 4.4.2 covers stack alignment for SIMD operations. We discuss alignment and SSE instructions in more detail in **CHAPTER 8**.

Aligning the stack in code can be achieved a number of ways, each with subtle differences, such as speed. One method is to subtract 8 from *rsp* upon entry into a function, but that also requires adding 8 back to *rsp* upon exiting. Another common method is to perform *rsp* AND -16 (0xF0). Doing so lowers *rsp* to the next multiple of 16 (an address that always ends in 0). For example, if we have the address 0x44 and we perform 0x44 AND 0xF0, the result is 0x40.

Another way to ensure alignment in GCC and Clang/LLVM is to pass the -mstackrealign flag to the compiler, which generates alternate prologue and epilogue code that aligns the stack as necessary.

▼ **Apple LLVM 8.0 - Custom Compiler Flags**

Setting		testing
Other C Flags		**-mstackrealign**
Other C++ Flags		-mstackrealign
Other Warning Flags		

Figure 6.7 mstackrealign flag in Xcode project settings

As we will notice in the **IMPLEMENTATIONS** section of this chapter, functions typically begin at an address ending in 0, indicating 16-byte alignment. Compilers achieve alignment in various ways. In Example 6.4, which is disassembly of the C++ Sum Program on macOS, notice that the compiler (Clang/LLVM) is using the NOP instruction (nopl) to align the stack (line 23), which is yet another option for a programmer. However, we do recommend allowing the compiler to align the stack automatically when possible.

LEARNING: Code the Sum Program in C++ (Example 6.1) using your preferred IDE and compile for 64-bit. Disassemble the object file and determine how your chosen compiler has performed 16-byte alignment. Refer to **APPENDIX C: DISASSEMBLY**.

Example 6.4 Stack alignment using NOP

```
 1  testing.o:
 2  (__TEXT,__text) section
 3  _main:
 4  0000000000000000    55                  pushq   %rbp
 5  0000000000000001    4889e5              movq    %rsp, %rbp
 6  0000000000000004    4883ec20            subq    $0x20, %rsp
 7  0000000000000008    c745fc00000000      movl    $0x0, -0x4(%rbp)
 8  000000000000000f    c745f802000000      movl    $0x2, -0x8(%rbp)
 9  0000000000000016    c745f404000000      movl    $0x4, -0xc(%rbp)
10  000000000000001d    8b7df8              movl    -0x8(%rbp), %edi
11  0000000000000020    8b75f4              movl    -0xc(%rbp), %esi
12  0000000000000023    e800000000          callq   0x28
13  0000000000000028    488b3d00000000      movq    (%rip), %rdi
14  000000000000002f    8945f0              movl    %eax, -0x10(%rbp)
15  0000000000000032    8b75f0              movl    -0x10(%rbp), %esi
16  0000000000000035    e800000000          callq   0x3a
17  000000000000003a    be00000000          movl    $0x0, %esi
18  000000000000003f    488945e8            movq    %rax, -0x18(%rbp)
19  0000000000000043    89f0                movl    %esi, %eax
20  0000000000000045    4883c420            addq    $0x20, %rsp
21  0000000000000049    5d                  popq    %rbp
22  000000000000004a    c3                  retq
23  000000000000004b    0f1f440000          nopl    (%rax,%rax)
24  __Z3sumii:
25  0000000000000050    55                  pushq   %rbp
26  0000000000000051    4889e5              movq    %rsp, %rbp
27  0000000000000054    897dfc              movl    %edi, -0x4(%rbp)
28  0000000000000057    8975f8              movl    %esi, -0x8(%rbp)
29  000000000000005a    8b75fc              movl    -0x4(%rbp), %esi
30  000000000000005d    0375f8              addl    -0x8(%rbp), %esi
31  0000000000000060    89f0                movl    %esi, %eax
32  0000000000000062    5d                  popq    %rbp
33  0000000000000063    c3                  retq
```

PROGRAMMING: The NOP instruction in Example 6.4 is a multi-byte variant. Specifically, 0F1F440000 is the 5 byte NOP sequence (instruction). Note that _main and __Z3sumii begin on addresses ending in zero—0x00 and 0x50, respectively. The _main function ends on 0x4b, and the NOP instruction takes up 5 bytes so that __Z3sumii begins on 0x50 (0x4b + 0x05 = 0x50). The variants of NOP are detailed in Intel's Instruction Set Reference, Volume 2B, Page 4-8, Table 4-9. The variants are also detailed in online sources (http://www.felixcloutier.com/x86/NOP.html).

Another important aspect of x86_64 conventions is extra space that is reserved on the stack. In Microsoft x64, the space is referred to as **shadow (home) space**, is 32 bytes in length, and is used to save parameter register values. You must reserve the space even if no parameters are passed. Shadow space is scratch space to store the values passed in *r8*, *r9*, *rcx*, and *rdx* if the registers are needed for subsequent function calls within a called function, though the space could be used for other purposes.

Example 6.5 provides an abstract description of stack contents in Microsoft x64 regarding shadow space.

Example 6.5 Microsoft x64 shadow space

Stack Contents	Description	
FunctionA parameters	size varies	Descending addresses with stack alignment as necessary
Shadow space (32 bytes)	allocated by FunctionA prologue for any subsequent function calls within FunctionA	
Return address (8 bytes)	pushed by CALL instruction in FunctionA	
Previous *rbp* value (8 bytes)	pushed in FunctionB prologue	
FunctionB parameters	size varies	
Shadow space (32 bytes)	allocated by FunctionB prologue for any subsequent function calls within FunctionB	

Example 6.6 shows the MASM prologue and epilogue disassembly for the x64 Sum Program's `main()` function when written in C++ in Visual Studio.

Example 6.6 x86_64 Sum program disassembly in MASM

Disassembly		Comments
		; main() prologue
push	rbp	; saving frame pointer
push	rdi	; callee saved register
sub	rsp,148h	; allocating enough stack space for main's local parameters + parameter space for any called function (largest is used) + shadow space + alignment
lea	rbp,[rsp+20h]	; sets frame pointer to *rsp* + 32 bytes meaning the frame boundary for main is followed by 32 bytes of shadow space that can be used to save parameter registers if any function calls exist in main
.		
.		
.		
.		; main() epilogue
lea	rsp,[rbp+128h]	; dereferencing main's reserved stack space, notice that *rsp* is set to main's frame pointer + 128h, which effectively dereferences all reserved memory as *rsp* was pointing to 32 bytes (20h) beyond *rbp*
pop	rdi	; restore callee saved register
pop	rbp	; restore previous frame pointer
ret		; exit function and pop return address into *rip*

As for AMD64, 32 bytes of shadow space does not exist, but rather 128 bytes beyond the return address (where *rsp* is pointing) is called the **red-zone**. The red-zone is temporary storage for function use and will not be tampered with by the system. If no PUSH, POP, or CALL instructions are used in the red-zone, and *rsp* is not modified, then *rsp* can be used to reference local variables and identifiers (for jumps and loops). The reason for the red-zone is to potentially optimize execution due to less adjustments of *rsp* for local variables, which saves clock cycles. Another use is the implementation of **leaf functions**, functions that make no calls, whose caller can use the red-zone to perform whatever computations are needed instead of actually issuing a call and dealing with the overhead.

Unlike Microsoft x64 shadow space, the AMD64 red-zone is not reserved by the programmer or compiler. The red-zone is simply a guarantee that system signals or interrupt handlers will not touch 128 bytes past *rsp*. However, function calls do clobber (destroy) the red-zone of a calling function. Thus, red-zone use is mainly limited to scratch space for leaf functions.

Some Useful Details

- If the Floating-Point Unit (FPU) stack is used, it must be clear upon entry into a function and upon exit, except for *st(0)*, which may be holding the return value. The FPU is discussed in **Chapter 8**.
- In 32-bit, addresses for pass-by-reference are passed on the stack. Registers serve as an intermediary to obtain the parameter address at run-time using the LEA instruction, which is then moved or pushed to the stack.

```
lea -0x8(%ebp), %eax  # a parameter address is loaded into eax
mov %eax, (%esp)         # address copied to where esp is pointing
```

In 64-bit, the address can be moved directly to a register for pass-by-reference.

```
lea -0x8(%rbp), %rdi  # a parameter address is loaded into rdi
```

- In 64-bit, if using varargs functions such as `printf()`, the *al* register, which is the low 8 bits of *rax*, is used to store the number of SSE registers used.
- Refer to the **Web Resources** for further detail on calling conventions. In particular, the reference by Agner Fog (http://www.agner.org/optimize/calling_conventions.pdf) and the **application binary interface (ABI)** documents such as http://refspecs.linuxfoundation.org/elf/x86-64-abi-0.99.pdf are the most useful in terms of comparing calling conventions and providing detailed overviews.

> **(!)** ATTENTION: An application binary interface (ABI) document is a formal document that defines low-level interfacing requirements for software. ABIs are published by companies and manufacturers such as Intel, AMD, and Microsoft.

Implementations

Throughout this chapter we have discussed the Sum Program (Example 6.1) and shown implementations of the program in different assemblers (Program 6.1). Examining and comparing the disassembly of C++ implementations in 32-bit versus 64-bit is also helpful. In this section, we compare cdecl, stdcall, and fastcall conventions in 32-bit. All code examples in this section were written in C++ using Xcode.

Program 6.2 *Sum program in C++*

```cpp
int sum(int, int);

int main() {
    int value1 = 2, value2 = 4, answer;
    answer = sum(value1, value2);
    return 0;
}

int sum(int value1, int value2){
    return value1 + value2;
}
```

> PROGRAMMING: If you are developing platform-specific code in Assembly or inline Assembly, you have the flexibility to implement functions in a way that is optimal, given your scenario. You may be able to write a sequence of instructions that is more efficient than what a high-level compiler can produce. For example, you can use registers to pass function parameters in 32-bit programs. You can minimize the instructions used to move values between memory locations and perform arithmetic. Depending on the data being passed, you can use one register to pass two values. The key is that you are in control.

Example 6.7 Sum Program `main()` Disassembly

32-bit (cdecl)			
1	chapter6`main:		
2	0x1f50 <+0>:	pushl	%ebp
3	0x1f51 <+1>:	movl	%esp, %ebp
4	0x1f53 <+3>:	subl	$0x18, %esp
5	0x1f56 <+6>:	movl	$0x0, -0x4(%ebp)
6	0x1f5d <+13>:	movl	$0x2, -0x8(%ebp)
7	0x1f64 <+20>:	movl	$0x4, -0xc(%ebp)
8	0x1f6b <+27>:	movl	-0x8(%ebp), %eax
9	0x1f6e <+30>:	movl	-0xc(%ebp), %ecx
10	0x1f71 <+33>:	movl	%eax, (%esp)
11	0x1f74 <+36>:	movl	%ecx, 0x4(%esp)
12	0x1f78 <+40>:	calll	0x1f90 ; sum
13	0x1f7d <+45>:	xorl	%ecx, %ecx
14	0x1f7f <+47>:	movl	%eax, -0x10(%ebp)
15	0x1f82 <+50>:	movl	%ecx, %eax
16	0x1f84 <+52>:	addl	$0x18, %esp
17	0x1f87 <+55>:	popl	%ebp
18	0x1f88 <+56>:	retl	

64-bit (AMD64)			
1	chapter6`main:		
2	0x100000f60 <+0>:	pushq	%rbp
3	0x100000f61 <+1>:	movq	%rsp, %rbp
4	0x100000f64 <+4>:	subq	$0x10, %rsp
5	0x100000f68 <+8>:	movl	$0x0, -0x4(%rbp)
6	0x100000f6f <+15>:	movl	$0x2, -0x8(%rbp)
7	0x100000f76 <+22>:	movl	$0x4, -0xc(%rbp)
8	0x100000f7d <+29>:	movl	-0x8(%rbp), %edi
9	0x100000f80 <+32>:	movl	-0xc(%rbp), %esi
10	0x100000f83 <+35>:	callq	0x100000fa0 ; sum
11	0x100000f88 <+40>:	xorl	%esi, %esi
12	0x100000f8a <+42>:	movl	%eax, -0x10(%rbp)
13	0x100000f8d <+45>:	movl	%esi, %eax
14	0x100000f8f <+47>:	addq	$0x10, %rsp
15	0x100000f93 <+51>:	popq	%rbp
16	0x100000f94 <+52>:	retq	

Different compilers will produce different low-level code to accomplish high-level statements, but notice that the 32-bit and 64-bit code in Example 6.7 is quite comparable. The 64-bit code is slightly more efficient, and both examples follow the calling conventions. Also, notice that the main() functions are 16-byte aligned, beginning on 0x1f50 and 0x100000f60, respectively (line 2).

In both scenarios, upon entry into main(), space is reserved for the three local parameters with SUB (line 4). Then the values are assigned with MOVs (lines 5–7) as shown in Example 6.8.

Example 6.8 Sum program `main()` disassembly, lines 4–7

32-bit			
4	0x1f53	subl	$0x18, %esp
5	0x1f56	movl	$0x0, -0x4(%ebp)
6	0x1f5d	movl	$0x2, -0x8(%ebp)
7	0x1f64	movl	$0x4, -0xc(%ebp)

64-bit			
4	0x100000f64	subq	$0x10, %rsp
5	0x100000f68	movl	$0x0, -0x4(%rbp)
6	0x100000f6f	movl	$0x2, -0x8(%rbp)
7	0x100000f76	movl	$0x4, -0xc(%rbp)

Leading up to the CALL is the first difference, as shown in Example 6.9. In 32-bit (lines 8–11), value1 and value2 are copied into registers (*eax, ecx*) and then copied from the registers to stack. The double move is required because MOV cannot transfer data from memory to memory. However, using PUSH could simplify the process. Comparatively, the 64-bit version (lines 8–9) simply moves the values to registers according to the AMD64 convention by using the first two parameter registers *edi* and *esi*. Since the values were declared as integers, which are 4 bytes in C++, *edi* and *esi* are used instead of *rdi* and *rsi*.

Example 6.9 Sum program `main()` disassembly, passing parameters

32-bit			
8	0x1f6b	movl	-0x8(%ebp), %eax
9	0x1f6e	movl	-0xc(%ebp), %ecx
10	0x1f71	movl	%eax, (%esp)
11	0x1f74	movl	%ecx, 0x4(%esp)

64-bit			
8	0x100000f7d	movl	-0x8(%rbp), %edi
9	0x100000f80	movl	-0xc(%rbp), %esi

Next are the implementations of the sum() function.

Example 6.10 Sum program `sum()` disassembly

32-bit (cdecl)	64-bit (AMD64)
1 chapter6`sum:`	1 chapter6`sum:`
2 0x1f90 <+0>: pushl %ebp	2 0x100000fa0 <+0>: pushq %rbp
3 0x1f91 <+1>: movl %esp, %ebp	3 0x100000fa1 <+1>: movq %rsp, %rbp
4 0x1f93 <+3>: subl $0x8, %esp	4 0x100000fa4 <+4>: movl %edi, -0x4(%rbp)
5 0x1f96 <+6>: movl 0xc(%ebp), %eax	5 0x100000fa7 <+7>: movl %esi, -0x8(%rbp)
6 0x1f99 <+9>: movl 0x8(%ebp), %ecx	6 0x100000faa <+10>: movl -0x4(%rbp), %esi
7 0x1f9c <+12>: movl %ecx, -0x4(%ebp)	7 0x100000fad <+13>: addl -0x8(%rbp), %esi
8 0x1f9f <+15>: movl %eax, -0x8(%ebp)	8 0x100000fb0 <+16>: movl %esi, %eax
9 0x1fa2 <+18>: movl -0x4(%ebp), %eax	9 0x100000fb2 <+18>: popq %rbp
10 0x1fa5 <+21>: addl -0x8(%ebp), %eax	10 0x100000fb3 <+19>: retq
11 0x1fa8 <+24>: addl $0x8, %esp	
12 0x1fab <+27>: popl %ebp	
13 0x1fac <+28>: retl	

First, notice that in both cases shown in Example 6.10 the `sum()` functions are 16-byte aligned, beginning on `0x1f90` and `0x100000fa0`, respectively (line 2). Then, take note of the customary prologue and epilogue code for the `sum()` stack frames (lines 2–3). Next, in both examples the values are copied to stack again within the `sum()` stack frame because the parameters are pass-by-value.

32-bit (lines 4–8)

- Space is reserved for local copies of the parameters (line 4).
- The values passed in `main()` via the stack are copied to registers (lines 5–6).
- The values are copied to the reserved space in `sum()`'s stack frame (lines 7–8).

64-bit (lines 4–5)

- The values are copied from parameter registers to stack within the red-zone.

Again, the 32-bit code has some inefficiencies/redundancies, which are partially due to the parameters being pass-by-value. One big difference between the two implementations is that in the 64-bit version of `sum()`, *rsp* is not adjusted with a SUB instruction. The red-zone has plenty of space for the computation and also no subsequent calls are made.

The values are then added and placed in the return register *eax* (lines 9–10 in 32-bit and lines 6–8 in 64-bit). Lastly, the local copies of the parameters are cleaned up in 32-bit by ADDing 8 bytes back to *esp* (line 11), followed by the POP of *ebp/rbp* and the RET instruction (lines 12–13 and lines 9–10, respectively).

Example 6.11 presents Program 6.2 when implemented using 32-bit stdcall and fastcall calling conventions. The implementations can be compared with the 32-bit (cdecl) and 64-bit (AMD64) conventions.

In stdcall, notice the `retl $0x8` instruction (line 14) in `sum()`. However, if you look closely at how Xcode chooses to handle the stdcall implementation (i.e., how values are pushed, *esp* adjustments) you may also notice that collectively the code negates the intended behavior of stdcall. Fastcall is essentially identical to the x86_64 example, with registers being used to pass the parameters (*ecx* and *edx*).

Example 6.11 Sum program `stdcall` versus `fastcall`

stdcall (32-bit)	fastcall (32-bit)
int __stdcall sum(int, int);	int __fastcall sum(int, int);

```
1   chapter6`main:
2   0x1f50 <+0>:   pushl   %ebp
3   0x1f51 <+1>:   movl    %esp, %ebp
4   0x1f53 <+3>:   subl    $0x18, %esp
5   0x1f56 <+6>:   movl    $0x0, -0x4(%ebp)
6   0x1f5d <+13>:  movl    $0x2, -0x8(%ebp)
7   0x1f64 <+20>:  movl    $0x4, -0xc(%ebp)
8   0x1f6b <+27>:  movl    -0x8(%ebp), %eax
9   0x1f6e <+30>:  movl    -0xc(%ebp), %ecx
10  0x1f71 <+33>:  movl    %esp, %edx
11  0x1f73 <+35>:  movl    %ecx, 0x4(%edx)
12  0x1f76 <+38>:  movl    %eax, (%edx)
13  0x1f78 <+40>:  calll   0x1f90          ; sum
14  0x1f7d <+45>:  subl    $0x8, %esp
15  0x1f80 <+48>:  xorl    %ecx, %ecx
16  0x1f82 <+50>:  movl    %eax, -0x10(%ebp)
17  0x1f85 <+53>:  movl    %ecx, %eax
18  0x1f87 <+55>:  addl    $0x18, %esp
19  0x1f8a <+58>:  popl    %ebp
20  0x1f8b <+59>:  retl
```

```
1   chapter6`main:
2   0x1f50 <+0>:   pushl   %ebp
3   0x1f51 <+1>:   movl    %esp, %ebp
4   0x1f53 <+3>:   subl    $0x18, %esp
5   0x1f56 <+6>:   movl    $0x0, -0x4(%ebp)
6   0x1f5d <+13>:  movl    $0x2, -0x8(%ebp)
7   0x1f64 <+20>:  movl    $0x4, -0xc(%ebp)
8   0x1f6b <+27>:  movl    -0x8(%ebp), %ecx
9   0x1f6e <+30>:  movl    -0xc(%ebp), %edx
10  0x1f71 <+33>:  calll   0x1f90          ; sum
11  0x1f76 <+38>:  xorl    %ecx, %ecx
12  0x1f78 <+40>:  movl    %eax, -0x10(%ebp)
13  0x1f7b <+43>:  movl    %ecx, %eax
14  0x1f7d <+45>:  addl    $0x18, %esp
15  0x1f80 <+48>:  popl    %ebp
16  0x1f81 <+49>:  retl
```

```
1   chapter6`sum:
2   0x1f90 <+0>:   pushl   %ebp
3   0x1f91 <+1>:   movl    %esp, %ebp
4   0x1f93 <+3>:   subl    $0x8, %esp
5   0x1f96 <+6>:   movl    0xc(%ebp), %eax
6   0x1f99 <+9>:   movl    0x8(%ebp), %ecx
7   0x1f9c <+12>:  movl    %ecx, -0x4(%ebp)
8   0x1f9f <+15>:  movl    %eax, -0x8(%ebp)
9   0x1fa2 <+18>:  movl    -0x4(%ebp), %ecx
10  0x1fa5 <+21>:  addl    %eax, %ecx
11  0x1fa7 <+23>:  movl    %ecx, %eax
12  0x1fa9 <+25>:  addl    $0x8, %esp
13  0x1fac <+28>:  popl    %ebp
14  0x1fad <+29>:  retl    $0x8
```

```
1   chapter6`sum:
2   0x1f90 <+0>:   pushl   %ebp
3   0x1f91 <+1>:   movl    %esp, %ebp
4   0x1f93 <+3>:   subl    $0x8, %esp
5   0x1f96 <+6>:   movl    %ecx, -0x4(%ebp)
6   0x1f99 <+9>:   movl    %edx, -0x8(%ebp)
7   0x1f9c <+12>:  movl    -0x4(%ebp), %ecx
8   0x1f9f <+15>:  addl    -0x8(%ebp), %ecx
9   0x1fa2 <+18>:  movl    %ecx, %eax
10  0x1fa4 <+20>:  addl    $0x8, %esp
11  0x1fa7 <+23>:  popl    %ebp
12  0x1fa8 <+24>:  retl
```

Summary

You should now have a better understanding of how functions are implemented at a low level. Calling conventions help standardize the use of registers and stack memory related to functions. We presented the most common calling conventions on x86 and x86_64; however, the insight you have gained into function implementation is transferable to other platforms. Understanding low-level details of functions will help you to optimize high-level code, adapt code based on resources available on a given system, and write efficient function calls.

Key Terms

application binary interface (ABI)
callee
caller
calling conventions
cdecl
epilogue
fastcall
functions
leaf functions
Little-Endian

Microsoft x64
procedures
prologue
red-zone
shadow (home) space
stack frame
stack memory
stdcall
Streaming SIMD Extensions (SSE)
System V AMD64 (AMD64)

Key Registers (32-bit, 64-bit)

ebp/rbp	base frame pointer: points to beginning of currently executing stack frame
esp/rsp	stack pointer: should always point to top of stack (most recently pushed value)
eax/rax	accumulator: used for function return value in most cases (not all cases; float return is one exception)
eip/rip	instruction pointer: points to next instruction to be executed

Code Review

PUSH	copies a value (memory or register) into the memory location pointed to by *esp/rsp* and decrements *esp* by 4 or *rsp* by 8
POP	copies the value pointed to by *esp/rsp* into a given destination (memory or register) and increments *esp* by 4 or *rsp* by 8
Push/Pop the *flags* register on/off the stack	PUSHF/POPF is for the 16-bit *flags* register; PUSHFD/POPFD (Intel) and PUSHFL/POPFL (AT&T) is for the 32-bit *eflags* register; and PUSHFQ/POPFQ is for the 64-bit *rflags* register
Push/Pop all general purpose registers on/off the stack	PUSHA/POPA is 16-bit; PUSHAD/POPAD (Intel) and PUSHAL/POPAL (AT&T) are 32-bit ordered *eax, ecx, edx, ebx, esp* (prior to push), *ebp, esi, edi*; no equivalent instruction exists for 64-bit so push/pop registers individually
CALL	pushes the address of the instruction directly following the CALL on the stack and transfers control to the called destination (usually indicated by a label)
LEA	Load Effective Address; calculates and loads the address (offset) of a memory operand at run-time
NOP	No Operation; takes up space in memory and uses clock cycles; has single-byte and multi-byte variants
RET	pops value from top of stack into *eip/rip*, which should be the location (address) of the instruction that was pushed on the stack by the related CALL instruction. Has two forms in 32-bit based on the calling convention used (1. cdecl, 2. stdcall): 1. RET 2. RET count Count is the number of bytes added to *esp* after completion of the return.

Platform Specific Notes

- Windows programmers make use of the PROC and ENDP directives to indicate the beginning and end of a procedure.
- In MASM on Windows, the calling convention (C, STDCALL) can be set via the .MODEL directive for the entire program or for individual PROC declarations for more granular control.

Program-wide	Procedure-specific
`.MODEL FLAT, STDCALL`	`sum PROC C`
	`    code`
`.MODEL FLAT, C`	`sum ENDP`

- In MASM on Windows, the USES directive is available in both 32-bit and 64-bit modes, which tells the assembler to generate PUSH and POP instructions for registers stated with the USES directive. The automatically generated instructions become part of the prologue and epilogue code on procedure entry and exit.

```
sum PROC STDCALL USES esi edi
    code
sum ENDP
```

- In macOS, function calls are 16-byte aligned in 32-bit and 64-bit.

Questions

Short Answer

1. A _____ is where a function's local variables are stored.
2. _____ define the process of low-level procedure implementation.
3. Using _____, the caller is responsible for cleaning up stack memory.
4. _____ registers are considered to be volatile because they will likely be used and overwritten in a function.
5. The _____ instruction implicitly pushes the subsequent instruction on the stack.
6. The _____ register points to the most recent item pushed on the stack.
7. _____ and _____ code are common lines of code upon entry to and exit from a function.
8. _____ and _____ instructions implicitly add and subtract from the stack pointer register as values are moved on and off the stack.
9. In 32-bit stdcall, the number of bytes to remove from the stack are stated with the _____ instruction.
10. The _____ register is typically used as the return register.
11. _____ is a 32-bit calling convention that uses registers to pass values if possible.
12. The x86_64 calling convention(s) attempt to pass some or all parameters via _____ instead of the stack.
13. Microsoft x64 reserves _____ bytes of shadow space, while AMD64 preserves _____ bytes of red-zone space.
14. _____ functions are functions that make no calls.
15. An _____ defines low-level (i.e., machine level) interfacing requirements for software.

True/False

1. Stack memory is allocated in increasing address space. (T/F)
2. In cdecl and stdcall, parameters are passed in right-to-left order. (T/F)
3. All procedure calls in 64-bit must be 16-byte aligned. (T/F)
4. The FPU stack must be clear upon function entry and exit. (T/F)
5. All x86_64 operations are 64-bits. (T/F)

Assignments

Use APPENDIX E: LINKING ASSEMBLY AND C++ to complete Assignments 6.1 and 6.2.

 LEARNING: Learning how to integrate Assembly with C++ will reinforce Chapter 6 concepts, while also helping you develop a useful programming skill. The assignments can be completed using your preferred calling convention.

In Assignments 6.1 and 6.2, the flow of the program should be driven by the _main function in the Assembly code. For example, in Assignment 6.1 you should call C++ functions *from* the Assembly code to get integer input and print integer output. Values entered on the C++ side are returned to the Assembly side, the calculation takes place, and then the sum is sent to a C++ function for output.

6.1 Sum (or any chosen arithmetic operation or set of operations)

Write a program that prompts the user for two integers, adds the integers, and displays the sum. Use C++ functions only to prompt for input and display output. Assembly code should control program flow, function calls, and arithmetic. Use appropriate accompanying text for the prompt and output statements.

6.2 Arithmetic and flags

Write a program that performs a series of three simple calculations (e.g., addition, subtraction, incrementing) using programmer-defined data. After each calculation, output the contents of the *eflags* register in hexadecimal (or binary) notation. Use a C++ function for the output and use Assembly for everything else. Use appropriate accompanying text for the output statements. To extend this assignment, interpret the *eflags* bits for relevant computation results (CF, OF, SF, ZF).

6.3 Sorting function in x86_64 (Challenge Assignment)

Write an x86_64 Assembly program that sorts a programmer-defined array. The size of the array and address of the array should be passed to the called sort function via registers. You can choose the sorting algorithm to be implemented. A simple example would be Bubble Sort. Test using 5 or 10 elements.

Program 6.3 x86_64 Implementation

The following implementations are examples of x86_64 Assembly for the Sum Program. The examples illustrate a few of the many possibilities in terms of implementation details. For example, the implementations are pass-by-reference. Also, in 64-bit GAS and NASM, we are taking advantage of **RIP-Relative Addressing**. In MASM, we also reserve 32 bytes of home space per the Microsoft x64 convention.

Program 6.3 *Sum program x86_64 implementations*

GAS	MASM	NASM
| ```
.data
num1: .quad 2
num2: .quad 4

.text
.globl _main, _sum
_main:

movq $10, %rax
decq %rax
movq $5, %rbx

leaq num1(%rip), %rdi
leaq num2(%rip), %rsi
callq _sum

addq %rbx, %rax
decq %rax

movq $0x2000001, %rax
movq $0, %rdi
syscall

_sum:
pushq %rbp
movq %rsp, %rbp
pushq %rbx
movq (%rdi), %rax
addq (%rsi), %rax
popq %rbx
popq %rbp
retq

.end
``` | ```
extrn ExitProcess : proc


.data
num1 QWORD 2
num2 QWORD 4

.code
_main PROC
mov rax, 10
dec rax
mov rbx, 5

lea rcx, num1
lea rdx, num2
call _sum

add rax, rbx
dec rax
mov rcx, 0
call ExitProcess
_main ENDP

_sum PROC
push rbp
push rbx
sub rsp, 20h
lea rbp, [rsp + 20h]
mov rax, [rcx]
add rax, [rdx]
lea rsp, [rbp]
pop rbx
pop rbp
ret
_sum ENDP
END
``` | ```
section .data
num1: dq 2
num2: dq 4

section .text
global _main, _sum
_main:

mov rax, 10
dec rax
mov rbx, 5

lea rdi, [rel num1]
lea rsi, [rel num2]
call _sum

add rax, rbx
dec rax


mov rax, 60
xor rdi, rdi
syscall

_sum:
push rbp
mov rbp, rsp
push rbx
mov rax, [rdi]
add rax, [rsi]
pop rbx
pop rbp
ret
``` |
```

String Instructions and Structures

Objectives

- Demonstrate string manipulation using string primitive instructions
- Apply repetition constructs to string primitive instructions
- Create composite datatypes using structures

Outline

Web Resources

- http://www.intel.com/content/www/us/en/processors/architectures-software-developer-manuals.html (Volume 1, Chapter 5 Instruction Set Summary, Section 5.1)
- http://www.nasm.us/doc/nasmdoc4.html#section-4.11.10 (NASM struct)
- https://msdn.microsoft.com/en-us/library/tydf8khh.aspx (MASM struct)
- https://sourceware.org/binutils/docs/as/Struct.html#Struct (GAS struct)

Introduction

The focus of Chapter 7 is strings and structures. We cover accessory instructions to string operations and five string primitive instructions that process string data, which exists in memory as byte arrays. Although you can complete most of the tasks using material presented in earlier chapters, the instructions presented here will allow you to accomplish the tasks with greater efficiency and less code. We also describe the composition and use of structures in Assembly.

Accessory Instructions

Before discussing string instructions, we must introduce two categories of instructions that you can use alongside the string instructions: direction and repetition instructions. Without an understanding of direction and repetition instructions, use of the string instructions may seem confusing and may even produce incorrect results.

The direction instructions, shown in Table 7.1, are for clearing and setting the **direction flag**. As mentioned in **CHAPTER 2**, the direction flag controls the left-to-right or right-to-left processing of strings when using string instructions, due to the automatic incrementing or decrementing of memory addresses.

Table 7.1 Direction flag instructions

Instruction	Description	Effect
CLD	Clears the direction flag	When repeating string operations, read characters in a left-to-right fashion (i.e., low-to-high memory addressing).
STD	Sets the direction flag	When repeating string operations, read characters in a right-to-left fashion (i.e., high-to-low memory addressing).

The CLD and STD instructions are most useful when used as control instructions to prepare for repetition. Repetition with string instructions works similarly to the JCXZ/JECXZ/JRCXZ instructions mentioned in **Chapter 5**. The **REP (repeat)** instruction has three forms, shown in Table 7.2, each using the *C* register as a counter.

Table 7.2 Repetition instructions

Instruction	Description	Effect
REP	Repeat while *cx/ecx/rcx* ≠ 0	A simple counter-based repetition that repeats while the C register is not zero.
REPE/REPZ	Repeat while *cx/ecx/rcx* ≠ 0 and ZF = 1	A counter-based repetition, but also requires ZF to be set for each repetition. The repetition stops when ZF is clear or the C register reaches zero.
REPNE/REPNZ	Repeat while *cx/ecx/rcx* ≠ 0 and ZF = 0	A counter-based repetition, but also requires ZF to be clear for each repetition. The repetition stops when ZF is set or the C register reaches zero.

The combination of a direction flag instruction and a repeat instruction sets up the process of automated data processing without the need for manually writing a loop. In order to better understand how repeat instructions work, the following list details the steps that occur automatically when REP or a variant is executed along with a string instruction.

1. The repeat instruction checks if the *C* register value is greater than zero. If the value is zero, the repeat process ends. If the value is greater than zero, the repeat process continues.
2. The string instruction executes, sets related flags depending on the result, and increments or decrements *si/esi/rsi* and *di/edi/rdi*, depending on the instruction and the direction flag.
3. In the case of REPE/REPNE and REPZ/REPNZ, the repeat instruction checks the flags to determine if a repeat should occur. If the flags indicate a repeat should not occur, the process ends.
4. If steps 2 and 3 (if applicable) were successful, the *C* register is decremented and return to step 1.

Before exploring the specific string instructions, consider the following scenario. Assume we have some data stored temporarily in memory and we wish to move (copy) the data to another location for further processing. Knowing that the data is 10 characters long, we can load the counter register, source memory address, and destination memory address accordingly. Then we can set the direction to process our text and finally execute the move. We cover the specifics in greater detail in the next section.

Example 7.1 Repetition in NASM

```
mov ecx, 10          ; set the counter for 10 characters
xor esi, esi         ; start address of source string (0h)
mov edi, 10000h      ; start address of destination
cld                  ; left-to-right string order
rep movsb            ; repeat BYTE MOVS until ECX=0
```

A more visual way of understanding the action of REP in Example 7.1 is shown in Example 7.2. We use the MOVS instruction due to its use of both *esi* and *edi*. As the REP instruction iterates through 10 characters, specified by the initial value in *ecx*, MOVSB increments *esi* and *edi* (because DF is clear) by 1 byte each iteration (the "b" suffix on MOVS is for BYTE). Once *ecx* becomes zero, the REP ends.

Example 7.2 Iterations of REP

Instruction	ECX	ESI	EDI
rep movsb	10	0x00000000	0x00010000
	9	0x00000001	0x00010001
	8	0x00000002	0x00010002
	7	0x00000003	0x00010003
	6	0x00000004	0x00010004
	5	0x00000005	0x00010005
	4	0x00000006	0x00010006
	3	0x00000007	0x00010007
	2	0x00000008	0x00010008
	1	0x00000009	0x00010009

String Primitive Instructions

Now that we have covered the basics of repetition, we examine five instructions for processing string data. **String primitive instructions** are similar to instructions discussed in earlier chapters (e.g., MOV, CMP), but string instructions are designed to deal with character arrays. Table 7.3 details each of the instructions.

Table 7.3 String primitive instructions

Instruction	Description
MOVS	MOVS is similar to the MOV instruction but is specifically for copying characters from one location to another. MOVS implicitly copies data starting at the memory location referenced by *si/esi/rsi* to the memory location referenced by *di/edi/rdi*.
CMPS	CMPS is similar to the CMP instruction but is specifically for comparing strings referenced by *si/esi/rsi* and *di/edi/rdi*. CMPS is best used with REPE/REPZ so that the comparison fails when a character in the source is not equal to the corresponding character in the destination.
SCAS	SCAS scans a string referenced by *di/edi/rdi* searching for the character stored in *al/ax/eax/rax*, depending on the instruction size suffix. SCAS is best used with REPNE/REPNZ so that the scan stops when the character is found.
STOS	STOS stores a value from *al/ax/eax/rax* into the location referenced by *di/edi/rdi*. STOS is best used to initialize arrays (of any kind) with default values by using REP.
LODS	LODS loads a value from the location referenced by *esi* into *al/ax/eax/rax*. LODS should not be used with a repeat instruction due to the repetitive overwriting of the accumulator register.

> **PROGRAMMING:** Each of the string instructions use the direction flag (DF) to either increment or decrement memory addresses in *(r/e)si* and *(r/e)di* by the specified number of bytes, so that the string instruction progresses through the array in the desired direction. An increment or decrement occurs even when REP does not accompany a string instruction.

MOVS

The **MOVS (move string)** instruction is similar to MOV with two differences: MOVS source and destination operands are assumed (e.g., *esi* and *edi*) and MOVS is suffixed with a size identifier no matter the Assembler. The registers *(r/e)si* and *(r/e)di* should contain memory addresses pointing to the data to be copied and the copy destination, respectively. In order for multiple characters to be copied in succession, MOVS increments or decrements (depending on DF) the memory addresses by the number of bytes indicated by the size suffix so that REP can continue to the next character.

Because string instructions can operate on data from 1 to 16 bytes in size, string instructions need to know how many bytes to read each repetition in order to address each character properly. So string instructions are accompanied by a size suffix in all Assemblers. Programmers using GAS are used to appending size suffixes to most instructions. Recall from **CHAPTER 3** the instruction suffix letters that signify operand size, shown again in Table 7.4.

Table 7.4 String instruction suffixes

Size	Suffix letter
byte (8 bits)	B
word (16 bits)	W
dword (32 bits)	D
qword (64 bits)	Q
octa (128 bits)	O

The basic invocation of MOVS is `MOVSS` (e.g., `MOVSQ`). But as previously described, MOVS is most useful when repeated. The REP MOVS combination is shown in Example 7.3 with the necessary accessory instructions.

Example 7.3 MOVS

GAS	MASM	NASM

`leal src, %esi`
`leal dst, %edi`
`movl $10, %ecx`
`cld`
`rep movsd`
	`lea esi, src`
	`lea edi, dst`
	`mov ecx, 10`
	`cld`
	`rep movsd`
		`lea esi, [src]`
		`lea edi, [dst]`
		`mov ecx, 10`
		`cld`
		`rep movsd`

The code in Example 7.3 assumes the existence of the `src` and `dst` variables, which are to be used for the data transfer. The first two instructions load the memory addresses of the variables into *esi* and *edi*, respectively. Next, the counter is set by storing 10 in *ecx*, signifying 10 repetitions/characters to be copied. Then, DF is cleared, signaling left-to-right data movement. Finally, MOVSD is executed accompanied by the REP instruction, which will execute MOVSD until *ecx* is zero. Remember, REP decrements *ecx* each iteration.

Figure 7.1 illustrates the steps taken by `rep movsd` in the code from Example 7.3.

CMPS

The **CMPS (compare string)** instruction is similar to the CMP instruction. Like MOVS, CMPS does not take operands but implicitly uses *(r/e)si* and *(r/e)di* for the memory addresses of the data to compare. Similarly, the CMPS instruction is most valuable when used in conjunction with REP. Executing CMPS without REP only compares a single character, not an entire string.

While MOVS uses REP in order to repeat sequential moves, CMPS acts like a sequential access algorithm you might implement with a high-level language in a programming class. CMPS needs to be repeated to move character by character through strings, but CMPS also must perform a check each iteration to determine whether or not the characters in the strings are equal. The REP instruction does not assist in any such comparisons, it simply repeats. To perform comparative checks, we must use one of the repeat variants (REPE/REPZ or REPNE/REPNZ).

For example, REPE/REPZ will only continue repeating if the characters are equal (i.e., ZF is set by the CMPS instruction). CMPS compares each corresponding character by performing an implicit subtraction of the character referenced by *(r/e)di* from the character referenced by *(r/e)si*, which modifies the processor flags, specifically ZF.

Figure 7.2 illustrates `repe cmps` comparing the strings, `"Johanna"` and `"Johnnie"`.

 PROGRAMMING: REPE and REPZ are synonymous instructions as they perform the same check. The same is true for REPNE and REPNZ.

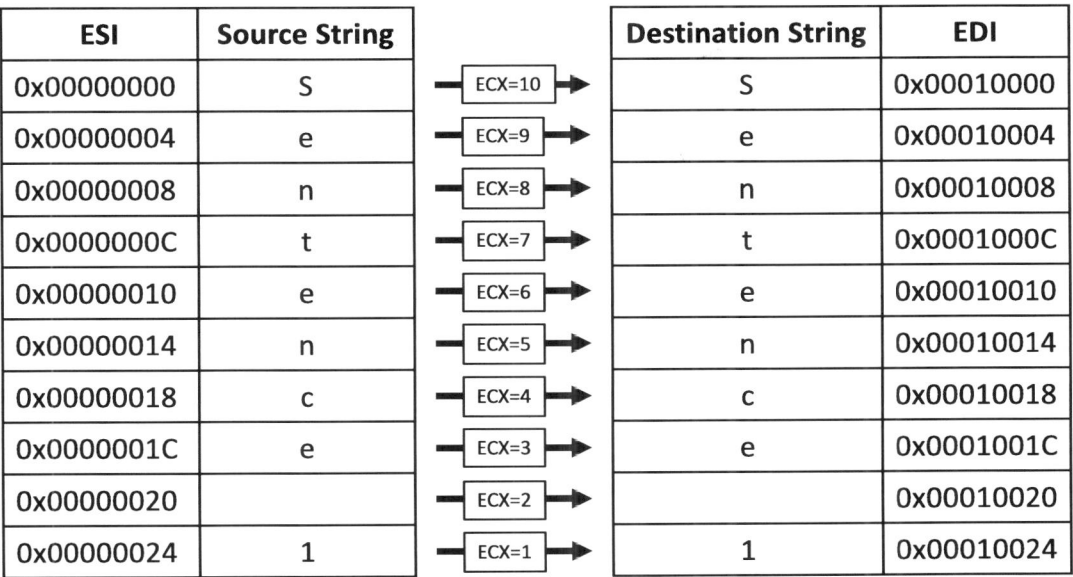

Figure 7.1 MOVSD step-by-step

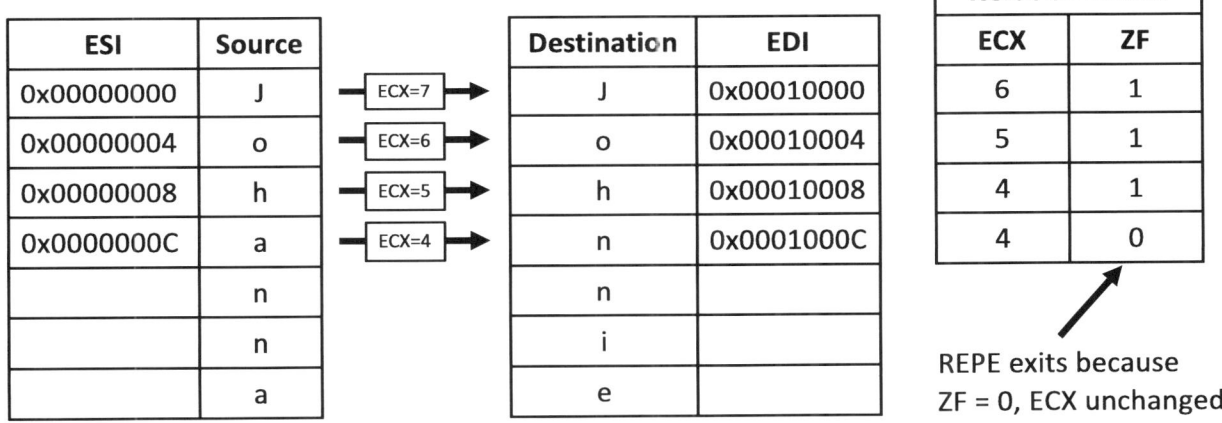

Figure 7.2 CMPSD step-by-step

Notice in Figure 7.2 how the CMPS instruction is executed first and *cx/ecx/rcx* is only decremented if the result of the string instruction indicates equality (ZF = 1). On the fourth iteration, CMPS sets ZF to 0, indicating inequality, and so the repetition ends and REPE does not decrement *ecx* to 3.

Immediately after the REPE CMPS operation you need to verify whether the two strings were equal or not equal. For strings of the same length, just ensure that ZF is set after the last iteration. You might mistakenly check the status of *(r/e)cx* in order to determine whether or not CMPS was successful: *(r/e)cx* being zero, indicating that the entire string was iterated and thus equal; or *(r/e)cx* being greater than zero, indicating that CMPS exited due to a non-equal comparison. Checking the counter register works for every instance except one: when the last character of the string is different. The counter will be zero because it has reached the last character, so a counter value of zero does not necessarily mean success. A set ZF does indicate success.

Using CMPS to determine if two strings are equal becomes slightly more difficult if the strings are different lengths. You can avoid the difficulty by testing the lengths prior to performing the comparison. Should you want to continue and execute CMPS on strings of different lengths, use the shorter of the two lengths as the counter value. Doing so ensures that the repetition does not exceed the memory bounds of the shorter string into neighboring data, which would lead to incorrect results. Remember, Assembly does not perform automatic bounds checking.

The basic invocation of CMPS is CMPS*s* (e.g., CMPSD). Program 7.1 demonstrates the use of CMPS with necessary precautions.

Program 7.1 *CMPS*

GAS	MASM	NASM
| ```
.data
src:
.ascii "Test sentence!\n\0"
.equ lenSrc, (. - src)
dst:
.ascii "Test sentence!\n\0"
.equ lenDst, (. - dst)


.text
.globl _main
_main:


# compare string lengths
movl $lenSrc, %eax
cmpl $lenDst, %eax
jne notequal


# when lengths are equal
# execute CMPS
leal src, %esi
leal dst, %edi
movl $lenSrc, %ecx
cld
repe cmpsb


# after CMPS, see if it
# ended successfully
jnz notequal


# equality things
jmp done


notequal:
# non-equality things


done:
pushl $0
subl $4, %esp
movl $1, %eax
int $0x80
.end
``` | ```
.386
.MODEL FLAT, stdcall
.STACK 4096
ExitProcess PROTO,
 dwExitCode:DWORD


.data
src DB "Test sentence",0
lenSrc EQU ($ - src)
dst DB "Test sentence",0
lenDst EQU ($ - dst)


.code
_main PROC


; compare string lengths
mov eax, lenSrc
cmp eax, lenDst
jne notequal


; when lengths are equal
; execute CMPS
lea esi, src
lea edi, dst
mov ecx, lenSrc
cld
repe cmpsb


; after CMPS, see if it
; ended successfully
jnz notequal


; equality things
jmp done


notequal:
; non-equality things


done:
INVOKE ExitProcess, 0
_main ENDP
END
``` | ```
SECTION .data
src: DB "Test sentence",0
lenSrc: EQU ($ - src)
dst: DB "Test sentence",0
lenDst: EQU ($ - dst)


SECTION .text
global _main
_main:


; compare string lengths
mov eax, lenSrc
cmp eax, lenDst
jne notequal


; when lengths are equal
; execute CMPS
lea esi, [src]
lea edi, [dst]
mov ecx, lenSrc
cld
repe cmpsb


; after CMPS, see if it
; ended successfully
jnz notequal


; equality things
jmp done


notequal:
; non-equality things


done:
mov eax, 1
mov ebx, 0
int 80h
``` |

In Program 7.1, two strings and symbols containing their lengths are declared. The lengths are first used to determine if both strings are the same number of bytes. If the lengths are not equal, we can immediately assert that the strings are not equal. If the lengths are equal, we begin preparing for the CMPS instruction. We load *esi* and *edi* with the memory addresses of the strings, copy the length to *ecx*, clear DF for left-to-right processing, and execute the CMPS instruction. CMPS iterates through each byte of the arrays and compares corresponding characters. If at any point the characters in corresponding slots do not match, CMPS will exit with ZF = 0. The subsequent JNZ instruction also ensures the final characters are equal by jumping to notequal if ZF = 0. However, the code in Program 7.1 will see CMPS finish successfully (ZF = 1) and fall through to jmp done because both strings are equal.
```

SCAS

The **SCAS (scan string)** instruction does not have a non-string counterpart as do the MOVS and CMPS instructions. SCAS is essentially a built-in sequential search algorithm. One potential difference between SCAS and a sequential search algorithm written in a high-level language is that SCAS only operates on a single character at a time as it iterates through a string. High-level implementations sometimes search for multi-character substrings within strings. But many high-level algorithms also search a character at a time.

The normal operation of SCAS is to iterate through a string, referenced by *(r/e)di*, until a target character stored in *al/ax/eax/rax* is found and then exit. The execution of SCAS is basically the opposite of CMPS. We want CMPS to repeat as long as each character pair is equal and thus use the REPE or REPZ instruction. SCAS needs to repeat as long as character pairs are not equal, which indicates the search character has not been found. So SCAS is usually executed with the REPNE or REPNZ instruction.

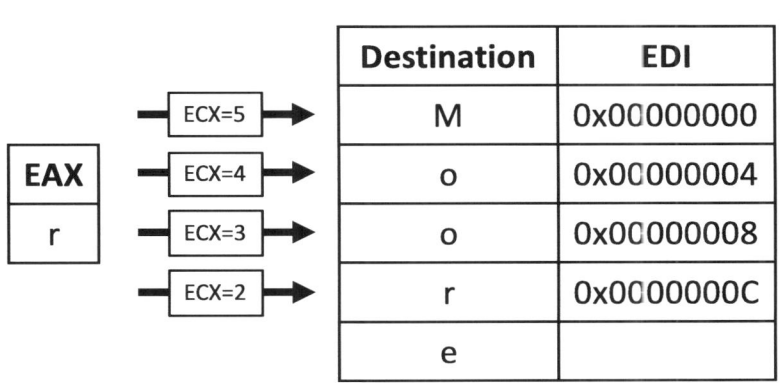

REPNE exits because ZF = 1, ECX decremented

Figure 7.3 SCASD step-by-step

Figure 7.3 illustrates the step-by-step execution of SCAS searching for the letter `'r'` in the string `"Moore"`.

> **PROGRAMMING:** With CMPS, REPE/REPZ does not decrement *(r/e)cx* when CMPS fails. But with SCAS, REPNE/REPNZ decrements *(r/e)cx* in both cases, success and failure.

The last step when scanning is determining whether or not SCAS found a match, which is accomplished in the same manner as with CMPS. If SCAS iterates through an entire string and does not find a match, the counter value is zero and ZF is clear (ZF = 0). If SCAS did find a match (e.g., Figure 7.3), the counter value could be zero or greater than zero, depending on the location of the match, but ZF will be set (ZF = 1). Similar to CMPS, use ZF as the sole indicator of success.

The basic invocation of SCAS is SCAS*S* (e.g., SCASW). Program 7.2 demonstrates use of the SCAS instruction.

Program 7.2 SCAS

GAS	MASM	NASM

```.data```
 ```src:```
 ```.ascii "Test sentence\0"```
 ```.equ lenSrc, (. - src)```
 ```search: .ascii "s"```
 	
 ```.text```
 ```.globl _main```
 ```_main:```
 	
 ```xor %eax, %eax```
 ```movb search, %al```
 ```leal src, %edi```
 ```movl $lenSrc, %ecx```
 ```cld```
 ```repne scasb```
 	
 ```# after SCAS, test for```
 ```# success```
 ```jnz notfound```
 	
 ```# found things```
 ```jmp done```
 	
 ```notfound:```
 ```# non-found things```
 	
 ```done:```
 ```pushl $0```
 ```subl $4, %esp```
 ```movl $1, %eax```
 ```int $0x80```
 ```.end```
	```.386```
	 ```.MODEL FLAT, stdcall```
	 ```.STACK 4096```
	 ```ExitProcess PROTO,```
	 ```dwExitCode:DWORD```
	
	 ```.data```
	 ```src BYTE "Test sentence",0```
	 ```lenSrc EQU ($ - src)```
	 ```search BYTE "s"```
	
	 ```.code```
	 ```_main PROC```
	
	 ```xor eax, eax```
	 ```mov al, search```
	 ```lea edi, src```
	 ```mov ecx, lenSrc```
	 ```cld```
	 ```repne scasb```
	
	 ```; after SCAS, test for```
	 ```; success```
	 ```jnz notfound```
	
	 ```; found things```
	 ```jmp done```
	
	 ```notfound:```
	 ```; non-found things```
	
	 ```done:```
	 ```INVOKE ExitProcess, 0```
	 ```_main ENDP```
	 ```END```
		```SECTION .data```
		 ```src: DB "Test sentence",0```
		 ```lenSrc: EQU ($ - src)```
		 ```search: DB "s"```
		
		 ```SECTION .text```
		 ```global _main```
		 ```_main:```
		
		 ```xor eax, eax```
		 ```mov al, [search]```
		 ```lea edi, [src]```
		 ```mov ecx, lenSrc```
		 ```cld```
		 ```repne scasb```
		
		 ```; after SCAS, test for```
		 ```; success```
		 ```jnz notfound```
		
		 ```; found things```
		 ```jmp done```
		
		 ```notfound:```
		 ```; non-found things```
		
		 ```done:```
		 ```mov eax, 1```
		 ```mov ebx, 0```
		 ```int 80h```

Program 7.2 is a simple sequential search for the character 's' in the string "Test sentence". Three variables are the string, the length of the string, and the search character. Because the search character must reside in the appropriate accumulator register (e.g., *al* for 8-bit, *ax* for 16-bit, etc.), we first clear *eax* with XOR. Since we are performing a byte search, the search character is loaded into *al*.

Unlike the previous string instructions, only *edi* is used with SCAS, as the source index. After the length of the string in bytes is loaded into *ecx*, we clear DF and execute SCASB. As discussed, once SCAS has finished we need to check ZF to determine if the search character was found or not. So we use the JNZ instruction to jump to the notfound label if ZF is clear (ZF = 0). In Program 7.2, the character 's' *is* found, so ZF is set (ZF = 1), JNZ fails, and execution falls through to the found section where we could notify the user or perform other tasks, but we simply jump to the done label.

STOS

The **STOS (store string)** instruction is useful for array initialization. STOS takes the value in the accumulator register and copies it into the memory location referenced by *(r/e)di*. In order to initialize more than one memory location (i.e., an entire array), use STOS in conjunction with REP.

Figure 7.4 illustrates using STOS to initialize a 5-element array with zeros.

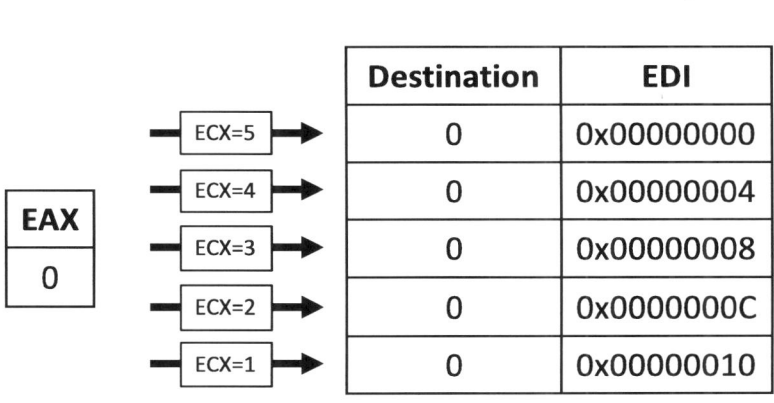

Figure 7.4 STOSD step-by-step

PROGRAMMING: STOS cannot use different values when initializing an array. The same value will be copied into each element of the array.

The basic invocation of STOS is STOS*s* (e.g., STOSO). Example 7.4 demonstrates use of the STOS instruction.

Example 7.4 STOS

GAS	MASM	NASM

xorl eax, eax
movb $0, %al
leal dst, %edi
movl $10, %ecx
cld
rep stosb
	xor eax, eax
	mov al, 0
	lea edi, dst
	mov ecx, 10
	cld
	rep stosb
		xor eax, eax
		mov al, 0
		lea edi, [dst]
		mov ecx, 10
		cld
		rep stosb

The code in Example 7.4 initializes a 10-element array, identified by dst, with the value zero. Since we execute STOS with the 'b' suffix, indicating bytes, we use *al* (a byte-sized register) to hold the value that will be copied into each element of the dst array.

LODS

The **LODS (load string)** instruction does the opposite of the STOS instruction. Instead of copying a value from the accumulator register into the address referenced by *(r/e)di*, LODS takes the value referenced by *(r/e)si* and copies it into the accumulator register. Unlike STOS and the other string instructions, you will likely never use LODS in conjunction with any of the repetition instructions due to repeated overwriting of the accumulator register. STOS is illustrated in Figure 7.5, which shows how *eax* is overwritten with each repetition.

The basic invocation of LODS is LODS*s* (e.g., LODSB). Example 7.5 shows a simple LODS example.

Example 7.5 LODS

GAS	MASM	NASM
movl $src, %esi lodsd	lea esi, src lodsd	lea esi, [src] lodsd

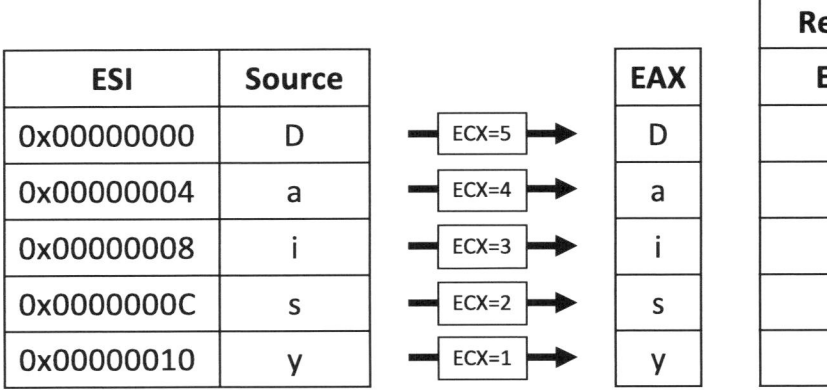

Figure 7.5 LODSD with REP step-by-step

The code in Example 7.5 copies the starting memory address of the `src` string to *esi* and then, via the LODSD instruction, copies the 32-bit (DWORD) character into *eax*. LODS was not executed with the REP instruction, therefore Example 7.5 only executes once and does not iterate through the entire `src` string.

Structures

A **structure**, or struct as it is commonly called, is a composite datatype. Just like structs in high-level languages, structs in Assembly are user-defined datatypes that contain multiple fields, or values, which can be different datatypes. Unlike arrays, where each element must be the same size, elements of a struct can be different sizes, as demonstrated in Example 7.6.

Example 7.6 Assembly structure in NASM

```
STRUC person
  .name: RESB 255
  .age:  RESD 1
  .size:
ENDSTRUC
```

In Example 7.6, the `name` field is a 255-BYTE array, and the `age` field is a single DWORD. Of particular note is the `size` field. Having an empty label at the end of a STRUC definition in NASM facilitates space reservation for a structure in the *uninitialized* program section. When reserving space for uninitialized variables, NASM needs to know how much space to reserve. Usually, space is reserved by indicating the number of bytes with a size directive (e.g., DB, DD, etc.), as is the case for primitive datatypes. But structs are not primitive.

Because structures do not have a single size directive telling the Assembler how many bytes the struct occupies as a whole, the Assembler needs to know both the starting position in memory (the struct's label, `person`) and the ending position in memory (the ending label, `size`). Just like using the *current location counter* with EQU to determine the length of an array, the empty `size` label allows NASM to determine the total size of a structure.

Given our basic overview of a structure, we can examine how to implement structs in a program. Because structs are not a built-in datatype, you must define them before you can declare any instances of the struct. The same is true in high-level languages. Definition of structs must be done outside of the *code* and *data* sections in what we might call the *absolute* section, or in a separate file to be included (using the INCLUDE directive, see **Code Review** for syntax). Doing so ensures that the structure is defined before instantiation.

Glaring differences exist in the Assembler syntaxes presented in Example 7.7. Both MASM and NASM have the ability to define and use structs in a similar fashion to high-level languages. However, GAS has no such construct. The `.struct` directive in GAS is simply used to define an absolute expression and assign it to the subsequent label (e.g., `name = 0` and `age = 10`). The labels can then be used in GAS code as normal identifiers by prefixing the label name with the dollar sign ($). Because GAS structs do not behave like structs in MASM or NASM, we do not discuss the GAS `.struct` directive any further.

Example 7.7 Structure definitions

GAS	MASM	NASM

```.struct 0```
```name:```
```.struct name + 10```
```age:```
	```person STRUCT```
	``` name DB 255 DUP(?)```
	``` age DD ?```
	```person ENDS```
		```STRUC person```
		``` .name: RESB 255```
		``` .age: RESD 1```
		``` .size:```
		```ENDSTRUC```

Both MASM and NASM implement the structure in Example 7.7 with an empty 255-byte array for `name` and an empty doubleword for `age`. When instantiating and manipulating structs in Assembly, use the same dot notation found in high-level languages. MASM uses dot notation implicitly, but NASM does not. In order to use dot notation in NASM, each member must be prefixed with a dot, as seen in Example 7.7 (do not confuse NASM `STRUC` member declarations with GAS directives). Without the dot prefixes, NASM cannot assemble the `STRUC` code.

With the structure defined in Example 7.7, we show an instantiation of the struct in Example 7.8. For MASM and NASM, we declare the `employee1` instance. Note the NASM syntax of `ISTRUC` and `IEND` to signify an **instance** of a structure.

Example 7.8 Structure declarations

MASM	NASM

```.DATA```
``` employee1 person <"Waldo",55>```
	```SECTION .data```
	``` employee1: ISTRUC person```
	``` AT person.name, DB "Waldo"```
	``` AT person.age, DD 55```
	``` IEND```

With both Assemblers, the instance is declared in the *data* section like other variables. MASM has a more compact syntax, but the same rules apply to both Assemblers: field values must be initialized in the order they were defined. In Example 7.8, two aspects of the NASM syntax are worth highlighting. First, the field specification that directly follows the AT macro must use `struct_name.member_name`. Second, the size directives used when declaring an `ISTRUC` are the *data* section size directives (e.g., DB, DD, etc.) instead of the *bss*-style (uninitialized) size directives used in the `STRUC` definition (e.g., RESB, RESD, etc.).

With the structure definition and declaration complete, we can discuss struct usage. The code in Example 7.9 copies the value in the `age` field to a register, which demonstrates dot notation in both Assemblers.

Example 7.9 Structure usage

MASM	NASM
```.CODE``` ``` mov eax, employee1.age```	```SECTION .text``` ``` mov eax, [employee1 + person.age]```

MASM uses the same notation as high-level languages, while NASM uses a method similar to that of arrays in Assembly. In order to access the value stored in a member field of a struct, NASM must dereference the appropriate memory location. As with arrays, the value is located by specifying a `[label + offset]`. The offset must be an absolute expression that results in a size in bytes. Therefore, we use `person.age` as the offset from the `employee1` label instead of `employee1.age`. The identifiers are simply referencing memory locations. The Assembler does not know the size of `employee1.age` without first determining `employee1` is of type `person` and then determining the size of `person.age`. Indirect referencing is not absolute and will produce an Assembly error. In NASM, use the definition label for the offset, not the declaration label.

 PROGRAMMING: Alignment directives (e.g., ALIGN, ALIGNB) are useful and sometimes necessary to ensure structures and structure members are aligned on appropriate boundaries.

The last example we consider with structures is declaring uninitialized structs. Example 7.10 shows code for an uninitialized array of structs, which in NASM requires using the `size` field and a variable (`empSize`) to contain the number of elements in the array.

Example 7.10 Array of uninitialized structures

MASM	NASM

`.DATA`
` empArr person 10 DUP(?)`
 	
`.CODE`
` mov eax, LENGTHOF empArr`
	`SECTION .bss`
	` empArr: RESB person.size*10`
	` empSize: EQU ($ - empArr) / person.size`

While NASM needs a symbol declared with EQU and/or the *current location counter* immediately after the array declaration, 32-bit MASM does not. MASM can determine the number of elements in an array dynamically by using the LENGTHOF directive (32-bit mode only). If using 64-bit MASM, you can use the same method as NASM (EQU and *current location counter*).

Summary

In this chapter we discussed various instructions for efficiently manipulating strings. String primitive instructions are most useful when combined with the appropriate accessory instructions to iterate through multi-character strings. Working with arrays of data, but specifically character arrays, should now be relatively straightforward. Furthermore, understanding how to work with structures in Assembly language provides an option for more complex object-oriented scenarios. Structs illustrate a point of similarity that MASM and NASM share with high-level languages, while GAS maintains a primitive approach.

Key Terms

CMPS (compare string)
direction flag
instance
LODS (load string)
MOVS (move string)

REP (repeat)
SCAS (scan string)
STOS (store string)
string primitive instructions
structure

Code Review

CLD	Clear the direction flag (DF)
CMPS	Compare strings (uses *si/esi/rsi* and *di/edi/rdi*)
INCLUDE	Preprocessor directive to include support files in a program. GAS: `.include "file.inc"`, NASM: `%include "file.inc"` MASM: `INCLUDE file.inc`
LODS	Load from a string (uses *si/esi/rsi*)
MOVS	Copy string (uses *si/esi/rsi* and *di/edi/rdi*)
REP	Repeat until *cx/ecx/rcx* = 0
REPE	Repeat as long as *cx/ecx/rcx* is not 0 and the character at *si/esi/rsi* is equal to the character at *di/edi/rdi*
REPNE	Repeat as long as *cx/ecx/rcx* is not 0 and the character at *si/esi/rsi* is not equal to the character at *di/edi/rdi*
REPNZ	Repeat as long as *cx/ecx/rcx* is not 0 and ZF is not set. Synonymous with REPNE.
REPZ	Repeat as long as *cx/ecx/rcx* is not 0 and ZF is set. Synonymous with REPE.
SCAS	Scan (search) for a character within a string (uses *di/edi/rdi*)

STD	Set the direction flag (DF)
STOS	Store to a string (uses *di/edi/rdi*)

Questions

Short Answer

1. Using STD before a repeat instruction ensures that the characters will be read _____.
2. In order to repeat while ZF is clear, you should use the _____ instruction.
3. When executing string instructions, you must append a size identifier, which is similar to how instructions are written when assembling with _____.
4. To work with characters 8 bytes in size, you must append the _____ character to a string primitive instruction.
5. The data required to be stored in *esi* and/or *edi* for string primitive instructions is _____.
6. Repeating CMPS with REPZ rather than REP is necessary because REPZ will only repeat if ZF is _____.
7. When using CMPSW, the address in *edi* will be incremented by _____ each iteration.
8. When repeating a string instruction, you must load the *C* register with the number of _____.
9. ZF will equal _____ each iteration that SCAS does not find the target character.
10. After executing SCAS, the most efficient way to proceed is to use the _____ instruction, which will execute the code branch for when the target character is not found.
11. Only one register is implicitly used for indirect addressing when executing STOS: _____.
12. LODS copies the value referenced by _____ and stores it in _____.
13. The _____ instruction(s) is/are the instruction(s) that is/are typically called with one of the repeat instructions.
14. Instead of using LEA when assembling with GAS, you can use the MOV instruction and prefix the variable with _____.
15. Calling MOVS with REPZ or REPNZ could have unintended effects such as exiting early because MOVS does not modify _____.

True/False

1. CLD clears the zero flag (ZF).
2. REPNE will repeat as long as ZF is set.
3. When repeating, the counter is decremented before the string instruction is executed.
4. When repeating CMPS, use REPNZ to continue repeating while the characters are equal.
5. STOS will initialize an array with whatever value is in the appropriate accumulator register.

Assignments

7.1 Copy cat

Write a program that compares two strings: `"Try harder"` and `"Try harder still"`. Determine if the strings are exactly the same, the same to a certain index, or completely different. The code must handle all three scenarios.

7.2 LOUD NOISES!

Write a program using the appropriate string primitive instructions that iterates through the string `"I DON'T KNOW WHAT WE'RE YELLING ABOUT!"` and converts each character to its lowercase counterpart and stores the resulting string in another location.

7.3 strstr() Disassembled

The C programming language has a function, `strstr()`, which searches for a substring inside of a string and returns the memory location of the first occurrence where the substring was found. Write a program that accomplishes the same goal, but returns the character index (the nth element) of the substring instead of the memory location.

CHAPTER 8

Floating-Point Operations

Objectives

- Distinguish between floating-point representations
- Convert values to IEEE floating-point representation
- Explain characteristics of floating-point storage
- Examine floating-point implementations/instruction sets
- Use floating-point instructions and manipulate floating-point values.

Outline

1. Web Resources
2. Introduction
3. Floating-Point Representation
   a. IEEE Representation
   b. Special Values
   c. Subnormal Numbers
   d. Rounding
4. Floating-Point Implementations
   a. x87
   b. MMX – A Tangent
   c. Streaming SIMD Extensions (SSE)
   d. XOP, FMA3/4, F16C – A Division
   e. Advanced Vector Extensions (AVX)
5. Summary
6. Key Terms
7. Key Registers
8. Code Review
9. Questions
   a. Short Answer
   b. True/False
10. Assignments

Web Resources

Wikis

- https://en.wikipedia.org/wiki/X87
- https://en.wikipedia.org/wiki/Streaming_SIMD_Extensions
- https://en.wikipedia.org/wiki/X86_instruction_listings#SSE_instructions
- https://en.wikipedia.org/wiki/Advanced_Vector_Extensions

Developer

- http://www.intel.com/content/dam/www/public/us/en/documents/manuals/64-ia-32-architectures-software-developer-vol-1-manual.pdf
- http://www.intel.com/content/dam/www/public/us/en/documents/manuals/64-ia-32-architectures-software-developer-instruction-set-reference-manual-325383.pdf
- https://software.intel.com/en-us/articles/introduction-to-intel-advanced-vector-extensions

Floating-Point Arithmetic

- https://docs.oracle.com/cd/E19957-01/806-3568/ncg_math.html (IEEE Arithmetic)
- http://babbage.cs.qc.cuny.edu/IEEE-754/ (IEEE 754 Analysis)

Introduction

This chapter provides an overview of floating-point operations on x86 and x86_64 architectures. We begin by discussing floating-point representation and storage with a focus on IEEE floating-point representation. Then, we present the development of floating-point implementations in chronological fashion using working examples. Included in the implementations are the x87 Floating-Point Unit, Streaming SIMD Extensions, and Advanced Vector Extensions. The content presented in this chapter provides a foundation for understanding floating-point architecture and for using floating-point instructions in programs.

> LEARNING: The programs in this chapter, Programs 8.1–8.8, are 32-bit programs. The CODE REVIEW section at the end of the chapter provides a 64-bit example of an investment calculator program.

Floating-Point Representation

In computing, **floating-point values** are data representations that approximate **real numbers** and are typically represented as a value with digits before and after a decimal point. A floating-point number is composed of the **significand** that represents a fixed number of significant digits, a base for scaling an exponent, and an exponent.

Given: 1.2345×10^4

1.2345	=	12345	x	10	4
floating point		significand		base	exponent

The idea is that a value can be represented by moving the "point" while scaling based on a number system such as decimal (base 10).

12345×10^0	1234.5×10^1	123.45×10^2	12.345×10^3	1.2345×10^4

This book assumes the reader is generally familiar with floating-point nomenclature and the mathematics related to floating-point arithmetic and fractions.

IEEE Representation

In 1985, the Institute of Electrical and Electronics Engineers (IEEE) published the technical standard **IEEE 754** for floating-point computation. The standard was updated in 2008 as IEEE 754-2008. Although other companies such as IBM and Cray have developed standards, IEEE 754 has remained the dominate floating-point representation in computing. IEEE 754 defines arithmetic formats for finite numbers, infinites, and special values such as "Not-a-Number" (NaN). The standard also defines rounding rules, operations, conditions for exception handling, and interchange formats among other specifics.

Table 8.1 shows common IEEE floating-point formats. Single precision, double precision, and double extended precision are the most common formats. Quadruple precision is defined in the IEEE standard but is generally not supported in hardware, while software support is sporadic and varied. For example, quadruple precision can be implemented as two double-precision values, but it is implemented as a `double` in Visual C++, a `long double` in GCC for PowerPC, and as non-standard types such as `__float128` in GCC or `_quad` in Intel's C/C++ compiler.

Table 8.1 IEEE 754 floating-point formats

Format	Sign bits	Exponent bits	Significand bits	Total bits	Exponent bias	Precision bits	Precision decimal digits	C++ data type
Single precision (binary32)	1	8	23	32	127	24	~7	float
Double precision (binary64)	1	11	52	64	1023	53	~16	double
Double extended (binary80)	1	15	63 + 1 (explicit leading bit)	80	16,383	64	~19	long double
Quadruple precision (binary128)	1	15	112	128	16,383	113	~34	long double, __float128, _Quad

As part of the IEEE binary formats, the exponent is stored with a bias. For example, single-precision exponents are 8 bits and the bias is 127. The bias is added to the actual exponent to ensure that the exponent is always stored as a positive value (unsigned). For single precision, the exponent range is -126 to 127, but with the bias added the exponent is stored as 1 to 254.

Floating-point values are also stored in **normalized** form. Normalization is achieved by moving the point until a single digit remains to the left of the point. The exponent then expresses the number of positions the point was moved left (positive) or right (negative). The result of normalization is that the first bit of a non-zero binary significand is always 1 and thus "implicit." The implicit bit is not stored in most formats, which makes one more bit available for precision. For example, in single-precision format, 23 bits are available for the significand, but 24 bits worth of precision can be stored. Double-extended format deviates from the pattern by keeping the leading significand bit explicitly stored.

To better understand IEEE representation and formats, we will walk through an example. Assume we wish to store the floating-point value 78.375 in binary single-precision format. Example 8.1 shows the steps for converting the value to IEEE 754 single-precision format.

Example 8.1 IEEE 754 conversion to single-precision format

Step	Value
Floating-point value	78.375
1. Assign sign bit: positive (0) or negative (1)	0
2. Convert number left of point to unsigned binary	78 = 1001110
3. Convert number right of point to binary using fractions and approximation. Each place corresponds to 2^n (Table 8.2 Negative powers of 2)	.375 = 3/8 3/8 = 0/2 + 1/4 + 1/8 + 0/n... binary = .011
4. Steps 1-3 formatted: sign + left.right	0 1001110.011
5. Normalize the significand (a binary 1 left of the point), generating an exponent for the binary point shift	0 1.001110011 x 2^6
6. Add bias to exponent and convert to binary	6 + 127 = 133 = 10000101
7. Steps 5-6 formatted: sign + exponent + fraction	0 10000101 1.001110011
8. Drop leading bit of significand (implicit) and pad fraction with trailing zeros to bit maximum	0 10000101 00111001100000000000000
9. Convert binary to hexadecimal	0100 0010 1001 1100 1100 0000 0000 0000 4 2 9 C C 0 0 0
10. Stored in memory (little-endian)	00 C0 9C 42

Table 8.2 Negative powers of 2

example decimal place values	.	3	7	5	0
negative powers of 2 (2^{-n})		2^{-1}	2^{-2}	2^{-3}	2^{-4}
decimal fraction		1/2	1/4	1/8	1/16
binary		0.1	0.01	0.001	0.0001

Special Values

In IEEE floating-point representation, special values exist that are worth noting. Special values include signed zeros, infinites, and Not-a-Number (NaN). In IEEE 754, the value zero is signed, which means two representations of zero exist: positive zero and negative zero. For most operations both zeros return equal results, but in some cases the results are different, such as 1/-0 (returns -∞), 1/+0 (returns +∞), and log(x). Table 8.3 shows the precision values in hexadecimal.

Not-a-Number (NaN) is a data type that represents undefined or imaginary values. NaNs fill various roles in floating-point computation. NaNs may be returned as the result of invalid operations, such as dividing by zero or computing the square root of a negative value. Most operations involving a NaN return a NaN. Technically, two types of NaNs exist: signaling and quiet. Signaling NaNs raise invalid operation **exceptions** as they propagate through floating-point operations, while quiet NaNs do not raise such exceptions. Exceptions are exceptional conditions that require special hardware or software processing. For example, compilers may fill uninitialized floating-point variables with signaling NaNs so operations prior to initialization result in exceptions. NaNs can have various encodings defined by compilers or programs, so the NaN values shown in Table 8.3 are only examples.

Table 8.3 IEEE 754 special values

Special value	Decimal value	Single precision	Double precision	Double extended
+0	0.0	0000 0000	00000000 00000000	00000000 00000000 00000000 00000000
-0	-0.0	8000 0000	80000000 00000000	80000000 00000000 00000000 00000000
+∞	Inf	7F80 0000	7FF00000 00000000	7FFF0000 00000000 00000000 00000000
-∞	-Inf	FF80 0000	FFF00000 00000000	FFFF0000 00000000 00000000 00000000
NaN	NaN	7FC0 0000	7FF80000 00000000	7FFF8000 00000000 00000000 00000000

Subnormal Numbers

Subnormal numbers, sometimes called **denormalized** numbers, provide the ability to store values beyond the normal range of the data type. For example, in single-precision format the smallest number in the normal range is 2^{-126} or 1.175×10^{-38}. If an operation such as a subtraction or division of small numbers near the boundary results in a number smaller than what can be stored, an **underflow** occurs. In the past, a harsh way of dealing with such a small number was to flush the value to zero. However, the IEEE 754 standard chose an alternative method called gradual underflow, which fills the gap toward zero beyond the smallest normal number. Such numbers are known as denormalized or subnormal numbers. In single-precision format, gradual underflow supports values as small as 2^{-149} or 1.401×10^{-45}. In other words, *very* small numbers can be stored. The tradeoff is that some precision is lost, but not as much as a round-off to zero.

In Example 8.2, the binary floating-point value $1.01011111000000000001111 \times 2^{-128}$ is in the subnormal range. Using gradual underflow, the number can still be stored by moving the point until the number is in the valid range. The new value $0.0101011111000000000011 \times 2^{-126}$ is a denormalized value that has lost some precision (note the two least significant 1s are lost), but it is closer to the original value than rounding to zero.

Example 8.2 Denormalized value

$1.0101111100000000000001111 \times 2^{-128}$
$0.10101111100000000000000111 \times 2^{-127}$
$0.010101111100000000000011 \times 2^{-126}$

Each precision format has maximum and minimum normal and subnormal values. For each precision format, Table 8.4 presents the normal range and Table 8.5 presents the subnormal range.

Table 8.4 Normal floating-point value range

Precision	Largest normal value	Smallest normal value
Single	$3.40282347 \times 10^{+38}$	$1.17549435 \times 10^{-38}$
Double	$1.7976931348623157 \times 10^{+308}$	$2.2250738585072014 \times 10^{-308}$
Double extended	$1.18973149535723176508575932662800070 \times 10^{+4932}$	$3.362103143112093506262677817321 7526 \times 10^{-4932}$

Table 8.5 Subnormal floating-point value range

Precision	Largest subnormal value	Smallest subnormal value
Single	$1.17549421 \times 10^{-38}$	$1.40129846 \times 10^{-45}$
Double	$2.2250738585072009 \times 10^{-308}$	$4.9406564584124654 \times 10^{-324}$
Double extended	$3.362103143112093506262677817321 7520 \times 10^{-4932}$	$6.475175119438025110924438958227 6466 \times 10^{-4966}$

Rounding

Technically, all floating-point values adhering to a format for computer storage are rational numbers with a terminating expansion (a finite series of digits right of the point). The fact that each format only has so many bits for precision means the expansion *must* terminate. So irrational numbers like π and non-terminating rational numbers must be approximated. If a number cannot be represented exactly in a given floating-point format, then the value must be rounded to another floating-point value that can be represented. An example is a value with more digits than available in the significand.

 ATTENTION: Whether or not a floating-point (fractional) value has a terminating expansion depends on the base. For example, in decimal (base 10) 1/2 (0.5) terminates, whereas 1/3 (0.333…) does not terminate. In binary (base 2), values that are powers of 2 are terminating, while everything else has an infinite binary expansion.

IEEE 754 specifies several rounding modes that we examine with examples. If we want to store the value 2.1234567890987654321 in 32-bit single-precision format, the value will have to be approximated since it has more digits than available in the format. Therefore, the value would be stored as 2.12345671653747559. Example 8.3 shows common rounding methods and the results of rounding the floating-point values π, 3.5, and -3.5, using a round-to-integer approach.

Example 8.3 Rounding modes

Rounding Modes	3.14159265358979324	3.5	-3.5
Round to nearest (even if equal)	3	4	-4
Round down toward -∞	3	3	-4
Round up toward +∞	4	4	-3
Round toward zero (truncate)	3	3	-3

The rounding method is taken into account when floating-point values are calculated or converted between formats. **Round to nearest** is the default rounding method on most systems. We discuss how to set the rounding method in the FLOATING-POINT IMPLEMENTATIONS section of this chapter for **x87**.

Floating-Point Implementations

The 8086 line of processors was not designed to perform floating-point arithmetic; stand-alone processors such as the 8086 and 80386 only handled integer arithmetic. To provide floating-point functionality, Intel developed coprocessor **floating-point units (FPU)**, such as the 8087 and 80387, which worked alongside the CPU. The FPU coprocessors implemented what is known as the x87 instruction set architecture. Beginning with the 80486/487, the FPU was integrated with the CPU. The FPU has continued to evolve beyond the x87 design with advancements like Streaming SIMD Extensions and Advanced Vector Extensions. This section provides a chronological overview and code examples of the major floating-point implementations for the x86 architecture.

x87

The **x87** instruction set is the floating-point architecture originally designed to work alongside the x86 architecture, though the designs are fundamentally different. x87 defines the instructions, registers, and floating-point formats available for floating-point computation. Table 8.6 introduces the x87 registers. This section only covers a small selection of x87 instructions in the code examples.

 ATTENTION: Refer to the IA-32 Intel Architecture Software Developer's Manual Volume 1 Chapter 8 for further reading, implementation details, and instruction details on x87.

Table 8.6 x87 Registers

FPU stack 80-bit registers	Other FPU registers
R7 R6 R5 R4 R3 R2 R1 R0	Last Instruction Pointer – 48 bits Last Data/Operand Pointer – 48 bits Status Register – 16 bits Control Register – 16 bits Tag Register – 16 bits Opcode Register – 11 bits

The general purpose registers for floating-point calculations are registers *R0–R7*. After an FPU instruction is executed, the memory addresses of the instruction and its operand (if used) are placed in the *Last Instruction Pointer* and *Last Data Pointer*, respectively. The purpose of storing the addresses of the last instruction and operand is to provide state information for exception handlers. Table 8.7 shows the length, purpose, and bit patterns for *R0-7* and the pointer registers.

Table 8.7 x87 General purpose, last instruction, and last operand registers

Register	Length	Purpose	Bits		
R0-7	80 bits	Holds floating-point values.	sign	exponent	significand
			79	78....64	63........0
Last Instruction Pointer	48 bits	Holds the address of the last non-control instruction executed.	segment selector	offset	
			47........32	31........0	
Last Data/ Operand Pointer	48 bits	Holds the address of the data/ operand of the last non-control instruction executed. Always a memory operand if used.	segment selector	offset	
			47........32	31........0	

> **PROGRAMMING:** The control instructions in x87 are FINIT/FNINIT, FCLEX/FNCLEX, FLDCW, FSTCW/FNSTCW, FSTSW/FNSTSW, FSTENV/FNSTENV, FLDENV, FSAVE/FNSAVE, FRSTOR, and WAIT/FWAIT. Any other instructions are non-control instructions. The instructions that interact with the Last Instruction Pointer and Data/Operand Pointer are FINIT/FNINIT (clears the registers), FSAVE/FNSAVE (clears the registers), FXSAVE, FSTENV/FNSTENV, FLDENV, FRSTOR, and FXRSTOR.

Two other FPU registers are particularly important to understand prior to reviewing code examples: the *Status Register* and the *Control Register*. The *Status Register* (Table 8.8) holds the current state of the FPU. A very important part of the *Status Register* is the **top-of-stack** bits (11-13) called TOP.

Table 8.8 x87 Status Register

Bits (16)													
15	14	13...11	10	9	8	7	6	5	4	3	2	1	0
FPU busy	condition code 3	TOP	condition codes			error status / interrupt request	stack fault	exception flags					
			2	1	0			P	U	O	Z	D	I

The FPU data registers (*R0-7*) behave as a circular stack. Any of the registers can serve as top-of-stack. If a value were to be loaded into *R0*, the next value loaded would wrap around to *R7*. Wrapping also happens in reverse when removing values from the stack. To enable such behavior, the data registers are not referenced by the programmer as *R0-7*, but rather *ST0-7* with *ST0* being top-of-stack (can be any of the *R* registers). The register currently serving as top-of-stack is maintained in the TOP field of the FPU *Status Register*.

Status Register bit specifics are as follows.

- **FPU busy (bit 15)**: set while the FPU is executing an instruction
- **Condition codes (bits 8–10 and 14)**: indicate results of floating-point arithmetic
- **TOP (bits 11–13)**: *R* register currently serving as top-of-stack
- **Error status (bit 7)**: set while an FPU exception is being handled
- **Stack fault (bit 6)**: FPU stack overflow or underflow has occurred (attempt to load a value into a register not free or store from a free register).
- **Exceptions (bits 0–5)**: P = precision, U = underflow, O = overflow, Z = zero divide, D = denormalized operand, I = invalid operation. P, U, and O are detected after an operation. Z, D, and I are detected prior to an operation.

Example 8.4 shows a snippet of x87 code (taken from Program 8.1) to demonstrate the use of FPU registers in code. Note that *ST#* is used instead of *R#*.

Example 8.4 FPU Register use in code

GAS	MASM	NASM
finit fldpi flds value fadd %st(1), %st	finit fldpi fld value fadd ST(0), ST(1)	finit fldpi fld DWORD [value] fadd ST0, ST1

The FPU *Control Register* (Table 8.9) has control bits for infinity, rounding, and precision. The register also contains exception mask bits. Each exception mask bit directly corresponds to an exception bit in the *Status Register*. The default state after an FPU initialization (FINIT) is that all mask bits are set (1) so that the FPU handles floating-point exceptions. If a mask bit is clear (0) and that interrupt is generated, the program must handle the exception. Bits 6, 7, 13, 14, and 15 are reserved/unused, and bit 12 (infinity control) is non-useful for modern x87 processors.

Table 8.9 x87 Control register

Bits (16)															
15	14	13	12	11	10	9	8	7	6	5	4	3	2	1	0
			Infinity control	Rounding control		Precision control				Exception masks					
										PM	UM	OM	ZM	DM	IM

Exception Masks: PM = precision, UM = underflow, OM = overflow, ZM = zero divide, DM = denormalized operand, IM = invalid operation.

The x87 FPU accepts values in seven different formats: single precision, double precision, double extended precision, word integer, doubleword integer, quadword integer, and packed **binary coded decimal (BCD)** integer. Table 8.10 shows the x87 datatypes by Assembler.

 LEARNING: Binary coded decimal (BCD) and some of its uses are presented in **Appendix H: ASCII and Decimal Arithmetic**.

Table 8.10 x87 Datatypes by Assembler

x87 FPU formats	GAS	MASM	NASM	Bits
Single precision	.float or .single	REAL4	DD	32
Double precision	.double	REAL8	DQ	64
Double extended	.tfloat (support varies)	REAL10	DT	80
Word integer	.word	WORD	DW	16
Doubleword integer	.long or .int	DWORD	DD	32
Quadword integer	.quad	QWORD	DQ	64
Packed BCD integer	not supported	TBYTE	DT (e.g., DT 42p)	80

By default, when a value is loaded into the FPU, the value is converted to double-extended format to take advantage of maximum precision. When values are stored to memory, they can be left as double extended or converted to a shorter format. The format can be controlled by altering the Precision Control field (PC) in the *Control Register* (Table 8.11).

> **PROGRAMMING:** Support for double-extended and packed BCD values can vary by platform and Assembler versions. For example, Clang's integrated assembler (used in Xcode) does not support the .tfloat directive, but modern versions of the GNU Assembler (GAS) do support the directive. The space needed for any of the floating-point types could be reserved in uninitialized space (.bss section). Some compilers create a "set" for a 10-byte value by using two longs and a short. And even though packed BCD does not have a supported datatype in GAS, it could be handled manually.

Table 8.11 Precision control

PC bits	Precision
00	single precision
01	reserved (not used)
10	double precision
11	double extended precision

The x87 FPU operates using **postfix** notation (like some calculators). With addition, for example, two values are placed on the stack and then the values are added. Another example is the expression (5 * 6) + 4, which would be evaluated as 5 6 * 4 +, meaning 5 and 6 are placed on the stack, multiply and pop, place 4 on the stack, then add and pop. Example 8.5 illustrates the expression using postfix notation.

Example 8.5 Postfix notation

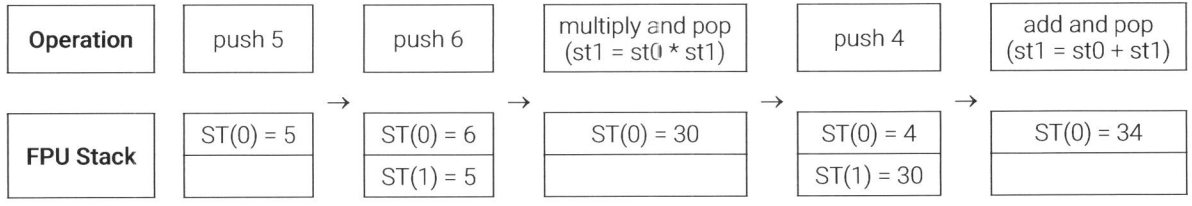

x87 FPU instructions start with the letter F. The second letter (B or I) indicates if the memory operand should be interpreted as packed BCD (B) or an integer (I). If neither is specified, then a floating-point format is assumed. For example, the load instruction FLD loads a real number, FILD an integer, and FBLD a packed BCD integer. To demonstrate the behavior of the x87 FPU and some basic floating-point instructions, consider Program 8.1, which assumes the Assembly code is linked to C++ code with implementations for _printFloat and _printDouble (see **APPENDIX E: LINKING ASSEMBLY AND C++**).

Program 8.1 *x87 FPU*

GAS	MASM	NASM
```.extern _printFloat``` ```.extern _printDouble```	```.686``` ```.MODEL FLAT, C``` ```.STACK 4096```	```extern _printFloat``` ```extern _printDouble```
```.data``` ```value: .float 1.2```	```_printFloat PROTO C``` ```_printDouble PROTO C```	```section .data``` ```value: dd 1.2```
```.bss``` ```.lcomm r_value, 4``` ```.lcomm f_result, 4``` ```.lcomm d_result, 8```	```.data``` ```value REAL4 1.2``` ```r_value REAL4 ?``` ```f_result REAL4 ?``` ```d_result REAL8 ?```	```section .bss``` ```r_value: resd 1``` ```f_result: resd 1``` ```d_result: resq 1```
```.text``` ```.globl _asmMain``` ```_asmMain:``` ``` push %ebp``` ``` movl %esp, %ebp```	```.code``` ```_asmMain PROC``` ``` push ebp``` ``` mov ebp, esp```	```section .text``` ```global _asmMain``` ```_asmMain:``` ``` push ebp``` ``` mov ebp, esp```
``` finit``` ``` fldpi``` ``` flds value``` ``` fadd %st(1), %st``` ``` fists r_value```	``` finit``` ``` fldpi``` ``` fld value``` ``` fadd ST(0), ST(1)``` ``` fist r_value```	``` finit``` ``` fldpi``` ``` fld DWORD [value]``` ``` fadd ST0, ST1``` ``` fist DWORD [r_value]```
``` fstps f_result``` ``` push $0``` ``` push f_result``` ``` call _printFloat``` ``` add $8, %esp```	``` fstp f_result``` ``` push 0``` ``` push f_result``` ``` call _printFloat``` ``` add esp, 8```	``` fstp DWORD [f_result]``` ``` push 0``` ``` push DWORD [f_result]``` ``` call _printFloat``` ``` add esp, 8```
``` fstpl d_result``` ``` push d_result + 4``` ``` push d_result``` ``` call _printDouble``` ``` add $8, %esp```	``` fstp d_result``` ``` push DWORD PTR [d_result + 4]``` ``` push DWORD PTR [d_result]``` ``` call _printDouble``` ``` add esp, 8```	``` fstp QWORD [d_result]``` ``` push DWORD [d_result + 4]``` ``` push DWORD [d_result]``` ``` call _printDouble``` ``` add esp, 8```
``` pop %ebp``` ``` ret``` ```.end```	``` pop ebp``` ``` ret``` ```_asmMain ENDP``` ```END```	``` pop ebp``` ``` ret```

We discuss Program 8.1 using the GAS version. The order of instructions we discuss is FINIT, FLDPI, FLDS, FADD, FISTS, FSTPS, and FSTPL. The FINIT instruction initializes the FPU and should be used when you want to set the FPU to its default state. Our example begins with *R3* as the current top-of-stack (Example 8.6), which will help to illustrate the circular nature of the FPU stack. So the TOP bits (11–13) in the *Status Register* are binary 011.

Example 8.6 x87 FPU stack

Data registers	Values	Stack registers
R7	nan	ST4
R6	nan	ST3
R5	0	ST2
R4	nan	ST1
R3	-inf	ST0 (TOP – 011)
R2	nan	ST7
R1	0	ST6
R0	0	ST5

FPU load instructions decrement TOP by one and place the value in the new top-of-stack register. FLDPI is an example of a load instruction, so TOP is decremented by one, then the value of π is placed in *ST0* (Example 8.7).

Example 8.7 x87 FPU stack after FLDPI

Data registers	Values	Stack registers
R7	nan	ST5
R6	nan	ST4
R5	0	ST3
R4	nan	ST2
R3	-inf	ST1
R2	3.1415926535€979324	ST0 (TOP − 010)
R1	0	ST7
R0	0	ST6

Example 8.8 x87 FPU stack after FLDS

Data registers	Values	Stack registers
R7	nan	ST6
R6	nan	ST5
R5	0	ST4
R4	nan	ST3
R3	-inf	ST2
R2	3.14159265358979324	ST1
R1	1.20000004768371582	ST0 (TOP − 001)
R0	0	ST7

FLDS (FLD) decrements TOP by one, then loads a floating-point value on the stack. Specifically, `flds value` loads a single-precision (float) of 1.2 using the `value` variable. Notice in Example 8.8 that the closest approximation of 1.2 that can be stored in double-extended format is the value on the stack in *ST0*.

FADD is an arithmetic instruction that adds the contents of two FPU registers. `fadd %st(1), %st` adds the contents of *ST(1)* and *ST(0)* and saves the result in *ST(0)* (Example 8.9). The top-of-stack register can be referenced in GAS code as *ST* or *ST(0)*.

 PROGRAMMING: GAS and MASM require the stack register number to be in parentheses, while NASM does not require parentheses.

Example 8.9 x87 FPU stack after FADD

Data registers	Values	Stack registers
R7	nan	ST6
R6	nan	ST5
R5	0	ST4
R4	nan	ST3
R3	-inf	ST2
R2	3.1415926535€979324	ST1
R1	4.34159270127350906	ST0 (TOP − 001)
R0	0	ST7

`fists r_value` is an example of a store instruction. Store instructions take the value in the current top-of-stack register and store it in memory. FST (`fst`) is the generic form of the store instruction. The second letter `'i'` tells the system to interpret the value as an integer. In GAS, the `'s'` at the end indicates single precision since the destination is 32 bits.

Table 8.12 shows examples of differences between store instructions in the Assemblers. GAS requires a suffix at the end of the instruction that corresponds to the datatype: `'s'` for single precision, `'l'` double precision (long), and `'t'` for double extended (ten-byte). Many FPU instructions have two versions: a version that just stores (copies), and a version that performs a store-and-pop (copy then increment TOP by one).

Table 8.12 x87 FPU store instruction comparison

Instruction	GAS	MASM	NASM
Store integer	`fists r_value`	`fist r_value`	`fist DWORD [r_value]`
Store float	`fsts f_value`	`fst f_value`	`fst DWORD [f_value]`
Store float and pop	`fstps f_value`	`fstp f_value`	`fstp DWORD [f_value]`
Store double and pop	`fstpl d_value`	`fstp d_value`	`fstp QWORD [d_value]`

`fists r_value` copies *ST(0)*, rounds to nearest, and stores in memory (`r_value` = 4).

FSTPS (FSTP) is an example of a store-and-pop instruction. Store-and-pop instructions store the value in the current top-of-stack register to memory, and then increment TOP by one. So, `fstps f_result` stores *ST(0)* to memory (`f_result`) in single-precision format, then increments TOP by one (pop). Notice that the pop does not actually delete the value, the register is just tagged as empty and TOP is incremented. A subsequent store would overwrite the value.

Example 8.10 x87 FPU stack after FSTPS

Data registers	Values	Stack registers
R7	nan	ST5
R6	nan	ST4
R5	0	ST3
R4	nan	ST2
R3	-inf	ST1
R2	3.14159265358979324	ST0 (TOP – 010)
R1	4.34159270127350906	ST7
R0	0	ST6

`fstpl d_result` stores *ST(0)* to memory (`d_result`) in double-precision format, then increments TOP by one (pop), as shown in Example 8.11.

Example 8.11 x87 FPU stack after FSTPL

Data registers	Values	Stack registers
R7	nan	ST4
R6	nan	ST3
R5	0	ST2
R4	nan	ST1
R3	-inf	ST0 (TOP – 011)
R2	3.14159265358979324	ST7
R1	4.34159270127350906	ST6
R0	0	ST5

In the **ROUNDING** section of this chapter, and in this **x87** section, we have mentioned the default rounding method of rounding to nearest (even). The Rounding Control (RC) bits (10–11) in the *Control Register* are 00 by default, which rounds to nearest (even). A programmer can manually set the bits to change the rounding method.

 ATTENTION: The rule for nearest (even) means the rounded result is closest to the infinitely precise result. But if two values are equally close, then the result is the *even* value, which will have a least significant bit of zero.

Program 8.2, written in GAS and commented, shows one way the rounding method could be changed programmatically. Comparable MASM and NASM versions can be found in the **CHAPTER 8 SUPPLEMENT**. Program 8.2 also introduces a few more x87 instructions: FSTCW (store control word), FLDCW (load control word), and FRNDINT (round to integer).

Program 8.2 *x87 FPU rounding control*

```
.data
default_cw:    .word 0x0000
nearest:       .word 0x0000
down:          .word 0x0400
up:            .word 0x0800
zero:          .word 0x0C00

.bss
.lcomm result, 4

.text
.globl _main
_main:

finit                      # initialize FPU
fstcw default_cw           # store initialized control word in default
movw default_cw, %ax       # move default control word to AX register
andb $0b11110011, %ah      # clear RC field (bits 10 and 11)
orw %ax, nearest           # set RC bits to 00 and store in nearest
orw %ax, down              # set RC bits to 01 and store in down
orw %ax, up                # set RC bits to 10 and store in up
orw %ax, zero              # set RC bits to 11 and store in zero

xor %ax, %ax               # sequence to verify bits
movw default_cw, %ax
movw nearest, %ax
movw down, %ax
movw up, %ax
movw zero, %ax

fldcw nearest              # set desired rounding mode

fldpi                      # load pi on the stack
frndint                    # round to integer (uses rounding mode)
fists result               # store from stack to memory
movl result, %eax          # mov rounded result to EAX

pushl $0
subl $4, %esp
movl $1, %eax
int $0x80
.end
```

LEARNING: The MASM and NASM versions of the GAS programs found throughout the rest of this chapter can be found in the **CHAPTER 8 SUPPLEMENT**. We only show one version in the main text so we can use inline comments to help explain instructions.

The x87 FPU has two more registers that hold information related to the FPU. The *Tag Register* (Table 8.13) indicates the contents of the FPU data registers (*R0-R7*). Tag registers can be useful to a programmer for checking contents without more complex instructions or decoding. The contents of the FPU *Tag Register* can be saved to memory with the FSTENV/FNSTENV or FSAVE/FNSAVE instructions. Software cannot directly modify the *Tag Register*.

Table 8.13 x87 Tag register

Bits (16)															
15	14	13	12	11	10	9	8	7	6	5	4	3	2	1	0
R7 tag		R6 tag		R5 tag		R4 tag		R3 tag		R2 tag		R1 tag		R0 tag	

If the tag bits are 00, the register contains a valid non-zero value. If the tag bits are 01, the register contains a zero or equivalent. If the tag bits are 10, the register contains a special value such as NaN, inf, -inf, and denormalized. If the tag bits are 11, the register is empty. FINIT and pop instructions tag registers as empty.

The final x87 FPU register is the *Opcode Register* (Table 8.14), which stores the opcode of the last non-control instruction executed. Only the first and second bytes of an instruction are used. An instruction's upper five bits of the first byte are the same for all FPU operations, so only the lower three bits of the first opcode byte are stored.

Table 8.14 x87 Opcode register

Bits (11)		
Instruction's 1st byte		Instruction's 2nd byte
7........3	2........0	7........0
	x87 Opcode register	

As with the *Last Instruction* and *Last Data Pointer Registers*, the *Opcode Register* provides state information for a programmer and exception handlers.

MMX – A Tangent

The reason we refer to this section as a Tangent is because **MMX technology** is not for floating-point operations, instead MMX uses the FPU registers for integer operations. Intel introduced MMX technology in 1996 with the P55C (80503) processor. A common misconception is that MMX is an acronym for terms such as MultiMedia eXtension, but it is simply an Intel Trademark. Processors with MMX capability have eight 64-bit registers available for integer operations and 47 additional instructions. The eight 64-bit registers, denoted by *MM0-7*, are aliases for the significand portion of the 80-bit FPU data registers *R0-7*.

 LEARNING: Refer to **APPENDIX G: USING CPUID** for information and code examples for determining what capabilities, and more specifically what floating-point capabilities, a processor supports.

Two major features introduced with MMX were **packed** integer data and the **single instruction, multiple data (SIMD)** model. The 64-bit MMX registers can hold packed bytes, words, and doublewords. Table 8.15 presents the MMX data formats.

Table 8.15 MMX data formats

Datatype	64 bits						
Packed doubleword integers (2)	63...............32			31...............0			
Packed word integers (4)	63........48		47........32	31........16		15........0	
Packed byte integers (8)	63...56	55...48	47...40	39...32	31...24	23...16	15...8	7...0

Data movement in and out of the MMX registers happens sequentially or in 64-bit chunks (quadwords), but arithmetic can be performed in parallel on the packed data. Operations in parallel on multiple data points with a single instruction *is* the SIMD model. For example, MOVQ (move quadword) can be used to move packed data into MMX registers, and then arithmetic instructions such as PADDSW (parallel add signed words) can add pairs of data with one instruction in one clock cycle.

Examine the GAS code in Program 8.3.

Program 8.3 MMX

```
.data
w1: .word 1, 2, 3, 4
w5: .word 5, 6, 7, 8
result: .quad 0

.text
.globl _main
_main:

movq w1, %mm0        # move quadword w1-w4 to MM0
movq w5, %mm1        # move quadword w5-w8 to MM1

paddsw %mm1, %mm0    # add packed signed words
movq %mm0, result    # move data to result

pushl $0
subl $4, %esp
movl $1, %eax
int $0x80
.end
```

movq w1, %mm0 moves a quadword (64 bits) to *mm0* starting at the identifier w1, which means w1–w4 is moved into *mm0*.

	mm0			
	word	word	word	word
movq w1, %mm0 →	1	2	3	4

We then do the same for w5–w8.

	mm1			
	word	word	word	word
movq w5, %mm1 →	5	6	7	8

We then add the packed signed word integers using PADDSW with *mm0* as the destination. Since the instructions only have two operands, one register serves as both a source and the destination.

MMX	word	word	word	word
mm0	1	2	3	4
mm1	5	6	7	8
`paddsw %mm1, %mm0`	↓	↓	↓	↓
mm0	6	8	A	C

We can then move the packed data from *mm0* to memory if desired (`movq %mm0, result`).

> **PROGRAMMING:** MMX and FPU instructions can be used in the same program even though they both use the same registers, but doing so introduces some overhead. When an MMX instruction is used, the FPU is set to accept MMX data and marks the entire x87 *Tag Register* as valid: each register tag is set to valid (00). Transitions between MMX and FPU operations can lead to data loss or meaningless results unless preventative steps are taken. The MMX state can be saved using the FPU instructions FSAVE/FXSAVE if you want to restore after a switch to FPU operations. To safely transition back to FPU operations, execute the EMMS instruction to set the FPU to accept FPU data and to set all the tags in the *Tag Register* to empty (11). Switching between MMX and FPU operations is costly in terms of clock cycles, so transition sparingly.

Much more could be said about MMX operations, but we have provided a brief introduction. For further reading, implementation, and instruction details refer to Chapter 9 in the IA-32 Intel Architecture Software Developer's Manual Volume 1 (see Developer links at beginning of this Chapter).

Streaming SIMD Extensions (SSE)

The next generation of floating-point architecture came with **Streaming SIMD Extensions (SSE)** and the Pentium III, which built upon MMX technology. The extension of MMX and the SIMD model to floating-point computation enabled improvements in graphics and networking applications. Where MMX handles packed integer data in 64-bit registers, SSE handles packed *and* scalar floating-point data in 128-bit registers. Keep in mind that packed operations provide implicit parallelism in programs. SSE has evolved over the years as computational capabilities have increased. Generations include SSE, SSE2, SSE3, SSSE3, and SSE4.

SSE instructions fall into four general categories.

- Packed and scalar floating-point instructions
- SIMD integer instructions
- State management instructions
- Cache control and instruction/memory ordering instructions

In this section we only briefly introduce a few SSE instructions. For further detail, see Chapters 10 and 11 in the IA-32 Intel Architecture Software Developer's Manual Volume 1.

The 128-bit SSE registers available in 32-bit mode are the XMM registers *xmm0–xmm7*. In 64-bit mode, eight more registers become available, *xmm8–xmm15*. We must note that the XMM registers are not aliased to any other registers, they are independent registers in SSE-compatible processors. XMM registers can only hold data, they cannot be used to address memory.

SSE also has a 32-bit control and status register called *MXCSR* (Table 8.16) that is similar to the x87 *Control* and *Status Registers*. *MXCSR* contains flag and mask bits for floating-point exceptions and rounding control, and various flags for controlling SIMD operations.

Table 8.16 SSE MXCSR (control and status) register

Bits (32)															
31............16	15	14–13	12	11	10	9	8	7	6	5	4	3	2	1	0
reserved	FZ	RC	PM	UM	OM	ZM	DM	IM	DAZ	PE	UE	OE	ZE	DE	IE

- **Exception flags (bits 0–5)**: IE = invalid operation, DE = denormalized operand, ZE = zero divide, OE = overflow, UE = underflow, PE = precision
- **DAZ (bit 6)**: denormalized operands are zeros; denormalized operands are converted to zero, maintains sign, not IEEE 754 compatible
- **Exception masks (bits 7–12)**: see Exception flags
- **Rounding Control (bits 13–14)**: similar behavior to x87 rounding control
- **FZ (bit 15)**: FZ = flush to zero; underflow results in a flush to zero, not IEEE 754 compliant

SSE only supports one data type: single-precision floating point (Table 8.17).

Table 8.17 SSE single-precision data

32-bit single precision	32-bit single precision	32-bit single precision	32-bit single precision
127................96	95................64	63................32	31................0

SSE2 expanded the datatypes to include double-precision floating point, quadword integers, doubleword integers, word integers (shorts), and byte integers, as shown in Table 8.18.

Table 8.18 SSE2 data formats

Datatype	128 bits															
Double quadword (1)	128															
Packed double-precision floating point (2)	64								64							
Packed quadword integers (2)	64								64							
Packed single-precision floating point (2)	32				32				32				32			
Packed doubleword integers (4)	32				32				32				32			
Packed word integers (8)	16		16		16		16		16		16		16		16	
Packed byte integers (16)	8	8	8	8	8	8	8	8	8	8	8	8	8	8	8	8

Consider a common graphics example. Assume we want to add two vectors (e.g., vectorA and vectorB), each with four single-precision floating-point values, and we want to store the result in one of the vectors.

```
float vectorA[] = {1.2, 3.4, 5.6, 7.8};
float vectorB[] = {7.8, 5.6, 3.4, 1.2};
```

To do the vector addition a traditional way in C++ would take at least four sequential lines of code or a loop, which is still four sequential addition operations.

Example 8.12 C++ Vector addition

```
# as individual statements
vectorA[0] = vectorA[0] + vectorB[0];
vectorA[1] = vectorA[1] + vectorB[1];
vectorA[2] = vectorA[2] + vectorB[2];
vectorA[3] = vectorA[3] + vectorB[3];

# as a loop
for(int i = 0; i <= 3; i++){
        vectorA[i] = vectorA[i] + vectorB[i];
}
```

Using SSE, a vector addition can happen in parallel with one instruction. In Program 8.4, we use the ADDPS instruction (add packed single precision) to perform a SIMD addition of two vectors.

> **PROGRAMMING:** Be careful with vector declarations in the context of a program. Vector data may need to be manually aligned on a 16-byte boundary using an ALIGN directive or else a memory access violation may occur. As mentioned in **CHAPTER 6**, functions in 64-bit mode require 16-byte alignment due to the use of 128-bit SSE operations. The same requirement is true for memory accesses with SSE.

Program 8.4 *SSE packed operations*

```
.data
.balign 16                # 16-byte alignment
vectorA: .float 1.2, 3.4, 5.6, 7.8
vectorB: .float 7.8, 5.6, 3.4, 1.2

.bss
.lcomm result, 128        # space for storing results

.text
.globl _main
_main:

movaps vectorA, %xmm0     # move aligned packed SP vectorA to XMM0
addps  vectorB, %xmm0     # add vectorB to XMM0
movaps %xmm0, result      # move data to result

pushl $0
subl $4, %esp
movl $1, %eax
int $0x80
.end
```

Program 8.4 produces the following result in *xmm0*: [9.0, 9.0, 9.0, 9.0].

SSE also introduced the ability to do **scalar** operations. Scalar operations were designed to replace x87 FPU functionality, so SSE scalar capabilities are similar to x87 FPU capabilities, but they are not identical. SSE did not provide constants like π or dedicated operations such as logs, sines, and cosines. SSE scalar instructions use the lower doubleword or quadword portions of the XMM registers to perform floating-point operations. For example, if *xmm0* is holding four 32-bit single-precision values and we use the MOVSS (move scalar single-precision) instruction to load a float value, only the lower doubleword of *xmm0* is modified.

Drawing from Program 8.5, the MOVSS (move scalar single-precision) and ADDSS (add scalar single-precision) instructions are only modifying the lower 32 bits of *xmm0*. Likewise, the MOVSD (move scalar double-precision) instruction is only modifying the lower 64 bits of *xmm0*.

> **PROGRAMMING:** As exemplified in Programs 8.4 and 8.5, most SSE instructions have two forms: scalar and packed. Examples are MOVSS and MOVPS, ADDSS and ADDPS, and so on. Most modern C++ compilers use SSE scalar instructions for floating-point computation, but do not automatically use SSE packed instructions to parallelize operations. Intel's C++ compiler is an exception. C++ compiler intrinsics (mentioned in **CHAPTER 9** and covered in **APPENDIX I: INTRINSICS**) can be used to utilize low-level SSE instructions to parallelize operations. If we were to examine the disassembly of the C++ code in Example 8.12, we would most likely find a loop with scalar operations instead of a SIMD packed operation.

Program 8.5 *SSE scalar operations*

```
.data
.balign 16
valueA: .float 1.2
pi: .double 3.14159265358979

.bss
.lcomm result, 4          # space for storing result

.text
.globl _main
_main:                    # scalar examples

movss   valueA, %xmm0     # move valueA to XMM0
addss   valueA, %xmm0     # add valueA to XMM0
movss   %xmm0, result     # store result
movl    result, %eax      # move result to EAX

movsd  pi, %xmm0          # move pi to XMM0

pushl $0
subl $4, %esp
movl $1, %eax
int $0x80
.end
```

In MMX, SSE, and SSE2, all arithmetic and comparison operations happen vertically across registers. For example, if we had four values in both *xmm0* and *xmm1* and wanted to add the values and then store the result in *xmm0*, the operation would work as shown in Table 8.19 and as demonstrated in Program 8.4.

Table 8.19 Vertical packed operations

xmm0	A3	A2	A1	A0
xmm1	B3	B2	B1	B0
operation	↓	↓	↓	↓
xmm0	C3	C2	C1	C0

SSE3 added the ability and instructions to compute horizontally across registers, as shown in Table 8.20 and demonstrated in Program 8.6.

Table 8.20 Horizontal packed operations

xmm	xmm1				xmm0			
packed data	B3	B2	B1	B0	A3	A2	A1	A0
operation	↓		↓		↓		↓	
xmm0	C3		C2		C1		C0	

Program 8.6 *SSE3*

```
.data
.balign 16
vectorA: .float 1.2, 3.4, 5.6, 7.8
vectorB: .float 7.8, 5.6, 3.4, 1.2

.text
.globl _main
_main:

movaps vectorA, %xmm0    # move vectorA to XMM0
movaps vectorB, %xmm1    # move vectorB to XMM1
haddps %xmm1, %xmm0      # horizontal add packed SP vectorB to vectorA

pushl $0
subl $4, %esp
movl $1, %eax
int $0x80
.end
```

Program 8.6 produces the following result in *xmm0*: [4.6, 13.4, 13.4, 4.6].

SSSE3 was a minor update that added new instructions, most of which optimize discrete operations. SSE4 was a major update that branched away from instructions only geared toward multimedia applications. Program 8.7 provides a few instructions to demonstrate the variety of operations available for floating-point and integer operations in SSE4.

In Program 8.7, the ROUNDPS instruction uses the immediate values (e.g., 1 and 2) to set the desired rounding mode: 1 rounds down and 2 rounds up. Also of particular interest is CVTPS2DQ, which is a convert instruction that converts (CVT) packed single-precision floats (PS) to (2) packed signed doubleword integers (DQ).

SSE and its evolution provided a new implementation for floating-point operations and established parallelism in multimedia applications. SSE, and more specifically SSE4, became the foundation upon which the next generation of floating-point operations would be built.

Program 8.7 *SSE4*

```
.data
.balign 16
vectorA: .float 1.2, 3.4, 5.6, 7.8
vectorB: .float 7.8, 5.6, 3.4, 1.2

.text
.globl _main
_main:

movaps  vectorA, %xmm0      # move aligned packed vectorA to XMM0
roundps $1, %xmm0, %xmm1    # round down(1) values in XMM0 and store in XMM1
cvtps2dq %xmm1, %xmm2       # convert SPF to int and store in XMM2

movaps  vectorB, %xmm3      # move aligned packed vectorB to XMM3
roundps $2, %xmm3, %xmm4    # round up(2) values in XMM3 and store in XMM4
cvtps2dq %xmm4, %xmm5       # convert SPF to int and store in XMM5

pmulld  %xmm2, %xmm5        # multiply doublewords and store in XMM5

pushl $0
subl $4, %esp
movl $1, %eax
int $0x80
.end
```

Program 8.7 produces the following result in *xmm5*: [8, 18, 20, 14].

 ATTENTION: Rely on the Intel manuals and other sources we have provided for lists and details of SSE instructions through the generations. Another good source with listings of SIMD instructions by generation is https://en.wikipedia.org/wiki/X86_instruction_listings#SIMD_instructions.

XOP, FMA3/4, F16C – A Division

After SSE4, Advanced Micro Devices (AMD) set about proposing the next SIMD extension dubbed SSE5. However, Intel decided to move to a new implementation, which we discuss in the next section. With the two microchip companies working on floating-point implementations, this section highlights a Division, a Wild West moment, for floating-point instructions.

Beginning in 2009, **eXtended OPerations (XOP)**, **fused multiply–add (FMA)** operations, and **F16C** (half-precision conversion) operations became integrated in processor lines such as AMD Bulldozer, AMD Piledriver, Intel Haswell, and Intel Broadwell.

XOP introduced instructions such as horizontal integer addition, multiply-accumulate, and a slew of vector instructions (e.g., compares, moves, shifts, rotates).

FMA added instructions for fused multiply–add, which means an expression such as `(a * b + c)` can happen in a single step. The difference between FMA3 and FMA4 is the number of operands in the instruction, with FMA3 having three operands and FMA4 having four operands. The full FMA operation is `destination = round(a * b + c)`. In FMA3, one of the registers used for a, b, or c is also used for the destination. In FMA4, the destination can be a fourth register.

 ATTENTION: Do not confuse fused multiply–add (FMA) with Intel's Fast Memory Access feature.

F16C instructions allow for converting between half-precision floating point (16 bits) and single-precision floating point (32 bits). Sometimes precision is not particularly important, so to save space, floating-point values can be stored with half precision, but must be converted to single precision for computation in SSE registers.

A lot of overlap exists between the above operations and what would eventually become the Advanced Vector Extensions (AVX) implementation. Thus, we move on from this relatively brief Division.

Advanced Vector Extensions (AVX)

Advanced Vector Extensions (AVX) was a major update to the x86 architecture based on the preceding SSE implementation. Processor support of AVX started around 2011. AVX is backward compatible with SSE. Three advanced extensions have been made thus far: AVX, AVX2, and AVX-512. The Advanced Vector Extensions considerably increase the register space and available instructions.

Table 8.21 AVX Register space

AVX	AVX-512	AVX2/AVX	
Bits	511....256	255....128	127....0
x86	ZMM0	YMM0	XMM0
	ZMM1	YMM1	XMM1
	ZMM2	YMM2	XMM2
	ZMM3	YMM3	XMM3
	ZMM4	YMM4	XMM4
	ZMM5	YMM5	XMM5
	ZMM6	YMM6	XMM6
	ZMM7	YMM7	XMM7
x86_64	ZMM8	YMM8	XMM8
	ZMM9	YMM9	XMM9
	ZMM10	YMM10	XMM10
	ZMM11	YMM11	XMM11
	ZMM12	YMM12	XMM12
	ZMM13	YMM13	XMM13
	ZMM14	YMM14	XMM14
	ZMM15	YMM15	XMM15
AVX-512	ZMM16 – 31	YMM16 – 31	XMM16 – 31

AVX extended the register space to include 256-bit YMM registers. In 32-bit mode, *ymm0-7*, and in 64-bit mode, *ymm0-15* (Table 8.21). Another new feature of AVX was a three-operand format. In SSE, most of the instructions, such as arithmetic, have two operands. In the case of SSE addition, as shown in our example programs, the two operands both serve as sources, but one operand also serves as the destination, so one operand is overwritten (a = a + b). In AVX, three operands are supported, so a third operand can serve as the destination, which leaves the sources intact (c = a + b).

AVX2 added more instructions, expanded instructions specifically for integers, and expanded three-operand support for FMA3 and FMA4 (d = a * b + c), bit manipulation, and multiplication.

AVX-512 further extends the register space to 512-bit ZMM registers and extends the number of registers *zmm0-31* (Table 8.21). AVX-512 also allows the legacy SSE and AVX instructions to operate on the additional sixteen registers *zmm16-31*, which are only available in 64-bit mode.

Datatype support in AVX extends the packed single-precision and double-precision floating-point types. For example, an AVX 256-bit YMM register can hold 8 single-precision floats or 4 double-precision floats. Although AVX is backward compatible with SSE, not all AVX instructions are available in all size combinations.

Program 8.8 provides a short example of AVX operations. Note that AVX instructions begin with the letter 'v'. For further information on AVX instructions, see the **WEB RESOURCES**.

Program 8.8 produces the following results in *ymm2*: [9, 9, 9, 9, 9, 9, 9, 9] and *xmm4*: [-1, -1, -1, -1].

Program 8.8 *AVX*

```
.data
.balign 16
vectorA: .float 1.2, 3.4, 5.6, 7.8, 8.9, 9.0, 0.9, 9.8
vectorB: .float 7.8, 5.6, 3.4, 1.2, 0.1, 0.0, 8.1, -0.8
vectorC: .long 1, 1, 1, 1
vectorD: .long -2, -2, -2, -2

.text
.globl _main
_main:                                  # AVX/AVX2 example

vmovaps    vectorA, %ymm0               # move vectorA to YMM0
vmovaps    vectorB, %ymm1               # move vectorA to YMM1
vaddps     %ymm0, %ymm1, %ymm2          # add vectorA and B, store in YMM2

vmovdqa    vectorC, %xmm3               # move vectorC to XMM3
vmovdqa    vectorC, %xmm4               # move vectorC to XMM4
vpsignd    vectorD, %xmm3, %xmm4        # negate sign of XMM3 values if vectorD
                                        #   values are < 0, store in XMM4
                                        # vpsign AVX support
                                        #   (CPUID for 128 or 256-bit capability)
pushl $0
subl $4, %esp
movl $1, %eax
int $0x80
.end
```

Summary

In this chapter we presented an overview of floating-point representation and implementation related to the x86 architecture. IEEE 754 serves as the standard of choice in computing for representation formats like single, double, and double-extended precision. We discussed and demonstrated the evolution of floating-point implementations from the x87 FPU to Streaming SIMD Extensions to Advanced Vector Extensions. Implementations for floating-point computation continue to evolve and do so at an accelerated pace. With a knowledge of floating-point architecture, writing low-level floating-point code can be a viable route when seeking efficiency and performance in areas of scientific computing, graphics, and game programming, among other areas.

Key Terms

Advanced Vector Extensions (AVX)
binary coded decimal (BCD)
exceptions
eXtended Operations (XOP)
F16C
floating point (values)
floating-point unit (FPU)
fused multiply–add (FMA)
IEEE 754
MMX technology
normalized
not-a-number (NaN)

packed (data and operations)
postfix
real numbers
round to nearest
scalar (data and operations)
significand
single instruction, multiple data (SIMD)
Streaming SIMD Extensions (SSE)
subnormal numbers
top-of-stack (TOP)
underflow
x87

Key Registers (32-bit, 64-bit)

st0-7	x87 floating-point stack registers
mm0-7	MMX packed integer registers
xmm0–7, 8–15	SSE registers for 32-bit and 64-bit
ymm0–7, 8–15	AVX registers for 32-bit and 64-bit
zmm0–15, 16–31	AVX-512 registers for 32-bit and 64-bit; includes *xmm* and *ymm* register expansion

Code Review

Three generations of floating-point implementations were introduced in this chapter: x87, SSE, and AVX. Most modern compilers are tuned to use SSE scalar instructions for basic floating-point arithmetic. The programs throughout **Chapter 8** are 32-bit, so this **Code Review** presents an investment calculator using SSE instructions in 64-bit mode. Program 8.9 is more similar to 64-bit floating-point code produced by C++ compilers.

The MASM and NASM versions of Program 8.9, as well as the C++ functions and investment formula, can be found in the **Chapter 8 Supplement**.

Program 8.9 x86_64 investment calculator

```
# This program calculates a monthly deposit needed to reach an investment
# value, given the future value, interest rate (%), and duration (months)
.extern _printString                    # declare external functions
.extern _printDouble
.extern _getDouble
.extern _getInt

.data
.balign 16                              # align data on 16-byte boundary
amountNeeded:    .double 0.0
interestRate:    .double 0.0
interest:        .double 0.0
monthlyPayment:  .double 0.0
duration:        .quad   0              # integer data
const100:        .double 100.0
const12:         .double 12.0
const1:          .double 1.0

amountMessage:   .asciz   "       Enter Amount Needed:  $"
interestMessage: .asciz   "       Enter Interest Rate:  "
durationMessage: .asciz   "Enter Duration (in months):  "
paymentMessage:  .asciz   "   Monthly Payment Amount:  $"

.text
.globl _asmMain
_asmMain:

pushq %rbp
movq  %rsp, %rbp                        # align stack pointer

leaq amountMessage(%rip), %rdi          # pass char* to print
callq _printString
callq _getDouble                        # get and store amountNeeded
movsd %xmm0, amountNeeded(%rip)
```

```
leaq interestMessage(%rip), %rdi        # pass char* to print
callq _printString
callq _getDouble                         # get interestRate as a %

divsd %xmm1, %xmm0
movsd %xmm0, interestRate(%rip)          # store rate as decimal value

leaq durationMessage(%rip), %rdi         # pass char* to print
callq _printString
callq _getInt                            # get and store duration
movq %rax, duration(%rip)

movsd const12(%rip), %xmm0               # interest = interestRate / const12
movsd interestRate(%rip), %xmm1
divsd %xmm0, %xmm1
movsd %xmm1, interest(%rip)

movsd interest(%rip), %xmm0              # investment formula (see Ch8 Supplement)
movsd amountNeeded(%rip), %xmm1
mulsd %xmm0, %xmm1                        # interest * amount needed, then store
movsd %xmm1, %xmm2

addsd const1(%rip), %xmm0                # add 1 to interest
movq duration(%rip), %rdi
callq _pow                               # pow(interest, duration)
subsd const1(%rip), %xmm0                # subtract 1 from result
vdivsd %xmm0, %xmm2, %xmm1               # complete formula with division
movsd %xmm1, monthlyPayment(%rip)

leaq paymentMessage(%rip), %rdi          # pass char* to print
callq _printString
movsd monthlyPayment(%rip), %xmm0
callq _printDouble                       # print monthlyPayment

popq %rbp
retq                                     # end _asmMain

_pow:                                    # pow function
pushq %rbp
movq %rsp, %rbp
movq %rdi, %rcx                          # use rcx for loop countdown
decq %rcx
movsd %xmm0, %xmm1

exp:                                     # multiply by value duration times
mulsd %xmm1, %xmm0
loop exp

popq %rbp
retq                                     # end _pow

.end
```

Questions

Short Answer

1. x86 processors use _____ format for floating-point representation.
2. In floating-point representation, the digits to the left and right of the "point" are known as the _____.
3. Exponent storage adds a _____ to an exponent because they are stored as _____ integers.
4. Floats are _____, which means the binary point is shifted until a single "1" is left of the point.
5. The 8087 FPU performs arithmetic using _____ format.
6. _____ is when a floating-point result is computed beyond the valid range.
7. The FPU coprocessor is denoted as _____.
8. The FPU *Control Register* dedicates two bits for rounding methods, meaning _____ possible rounding methods exist.
9. The FPU register stack has _____ registers that are _____ bits wide.
10. Streaming SIMD Extensions allow for _____ instructions to operate on _____ data.
11. MMX technology introduced _____ datatypes.
12. Advanced Vector Extensions have added _____ and _____ registers.
13. AVX allows for _____ operand instructions.
14. The hardware implementation of `destination = a + (b * c)` is known as _____.
15. The SIMD `"movss"` instruction indicates the instruction is the _____ version.

True/False

1. The FPU can perform operations on non-numbers (NaNs). (T/F)
2. All exceptions detected by the FPU are always handled automatically. (T/F)
3. SSE added XMM registers 128 bits wide. (T/F)
4. AVX is backward compatible with SSE. (T/F)
5. Generally, floating-point implementations can also operate on integers. (T/F)

Assignments

The following C++ code is provided for Assignments 8.1 and 8.2. The C++ code should *not* be modified in completing the assignments.

Mac (Xcode)	Windows (Visual Studio)/Linux (g++)

<pre>#include <iostream>
using namespace std;
 	
extern "C" void asmMain();
 	
extern "C" double getDouble(){
    double d;
    std::cin >> d;
    return d;
}
 	
extern "C" void printString(char* s){
    std::cout << s;
    return;
}
 	
extern "C" void printDouble(double d){
    cout << d << endl;
}
 	
// main stub driver
int main(){
    asmMain();
    return 0;
}</pre>
	<pre>#include <iostream>
	using namespace std;
	
	extern "C" void _asmMain();
	
	extern "C" double _getDouble() {
	    double d;
	    std::cin >> d;
	    return d;
	}
	
	extern "C" void _printString(char* s) {
	    std::cout << s;
	    return;
	}
	
	extern "C" void _printDouble(double d) {
	    cout << d << endl;
	}
	
	// main stub driver
	int main() {
	    _asmMain();
	    return 0;
	}</pre>

8.1 Computing the volume of a cylinder (x87)

Given the C++ code, write a program to compute the volume of a cylinder using the x87 FPU. Prompt the user for the radius and the height; then compute and display the volume. Link your Assembly code with the C++ functions to prompt for input and to display output. The Assembly code should control program flow, function calls, and floating-point arithmetic. All variables must be declared in Assembly. Use appropriate accompanying text for the prompt and output statements; the strings must also be declared in Assembly.

Volume of a cylinder: $V=\pi r^2 h$

8.2 Computing orbital velocity (SSE scalar)

Given the C++ code, write a program to compute the orbital velocity of an object orbiting Earth using SSE scalar instructions. Prompt the user for the distance (in meters) of the object from the surface of the earth; then compute and display the orbital velocity in both meters/sec (m/s) and miles per hour (mph). Link your Assembly code with the C++ functions to prompt for input and to display output. Assembly code should control program flow, function calls, and floating-point arithmetic. All variables must be declared in Assembly. Use appropriate accompanying text for the prompt and output statements; the strings must also be declared in Assembly.

Orbital velocity (v): $\quad v = \sqrt{\dfrac{Gm_e}{r}}$

Where:

Gravitational constant (G) $\approx 6.6741 \times 10^{-11}$ (N m^2 kg^{-2})
Mass of Earth (m$_e$) $\approx 5.9722 \times 10^{24}$ (kg)
Radius (r) is the distance in meters to the object from the center of Earth. The distance from the center of the Earth to the surface is about 6.371×10^6 meters, which must be added to the distance of the object from the surface of the Earth. Given the units, the *orbital velocity (v)* is in meters/sec (m/s).

Miles per hour (mph) = m/s ÷ 0.44704

8.3 Normalizing vectors (Challenge Assignment)

Write a 32-bit or 64-bit stand-alone Assembly program that defines a 2d vector and a 3d vector, then normalizes both vectors. This is a task that could be accomplished any number of ways, but we encourage the use of MMX, SSE, and/or AVX instructions to parallelize operations. You can choose the values of the vectors. This assignment could be expanded by also computing a reflection vector.

Formula to normalize a vector: $\check{V}= \dfrac{V}{|V|}$ where $|V|$ is the length of vector V.

Formulas for computing vector length: 2D: $|V| = \sqrt{x^2 + y^2}$ and 3D: $|V| = \sqrt{x^2 + y^2 + z^2}$

Chapter 8 Programs

The following programs are comparative MASM and NASM versions of the GAS programs presented in **CHAPTER 8**. Program 8.1 assumes the Assembly code is linked to C++ code with implementations for `_printFloat` and `_printDouble`. Note in Program 8.1 that the C++ functions are prefixed with an underscore for Windows/Visual Studio and Linux/g++. Programs 8.2 through 8.8 are stand-alone Assembly programs. Also, take note of the processor and extension directives in the MASM programs (e.g., .686, .MMX, .XMM).

Program 8.1a *C++ Functions*

```
// for Xcode on macOS (Clang/LLVM)
#include <iostream>
#include <iomanip>
using namespace std;

extern "C" void asmMain();

extern "C" void printFloat(float f){
    cout << setprecision(7) << f << endl;
}

extern "C" void printDouble(double d){
    cout << setprecision(15) << d << endl;
}

int main(){
    asmMain();
    return 0;
}
```

```
// for Visual Studio on Windows and g++ on Linux (e.g., Ubuntu)
#include <iostream>
#include <iomanip>
using namespace std;

extern "C" void _asmMain();

extern "C" void _printFloat(float f){
    cout << setprecision(7) << f << endl;
}

extern "C" void _printDouble(double d){
    cout << setprecision(15) << d << endl;
}

int main(){
    _asmMain();
    return 0;
}
```

Program 8.1b *x87 FPU*

GAS	MASM	NASM
| ```
.extern _printFloat
.extern _printDouble

.data
value: .float 1.2

.bss
.lcomm r_value, 4
.lcomm f_result, 4
.lcomm d_result, 8

.text
.globl _asmMain
_asmMain:
push %ebp
movl %esp, %ebp

finit
fldpi
flds value
fadd %st(1), %st
fists r_value

fstps f_result
push $0
push f_result
call _printFloat
add $8, %esp

fstpl d_result
push d_result + 4
push d_result
call _printDouble
add $8, %esp

pop %ebp
ret
.end
``` | ```
.686
.MODEL FLAT, C
.STACK 4096

_printFloat  PROTO C
_printDouble PROTO C

.data
value    REAL4 1.2
r_value  REAL4 ?
f_result REAL4 ?
d_result REAL8 ?

.code
_asmMain PROC
push ebp
mov ebp, esp

finit
fldpi
fld value
fadd ST(0), ST(1)
fist r_value

fstp f_result
push 0
push f_result
call _printFloat
add esp, 8

fstp d_result
push DWORD PTR [d_result + 4]
push DWORD PTR [d_result]
call _printDouble
add esp, 8

pop ebp
ret
_asmMain ENDP
END
``` | ```
extern _printFloat
extern _printDouble

section .data
value: dd 1.2

section .bss
r_value: resd 1
f_result: resd 1
d_result: resq 1

section .text
global _asmMain
_asmMain:
push ebp
mov ebp, esp

finit
fldpi
fld DWORD [value]
fadd ST0, ST1
fist DWORD [r_value]

fstp DWORD [f_result]
push 0
push DWORD [f_result]
call _printFloat
add esp, 8

fstp QWORD [d_result]
push DWORD [d_result + 4]
push DWORD [d_result]
call _printDouble
add esp, 8

pop ebp
ret
``` |
```

Program 8.2 *x87 FPU Rounding control*

GAS	MASM	NASM
`.data`	`.686`	`section .data`
`default_cw: .word 0x0000`	`.MODEL FLAT, C`	`default_cw:  dw 0000h`
`nearest:    .word 0x0000`	`.STACK 4096`	`nearest:    dw 0000h`
`down:       .word 0x0400`		`down:       dw 0400h`
`up:         .word 0x0800`	`ExitProcess PROTO stdcall,`	`up:         dw 0800h`
`zero:       .word 0x0C00`	`dwExitCode:DWORD`	`zero:       dw 0C00h`
`.bss`	`.data`	`section .bss`
`.lcomm result, 4`	`default_cw   WORD 0000h`	`result: resd 1`
	`nearest      WORD 0000h`	
`.text`	`down          WORD 0400h`	`section .text`
`.globl _main`	`up            WORD 0800h`	`global _main`
`_main:`	`zero          WORD 0C00h`	`_main:`
	`result DWORD ?`	
`finit`		`finit`
`fstcw default_cw`	`.code`	`fstcw WORD [default_cw]`
`movw default_cw, %ax`	`_main PROC`	`mov ax, [default_cw]`
`andb S0b11110011, %ah`		`and ah, 11110011b`
`orw %ax, nearest`	`finit`	`or [nearest], ax`
`orw %ax, down`	`fstcw default_cw`	`or [down], ax`
`orw %ax, up`	`mov ax, default_cw`	`or [up], ax`
`orw %ax, zero`	`and ah, 11110011b`	`or [zero], ax`
	`or nearest, ax`	
`xor %ax, %ax`	`or down, ax`	`xor ax, ax`
`movw default_cw, %ax`	`or up, ax`	`mov ax, [default_cw]`
`movw nearest, %ax`	`or zero, ax`	`mov ax, [nearest]`
`movw down, %ax`		`mov ax, [down]`
`movw up, %ax`	`xor ax, ax`	`mov ax, [up]`
`movw zero, %ax`	`mov ax, default_cw`	`mov ax, [zero]`
	`mov ax, nearest`	
`fldcw nearest`	`mov ax, down`	`fldcw [nearest]`
	`mov ax, up`	
`fldpi`	`mov ax, zero`	`fldpi`
`frndint`		`frndint`
`fists result`	`fldcw nearest`	`fist DWORD [result]`
`movl result, %eax`		`mov eax, [result]`
	`fldpi`	
`pushl $0`	`frndint`	`mov eax, 1`
`subl S4, %esp`	`fist result`	`mov ebx, 0`
`movl S1, %eax`	`mov eax, result`	`int 80h`
`int $0x80`		
`.end`	`INVOKE ExitProcess, 0`	
	`_main ENDP`	
	`END`	

Program 8.3 MMX

GAS	MASM	NASM
| ```
.data
w1: .word 1, 2, 3, 4
w5: .word 5, 6, 7, 8
result: .quad 0

.text
.globl _main
_main:

movq w1, %mm0
movq w5, %mm1

paddsw %mm1, %mm0
movq %mm0, result

pushl $0
subl $4, %esp
movl $1, %eax
int $0x80
.end
``` | ```
.686
.MMX
.MODEL FLAT, C
.STACK 4096

ExitProcess PROTO stdcall,
dwExitCode:DWORD

.data
w1 WORD 1, 2, 3, 4
w5 WORD 5, 6, 7, 8
result QWORD 0

.code
_main PROC

lea eax, w1
lea ebx, w5
movq mm0, [eax]
movq mm1, [ebx]

paddsw mm0, mm1
movq result, mm0

INVOKE ExitProcess, 0
_main ENDP
END
``` | ```
section .data
w1: dw 1, 2, 3, 4
w5: dw 5, 6, 7, 8
result: dq 0

section .text
global _main
_main:

movq mm0, [w1]
movq mm1, [w5]

paddsw mm0, mm1
movq [result], mm0

mov eax, 1
mov ebx, 0
int 80h
``` |
```

Program 8.4 SSE Packed operations

GAS	MASM	NASM
| ```
.data
.balign 16
vectorA: .float 1.2, 3.4, 5.6,
7.8
vectorB: .float 7.8, 5.6, 3.4,
1.2

.bss
.lcomm result, 128

.text
.globl _main
_main:

movaps vectorA, %xmm0
addps  vectorB, %xmm0
movaps %xmm0, result

pushl $0
subl $4, %esp
movl $1, %eax
int $0x80
.end
``` | ```
.686
.XMM
.MODEL FLAT, C
.STACK 4096

ExitProcess PROTO stdcall,
dwExitCode:DWORD

.data
ALIGN 16
vectorA REAL4 1.2, 3.4, 5.6,
7.8
vectorB REAL4 7.8, 5.6, 3.4,
1.2
result  REAL4 ?, ?, ?, ?

.code
_main PROC

movaps xmm0, vectorA
addps  xmm0, vectorB
movaps result, xmm0

INVOKE ExitProcess, 0
_main ENDP
END
``` | ```
section .data
align 16
vectorA: dd 1.2, 3.4, 5.6,
7.8
vectorB: dd 7.8, 5.6, 3.4,
1.2

section .bss
result: resd 4

section .text
global _main
_main:

movaps xmm0, [vectorA]
addps  xmm0, [vectorB]
movaps [result], xmm0

mov eax, 1
mov ebx, 0
int 80h
``` |
```

Program 8.5 *SSE Scalar operations*

GAS	MASM	NASM
``.data
.balign 16
valueA: .float 1.2
pi: .double
3.14159265358979

.bss
.lcomm result, 4

.text
.globl _main
_main:

movss   valueA, %xmm0
addss   valueA, %xmm0
movss   %xmm0, result
movl   result, %eax

movsd pi, %xmm0

pushl $0
subl $4, %esp
movl $1, %eax
int $0x80
.end``` | ```.686
.XMM
.MODEL FLAT, C
.STACK 4096

ExitProcess PROTO stdcall,
dwExitCode:DWORD

.data
ALIGN 16
valueA REAL4 1.2
pi   REAL8 3.14159265358979
result REAL4 ?

.code
_main PROC

movss   xmm0, valueA
addss   xmm0, valueA
movss   result, xmm0
mov   eax, result

movsd   xmm0, pi

INVOKE ExitProcess, 0
_main ENDP
END``` | ```section .data
align 16
valueA: dd 1.2
pi: dq 3.14159265358979

section .bss
result: resd 1

section .text
global _main
_main:

movss   xmm0, [valueA]
addss   xmm0, [valueA]
movss   [result], xmm0
mov   eax, DWORD [result]

movsd   xmm0, [pi]

mov eax, 1
mov ebx, 0
int 80h``` |

Program 8.6 *SSE3*

GAS	MASM	NASM
``.data
.balign 16
vectorA: .float 1.2, 3.4,
5.6, 7.8
vectorB: .float 7.8, 5.6,
3.4, 1.2

.text
.globl _main
_main:

movaps vectorA, %xmm0
movaps vectorB, %xmm1
haddps %xmm1, %xmm0

pushl $0
subl $4, %esp
movl $1, %eax
int $0x80
.end``` | ```.686
.XMM
.MODEL FLAT, C
.STACK 4096

ExitProcess PROTO stdcall,
dwExitCode:DWORD

.data
ALIGN 16
vectorA REAL4 1.2, 3.4, 5.6, 7.8
vectorB REAL4 7.8, 5.6, 3.4, 1.2

.code
_main PROC

movaps xmm0, vectorA
movaps xmm1, vectorB
haddps xmm0, xmm1

INVOKE ExitProcess, 0
_main ENDP
END``` | ```section .data
align 16
vectorA: dd 1.2, 3.4,
5.6, 7.8
vectorB: dd 7.8, 5.6,
3.4, 1.2

section .text
global _main
_main:

movaps xmm0, [vectorA]
movaps xmm1, [vectorB]
haddps xmm0, xmm1

mov eax, 1
mov ebx, 0
int 80h``` |

Program 8.7 *SSE4*

GAS	MASM	NASM
| ```
.data
.balign 16
vectorA: .float 1.2, 3.4,
5.6, 7.8
vectorB: .float 7.8, 5.6,
3.4, 1.2

.text
.globl _main
_main:

movaps  vectorA, %xmm0
roundps $1, %xmm0, %xmm1
cvtps2dq %xmm1, %xmm2

movaps  vectorB, %xmm3
roundps $2, %xmm3, %xmm4
cvtps2dq %xmm4, %xmm5

pmulld  %xmm2, %xmm5

pushl $0
subl $4, %esp
movl $1, %eax
int $0x80
.end
``` | ```
.686
.XMM
.MODEL FLAT, C
.STACK 4096

ExitProcess PROTO stdcall,
dwExitCode:DWORD

.data
ALIGN 16
vectorA REAL4 1.2, 3.4,
5.6, 7.8
vectorB REAL4 7.8, 5.6,
3.4, 1.2

.code
_main PROC

movaps  xmm0, vectorA
roundps xmm1, xmm0, 1
cvtps2dq xmm2, xmm1

movaps  xmm3, vectorB
roundps xmm4, xmm3, 2
cvtps2dq xmm5, xmm4

pmulld  xmm5, xmm2

INVOKE ExitProcess, 0
_main ENDP
END
``` | ```
section .data
align 16
vectorA: dd 1.2, 3.4, 5.6,
7.8
vectorB: dd 7.8, 5.6, 3.4,
1.2

section .text
global _main
_main:

movaps  xmm0, [vectorA]
roundps xmm1, xmm0, 1
cvtps2dq xmm2, xmm1

movaps  xmm3, [vectorB]
roundps xmm4, xmm3, 2
cvtps2dq xmm5, xmm4

pmulld  xmm5, xmm2

mov eax, 1
mov ebx, 0
int 80h
``` |
```

Program 8.8 *AVX*

GAS	MASM	NASM

```.data```
```.balign 16```
```vectorA: .float 1.2, 3.4,```
```5.6, 7.8, 8.9, 9.0, 0.9, 9.8```
```vectorB: .float 7.8, 5.6,```
```3.4, 1.2, 0.1, 0.0, 8.1, -0.8```
```vectorC: .long 1, 1, 1, 1```
```vectorD: .long -2, -2, -2, -2```
 	
```.text```
```.globl _main```
```_main:```
 	
```vmovaps   vectorA, %ymm0```
```vmovaps   vectorB, %ymm1```
```vaddps   %ymm0, %ymm1, %ymm2```
 	
```vmovdqa   vectorC, %xmm3```
```vmovdqa   vectorC, %xmm4```
```vpsignd   vectorD, %xmm3,```
```%xmm4```
 	
```pushl $0```
```subl $4, %esp```
```movl $1, %eax```
```int $0x80```
```.end```
	```.686```
	```.XMM```
	```.MODEL FLAT, C```
	```.STACK 4096```
	
	```ExitProcess PROTO stdcall,```
	```dwExitCode:DWORD```
	
	```.data```
	```vectorA REAL4 1.2, 3.4, 5.6, 7.8,```
	```8.9, 9.0, 0.9, 9.8```
	```vectorB REAL4 7.8, 5.6, 3.4, 1.2,```
	```0.1, 0.0, 8.1, -0.8```
	```vectorC DWORD 1, 1, 1, 1```
	```vectorD DWORD -2, -2, -2, -2```
	
	```.code```
	```_main PROC```
	
	```lea eax, vectorA```
	```lea ebx, vectorB```
	```vmovups ymm0, YMMWORD PTR [eax]```
	```vmovups ymm1, YMMWORD PTR [ebx]```
	```vaddps ymm2, ymm1, ymm0```
	
	```lea eax, vectorC```
	```lea ebx, vectorD```
	```vmovdqa xmm3, XMMWORD PTR [eax]```
	```vmovdqa xmm4, XMMWORD PTR [ebx]```
	```vpsignd xmm4, xmm3, vectorD```
	
	```INVOKE ExitProcess, 0```
	```_main ENDP```
	```END```
		```section .data```
		```align 16```
		```vectorA: dd 1.2, 3.4, 5.6,```
		```7.8, 8.9, 9.0, 0.9, 9.8```
		```vectorB: dd 7.8, 5.6, 3.4,```
		```1.2, 0.1, 0.0, 8.1, -0.8```
		```vectorC: dd 1, 1, 1, 1```
		```vectorD: dd -2, -2, -2, -2```
		
		```section .text```
		```global _main```
		```_main:```
		
		```vmovaps ymm0, [vectorA]```
		```vmovaps ymm1, [vectorB]```
		```vaddps ymm2, ymm1, ymm0```
		
		```vmovdqa xmm3, [vectorC]```
		```vmovdqa xmm4, [vectorC]```
		```vpsignd xmm4, xmm3,```
		```vectorD]```
		
		```mov eax, 1```
		```mov ebx, 0```
		```int 80h```

Program 8.8 GAS and NASM versions use aligned data and thus the VMOVAPS (vector move aligned packed single-precision) instruction for moving vectorA and vectorB to *ymm* registers. The MASM version uses unaligned data and thus the VMOVUPS (vector move unaligned packed single-precision) instruction. The MASM program also demonstrates storing the address of a vector in a register and then using the YMMWORD and XMMWORD directives to move data. Alignment requirements, available directives, and data manipulation approaches will vary by platform. Consult the documentation for your chosen platform for specific details.

Investment Calculator (x86_64)

This section presents Program 8.9 – x86_64 Investment Calculator as shown in the **CHAPTER 8 CODE REVIEW** section for GAS. To link the C++ and Assembly code, see the 64-bit notes in **APPENDIX E: LINKING ASSEMBLY AND C++** for your chosen development environment.

Investment formula: $monthlyPayment = \dfrac{(interest * amountNeeded)}{(pow\ ((interest + 1),\ duration) - 1)}$

Program 8.9a *x86_64 Investment calculator, C++ functions*

```cpp
// for Xcode on macOS (Clang/LLVM)
#include <iostream>
#include <iomanip>

extern "C" void asmMain();

extern "C" void printString(char* s){
    std::cout << s;
    return;
}

extern "C" void printDouble(double d){
    std::cout.setf(std::ios::fixed);
    std::cout.setf(std::ios::showpoint);
    std::cout.precision(2);
    std::cout << d << std::endl;
    return;
}

extern "C" double getDouble(){
    double d;
    std::cin >> d;
    return d;
}

extern "C" int getInt(){
    int i;
    std::cin >> i;
    return i;
}

//main stub driver
int main(){
    asmMain();
    return 0;
}

// for Visual Studio on Windows and g++ on Linux (e.g., Ubuntu)
#include <iostream>
#include <iomanip>

extern "C" void _asmMain();

extern "C" void _printString(char* s){
    std::cout << s;
    return;
}

extern "C" void _printDouble(double d){
    std::cout.setf(std::ios::fixed);
    std::cout.setf(std::ios::showpoint);
    std::cout.precision(2);
    std::cout << d << std::endl;
    return;
}

extern "C" double _getDouble(){
    double d;
    std::cin >> d;
    return d;
}

extern "C" int _getInt(){
    int i;
    std::cin >> i;
    return i;
}

//main stub driver
int main(){
    _asmMain();
    return 0;
}
```

Take special note of some unique differences in the MASM version.

- The first message (`amountMessage`) starts with a carriage return and line feed (13, 10).
- The `_asmMain` and `_pow` functions must reserve 32 bytes of shadow space or an exception occurs.
- *rip*-relative addressing is not explicitly used in MASM code.

Program 8.9b *x86_64 Investment calculator, GAS*

Part 1	Part 2

<pre>.extern _printString
.extern _printDouble
.extern _getDouble
.extern _getInt
 	
.data
.balign 16
amountNeeded: .double 0.0
interestRate: .double 0.0
interest: .double 0.0
monthlyPayment: .double 0.0
duration: .quad   0
const100:   .double 100.0
const12:   .double 12.0
const1:   .double 1.0
 	
amountMessage: .asciz
"   Enter Amount Needed: $"
interestMessage: .asciz
"   Enter Interest Rate: "
durationMessage: .asciz
"Enter Duration (in months):   "
paymentMessage: .asciz
"   Monthly Payment Amount: $"
 	
.text
.globl _asmMain
_asmMain:
 	
pushq %rbp
movq   %rsp, %rbp
 	
leaq amountMessage(%rip), %rdi
callq _printString
callq _getDouble
movsd %xmm0, amountNeeded(%rip)
 	
leaq interestMessage(%rip), %rdi
callq _printString
callq _getDouble
 	
movsd const100(%rip), %xmm1
divsd %xmm1, %xmm0
movsd %xmm0, interestRate(%rip)</pre>
	<pre>leaq durationMessage(%rip), %rdi
	callq _printString
	callq _getInt
	movq %rax, duration(%rip)
	
	movsd const12(%rip), %xmm0
	movsd interestRate(%rip), %xmm1
	divsd %xmm0, %xmm1
	movsd %xmm1, interest(%rip)
	
	movsd interest(%rip), %xmm0
	movsd amountNeeded(%rip), %xmm1
	mulsd %xmm0, %xmm1
	movsd %xmm1, %xmm2
	
	addsd const1(%rip), %xmm0
	movq duration(%rip), %rdi
	callq _pow
	subsd const1(%rip), %xmm0
	vdivsd %xmm0, %xmm2, %xmm1
	movsd %xmm1, monthlyPayment(%rip)
	
	leaq paymentMessage(%rip), %rdi
	callq _printString
	movsd monthlyPayment(%rip), %xmm0
	callq _printDouble
	
	popq %rbp
	retq
	
	_pow:
	pushq %rbp
	movq %rsp, %rbp
	movq %rdi, %rcx
	decq %rcx
	movsd %xmm0, %xmm1
	
	exp:
	mulsd %xmm1, %xmm0
	loop exp
	
	popq %rbp
	retq
	
	.end</pre>

Program 8.9c *x86_64 Investment calculator, MASM*

Part 1	Part 2
| ```
ExitProcess PROTO
_printString PROTO
_printDouble PROTO
_getDouble PROTO
_getInt PROTO


.data
align 16
amountNeeded    REAL8 0.0
interestRate    REAL8 0.0
interest        REAL8 0.0
monthlyPayment  REAL8 0.0
duration        QWORD 0
const100        REAL8 100.0
const12         REAL8 12.0
const1          REAL8 1.0


amountMessage   BYTE
13, 10, "        Enter Amount Needed:  $".0
interestMessage BYTE
"       Enter Interest Rate:   ",0
durationMessage BYTE
"Enter Duration (in months):   ",0
paymentMessage  BYTE
"    Monthly Payment Amount:  $",0


.code
_asmMain PROC

push rbp
sub rsp, 20h
lea rbp, [rsp + 20h]

lea rcx, amountMessage
call _printString
call _getDouble
movsd amountNeeded, xmm0

lea rcx, interestMessage
call _printString
call _getDouble

movsd xmm1, const100
divsd xmm0, xmm1
movsd interestRate, xmm0
``` | ```
lea rcx, durationMessage
call _printString
call _getInt
mov duration, rax

movsd xmm0, const12
movsd xmm1, interestRate
divsd xmm1, xmm0
movsd interest, xmm1

movsd xmm0, interest
movsd xmm1, amountNeeded
mulsd xmm1, xmm0
movsd xmm2, xmm1

addsd xmm0, const1
mov rcx, duration
call _pow
subsd xmm0, const1
vdivsd xmm1, xmm2, xmm0
movsd monthlyPayment, xmm1

lea rcx, paymentMessage
call _printString
movsd xmm0, monthlyPayment
call _printDouble

lea rsp, [rbp]
pop rbp
ret
_asmMain ENDP

_pow PROC
push rbp
sub rsp, 20h
lea rbp, [rsp + 20h]
dec rcx
movsd xmm1, xmm0

exp:
mulsd xmm0, xmm1
loop exp

lea rsp, [rbp]
pop rbp
ret
_pow ENDP

END
``` |

Program 8.9d *x86_64 Investment calculator, NASM*

Part 1	Part 2
<pre>extern _printString
extern _printDouble
extern _getDouble
extern _getInt

section .data
align 16
amountNeeded: dq 0.0
interestRate: dq 0.0
interest: dq 0.0
monthlyPayment: dq 0.0
duration: dq 0
const100:   dq 100.0
const12:   dq 12.0
const1:   dq 1.0

amountMessage: db
"   Enter Amount Needed: $",0
interestMessage: db
"   Enter Interest Rate: ",0
durationMessage: db
"Enter Duration (in months):   ",0
paymentMessage: db
"   Monthly Payment Amount: $",0

section .text
global _asmMain
_asmMain:

push   rbp
mov rbp, rsp

lea rdi, [rel amountMessage]
call _printString
call _getDouble
movsd [rel amountNeeded], xmm0

lea rdi, [rel interestMessage]
call _printString
call _getDouble

movsd xmm1, [rel const100]
divsd xmm0, xmm1
movsd [rel interestRate], xmm0</pre> | <pre>lea rdi, [rel durationMessage]
call _printString
call _getInt
mov [rel duration], rax

movsd xmm0, [rel const12]
movsd xmm1, [rel interestRate]
divsd xmm1, xmm0
movsd [rel interest], xmm1

movsd xmm0, [rel interest]
movsd xmm1, [rel amountNeeded]
mulsd xmm1, xmm0
movsd xmm2, xmm1

addsd xmm0, [rel const1]
mov rdi, [rel duration]
call _pow
subsd xmm0, [rel const1]
vdivsd xmm1, xmm2, xmm0
movsd [rel monthlyPayment], xmm1

lea rdi, [rel paymentMessage]
call _printString
movsd xmm0, [rel monthlyPayment]
call _printDouble

pop rbp
ret

_pow:
push rbp
mov rbp, rsp
mov rcx, rdi
dec rcx
movsd xmm1, xmm0

exp:
mulsd xmm0, xmm1
loop exp

pop rbp
ret</pre> |

Inline Assembly and Macros

Objectives

- Examine usefulness of inline Assembly
- Create inline Assembly statements
- Compare macros with function calls
- Create Assembly macros

Outline

Web Resources

Wikis

- http://wiki.osdev.org/Inline_Assembly
- https://en.wikipedia.org/wiki/Memory_ordering

Developer

- https://msdn.microsoft.com/en-us/library/4ks26t93.aspx (Microsoft Inline Assembler)
- https://gcc.gnu.org/onlinedocs/gcc/Using-Assembly-Language-with-C.html (Clang/GCC)
- https://gcc.gnu.org/onlinedocs/gcc/Machine-Constraints.html (x86 Machine Constraints)
- http://www.ibm.com/developerworks/library/l-ia/ (Inline Assembly for x86 in Linux)
- https://sourceware.org/binutils/docs/as/Macro.html (GAS Macros)
- https://msdn.microsoft.com/en-us/library/d4chx59e.aspx (MASM Macros)
- http://www.nasm.us/doc/nasmdoc4.html (NASM Macros)

Introduction

The purpose of this chapter is to familiarize you with the programming concepts of inline Assembly and macros. First, we discuss the usefulness of inline Assembly followed by some code examples and cautions associated with inline Assembly. Second, we compare macros with functions and then present examples of writing Assembly macros. The techniques presented in this chapter give a programmer more options when writing and fine-tuning programs.

Inline Assembly

Inline Assembly is a way of embedding Assembly code into a high-level language. Throughout this book we have used C++ for high-level context and examples, which remains the same for this chapter. Although a language like C++ is extremely flexible and powerful, sometimes a programmer wants or needs to code closer to the metal. Example situations are programmer-controlled optimizations and hardware control.

One way to integrate Assembly with high-level code is to follow the process discussed in **Chapter 6** and **Appendix E: Linking Assembly and C++**: to create an Assembly file with the desired Assembly code written as functions and then call the functions from C++. However, the function and linking approach has some overhead in terms of setup and function calls. Writing inline Assembly is an alternative and potentially simpler approach, depending on the situation. It always depends.

Compiler Specifics

Writing inline Assembly assumes we are working with a high-level codebase, so we are dealing with compilers as opposed to assemblers. Compiler support and available features for inline Assembly vary from compiler to compiler. When discussing Assembly throughout this book, we have provided examples for the three most common assemblers: GAS, MASM, and NASM. As we move the discussion to compilers, we provide inline Assembly examples for **Clang**, **GCC**, and **Visual C++**. Doing so provides useful examples for most OS platforms. In most cases, Clang and GCC are identical in form and function.

> **!** ATTENTION: Clang is the default compiler in Xcode as of version 4.2. Clang also can be used on Linux and Windows. Clang and GCC use the AT&T Assembly syntax by default (can be switched to Intel syntax), while Visual C++ uses Intel syntax.

Inline Assembly code is assembled differently depending on the compiler. In Xcode, Clang is paired with the LLVM integrated assembler, which handles inline Assembly statements. GCC, as part of the translation pipeline (see **Chapter 1**), creates an Assembly file from the high-level code before translation to machine code. So assuming the inline Assembly code is not modified or optimized out during compilation, GCC copies inline Assembly code to the Assembly output (.s) file, which is then passed along to the GNU assembler (GAS) with the rest of the code. In Microsoft's Visual Studio, Visual C++ has and uses a built-in assembler to handle inline Assembly statements, as opposed to using a separate assembler such as MASM.

> LEARNING: Microsoft's x64 C/C++ compiler does not support inline Assembly and instead uses compiler intrinsics that map to low-level instructions. Intrinsics are discussed in **Appendix I: Intrinsics**.
> https://msdn.microsoft.com/en-us/library/wbk4z78b.aspx

Inline Statements

C++ compilers often provide a keyword for inline statements such as `asm` or `__asm`. Let us start with a simple inline Assembly statement. Example 9.1 sends an interrupt to set a debugging breakpoint at runtime.

Example 9.1 Inline Assembly interrupt

Clang/GCC	Visual C++
`asm ("int $3");`	`__asm int 3`

Like Assembly more generally, inline Assembly has many subtle complexities. Examine the inline Assembly templates in Table 9.1 and the comparative examples in Table 9.2.

Table 9.1 Inline Assembly templates

Clang/GCC basic	`asm ("instruction 1 \n\t instruction 2");`
	
	`asm ("instruction 1 \n\t"`
	`      "instruction 2" ;`

Clang/GCC extended	`asm ("instruction 1 \n\t"`
	`      "instruction 2"`
	`       : output operands`
	`       : input operands`
	`       : clobbers);`

Visual C++ single statement	`__asm instruction 1`
Visual C++ block	`__asm {instruction 1` `          instruction 2};`

Table 9.2 Inline Assembly examples

Clang/GCC basic	`asm ("movl $42, %eax \n\t inc %eax");`
	
	`asm ("movl $42, %eax \n\t"`
	`      "inc %eax");`

Clang/GCC extended	`asm ("movl $42, %%eax \n\t"`
	`      "inc %%eax"`
	`       :`
	`       :`
	`       : "%eax");`

Visual C++ single statement	`__asm mov eax, 42`
Visual C++ block	`__asm {mov eax, 42` `          inc eax};`

In Clang/GCC, the `asm` keyword is followed by parentheses, the code is in quotes as a string, and the semicolon is required. The newline and tab characters (`\n\t`) separate statements in the string. In Visual C++, the `__asm` keyword can be followed by braces if it contains multiple statements or omitted if a single statement, quotes are not used, and the semicolon is optional.

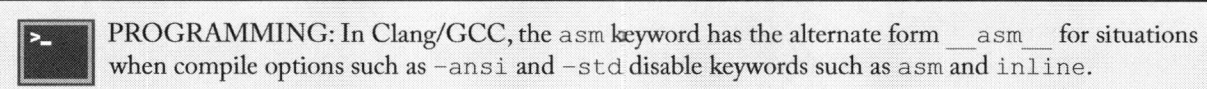 PROGRAMMING: In Clang/GCC, the `asm` keyword has the alternate form `__asm__` for situations when compile options such as `-ansi` and `-std` disable keywords such as `asm` and `inline`.

Notice that Clang and GCC have basic and extended forms. **Basic asm** should be avoided whenever possible as it may behave inconsistently when accessing global variables, and it assumes no changes are made to general purpose registers. However, basic asm does not have to be in a C/C++ function, so it can be used to issue assembler directives and write global Assembly functions. Also, C/C++ functions declared as `naked` (no prologue and epilogue code is generated by the compiler) require use of basic asm in order write the custom prologue and epilogue code for such functions. **Extended asm** allows for more fine-tuned control of outputs, inputs, and register usage. For consistency, the remainder of this section uses extended asm for Clang/GCC. Extended asm in Clang/GCC and all inline Assembly in Visual C++ must exist inside a C/C++ function.

> ⚠ ATTENTION: GCC does not parse inline Assembly instructions and does not even know if statements are valid. Clang/LLVM is better at issuing debug information about invalid inline Assembly syntax, but decrypting error messages or locations can be difficult due to the template design of asm statements and the fact that debuggers (e.g., GDB, LLDB) do not step through inline Assembly instructions; the entire asm statement is treated as a single step. To step through inline statements, you can manually add "int $3" instructions anywhere you want a breakpoint for debugging. Visual Studio does allow for stepping through x86 inline Assembly without the use of INT.

Program 9.1 *Simple inline Assembly*

Clang/GCC	Visual C++

```#include <iostream>```
```using namespace std;```
 	
```int main(){```
 	
```int var1 = 1234, var2;```
 	
```   asm ("mov %1, %%eax \n\t"```
```   "add $2, %%eax \n\t"```
```   "mov %%eax, %0 \n\t"```
```   :"=r" (var2)   /* %0: Out */```
```   :"r" (var1)   /* %1: In */```
```   :"%eax"   /* Overwrite */```
```   );```
 	
```   cout << var2 << endl;```
```   return 0;```
```}```
	```#include <iostream>```
	```using namespace std;```
	
	```int main(){```
	
	```int var1 = 1234, var2;```
	
	``` __asm {mov eax, var1```
	``` add eax, 2```
	``` mov var2, eax```
	``` }```
	
	``` cout << var2 << endl;```
	``` return 0;```
	```}```

Program 9.1 is a short program for comparing how access to variables is handled and several other specifics of inline Assembly.

> PROGRAMMING: Comments in inline Assembly can follow either stand-alone Assembly or C++ formats, though we highly recommend the latter for consistency.

First, recognize that the inline Assembly statement is inside a C++ function, the main function. Parameter access varies by compiler. In Visual C++, you can directly refer to accessible C variables (e.g., var1 is simply var1). In Clang/GCC, parameter access is more complex. Input and output (I/O) variables used in inline statements must be stated in the input and output lists in the assembler template. I/O lists can be empty and are maxed at 30 total.

Clang/GCC format for inputs and outputs

```
[asmSymbolicName] "constraint" (CvariableName)
```

The asmSymbolicName can be any valid identifier name, including already defined variables such as the C variable name that the I/O operand references. **Constraints** provide information related to the use and placement of the operand. Constraints are a letter or series of letters (see Machine Constraints in the **Web Resources**). Output constraints start with a modifier, which is then followed by a letter or a series of letters. The two most common modifiers are '=' (meaning the operand will be overwritten) and '+' meaning the operand will both be read from and written to (the parameter is both an input and an output). Use '&' to avoid overlapping use of registers for inputs and outputs throughout the inline Assembly.

Another part of the Clang/GCC inline Assembly template is the **clobbers** list. The clobbers list identifies registers that will be used as part of the inline Assembly instructions, and for which instructions are generated to save the initial values and restore them upon `asm` statement completion. Compilers also avoid using clobbered registers when selecting registers for input and output operands. Not listing registers used in inline Assembly statements is likely to lead to unintended consequences and problems in your code!

> 📖 **LEARNING:** Refer to the GCC documentation on extended asm for more specific content on material presented in this section. For example, special clobber arguments such as `"cc"` and `"memory"`.
> https://gcc.gnu.org/onlinedocs/gcc/Extended-Asm.html

Examine the code snippets in Example 9.2 and assume the line of code `int var1 = 1234, var2;` precedes each `asm` statement. The code moves the input parameter (`var1`) to *eax*, adds 2, and stores the value in the output parameter (`var2`).

Example 9.2 Inline parameter access in Clang/GCC

Example	Code	Disassembly
9.2.1 Zero-based position and Register constraint with clobber	```asm (" mov %1, %%eax \n\t" " add $2, %%eax \n\t" " mov %%eax, %0 \n\t" : "=r" (var2) : "r" (var1) : "%eax");```	```movl $0x4d2, 0x1c(%esp) movl 0x1c(%esp), %edx movl %eax, 0x14(%esp) movl %edx, %eax addl $0x2, %eax movl %eax, %edx movl %edx, 0x18(%esp)```
9.2.2 Zero-based position and Register constraint without clobber	```asm (" mov %1, %%eax \n\t" " add $2, %%eax \n\t" " mov %%eax, %0 \n\t" : "=r" (var2) : "r" (var1) :);```	```movl $0x4d2, 0x1c(%esp) movl 0x1c(%esp), %edx movl %edx, %eax addl $0x2, %eax movl %eax, %edx movl %edx, 0x18(%esp)```
9.2.3 Symbolic Names and Memory constraint with clobber	```asm (" mov %[asm_var2], %%eax \n\t" " add $2, %%eax \n\t" " mov %%eax, %[asm_var1] \n\t" : [asm_var2] "=m" (var2) : [asm_var1] "m" (var1) : "%eax");```	```movl $0x4d2, 0x1c(%esp) movl %eax, 0x14(%esp) movl 0x1c(%esp), %eax addl $0x2, %eax movl %eax, 0x18(%esp)```
9.2.4 Symbolic Names and Register and Memory constraints without clobber	```asm (" mov %[var2], %%eax \n\t" " add $2, %%eax \n\t" " mov %%eax, % var1] \n\t" : [var2] "=rm" var2) : [var1] "rm" (var1) :);```	```movl $0x4d2, 0x1c(%esp) movl 0x1c(%esp), %edx movl %edx, 0x14(%esp) movl 0x14(%esp), %eax addl $0x2, %eax movl %eax, 0x18(%esp)```

In Examples 9.2.1 and 9.2.2, we use zero-based position, meaning no symbolic names are used for the parameters in the Assembly and so parameters are referred to beginning with `%0` for the first output parameter. The number increases by one for each output parameter and continues until the last input parameter. In Example 9.2.3, we use a symbolic name that differentiates between the parameters as referenced in the inline Assembly (`asm_var#`) and the C instance of the variables (`var#`). In Example 9.2.4, we use the same symbolic C names in the Assembly.

In Examples 9.2.1 and 9.2.2, we identify the parameter constraints as `'r'`, meaning the parameters should be placed in a general purpose integer register prior to statement execution. As shown in the disassembly, the compiler chose *edx* as the register to satisfy the constraints. In Example 9.2.3, we use the `'m'` constraint, indicating memory access will suffice, so a register is not used as an in-between. As shown in the disassembly for 9.2.3, the value is moved directly from its memory location to *eax*. In example 9.2.4, we identify both register and memory as constraints, which again the disassembly reveals.

Table 9.3 presents common x86 constraints (support of listed and non-listed constraints is machine dependent and will vary).

Table 9.3 Common x86 inline constraints

Constraint	Meaning
r or R	a general purpose register
q	lower 8 bits of supported registers (e.g., *al*)
Q	upper 8 bits of supported registers (e.g., *ah*)
a, b, c, d	*ax/eax/rax, bx/ebx/rbx, cx/ecx/rcx, dx/edx/rdx*
S	*si/esi/rsi*
D	*di/edi/rdi*
A	*ax/eax/rax* and *dx/edx/rdx* for doubleword results
f	any x87 FPU stack register
t	Top of x87 FPU stack (*st0*)
u	second from Top of x87 FPU stack (*st1*)
y	any MMX register
x	any SSE register
m	any memory operand
o	*offsettable* memory operand
V	not *offsettable* memory operand
g	any general register, memory, or immediate allowed
X	any operand whatsoever
p	an operand that is a valid memory address (pointer)
i	an immediate constant integer operand (e.g., `"i"` `(5)`)
F	an immediate constant floating-point operand

In Examples 9.2.1 and 9.2.3, we state that *eax* will be clobbered, overwritten, in the Assembly instructions. As a result, **instructions** are generated to save the value of *eax* so it can be restored after execution.

In AT&T Assembly syntax, registers begin with `%`. Notice in the inline Assembly that parameters start with a single percent sign (`%`) and registers with two (`%%`). The `%` character outputs specific other characters in inline Assembly code (i.e., a form of escape character). `"%%"` outputs a single `'%'` in code; `"%="` outputs a unique number for every instance of the `asm` statement in the codebase (useful for creating and referring to labels); while `"%{"`, `"%|"`, and `"%}"` output the trailing characters to the Assembly code, since the characters have reserved meaning regarding assembler dialects. So, to produce `"%eax"` the inline equivalent is `"%%eax"`. As for registers in the clobbers list, only one `%` is required.

With regard to floating-point inline Assembly, we have provided Program 9.2, which presents x87 and SSE scalar examples to help you get started.

Program 9.2 *Floating-point inline Assembly*

Clang/GCC	Visual C++
| ```cpp
#include <iostream>
using namespace std;

int main(){

float var = 0;

// x87 floating-point example
    asm("finit \n\t"
        "fldpi \n\t"
        "fsqrt \n\t"
        "fstps %[var]"
        :[var] "=m" (var)
        :
        :
        );

    cout << var << endl;

// SSE scalar example
    var = 1.2;

    asm("movss %0, %%xmm0 \n\t"
        "addss %0, %%xmm0 \n\t"
        "movss %%xmm0, %0 \n\t"
        : "+x" (var)
        :
        : "%xmm0"
    );

    cout << var << endl;

    return 0;
}
``` | ```cpp
#include <iostream>
using namespace std;

int main(){

float var = 0;

// x87 floating-point example
    __asm{finit
            fldpi
            fsqrt
            fstp var
    };

    cout << var << endl;

// SSE scalar example
    var = 1.2;

    __asm{movss xmm0, var
            addss xmm0, var
            movss var, xmm0
    };

    cout << var << endl;

    return 0;
}
``` |

Assembly Dialects

As already mentioned, Clang and GCC use the **AT&T syntax** by default, and Visual C++ uses the **Intel syntax**. However, both Clang and GCC support multiple Assembly dialects for inline Assembly. The advantage of switching from AT&T to Intel syntax is that you may find the code more readable. Compare the two inline Assembly statements in Example 9.3.

Example 9.3 Clang/GCC inline Assembly dialects

AT&T dialect	Intel dialect
| ```cpp
asm(".att_syntax \n\t"
    "mov $5, %%eax \n\t"
    "mov $3, %%ebx \n\t"
    "add %%ebx, %%eax \n\t"
    :
    :
    : "%eax", "%ebx"
    );
``` | ```cpp
asm(".intel_syntax \n\t"
    "mov eax, 5 \n\t"
    "mov ebx, 5 \n\t"
    "add eax, ebx \n\t"
    :
    :
    : "eax", "ebx"
    );
``` |

As Example 9.3 illustrates, an easy way to use a particular syntax for an inline Assembly statement is to identify the syntax you want to use with the first directive (.att_syntax or .intel_syntax).

PROGRAMMING: The Assembly dialect (att or intel) can be set as a compile option for Clang and GCC by using the -masm option control.

For x86 targets, Clang/GCC supports multiple dialects, which is useful if your code needs to support both AT&T and Intel syntaxes. The code takes on the form {dialect0 | dialect1...} and samples are shown in Example 9.4.

Example 9.4 Multiple dialects in Clang/GCC

```
asm("mov{l $5, %%ebx | ebx, 5} \n\t"
    "mov{l $3, %%ecx | ecx, 3} \n\t"
    "xchg{l}\t {%%}ebx,\t {%%}ecx \n\t"
    :
    :
    :
    );
```

A couple of other possibilities are evident in Example 9.4. First is the use of the size suffix 'l' for long in AT&T syntax. Second is the use of the '\t' between parts of an instruction (in the xchg instruction).

Cautions

The use of inline Assembly demands some caution. First and most important is portability. One purpose of a language like C++ is cross-platform development. But as soon as you write an inline Assembly statement, compatibility becomes an issue. If cross-platform support is necessary for a program, the code must be architected in a way that it handles inline Assembly components correctly (via use of defines, includes, headers, etc.).

A second caution is that of directive support. While the x86 instruction set is generally supported in inline Assembly, assembler directive support varies. For example, remember Visual C++ uses an integrated assembler, not MASM, so the directives supported are different. Data directives (e.g., DB/BYTE, DD/DWORD) are not supported since data must be declared in the C++ code. Other MASM directives such as MACRO, REPT, DUP, and STRUCT are not supported by the Visual C++ inline assembler, while directives such as EVEN and ALIGN are supported. Consult the documentation for your specific compiler and integrated assembler for information on directive support.

A third major caution is that of optimization. Optimization generally has two forms: software (compiler optimizations) and hardware (CPU optimizations). Regarding compiler optimization, running inline Assembly code in Debug mode may look and behave close to what you are expecting, though the compiler may add steps such as saving register data, creating variable copies based on constraints, and aligning the stack. But in Release mode, sophisticated optimizers often reorganize code and eliminate what the compiler considers to be unnecessary steps and outputs.

Several measures can be taken to limit optimizations and keep your inline Assembly intact and executing as written. One measure is to declare the asm statement as **volatile,** as shown in Example 9.5. This disables some compiler optimizations, however CPU optimizations may still take place. For Clang/GCC, basic inline Assembly is implicitly volatile, whereas extended Assembly is not.

Example 9.5 asm volatile

```
asm volatile ("movl $42, %%eax \n\t"
              "inc %%eax"
              :
              :
              : "%eax");
```

Another measure is to use what are known as **memory barriers** or **fences,** which are most applicable to modern processors with multi-threading. The purpose of barriers/fences is to prevent reordering of instructions by the compiler or CPU. An in-depth discussion of volatile and barriers is beyond the scope of this chapter, but we have provided some formal and informal online sources in a LEARNING note to get you started.

Inline Assembly can be a useful tool for a programmer, but its use does warrant careful consideration.

LEARNING: This list contains links to volatile and memory barrier documentation. The sources are meant to provide a starting point.

- https://gcc.gnu.org/onlinedocs/gcc/Extended-Asm.html#Volatile
- https://brooker.co.za/blog/2013/01/06/volatile.html
- https://en.wikipedia.org/wiki/Memory_barrier
- https://www.kernel.org/doc/Documentation/memory-barriers.txt
- http://bruceblinn.com/linuxinfo/MemoryBarriers.html
- http://yarchive.net/comp/linux/memory_barriers.html
- https://msdn.microsoft.com/en-us/library/f20w0x5c(v=vs.140).aspx

Macros

Assembly macros are another coding technique that can be useful to a programmer. A **macro** can be thought of as a module, a sequence of instructions, that is invoked by name. Assembly macros work like C++ *inline* functions (not to be confused with inline Assembly statements), which, when called, replace the original call line with the sequence of statements/instructions that comprise the macro. Such is the case for every instance the macro is invoked.

Macros versus Functions

What is the difference between a function (**Chapter 6**) and a macro? Functions are best for long sequences of repeatable code. Only one instance of a function exists and when the function is called, control transfers to the function in memory. The overhead of passing parameters, setting up and cleaning up stack space, and so on is more efficient than having multiple instances of long or complex functions.

Macros are best for short and simple sequences of repeatable code. When a program is assembled, the assembler replaces every instance of the macro name with the sequence of instructions the macro represents. The result is multiple instances of the same code sequence, but the overhead of a function call is alleviated. What macros and functions have in common is that they both allow arguments (parameters). In the case of a function, arguments are passed at runtime. In the case of a macro, arguments are placed at assembly time.

Defining and Calling Macros

Table 9.4 shows the general macro syntax for the three assemblers. It is worth noting how the arguments are referenced within a macro. GAS prefixes arguments with a \ as in \arg1, NASM uses [%#] with the # starting at 1, while in MASM the argument name is unmodified.

Table 9.4 Assembly macro syntax

GAS	`.macro identifier arg1, arg2...`
	`# instructions`
	`# args referenced as \arg1, \arg2...`
	`.endm`

MASM	`identifier MACRO arg1, arg2...`
	`; instructions`
	`; args referenced as arg1, arg2...`
	`ENDM`

NASM	`%macro identifier argCount`
	`; args referenced as [%1], [%2]...`
	`%endmacro`

In Program 9.3, we demonstrate a simple addition macro.

Program 9.3 *Addition macro*

GAS	MASM	NASM

```.macro intAdd dest,```
 ```source1, source2```
 ```   movl \source1, %eax```
 ```   addl \source2, %eax```
 ```   movl %eax, \dest```
 ```.endm```
 	
 ```.data```
 ```intA: .long 2```
 ```intB: .long 4```
 ```intC: .long 3```
 ```intD: .long 7```
 ```result: .long 0```
 	
 ```.text```
 ```.globl _main```
 ```_main:```
 	
 ```intAdd result, intA, intB```
 ```intAdd result, intC, intD```
 	
 ```pushl $0```
 ```subl $4, %esp```
 ```movl $1, %eax```
 ```int $0x80```
 ```.end```
	```.386```
	 ```.MODEL FLAT, stdcall```
	 ```.STACK 4096```
	
	 ```ExitProcess PROTO,```
	 ```dwExitCode:DWORD```
	
	 ```intAdd MACRO dest, source1,```
	 ```source2```
	 ``` mov eax, source1```
	 ``` add eax, source2```
	 ``` mov dest, eax```
	 ```ENDM```
	
	 ```.DATA```
	 ```intA DWORD 2```
	 ```intB DWORD 4```
	 ```intC DWORD 3```
	 ```intD DWORD 7```
	 ```result DWORD 0```
	
	 ```.CODE```
	 ```_main PROC```
	
	 ```intAdd result, intA, intB```
	 ```intAdd result, intC, intD```
	
	 ```INVOKE ExitProcess, 0```
	 ```_main ENDP```
	 ```END```
		```%macro intAdd 3```
		 ``` mov eax, [%2]```
		 ``` add eax, [%3]```
		 ``` mov [%1], eax```
		 ```%endmacro```
		
		 ```section .data```
		 ```intA: dd 2```
		 ```intB: dd 4```
		 ```intC: dd 3```
		 ```intD: dd 7```
		 ```result: dd 0```
		
		 ```section .text```
		 ```global _main```
		 ```_main:```
		
		 ```intAdd result, intA,```
		 ```intB```
		 ```intAdd result, intC,```
		 ```intD```
		
		 ```mov eax, 1```
		 ```mov ebx, 0```
		 ```int 80h```

In Program 9.3, the only lines of code in _main are the calls to the intAdd macro. When assembled and executing, the code would look like the instructions shown in Example 9.6 within _main.

Example 9.6 Expanded program 9.3 addition macros

GAS	MASM	NASM

```_main:```
 	
 ```movl intA, %eax```
 ```addl intB, %eax```
 ```movl %eax, result```
 ```movl intC, %eax```
 ```addl intD, %eax```
 ```movl %eax, result```
	```_main PROC```
	
	 ```mov eax, intA```
	 ```add eax, intB```
	 ```mov result, eax```
	 ```mov eax, intC```
	 ```add eax, intD```
	 ```mov result, eax```
		```_main:```
		
		 ```mov eax, DWORD [intA]```
		 ```add eax, DWORD [intB]```
		 ```mov [result], eax```
		 ```mov eax, DWORD [intC]```
		 ```add eax, DWORD [intD]```
		 ```mov [result], eax```

Macros can be placed outside or inside segments, but stay consistent with the style. Another good way to handle macros is to place all macros or related macros in a separate file and then include the file via the INCLUDE Assembly directive (see **Chapter 7 Code Review**).

An additional characteristic of macros in MASM is that arguments can be set as required.

MASM

```
identifier MACRO arg1:REQ
```

Macros are useful for a variety of purposes, but some good examples are custom prologue and epilogue routines, parameter passing for functions, and a simple way of naming and writing repetitive but complex single-line instructions.

Summary

In this chapter we showed how to use inline Assembly in C++ programs and macros in Assembly programs. Inline Assembly and macros are techniques that can offer programming solutions for specific tasks. As with all programming techniques, it is important to consider pros and cons, such as compatibly and overhead. To maintain your programmer dignity, do not confuse C++ inline functions with inline Assembly, as the former is the C++ equivalent of Assembly macros.

Key Terms

AT&T syntax

basic asm

Clang

clobbers

constraints

extended asm

GCC

inline Assembly

Intel syntax

macro

memory barriers (fences)

Visual C++

volatile

Questions

Short Answer

1. Many compilers use _____ assemblers to handle inline Assembly.
2. Inline Assembly statements generally begin with the _____ prefix.
3. Clang and GCC support two forms of inline Assembly: _____ and _____.
4. _____ provide information related to the use and placement of I/O operands.
5. In Clang/GCC inline Assembly, output operands require a _____ that indicates read/write status.
6. An "rm" constraint indicates that both a _____ and _____ are constraints of the operation.
7. The _____ constraint is necessary to indicate an SSE register placement.
8. With regard to Assembly code, AT&T and Intel are formally known as _____.
9. While generally supportive of the x86 instruction set, integrated assembler support of _____ is more limited.
10. Compiler optimizations can potentially be limited by the use of _____.
11. The Assembly equivalent of an `inline` C++ function is a _____.
12. Functions and macros both allow for _____.
13. Assembly macros are invoked in GAS, MASM, and NASM by stating the macro _____ followed by comma-separated arguments.
14. Macros can be placed inside or outside of Assembly program _____.
15. The REQ attribute can be used to require a macro argument in the _____ assembler.

True/False

1. The interrupt code for a debugging breakpoint is 1. (T/F)
2. In Visual C++ inline Assembly, registers used must be listed as clobbered. (T/F)
3. A variable name used in C++ code also can be used as a symbolic name in Clang/GCC inline Assembly. (T/F)
4. The use of the `volatile` keyword in an `asm` statement guarantees that absolutely no optimizations will happen regarding that portion of the code. (T/F)
5. The MACRO directive is allowed in Visual C++ inline Assembly. (T/F)

Assignments

9.1 Inline Assembly and floating-point arithmetic

Write a C++ program with inline Assembly. The C++ code should get two floating-point values from the user. Then with inline Assembly, perform three different arithmetic operations using a combination of the user parameters and FPU/SSE/AVX instructions. After each computation, save the result in a programmer-defined variable. Print the results to the console using C++. You can choose the arithmetic operations. You also are encouraged to use constants such as π, and instructions such as FSQRT, SQRTSS, and SQRTSD.

9.2 Macros and floating-point arithmetic

Write an Assembly program that defines three macros and tests (invokes) each. Macro #1 should perform floating-point subtraction on two parameters. Macro #2 should perform floating-point multiplication on two parameters. Macro #3 is your choice. You can use programmer-defined data for the parameters, and the results should either be stored in memory or printed to the console. All code should be written in Assembly.

9.3 Encryption with inline Assembly (Challenge Assignment)

Write a C++ program that takes a text file as input, allows the user to select whether to encrypt or decrypt, then uses inline Assembly to encrypt or decrypt the data, and finally prints the desired version of the file. The encryption/decryption process must be a minimum of five steps. Consider using techniques such as XOR and bit shifting as possibilities for character encryption.

Advanced Processor and System Architecture

Objectives

- Examine relevant connections between computer architecture and OS architecture
- Identify system management registers
- Distinguish between processor modes
- Distinguish between memory models
- Generate system calls using Assembly instructions, libraries, and APIs
- Use varying paths for handling system calls

Outline

1. Web Resources
2. Introduction
3. Processor and System Capabilities
   a. System Registers
   b. Processor Modes
   c. Memory Models
   d. Code Example
4. Interrupts and System Calls
   a. Software Interrupts
   b. Hardware Interrupts
   c. Using INT (Old School)
   d. SYSENTER, SYSCALL, and Libraries/APIs (New School)
5. Summary
6. Key Terms
7. Code Review
8. Questions
   a. Short Answer
   b. True/False
9. Assignments

Web Resources

Wikis

- https://en.wikipedia.org/wiki/X86#Operating_modes
- https://en.wikipedia.org/wiki/X86_memory_segmentation
- https://en.wikipedia.org/wiki/System_call
- https://en.wikipedia.org/wiki/Global_Descriptor_Table
- http://wiki.osdev.org/GDT_Tutorial
- https://en.wikipedia.org/wiki/Interrupt
- http://wiki.osdev.org/Interrupt_Descriptor_Table

Developer

- http://www.intel.com/content/www/us/en/processors/architectures-software-developer-manuals.html (Intel Developer Manuals)
- https://github.com/hjl-tools/x86-psABI/wiki/X86-psABI (AMD64 ABI)
- https://msdn.microsoft.com/library/windows/desktop/hh920508.aspx (Windows API Index)

Introduction

Chapter 10 satisfies two objectives and is crucially important to the overall understanding of Assembly programming and computer architecture. The first objective is to supplement other content in the book (especially **Chapter 2**) with further detail on processor and system architecture. We introduce system registers, processor modes, and memory models. The second objective is to introduce the programming topics of interrupts and system calls (alluded to in **Chapter 9**), which enhance your ability to accomplish low-level tasks. The programs and examples illustrate how system calls can be invoked in a variety of ways on a variety of platforms. Get ready to enter a rabbit hole and beware the acronyms.

Processor and System Capabilities

System Registers

In **Chapter 2** we introduced the registers available in x86 and x86_64 architectures. However, we did not discuss certain registers that are specifically for system needs. In this section, we briefly introduce some of the x86 system registers and re-introduce segment registers. Knowledge of system registers will help you understand other portions of this chapter.

System registers include the following:

- **Control registers** – indicate the processor mode and characteristics of executing tasks
  - ∘ *cr0* through *cr4*; *cr1* is reserved
  - ∘ *cr8* aka Task Priority Register (*tpr*) – used to prioritize external interrupts, 64-bit only
- **Memory-management registers** – specify locations of descriptor tables used in Protected Mode
  - ∘ *gdtr* – Global Descriptor Table Register
  - ∘ *ldtr* – Local Descriptor Table Register
  - ∘ *idtr* – Interrupt Descriptor Table Register
  - ∘ *tr* – Task Register
- **Machine-specific registers (MSRs)** – used to control and report processor performance. Some are specifically related to system calls (more on MSRs later).

> **PROGRAMMING:** Each of the memory management registers has corresponding load and store instructions: LGDT/SGDT, LLDT/SLDT, LIDT/SIDT, and LTR/STR. The load instructions are *only* used by system software to load the registers with the linear memory addresses of the descriptor tables. At startup, all memory management registers default to `0x0h` and have a size limit of `0xFFFFh`. Once *gdtr* and *idtr* are loaded with actual values as part of processor initialization, they do not change, whereas *ldtr* and *tr* can change as tasks are switched. The store instructions are also for use by system software, but they can be used by application software if necessary.

Segment registers are 16 bits wide and include the code segment (*cs*), data segment (*ds*), stack segment (*ss*), extra segment (*es*), and two other general segment registers—*fs* and *gs*—that were added with the Intel 80386. *es* is the default segment for string operations (e.g., MOVS, CMPS, SCAS), while *fs* and *gs* have no formal hardware-defined use.

For the system and segment registers, we discuss some of their uses within the context of processor modes, memory models, and system calls. Access to system registers is meant for system software, not application software. The same is generally true for segment registers, but the segment registers do have some uses in application software.

Processor Modes

Throughout the x86 era, processor modes have evolved along with the instruction set and system capabilities. Table 10.1 shows the primary processor modes for x86/x86_64, the first processor to support the mode, and addressable memory space. Some other x86 modes exist, such as System Management mode and Virtual 8086 mode. However, we focus on attributes of the primary modes, namely **Real Mode**, **Protected Mode**, and **Long Mode**. Intel documentation usually refers to Long Mode as **IA-32e**.

Table 10.1 Processor modes

Mode	Real Mode	Protected Mode	386 Protected Mode	Long Mode
First Processor	Intel 8086	Intel 80286	Intel 80386	AMD Opteron
Addressable Memory	2^{20} (1 megabyte)	2^{24} (16 megabytes)	2^{32} (4 gigabytes)	2^{48} (256 terabytes) 2^{64} (16 exabytes)*

The Intel 8086 was the 16-bit processor that introduced the x86 ISA. The 8086 operated in Real Mode, which means the physical memory space, I/O channels, and hardware peripherals allow direct software access. Such unfettered access is necessary when software needs to directly communicate with hardware for tasks such as system startup (booting).

 ATTENTION: Modern x86 and x86_64 processors start the boot process in Real Mode as a way of dealing with backward compatibility, but then quickly switch to Protected Mode or Long Mode. Most modern processors use UEFI for hardware setup, but are backward compatible with BIOS.

All x86 processors beginning with the Intel 80286 offer Protected Mode, which is the default mode for 32-bit x86 systems. The protected mode introduced with the i286 had some limitations. Once in Protected Mode, the processor could not be switched back to Real Mode. Memory accesses were complicated, which consumed clock cycles, making it slow. And addressable memory was still fairly limited. Protected Mode was enhanced for the Intel 80386, which solved the aforementioned issues and is the protected mode used by modern processors, with occasional improvements.

Long Mode, introduced with the AMD Opteron, is the processor mode that enables access to the x86_64 instruction set and registers. Long Mode requires a 64-bit operating system. *Currently, memory addresses only use 48 of the available 64 bits, so up to 256 terabytes of memory can be addressed even though the theoretical limit is 16 exabytes. Long Mode has sub-modes; one is **64-bit Mode** for 64-bit programs, and the other is **Compatibility Mode**, which is an enhanced Protected Mode for 32-bit and 16-bit programs. When not in Long Mode, x86_64 processors still support Real and Protected Modes.

 LEARNING: Appendix G: Using CPUID discusses extended attributes, which programs can use to determine if a processor supports Long Mode.

Memory Models

The memory model used in a computer system is determined by the processor modes available and what the operating system supports. Two general models are **segmented** and **flat**. The segmented memory model divides the address space into segments (sections). The segments can be used for different parts of a program, such as a segment for data and a segment for code. Addresses are referred to by indicating the segment base address and then adding an offset.

The flat memory model presents the memory space to the programmer and program as a single contiguous space. The flat model is sometimes called the **linear** model. All memory addresses can be referred to directly in a linear fashion, as opposed to indicating a segment and an offset within the segment. Most computer architectures use a flat model, while the x86 architecture has transitioned between models over time.

In both models, the goal is to map a logical address (an abstracted reference) to a physical address (the actual location). x86 16-bit systems use a segmented memory model, as do 32-bit systems in Real Mode. x86 systems in Protected Mode use a segmented model that is presented as a flat model. And x86_64 systems use a flat memory model.

Example 10.1 illustrates how segmented addressing works in x86 Real Mode. Assume we are in 16-bit, we have a memory *data segment* that starts at 1234h, and the location of the item we want to refer to is offset 5678h from the beginning of the *data segment*. The first part of the address is known as the **segment selector**, and the second part is the offset. In code, we could refer to the item's address as 1234h:5678h, but that is not the physical address.

Example 10.1 Real Mode addressing

Logical address	1234h:5678h		
Step 1	1234h	* 16	= 12340h
Step 2	12340h	+ 5678h	= **179B8h**

← Physical address

Recall from **CHAPTER 1** that each hexadecimal digit is four bits. So, 1234h = 0001 0010 0011 0100b. Recall from Table 10.1 that the address space in Real Mode is 2^{20}, and thus a physical address is 20-bits. The segment selector is only 16-bits, so the last four bits are automatically set to zeros. Another way to think about it is that the selector is multiplied by 16, resulting in 12340h. The value is then added to the 16-bit offset—in our example 5678h, resulting in the physical address 179B8h.

In x86, the segment selector is typically not stated as an explicit value (1234h), but is usually one of the 16-bit segment registers that holds the segment base address. So assuming 1234h is a segment base address, we might store the value in the *gs* register and then refer to the address above as gs:5678h.

Addressing in 32-bit x86 Protected Mode has some similarities and differences with Real Mode segmented memory. First, the segmented memory model is still used in Protected Mode, but additional layers of abstraction present the memory space more like a linear model. One abstraction is the use of descriptors, and a second abstraction is paging.

As mentioned in the first ATTENTION note, more modern x86 processors start in Real Mode and then switch to Protected Mode. As part of the boot process, the system sets up descriptors, such as the **Interrupt Descriptor Table (IDT)**, **Global Descriptor Table (GDT)**, **Local Descriptor Table (LDT)**, **Task State Segment (TSS)** descriptor, a **Code Segment Descriptor**, and a **Data Segment Descriptor**. The GDT and LDTs are data structures that detail memory segments: base addresses, sizes, and access privileges. The GDT is intended for global and shared segments, while running programs/processes may have their own LDT. The TSS is where data such as register values, I/O permissions, and stack pointers for tasks are stored to support multitasking (suspending and switching tasks). We discuss the IDT and TSS in later sections.

 LEARNING: For detailed information on the boot process and mode switching for x86/x86_64, see the Intel Developers Manual Volume 3A sections 9.8, 9.9, and 9.10. After the tables are set up, Protected Mode is enabled in the *cr0* register. The *cr0* register is 32 bits wide in 32-bit mode, and 64 bits wide in 64-bit mode. The two *cr0* bits relevant to our discussion are Protected Mode Enable (PE, bit 0) and Paging (PG, bit 31).

To illustrate Protected Mode segmented addressing, let us assume we have the same setup as Example 10.1, with a logical address of 1234h:5678h. The segment selector in this case does not refer to a segment, but rather an index in the GDT. Every entry in the GDT is 8 bytes in 32-bit and 16 bytes in 64-bit.

Example 10.2 Protected Mode addressing

Logical Address → 1234h:5678h

Step 1	1234h	lookup in GDT	= 90120h
Step 2	90120h	+ 05678h	= 95798h

Physical Address ↑

GDT (Step 1) ← TI

NULL	00h
Base Address	08h
Base Addresses	...
Base Address = 90120h	1234h

← index

Example 10.2 is in 16-bit, so keep in mind that in 32-bit the base addresses and offsets are 32 bits. Also, as in Example 10.1, the segment selector is contained in one of the segment registers. A Protected Mode segment selector contains three pieces of information as shown in Table 10.2.

Table 10.2 Segment selector contents

Bits	15...3	2	1...0
Contents	index	table indicator (TI)	requested privilege level (RPL)

The RPL will either be 0 for kernel access or 3 for user (application) access. The TI will be 0 for GDT or 1 for LDT. The index is the location to look up in either the GDT or LDT.

The values stored in segment registers are set by the system and depend on the memory model in use, the operating system in use, and the currently executing program. In 32-bit, typically the *ds*, *ss*, and *es* registers all point to the same location. That is, they all contain the same segment selector as they are all types of data storage organized in the same segment by the system. *fs* and *gs* are for programmer use and so are usually 0x0h by default, indicating the beginning of the address space, although they also may be set to the same selector as *ds*. *cs* holds the selector for the code segment, which is the segment where currently executing instructions are stored.

 LEARNING: As mentioned in previous chapters, the Instruction Pointer register (*ip/eip*) points to the address of the next instruction to be fetched and executed. But in x86, *ip/eip* actually contains an offset to an instruction inside the code segment. So the actual address fetched by the processor is a combination of *cs:ip/eip*, where *cs* is the code segment selector and *ip/eip* is the offset.

Paging adds another layer of abstraction and translation in x86 systems. We do not intend to go into extreme detail on paging mechanisms, but here are the basics. Almost all modern operating systems use paging, which means the PG bit (31) in *cr0* is set (1). When paging is enabled, *cr3* is used to translate linear virtual addresses into physical addresses. One of the items *cr3* contains is the physical address of the first page directory for the current task. Figure 10.1 presents how x86 paging is organized and 32-bit virtual addresses are constructed.

32-bit x86 uses a multi-level paging mechanism. A **page** is usually 4 kilobytes that appears to the system as continuous memory space. Page sizes of 2mb and 4mb are also supported if the **Page Size Extension (PSE)**, bit 4 in *cr4*, is set. A **page table** is an array of 1,024 32-bit entries, meaning a page table fits into a page. Each of the entries in a page table points to the physical address of a page. The third level is a **page directory**, which is also 1,024 32-bit entries, each of which points to a page table.

	Virtual Address (32-bit)				
Bits	31...22	...	21...12	...	11...0
Contents	index to page directory	...	index to page table	...	index to page

	page directory	page table	page (4kb)
cr3 →	. . .	. . . .	. . .
	32-bit entry →		
	.	32-bit entry →	data
	. . .	. . .	.

Addressable space	1,024 entries	x	1,024 entries	x	4,096 (4kb)
				=	4,294,967,296 bytes (4gb)

Figure 10.1 x86 Paging

When an address is fetched, the data is accessed in the following manner. *cr3* points to the base address of the active page directory. The upper 10 bits of the 32-bit virtual address point to the indexed location in the page directory. Bits 12 through 21 are used to index into the page table pointed to by the entry in the page directory. Bits 0 through 11 are used to index into the page file pointed to by the entry in the page table.

The virtual address, along with *cr3* and the 32-bit entries, allows data for programs to be stored in files using the flat model that represents the entire address space 2^{32} (4gb). Page files are stored in secondary storage (disk) and are moved to main memory (RAM) and cache as needed. If the data is not found in cache or RAM, then a **page fault** occurs and the page is retrieved from secondary storage. When paging is enabled, segmentation has little purpose. Every program has its own space separate from other programs, but each has virtual access to the full address space, a clever and powerful illusion.

 ATTENTION: Paging is transparent to programs and the user. In a flat model with paging enabled, a virtual address is essentially seen as a linear address in a linear address space. In reality, the linear space is divided into pages mapped to virtual memory mapped to physical memory **frames** (which hold a page).

Addressing in 64-bit x86_64 removes segmentation almost entirely. Segmentation is not used in Long Mode, and segment register use varies. The *cs*, *ds*, *ss*, and *es* segment registers will either be forced to 0x0h or will be treated as zero (regardless of associated segment descriptors) and the addressable space limit will be extended to 2^{64}. The result is a flat address space for code, data, and stack. Debuggers may not even show the segment registers. But *fs* and *gs* can be used for special purposes. On Microsoft Windows, *gs* is used to point to thread blocks for running threads, and the Linux kernel uses *gs* to store CPU data. Segment registers are still used for tasks running in Compatibility Mode.

Paging in x86_64 also changes by adding another level. *cr3* points to a **page directory pointer table**, which contains page directory entries to page directories. A bit is taken from the page table, and the page directory indexes to create a 2-bit index value for the pointer table.

Code Example

Typically, x86 Assembly instructions implicitly use the appropriate segment register based on the instruction, which means in most cases we do not have to indicate the segment. For example, stack instructions such as PUSH and POP implicitly use the stack segment selector in the *ss* register, and data access instructions such as MOV use the data segment selector in the *ds* register.

Program 10.1 shows a variety of ways segment selectors can be used to address memory in x86 Assembly. Again, segment selectors are usually not required, but Program 10.1 illustrates their explicit use. Similar NASM and MASM versions are in the **Chapter 10 Supplement**.

Program 10.1 *Using segment selectors*

GAS (32-bit)

```
.data
array: .long 3, 2, 6, 4, 1

.text
.globl _main
_main:

movl $array, %eax        #1 array address to eax
movl 4(%eax), %ebx       #2 second element to ebx
movl %ds:array, %ecx     #3 first element to ecx
movl %ds:array+8, %edx   #4 third element to edx

movl %gs, %esi           #5 gs to esi
movl $42, %gs:(%esi)     #6 42 to gs:(offset in esi)
movl %gs:(%esi), %edi    #7 gs:offset to edi
movl $43, %gs:0x04h      #8 43 to gs:offset
movl %gs:0x04h, %edi     #9 gs:offset to edi

pushl $0
subl $4, %esp
movl $1, %eax
int $0x80
.end
```

Line #1 moves the address of the first array element to *eax*. In line #2 we show the typical way a value might be moved by using the address contained in *eax* plus an offset. Since the array is in the data segment, we can prefix the identifier (`array`) with the segment register that contains the data segment selector (`ds`) as shown in #3 and #4.

> **PROGRAMMING:** If using the MASM Assembler, a data move based on a linear address is one of the occasions when a segment selector is *required*. An example of a move with a linear address would be `mov eax, ds:[0Fh]`. See the MOV comparison with GAS and NASM syntax in **APPENDIX A**.

Lines #5 through #9 show some ways the *gs* register could be used in macOS and are purely illustrative of syntax. Such use is not recommended since Linux and Windows use *fs* and *gs* for system purposes. Line #5 moves the default value stored in *gs* to *esi*. Though the two registers contain the same binary value, in line #6 we move the immediate value 42 to the segment location stored in *gs* plus the offset stored in *esi*. We then grab the value as it exists (42) and move it to the *edi* register in line #7. Lines #8 and #9 show how to do the same thing, but with a literal offset value (0x04h). Again, the code is just simple examples of syntax and use.

> **ATTENTION:** Throughout the remainder of this chapter we refer to masOS and BSD operating systems collectively. Although the macOS kernel, XNU, is a hybrid of Mach and FreeBSD, the code examples provided for macOS also generally apply to BSD systems.

Interrupts and System Calls

Software Interrupts

An **interrupt** is a signal to the processor that something needs immediate attention. Broadly, there are two types of interrupts: hardware and software. Our primary focus is on **software interrupts**. One form of a software interrupt is when an *application* sends a signal to the processor. Using the INT instruction in an application is an explicit way of generating a software interrupt. Another form of software interrupt is called an **exception (trap)**, which happens as a processor is executing instructions and situations occur that are not or cannot be handled by the executing application.

> **LEARNING:** Learning about interrupts is most important if you intend to write system software (OSs, drivers, utilities). As for application developers, knowledge of interrupts helps with understanding the evolution of system calls. On older 16/32-bit x86 systems, an interrupt was the primary way of asking the OS to do something hardware or software related. Newer 32/64-bit x86 systems have moved away from using interrupts for system tasks and instead use more efficient x86/x86_64 instructions. Read on …

A good example of a software exception is division by zero. Multiple possibilities exist for handling this circumstance. Look at the following C++ code examples.

Example 10.3 Division by zero without exception

```
int divide(int numerator, int denominator){
    if (denominator == 0) {
        cout << ("ERROR: Cannot divide by zero.\n");
        return 1;
    }
    else
        return numerator / denominator;
}
```

Example 10.3 shows a simplistic and relatively meaningless way to handle a potential exception: an `if` statement that outputs a statement to the console, but provides no real indication to the system that an exception took place. Example 10.4 shows a better way to deal with the situation in C++ by using a try-catch block and throwing an exception. A message is still sent to the console, but having an **exception handler** (catch) deal with the situation has meaning for the system.

Example 10.4 Division by zero with exception

```
int divide(int numerator, int denominator){
    if (denominator == 0) {
        throw string("ERROR: Cannot divide by zero.\n");
    }
    else
        return numerator / denominator;
}
in main...
    try {quotient = divide(num1, num2);
        cout << "The quotient is: " << quotient << endl;
    }
    catch (string exceptionString) {
        cout << exceptionString;
    }
```

But what if we do not handle division by zero with our own software exception handler? When the processor attempts to execute the division instruction with a zero as denominator, the processor generates an interrupt and handles the exception itself, since division by zero is a standard processor exception (Table 10.3).

Table 10.3 x86 Interrupts

INT_NUM	Description	INT_NUM	Description
0x00	Division by zero	0x0B	Segment not present
0x01	Debug exception	0x0C	Stack fault
0x02	Non-maskable interrupt	0x0D	General protection fault
0x03	Debug breakpoint	0x0E	Page fault
0x04	Overflow	0x0F	Reserved
0x05	Bounds/range exceeded	0x10	x87 floating-point fault
0x06	Invalid opcode	0x11	Alignment check
0x07	Co-processor (FPU)/device not available	0x12	Machine check
0x08	Double fault	0x13	SIMD exception
0x09	Co-processor segment overrun	0x14	Virtualization exception
0x0A	Invalid Task State Segment	0x15 – 0xFF	System/user-defined interrupts

> ⚠ **ATTENTION:** Exception handling may differ depending on whether the CPU or FPU is handling the computation. If the data types are integers as in Example 10.3, the CPU will throw an arithmetic division exception with code 0x0h, and the program will terminate/crash. If the data types are floats, the FPU may handle the exception more smoothly by returning infinity (INF) and then continuing processing.

In the **MEMORY MODELS** section, we introduced the Interrupt Descriptor Table. In Real Mode, the IDT is known as the **Interrupt Vector Table (IVT)**, but we will focus on how interrupts work in 32-bit and 64-bit modes. Traditionally, the IVT is the first structure in physical memory ranging from address 0x0000h to 0x03FFh in 16-bit, 0x07FFh in 32-bit, and 0x03FFFh in 64-bit. However, in 32-bit and 64-bit modes, the IDT may reside anywhere, and the *idtr* register stores the physical base address and the length in bytes of the IDT.

Table 10.4 *IDTR* contents

Bits	47(79) ... 16	15 ... 0
Contents	32(64)-bit linear base address	16-bit table size limit

The IDT in 32-bit mode is an array of 8-byte descriptors known as interrupt gates, trap gates, and task gates (we will just use the general term *interrupt*). The standard IDT is 256 entries, meaning the IDT size is 2kb (256 * 8). In 64-bit modes (Long Mode and Compatibility Mode), the IDT descriptors are 16-bytes with some contents changed and added. The size increase is mostly to maintain alignment for *rip*-relative addressing.

An 8-byte interrupt descriptor in 32-bit Protected Mode has the structure presented in Table 10.5. The **Descriptor Privilege Level (DPL)**, similar to the RPL for segment selectors, is 0 for kernel access or 3 for application access. *D* (bit 11 in byte 6) is the size of the interrupt gate; 1 meaning 32-bit and 0 meaning 16-bit. *P* (bit 15 in byte 6) is the segment present flag. The *Target Segment Selector* (bytes 3–4) is the segment selector for the destination code segment where the **Interrupt Service Routine (ISR)** is located. The *Offset in Target Segment* (bytes 7–8) is the offset to the ISRs entry point within the target segment.

Table 10.5 32-bit IDT descriptor contents

Bits	31 ... 16	15	14 13	12 .. 8	7..5	4 ... 0
Contents	Offset in target tegment	P	DPL	0D110	000	Reserved
Byte	8	7		6		5

Bits	31 ... 16	15 ... 0
Contents	Target segment selector	Offset in target segment
Byte	4	3	2	1

Servicing an interrupt is a somewhat complex operation. When an interrupt is generated in a 32-bit mode, the following process takes place.

1. The CPU multiplies the interrupt number (e.g., `int 3`) times 8 since each descriptor is 8 bytes wide (e.g., 3 * 8) and adds the value to the base address of the IDT (stored in *idtr*).
2. A compare takes place between the value from Step 1 and the size of the IDT, which is stored in *idtr*. The test verifies that the interrupt is valid. If the interrupt is invalid a **General Protection (GP) exception** is generated.
3. If the interrupt is valid, the 8-byte descriptor stored at the address calculated in Step 1 is fetched. As shown in Table 10.5, the descriptor contains all the information related to the ISR (handler).

32-bit Scenario 1

If the handler is to be executed at a lower **Privilege Level (PL)** (e.g., the application running is at PL 3 and the interrupt is to execute at PL 0):

4. The stack segment selector (*ss*) and stack pointer (*esp*) used by the ISR are fetched from the TSS in the GDT.
5. The processor pushes the stack segment selector (*ss*) and stack pointer (*esp*) of the interrupted procedure on the newly active stack.
6. The processor pushes the current state of *eflags*, *cs*, and *eip* on the active stack.
7. Some interrupts (8, 10-14, 17-18) contain an error code and if so the code value is pushed to the active stack after *eip*.

32-bit Scenario 2

If the handler is to be executed at the same privilege level (e.g., the application and interrupt are both at PL 3):

4. The processor pushes the current state of *eflags*, *cs*, and *eip* on the active stack.
5. Some interrupts (8, 10–14, 17–18) contain an error code, and if so the code value is pushed to the active stack after *eip*.

Then the interrupt routine executes. Upon completion, the IRET instruction is used to return from an interrupt. The IRET instruction is a special form of RET that restores (POPs) the register states such as *eip*, *cs*, and *eflags* so the interrupted task can pick up exactly where it left off. The number of pops performed by IRET matches the pushes based on the privilege level scenarios.

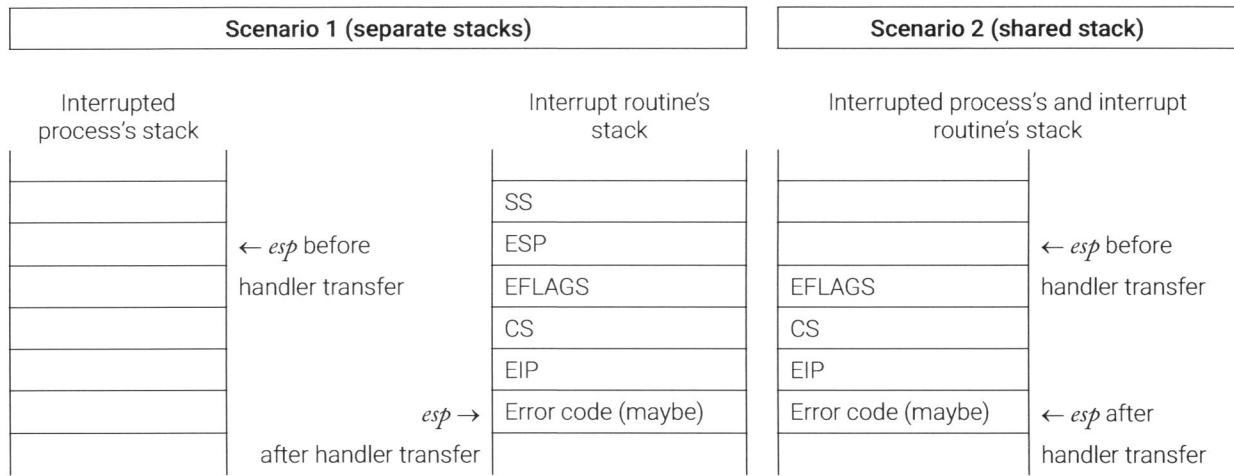

Figure 10.2 32-bit stack scenarios for interrupts

Figure 10.2 illustrates the stack scenarios for handling interrupts in 32-bit x86. In *Scenario 1*, the interrupted process and the interrupt routine have different stacks. In *Scenario 2*, the interrupted process and the interrupt routine share the same stack.

When a software interrupt is generated in one of the 64-bit modes, the process is similar but with some differences. The interrupt routines are 64-bit code. The IDT entries are 16 bytes each with some content changes, the most significant being a 3-bit field representing the **Interrupt Stack Table (IST)**, which is discussed further in *64-bit Scenario 4*.

 ATTENTION: Interrupts serviced in Compatibility Mode, an enhanced 32-bit mode that is a submode of 64-bit Long Mode, are defined as 64-bit interrupt gates and routines.

When an interrupt occurs in 32-bit, the amount of data pushed on the stack depends on whether a change in privilege level takes place as shown in Figure 10.2. 64-bit mode interrupts are more consistent as *ss:rsp* is always pushed to the stack and a placeholder is used for the error code if none accompanies the interrupt. As with procedure calls in 64-bit, interrupt calls and returns maintain 16-byte alignment for optimal use of *xmm* registers.

IRET in 64-bit generally has the same behavior except that the POPs are 64-bit values. One difference is that because *ss:rsp* is always pushed to the stack for 64-bit interrupts, IRET always pops *ss:rsp* in 64-bit Mode, but will only pop *ss:rsp* in Compatibility Mode in the case of a privilege level change. Thus, backward compatibility is maintained.

64-bit processors have four possible stack scenarios when servicing interrupts.

64-bit Scenario 1

When the processor is in a legacy 32-bit mode, stack switching behaves as described previously in the 32-bit scenarios.

64-bit Scenario 2

In 64-bit Compatibility Mode, stack switches in the case of a change in privilege level are slightly different than *32-bit Scenario 1*, specifically Step 4 is different. *rsp* is updated with a new value from the TSS, but *ss* is set to NULL and its RPL field is set to the interrupt's privilege level so nested interrupts can be handled. Upon returning, the interrupted values of *ss* and *rsp* are restored.

64-bit Scenario 3

In 64-bit Mode, if the IST 3-bit index is zero (000b), *64-bit Scenario 2* is followed.

64-bit Scenario 4

In 64-bit Mode, if the IST index is not zero (001b–111b) the IST switching mechanism is used. Operating on a known good stack is important for certain interrupts. In 32-bit mode, the switch to a known good stack is achieved via **task gates** in the IDT; in 64-bit mode the switch is achieved via the IST.

 LEARNING: Task gates are a form of interrupt that are handled like an ordinary task switch by using the interrupt's corresponding entry in the TSS. The link back to the interrupted task is stored in the *Previous TSS link field* of the handler's TSS entry. Other interrupts are disabled in task gates. Examples of task gates are Non-Maskable Interrupt (NMI), Double Fault, and Machine Check.

The IST is a section within the TSS specifically for 64-bit stack switching. The IST field is 3 bits in a 64-bit IDT entry, so the max value is 111b, and seven corresponding pointers in the TSS's IST exist. Each pointer in the IST points to a valid stack location that can be loaded into *rsp* as the new stack location for handling the interrupt. Figure 10.3 offers a simplified visual of the 64-bit IST implementation.

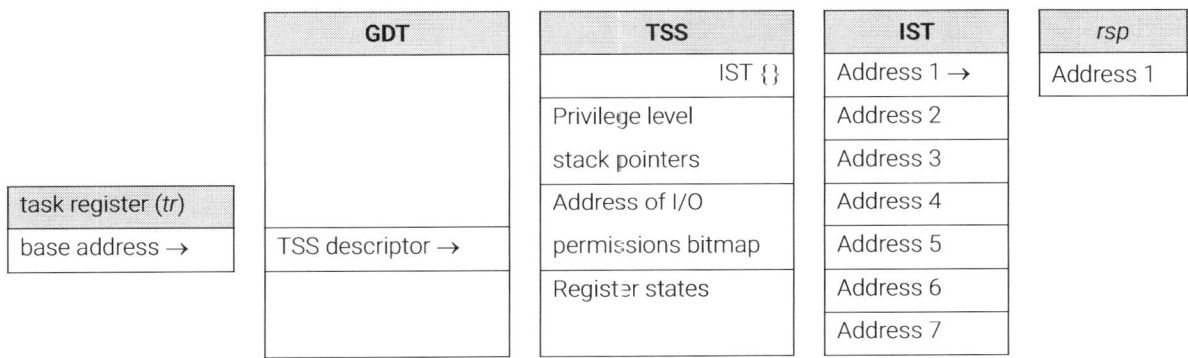

Figure 10.3 – 64-bit interrupt stack table (IST) implementation

The Task Register (*tr*) holds the address of the TSS descriptor in the GDT. The TSS descriptor contains the address of the Task State Segment. Within the TSS is the IST, which is a collection of good stack addresses, one of which will be loaded into *rsp* if the IST field in an interrupt descriptor entry is not zero.

Aside from the IST aspect, the steps in *64-bit Scenario 4* resemble *64-bit Scenario 2*. With the good stack location in *rsp*, the *ss* register is set to NULL and the RPL is set to the current privilege level. The interrupted process's *ss*, *rsp*, *rflags*, *cs*, and *rip* values are pushed to the new stack, and the interrupt is processed.

Hardware Interrupts

A **hardware interrupt** also sends a signal to the processor, but the signal is from a device in communication with the system via an **interrupt request line (IRQ)**. IRQ lines provide a means of communication between the processor and hardware devices. A processor has a limited number of IRQ lines for hardware interrupts. The hardware lines to the processor are connected through a *Programmable Interrupt Controller (PIC)*. Older x86 systems used two of Intel's 8259 PICs, which supported eight IRQ lines each and were noted as IRQ0–IRQ15.

Modern x86 systems use Intel's *Advanced Programmable Interrupt Controller (APIC)*, which is much more flexible in terms of routing interrupts in multi-processor systems. APICs theoretically support up to 255 interrupt lines, though most systems currently support 24 IRQs. The older PCs had set IRQ lines, such as IRQ0 for the system clock and IRQ14 as the primary ATA channel for disks. The newer APICs are fully programmable. But most operating systems maintain the standard IRQ numbering scheme.

Using INT (Old School)

Beginning with the Bubble Sort example in **Chapter 1 Code Review** all the way through Program 10.1 in this chapter, the last instruction in all stand-alone 32-bit GAS and NASM programs is "int $0x80" and "int 80h", respectively. The first inline assembly code example in Chapter 9 (Example 9.1) was "int $3" for Clang/GCC and "int 3" for Visual C++. Here we present more examples of using INT.

As mentioned in the LEARNING note at the beginning of the **Software Interrupts** section, using an explicit interrupt is an older way of performing system tasks on 16/32-bit x86 systems. So a lot of code examples found online and elsewhere use INT for system calls. A **system call** is a request to the operating system **kernel** to do something, sometimes via an **application programming interface (API)** as in Windows. System calls can be made on 32-bit Unix/Linux systems by using "int 80h". Microsoft DOS used "int 21h" and later iterations of Windows (e.g., 2000, XP) used "int 2Eh".

 LEARNING: We use macOS and Linux to illustrate the INT instruction since its use has remained consistent and straightforward over time. For the Windows examples, we use the Windows API for consistency and because it is the practical and modern approach.

The process of handling a system call via "int 80h" is as follows.

1. INT is executed.
2. The processor switches from running at PL3 (application) to PL0 (kernel).
3. The INT 80h routine is located via an IDT descriptor.
4. Control transfers to the kernel to handle the request indicated by the system call number.
5. The task is performed.
6. The privilege level is reset to PL3.
7. Control is returned to the calling program.

Program 10.2 shows examples of INT in GAS. A similar program for NASM is in the **Chapter 10 Supplement**.

We start Program 10.2 by signaling the processor with a debug breakpoint (int $3). When running the program in *Debug* mode, execution will halt at int $3, and then we can step through the program. In graphical development environments such as Xcode and Visual Studio, you can set a breakpoint visually, while in command-line debuggers such as GDB and LLDB, a breakpoint can easily be set at any label. Using INT 3 is a programmatic way of setting a breakpoint, but it is for debugging use only.

Program 10.2 prints the string "Computer Architecture" twice: first by using a system call, and second by using a system call implemented as a function. A system call must be accompanied by what you want the system to do, such as write to console or read from a file. The desired action is indicated by a **system call number**. The call number and necessary arguments are placed in registers, on the stack, or a combination of both, depending on the system.

 LEARNING: The **Chapter 10 Supplement** contains information on system call tables and relevant links to online sources.

When using INT in 32-bit mode on macOS/BSD, arguments go on the stack and the call number goes in *eax*. On Linux, registers are used for arguments and the call number.

- **macOS/BSD**: push arguments on the stack in reverse order; move call number to *eax*; send INT.
- **Linux**: move arguments to registers in the order *ebx*, *ecx*, *edx*, *esi*, *edi*, and *ebp*; move call number to *eax*; send INT.

Program 10.2 *Debug and system write interrupts*

GAS (32-bit)

```
.data
output:    .ascii "Computer Architecture\n"
.equ len, (. - output)

.text
.globl _main
_main:              # Print "Computer Architecture"

int $3              # Set breakpoint (remove if desired)
pushl $len          # String length
pushl $output       # String address
pushl $1            # Print to STDOUT (File Descriptor 1, FD1)
pushl $0            # Extra push to align stack
movl $4, %eax       # Use SYSCALL 4 (WRITE), prints to screen
int  $0x80          # system call interrupt
addl $16, %esp      # Clean up stack

pushl $len          # BSD assumes that a function calls INT 80h
pushl $output       # as opposed to issuing INT 80h directly
pushl $1            # Print using kernel call
movl $4, %eax
call _kernel
addl $12, %esp

pushl $0            # return value
subl $4, %esp       # align stack
movl $1, %eax       # call number for exit
int $0x80           # system call interrupt

_kernel:            # For any system call
   int $0x80
   ret

.end
```

Example 10.5 System write with INT

macOS/BSD – GAS		Linux – NASM	
pushl $len	# length	mov ebx, 1	; FD
pushl $output	# address	mov ecx, output	; address
pushl $1	# FD	mov edx, len	; length
pushl $0	# align	mov eax, 4	; call number
movl $4, %eax	# call number	int 80h	
int $0x80			

Example 10.5 shows how system calls are similar to function calls. System calls are calls to routines (functions) via an interrupt gate. The Linux example is similar to the 32-bit *fastcall* convention. The macOS/BSD example is similar to the *cdecl* convention: stack is used and parameters are passed in reverse order, which is clear when looking at the system write prototype in the syscalls.master file for BSD.

```
4...{user_ssize_t write(int fd, user_addr_t cbuf, user_size_t nbyte);}
```

Referring to Program 10.2 and Example 10.5, we first push the length of the string on the stack; second, the location of the string; third, the file descriptor for STDOUT (1); fourth, the stack is aligned (a macOS 32-bit requirement); and then we place the value for the system call to perform a write in *eax*. With the arguments and call number set, we issue the system call with "int $0x80". The string prints to the console and in code we adjust the stack pointer 4 bytes for every argument passed for cleanup.

Notice the return value (user_ssize_t) in the system write prototype. Most system calls return a value, usually in *eax/rax*. If you check the state of *eax* after the interrupts in Program 10.2, you will notice the value 0x16h (22d), which means 22 characters were printed. Other system calls, such as a request for the system time, will place the days, hours, minutes, and so on in various registers. For specifics on system call return values, refer to the system call information for your chosen platform (again, see the **CHAPTER 10 SUPPLEMENT**).

In Program 10.2, the _kernel function shows how to issue a system call via a function, which is useful in any system but is how system calls are expected in macOS/BSD. Notice that if the interrupt is issued via a function that contains the INT and a RET, the extra PUSH to align the stack is not needed.

Program 10.3 provides another example of using INT. In Program 10.3, we get the process ID of the program and print it to the console. The system call number to query for the process ID (0x14h) is loaded into *eax*, the interrupt is issued, and the process ID is returned in *eax*. We then go through a loop converting the numeric value into printable ASCII characters. Then we use INT as we did in Program 10.2 to print the process ID to console.

INT has some necessary and positive uses for low-level programming, but methods evolve. Using INT to achieve system calls is possible, but there is some considerable overhead.

Program 10.3 *Print process ID with INT*

GAS (32-bit)

```
.data
    decimal: .long 10
.bss
.lcomm PID, 4     # Reserve 4 bytes for a process id

.text
.globl _main
_main:                      # Print Process ID

movl $0x14, %eax            # GET_PID call
int $0x80                   # syscall
                            # process ID is returned in EAX
movl $(PID+4), %edi         # Pointer to end of PID string
convert:
    xorl    %edx, %edx
    divl    decimal         # Divide by 10
    addl    $48, %edx       # Add 48 to remainder
    movb    %dl, (%edi)     # Store
    decl    %edi            # Next digit
    cmpl    $0, %eax        # Is EAX = 0?
    jg      convert         # If greater than 0, more digits

pushl $6                    # string length
pushl $PID                  # string address
pushl $1                    # file descriptor STDOUT (1)
pushl $0                    # align stack
movl $4, %eax               # system call 4 (write)
int $0x80                   # system call
addl $16, %esp             # clean stack

pushl $0                    # return value
subl $4, %esp              # align stack
movl $1, %eax               # system call 1 (exit)
int $0x80                   # system call
.end
```

SYSENTER, SYSCALL, and Libraries/APIs (New School)

Beginning with the Pentium II processor, Intel introduced instructions to perform **fast system calls**. SYSENTER and its counterpart SYSEXIT were the first instructions, and they are supported in 32-bit and 64-bit modes. SYSCALL and its counterpart SYSRET were introduced with 64-bit mode (Long Mode) and are supported in 64-bit modes. The instructions are referred to as "fast calls" because of the *intention* to handle privilege level (PL) switches more efficiently.

 PROGRAMMING: SYSENTER/SYSCALL and their counterparts SYSEXIT/SYSRET are not used as a CALL/RET pair. The instructions are counterparts for switching to privilege level 0 and switching back to privilege level 3.

This topic, like many advanced architecture topics, is a deep and twisted rabbit hole that you can explore further via the Resources in the **CHAPTER 10 SUPPLEMENT**. Responsibility for handling the PL switch context lies with the operating system. So what does that mean? In some cases, fast calls are faster than the INT method and in some cases fast calls are slower. The implementation is mostly OS-dependent, but the processor pipeline also affects the speed.

If you look into system call methods online or elsewhere, you will find many examples (most outdated) and opinions on what method is best. Keep in mind that the way system calls work in one version of an OS (and its myriad of context details) probably differs from how it works in past or future versions.

For example, although past versions of the Linux kernel (e.g., 2.6, 3.x.y) had very different methods for handling INT, SYSENTER, and SYSCALL, more modern releases (e.g., 4.x.y., as of this writing) have merged the implementations such that they are essentially interchangeable. The kernel provides one path for handling system calls whether it is initiated with INT, SYSENTER, or SYSCALL.

The same is true in Windows-land, but the implementation is different. The INT instruction is rarely directly used anymore in user space since system calls can easily be issued in Assembly code through the Windows API. The Windows API is actually built on top of the Windows Native API (`ntdll.dll`). The Native API routines for system calls are low-level routines written in C and Assembly using INT, SYSENTER, and SYSCALL. The point is that whether in Windows, Linux, or macOS/BSD-land, system calls are usually achieved with wrapper functions in libraries or APIs that have multiple layers of abstraction. The abstractions are not just between the user code and the processor, but also between the user code and the kernel.

All of the example Windows (MASM) programs throughout this book have used a Windows API call to exit (similar to exiting with INT in GAS and NASM). Recall the following 32-bit MASM code snippets.

```
ExitProcess PROTO, dwExitCode:DWORD
; code
INVOKE ExitProcess, 0
```

`ExitProcess` is a function in the Windows API that exists as a system call in `Kernel32.lib/dll` and ends the calling process. The first line in the snippet is the function prototype, which signals our intent to use the method. The second line is where we INVOKE (a form of CALL) the system procedure.

Program 10.4 shows 32-bit examples of using the Windows API to achieve output similar to Programs 10.2 and 10.3. Program 10.4 also shows the difference between CALL and INVOKE, the latter being a simpler way of writing the call and passing arguments. Three Windows API functions we use are `MessageBox`, `GetCurrentProcessId`, and `ExitProcess`. Example 10.6 shows the C++ prototypes for the methods. All methods are invoked via the WinAPI, but the routines exist in different libraries.

Program 10.4 *Windows API calls*

MASM (32-bit)

```
.386
.MODEL FLAT, stdcall
.STACK 4096

GetCurrentProcessId PROTO
ExitProcess PROTO, dwExitCode:DWORD
MessageBoxA PROTO, hwnd:DWORD, text:DWORD, caption:DWORD, buttons:DWORD

.DATA
output BYTE "Computer Architecture",0
caption BYTE "Message", 0
decimal DWORD 10
PID DWORD ?

.CODE
_main PROC                         ; Print "Computer Architecture"

   push 0                          ; MB_OK (0 = OK button only)
   push OFFSET caption             ; lpCaption
   push OFFSET output              ; lpText
   push 0                          ; hWnd handle owner window (0 = no owner)
   call MessageBoxA

   INVOKE GetCurrentProcessId
   mov PID, eax

   mov edi, OFFSET [PID+3]         ; Pointer to end of PID string
convert:
   xor     edx, edx
   div     decimal                 ; Divide by 10
   add     edx, 48                 ; Add 48 to remainder
   mov     BYTE PTR [edi], dl      ; Store
   dec     edi                     ; Next digit
   cmp     eax, 0                  ; Is EAX = 0?
   jg      convert                 ; If greater than 0, more digits

   INVOKE MessageBoxA, 0, OFFSET PID, OFFSET caption, 0

INVOKE ExitProcess, 0
_main ENDP
END
```

Example 10.6 Windows API C++ prototypes

Function	MessageBox	ExitProcess and GetCurrentProcessId
Library	User32.lib/dll	Kernel32.lib/dll

Prototype	`int WINAPI MessageBox(`
	`  _In_opt_ HWND    hWnd,`
	`  _In_opt_ LPCTSTR lpText,`
	`  _In_opt_ LPCTSTR lpCaption,`
	`  _In_     UINT    uType`
	`);`
		`VOID WINAPI ExitProcess(`
		`  _In_ UINT uExitCode`
		`);`
		
		`DWORD WINAPI GetCurrentProcessId(void);`

PROGRAMMING: The INVOKE directive is available in MASM 32-bit but *not* available in MASM 64-bit. When programming for Microsoft x64 you *must* use the CALL instruction after placing the parameters in the appropriate locations. See **CHAPTER 6 TABLE 6.1** and **CHAPTER 10 PROGRAM 10.8**.

One subtle difference in converting the PID to ASCII for output is that in MASM (and NASM) we shift 3 bytes, whereas in Program 10.3 for GAS we shifted 4 bytes. Be aware that the values and ways to handle the output string can vary since the length of process IDs is system dependent.

 ATTENTION: Use libraries or APIs when possible for system calls, as opposed to Assembly instructions. Two major advantages of doing so are consistency and portability.

The general low-level process for invoking a *system call* is consistent.

1. Save the current context.
2. Change the privilege level (to PL0).
3. Load and execute the system routine.
4. Reset the privilege level (to PL3).
5. Return to a valid location (usually where the calling procedure left off).

But what if we could perform a system call without having to switch PLs and save context? We can and often do, though it is transparent to the programmer. In Linux-land, the kernel creates a virtual memory page known as the **virtual dynamic shared object (VDSO)**, which is linked to all user processes in memory. The VDSO contains common system call routines. When an application in user space makes a system call, whether through a library (e.g., *libc*, *glibc*, *unistd*) as is typically the case, or directly via an Assembly instruction, what is actually invoked (`__kernel_vsyscall`) is fairly abstracted. The VDSO is a clever solution in that it is provided to the user space *by* the kernel, so it can execute the system routines like normal function calls and does not require a context or PL switch. But keep in mind that not all system routines are in the VDSO.

 ATTENTION: Methods of speeding up system calls vary by platform and version. Older Linux kernels have `vsyscall`, which is more limited than VDSO. macOS has traditionally had `commpage`, but has moved to other mechanisms for handling system routines (libraries and the x86_64 ABI). Windows uses dynamic libraries (DLLs). System routines are abstracted in many ways and this changes over time.

Operating systems do use machine-specific registers (MSRs)—mentioned at the beginning of the chapter—in the kernel initialization process. MSRs are used to facilitate fast system calls and have their own instructions for reading and writing to the registers (RDMSR/WRMSR). Do *not* mess with the MSRs.

Machine-specific registers include the following registers.

- 32-bit
  - IA32_SYSENTER_CS – holds the segment selector for the PL0 (kernel) code segment;
  - IA32_SYSENTER_EIP – holds the address of the first instruction of the desired system routine;
  - IA32_SYSENTER_ESP – holds the address of the PL0 stack.
- 64-bit
  - IA32_STAR – holds *cs* and *ss* for both the PL0 code (target) and the PL3 code (caller);
  - IA32_LSTAR – holds the address of the first instruction of the desired system routine;
  - IA32_FMASK – holds an *rflags* mask value.

As detailed in the MSR list, MSRs hold addresses and relevant information used in context switching for routines. Operating systems query the MSRs during initialization to formulate the system call path that will be used once the system is up and running.

With the different system call approaches in mind, we present the following programs. Note that argument passing with SYSENTER is similar to INT, but SYSCALL is different.

Program 10.5: a 32-bit program using SYSENTER for Ubuntu Linux (NASM).

> **32-bit SYSENTER**: Move arguments to registers in the order *ebx, ecx, edx, esi, edi*, and *ebp*; move call number to *eax*, issue SYSENTER; value returned in *eax*.

Program 10.6: 64-bit programs using SYSCALL for macOS/BSD (GAS) and Ubuntu Linux (NASM).

> **64-bit SYSCALL (AMD64)**: Move arguments to registers in the order *rdi, rsi, rdx, r10, r8*, and *r9*; move call number to *rax*; issue SYSCALL; value returned in *rax* (negative value indicates error).

Program 10.7: a 32/64-bit program in C++ using the *unistd* and *libc* libraries for macOS/BSD and Linux; and the Windows API for Windows.

Program 10.8: a 64-bit MASM Assembly implementation of Program 10.7 using the Windows API.

> **Microsoft x64**: Move parameters to registers in the order *rcx, rdx, r8*, and *r9*; additional parameters passed on the stack in reverse order; issue CALL; value typically returned in *rax*.

 PROGRAMMING: Refer to **Appendix G: Using CPUID** for detecting processor support for SYSENTER.

Program 10.5 shows how SYSENTER works on 32-bit Linux. Program 10.5 prints a message to console just like Program 10.2, however SYSENTER has replaced INT. SYSENTER introduces a different kind of overhead: we must save register and stack context to stack so we can restore the context upon return, and we must create a return point (`sysenter_ret`).

Program 10.5 SYSENTER

Linux (NASM 32-bit)

```
section .data
output: DB "Computer Architecture",0Ah
len: EQU ($ - output)

section .text
global _main
_main:

mov ebx, 1
mov ecx, output
mov edx, len
mov eax, 4

push sysenter_ret
push  ecx
push  edx
push  ebp
mov   ebp, esp
sysenter
sysenter_ret:

mov eax, 1
mov ebx, 0
int 80h
```

Program 10.6 shows how SYSCALL works on 64-bit macOS/BSD and Linux by writing to a file. Unlike our 32-bit Programs 10.2 and 10.5, in 64-bit avoid use of the EQU directive. Important differences between the macOS/BSD and Linux versions are (1) the system call numbers are different, (2) *rip*-relative addressing syntax is different regarding the len variable, and (3) the number systems are different for file flags as macOS/BSD uses hexadecimal and Linux uses octal.

The **CHAPTER 10 SUPPLEMENT** contains commented versions of Program 10.6 and more specifics on the system call numbers and the system call classes used in XNU (e.g., 0x2000001 for Unix/BSD, 0x1000001 for Mach).

Program 10.6 – *SYSCALL on 64-bit systems*

SYSCALL on macOS/BSD (GAS 64-bit)	SYSCALL on Linux (NASM 64-bit)
| ```
.data
output: .ascii "Computer Architecture\n"
len: .quad (. - output)
file_name: .asciz "output.txt"
file_handle: .long 0

.text
.globl _main
_main:

# write to console
movq $0x2000004, %rax
movq $1, %rdi
leaq output(%rip), %rsi
movq len(%rip), %rdx
syscall

# create and open file
movq $0x2000005, %rax
leaq file_name(%rip), %rdi
movq $0x0201, %rsi
movq $0666, %rdx
syscall
movq %rax, file_handle(%rip)

# write to file
movq $0x2000004, %rax
movq file_handle(%rip), %rdi
leaq output(%rip), %rsi
movq len(%rip), %rdx
syscall

# close file
movq $0x2000006, %rax
movq file_handle(%rip), %rdi
syscall

# exit
movq $0x2000001, %rax
movq $0, %rdi
syscall
.end
``` | ```
section .data
output: DB "Computer Architecture",0Ah
len: DQ ($ - output)
file_name: DB "output.txt",0
file_handle: DD 0

section .text
global _main
_main:

# write to console
mov rax, 1
mov rdi, 1
lea rsi, [rel output]
mov rdx, [len]
syscall

# create and open file
mov rax, 2
lea rdi, [rel file_name]
mov rsi, 0101o
mov rdx, 0666o
syscall
mov [rel file_handle], rax

# write to file
mov rax, 1
mov rdi, [rel file_handle]
lea rsi, [rel output]
mov rdx, [len]
syscall

# close file
mov rax, 3
mov rdi, [rel file_handle]
syscall

# exit
mov rax, 60
xor rdi, rdi
syscall
``` |

Program 10.7 shows how libraries and APIs can be used to make system calls in C++. On the Unix-like side, we show how to use *unistd* and *libc* to initiate system calls. The functions open(), read(), write(), and close() are wrapper functions that will be processed as deemed appropriate by the kernel. We assume a file exists called input.txt, which contains characters. We set the number of characters to be read and written to 13. So if the file contained the phrase "Computer Architecture," the phrase "Computer Arch" would be printed. The Windows version of Program 10.7 is an example of using the Windows API in C++.

Program 10.7 *Library and API system calls*

macOS/BSD and Linux (C++ 32/64-bit)	Windows API (C++ 32/64-bit)
| ```cpp
#include <unistd.h>
#include <fcntl.h>

int main()
{
    const int num = 13;
    char inputFile[] = "input.txt";
    char buffer[num + 1] = {NULL};

    //open file
    int FD = open(inputFile, O_RDONLY);

    //read file
    read(FD, buffer, num);

    //print to STDOUT
    write(STDOUT_FILENO, buffer, num);

    //close file
    close(FD);

    return 0;
}
``` | ```cpp
#include <Windows.h>
using namespace std;

int main()
{
    const int num = 13;
    char inputFile[] = "input.txt";
    char caption[] = "Message";
    char buffer[num + 1] = {NULL};
    DWORD charsRead = 0;

    //open file
    HANDLE FD = CreateFile(inputFile,
            GENERIC_READ,
            0,
            NULL,
            OPEN_EXISTING,
            FILE_ATTRIBUTE_NORMAL,
            NULL);

    //read file
    bool read = ReadFile(FD,
                buffer,
                num,
                &charsRead,
                NULL);

    //print to Message Box
    int button = MessageBox(0,
                buffer,
                caption,
                MB_OK);

    //close file
    bool closed = CloseHandle(FD);
    return 0;
}
``` |

Program 10.8 shows a Windows version of Program 10.7, but written in MASM 64-bit Assembly. Refer to the **CHAPTER 6** discussion on Microsoft x64 for a deeper explanation of calling functions in Windows 64-bit. We have fully commented the program and broken down the steps to assist learning, such as the allocation of stack space and why (e.g., could do "`sub rsp, 48h`" instead of 3 SUB steps) and the arithmetic for parameter locations on the stack.

Summary

Well, you made it to the other end of this particular rabbit hole. A lot more detail exists in the world of processor and system architecture, but this overview should provide you with the necessary information to get you started with system calls and low-level systems programming. We also broadly discussed system capabilities regarding processor modes and memory models. If you are interested in exploring the topics further, start with the **CHAPTER 10 SUPPLEMENT**, but do not hold us accountable for where you end up or the mental toll the paths may take.

Program 10.8 *Windows API calls in Microsoft x64 Assembly*

Windows (MASM 64-bit)

```
extrn ExitProcess : proc
extrn MessageBoxA : proc
extrn CreateFileA : proc     ; A = ANSI, W = Unicode
extrn ReadFile : proc
extrn CloseHandle : proc
extrn GetLastError : proc    ; for troubleshooting if needed

.DATA
num QWORD 13
inputFile BYTE "input.txt",0
caption BYTE "Message", 0
buffer BYTE 14 DUP (0)

;return data
FD QWORD ?
read QWORD ?
charsRead QWORD 0
button QWORD ?
closed QWORD ?

.CODE
_main PROC                              ; Print "Computer Arch"

  sub rsp, 10h                          ; reserve for return and rbp
  sub rsp, 18h                          ; reserve for parameters
  sub rsp, 20h                          ; reserve shadow space for regs

  lea rcx, inputFile                    ; address of file name
  mov rdx, 80000000h                    ; constant for GENERIC_READ
  xor r8, r8                            ; 0 share mode
  xor r9, r9                            ; 0 security
  mov QWORD PTR [rsp+48h-28h], 3        ; reverse order, 3 open existing
  mov QWORD PTR [rsp+48h-20h], 80h      ; flags FILE_ATTRIBUTE_NORMAL
  mov QWORD PTR [rsp+48h-18h], 0        ; 0 template
  call CreateFileA
  mov FD, rax                           ; save handle

  mov rcx, FD                           ; pass FD
  lea rdx, buffer                       ; pass address of buffer
  mov r8, num                           ; pass buffer size
  lea r9, charsRead                     ; pass address of charsRead
  mov QWORD PTR [rsp+48h-28h], 0        ; 0 overlap
  call ReadFile
  mov read, rax                         ; save characters read

  xor rcx, rcx                          ; 0 handle owner
  lea rdx, buffer                       ; pass text address
  lea r8, caption                       ; pass caption address
  xor r9, r9                            ; 0 MB_OK
  call MessageBoxA
  mov button, rax                       ; save button clicked

  mov rcx, FD                           ; pass handle
  call CloseHandle
  mov closed, rax                       ; save status

  add rsp, 48h                          ; clean up stack

  mov rcx, 0                            ; return value
  call ExitProcess                      ; exit

_main ENDP
END
```

Key Terms

64-bit mode
application programming interface (API)
code segment descriptor
compatibility mode
control registers
data segment descriptor
descriptor privilege level (DPL)
exception (trap)
exception handler
fast system calls
flat (linear) memory model
frame (memory)
general protection (GP) exception
Global Descriptor Table (GDT)
hardware interrupt
interrupt
Interrupt Descriptor Table (IDT)
interrupt request line (IRQ)
interrupt service routine (ISR)
interrupt stack table (IST)
interrupt vector table (IVT)
kernel

Local Descriptor Table (LDT)
long mode (IA-32e)
machine-specific registers (MSRs)
memory management registers
page (paging)
page directory
page directory pointer table
page fault
page size extension (PSE)
page table
privilege level (PL)
protected mode
real mode
segment selector
segment registers
segmented memory model
software interrupt
system call
system call number
task gates
task state segment (TSS)
virtual dynamic shared object (VDSO)

Code Review

INT	Signal a software interrupt
IRET	Special form of RET for returning from an interrupt routine
SYSENTER	Intel's initial fast system call instruction
SYSEXIT	Counterpart to SYSENTER
SYSCALL	Fast system call for x86_64
SYSRET	Counterpart to SYSCALL
CALL	Used to issue a call to a routine
INVOKE	MASM32 directive used to simplify writing Windows API calls

Questions

Short Answer

1. The typical x86 32-bit system runs in _____ mode.
2. x86_64 systems use the _____ memory model.
3. The _____ register holds an offset to an instruction location within the Code Segment.
4. Two forms of abstraction in modern memory architecture are _____ and _____.
5. Virtual memory pages are designed to fit into equally sized physical memory _____.
6. _____ is a signal initiated by the processor caused by a situation that cannot be handled by the current application.
7. Interrupts are slowed by saving context and switching _____.

8. Certain interrupts require a known good _____, for which locations are maintained in the IST.
9. IRQ lines are used for _____ interrupts.
10. The INT instruction is one way a system call can be issued to the _____.
11. The _____ instruction can only be used in 64-bit mode to make system calls.
12. Libraries and APIs offer a more consistent and _____ way to issue system calls.
13. _____ are used in kernel initialization to facilitate abstracted management of system routines.
14. Unix-like systems adhere to the _____ ABI for the implementation of 64-bit system calls.
15. The _____ calling convention uses the *rcx* register for passing parameters.

True/False

1. System registers do not have corresponding load and store instructions in order to limit access. (T/F)
2. Real Mode is no longer used in x86 and x86_64 systems. (T/F)
3. Exception handlers are functions (software routines). (T/F)
4. All 64-bit interrupts are executed as 64-bit routines, including in Compatibility Mode. (T/F)
5. The INVOKE directive is available in all Assemblers. (T/F)

Assignments

10.1 Working with Files

Create a file somewhere on your system with read-only permissions for users (4440). Using your preferred platform and Assembler, write a program that uses system calls to *copy* the file to a new location. Retrieve the file handles of both files, copy the contents, and set the new file permissions to read/write for users (6660). Do not change the original file. Display a message to let the user know the copy was successful. You may use any of the system call methods discussed in the chapter, but the entire program must be written in Assembly.

10.2 Date and Time

Using your preferred platform and Assembler, write a program that uses system calls to retrieve the current date and time and then print the date and time to screen (console or message box). You are allowed to use any of the system call methods discussed in this chapter, but the entire program must be written in Assembly. Libraries and APIs in high-level languages make this task fairly simple, however retrieving and formatting time in Assembly is more challenging. In other words, this is not as simple as it sounds.

10.3 CPUID and Vendor ID (Challenge Assignment)

The last PROGRAMMING note in the chapter says to refer to Appendix G: Using CPUID for detecting processor support for the SYSENTER instruction. However, before using CPUID it might be best to detect if CPUID itself is supported on a system. This assignment will give you a better understanding of detecting CPU features.

Using your preferred platform and Assembler, write a program that determines if your system supports the CPUID instruction and then prints whether CPUID is supported or not to screen (console or message box). The entire program must be written in Assembly (whereas Appendix G mixes CPUID and C++).

Any modern system will support CPUID, so along with the statement of support include the *vendor ID* as part of the output statement. An example of a *vendor ID* is "GenuineIntel." We recommend three sources for help.

- Appendix G: Using CPUID
- https://en.wikipedia.org/wiki/CPUID
- http://wiki.osdev.org/CPUID

Remember, you can always refer to the formal Intel documentation on the CPUID instruction.

Chapter 10 Programs and Resources

Programs

Program 10.1 *Using segment selectors*

MASM (32-bit)	NASM (32-bit)
| ```
.386
.MODEL FLAT, stdcall
.STACK 4096
ExitProcess PROTO, dwExitCode:DWORD

.DATA
array DWORD 3, 2, 6, 4, 1
.CODE
_main PROC
    mov eax, OFFSET array
    mov ebx, [eax+4]
    mov ecx, ds:[array]
    mov edx, ds:[array+8]
    INVOKE ExitProcess, 0
_main ENDP
END
``` | ```
section .data
array: dd 3, 2, 6, 4, 1

section .text
global _main
_main:

mov eax, array
mov ebx, [eax+4]
mov ecx, [ds:array]
mov edx, [ds:array+8]

mov eax, 1
mov ebx, 0
int 80h
``` |

Program 10.2 *Debug and system write interrupts*

NASM (32-bit)
| ```
section .data
output: DB "Computer Architecture",0Ah
len: EQU ($ - output)

section .text
global _main
_main:            ; Print "Computer Architecture"

;int 3h           ; Set breakpoint (remove if desired)
mov ebx, 1        ; File descriptor STDOUT (1)
mov ecx, output ; String address
mov edx, len    ; String length
mov eax, 4        ; Use SYSCALL 4 (WRITE), prints to screen
int 80h           ; SYSCALL

mov eax, 1
mov ebx, 0
int 80h
``` |
```

Program 10.3 *Print process ID with INT*

NASM (32-bit)

```
section .data
    decimal: dd 10
section .bss
    PID: resd 1

section .text
global _main
_main:                       ; Print Process ID

mov eax, 14h                 ; GET_PID call
int 80h                      ; system call
                             ; process ID is returned in EAX

mov edi, PID+3               ; Pointer to end of PID string

convert:
    xor     edx, edx
    div     DWORD [decimal] ; Divide by 10
    add     edx, 48          ; Add 48 to remainder
    mov     BYTE [edi], dl  ; Store
    dec     edi              ; Next digit
    cmp     eax, 0           ; Is EAX = 0?
    jg      convert          ; If greater than 0, more digits

mov ebx, 1          ; File descriptor STDOUT (1)
mov ecx, PID        ; String address
mov edx, 6          ; String length
mov eax, 4          ; system call 4 (WRITE), prints to screen
int 80h             ; system call

mov eax, 1           ; system call 1 (exit)
mov ebx, 0           ; return value
int 80h              ; system call
```

Program 10.6a *SYSCALL on 64-bit systems*

GAS (64-bit)

```
.data
output:     .ascii "Computer Architecture\n"
len: .quad (. - output)
file_name: .asciz "output.txt"
file_handle: .long 0

.text
.globl _main
_main:

movq $0x2000004, %rax       # system write (4)
movq $1, %rdi               # file handle STDOUT (1)
leaq output(%rip), %rsi     # address
movq len(%rip), %rdx        # length
syscall

movq $0x2000005, %rax       # system open (5)
leaq file_name(%rip), %rdi  # path
movq $0x0201, %rsi          # flags (02=O_CREAT, 01=O_WRONLY)
movq $0666, %rdx            # mode (permissions)
syscall
movq %rax, file_handle(%rip)

movq $0x2000004, %rax       # system write (4)
movq file_handle(%rip), %rdi # file handle
leaq output(%rip), %rsi     # address
movq len(%rip), %rdx        # length
syscall

movq $0x2000006, %rax       # system close (6)
movq file_handle(%rip), %rdi # file handle
syscall

movq $0x2000001, %rax       # system exit (1)
movq $0, %rdi               # return value
syscall
.end
```

Program 10.6b *SYSCALL on 64-bit systems*

NASM (64-bit)

```
section .data
output: DB "Computer Architecture",0Ah
len: DQ ($ - output)
file_name: DB "output.txt",0Ah
file_handle: DD 0

section .text
global _main
_main:

mov rax, 1                  ; system write (1)
mov rdi, 1                  ; file handle STDOUT (1)
lea rsi, [rel output]       ; address
mov rdx, [len]              ; length
syscall

mov rax, 2                  ; system open (2)
lea rdi, [rel file_name]    ; path
mov rsi, 0101o              ; flags (01=O_CREAT, 01=O_WRONLY)
mov rdx, 0666o              ; mode (permissions)
syscall
mov [rel file_handle], rax

mov rax, 1                  ; system write (1)
mov rdi, [rel file_handle]  ; file handle
lea rsi, [rel output]       ; address
mov rdx, [len]              ; length
syscall

mov rax, 3                  ; system close (3)
mov rdi, [rel file_handle]  ; file handle
syscall

mov rax, 60                 ; system exit
xor rdi, rdi                ; return value
syscall
```

Resources

Formal Documentation

The formal documentation for Intel and AMD can also be found via the book website. The formal documentation is the best place to start for help in understanding registers and instructions related to interrupts and system calls. Relevant information is scattered throughout multiple volumes and chapters of the Intel manual, so we recommend downloading the combined volume and doing text searches for the desired topic.

Intel 64 and IA-32 Architectures Software Developer's Manual
http://www.intel.com/content/www/us/en/processors/architectures-software-developer-manuals.html

System V Application Binary Interface, AMD64 Architecture Processor Supplement
https://github.com/hjl-tools/x86-psABI/wiki/X86-psABI

Microsoft Windows API Index
https://msdn.microsoft.com/library/windows/desktop/hh920508.aspx

System Call Tables

The location of system call tables and numbers varies by system. Here is a list of file names and potential locations on macOS/BSD and Linux systems.

MacOS/BSD

Files: `syscalls.h, fcntl.h`
Found at: `/usr/include/sys`

File: `syscalls.master`
http://opensource.apple.com/source/xnu/xnu-3248.50.21/bsd/kern/syscalls.master

File: `syscall_sw.h`
Purpose: code defining the system call classes (e.g., `0x2000001` for Unix/BSD, `0x1000001` for Mach)
http://opensource.apple.com/source/xnu/xnu-3248.50.21/osfmk/mach/i386/syscall_sw.h

64-bit System Call Table Reference
https://sigsegv.pl/osx-bsd-syscalls/

Other References
https://www.freebsd.org/doc/en_US.ISO8859-1/books/developers-handbook/x86-system-calls.html

Linux

Files: `syscall_32.tbl, syscall_64.tbl`
Found at: `/arch/x86/entry/syscalls`

File: `fcntl.h`
Found at: `/usr/include/` or `/usr/include/bits`

System Call Table References:
http://lxr.linux.no/linux+v4.6.4/arch/x86/entry/syscalls/
http://syscalls.kernelgrok.com (32-bit only)
http://www.escapin.it/assembler/asm_syscall.pdf (32-bit only)

Windows

DOS API: https://en.wikipedia.org/wiki/MS-DOS_API
Porting DOS calls to WinAPI: https://msdn.microsoft.com/en-us/library/aa984837(v=vs.71).aspx
Native API 32-bit: http://j00ru.vexillium.org/ntapi/
Native API 64-bit: http://j00ru.vexillium.org/ntapi_64/

Other Online Resources

Linux Inside – Interrupts
https://0xax.gitbooks.io/linux-insides/content/interrupts/

Linux Inside – System Calls
https://0xax.gitbooks.io/linux-insides/content/SysCall/

The Definitive Guide to Linux System Calls
http://blog.packagecloud.io/eng/2016/04/05/the-definitive-guide-to-linux-system-calls/

Virtual Dynamic Shared Object (VDSO) man page
http://man7.org/linux/man-pages/man7/vdso.7.html

LKML.ORG thread on merging system call paths in Linux
https://lkml.org/lkml/2015/9/1/562

LKML.ORG thread on sysenter and performance in Linux
https://lkml.org/lkml/2002/12/9/13
https://lkml.org/lkml/2002/12/18/218

Sysenter Based System Call Mechanism in Linux 2.6 (outdated, but useful explanation)
http://articles.manugarg.com/systemcallinlinux2_6.html

Nt vs. Zw – Clearing Confusion on the Native API
http://www.osronline.com/article.cfm?id=257

## CHAPTER 11

Other Architectures

Objectives

- Contrast CISC and RISC architectures
- Explore alternative architecture designs
- Analyze Assembly programs for architectures other than x86
- Identify future trends in computer architecture

Outline

Web Resources

Wikis

- https://en.wikipedia.org/wiki/Category:Instruction_set_architectures
- https://en.wikipedia.org/wiki/ARM_architecture
- https://en.wikipedia.org/wiki/Atmel_AVR
- https://en.wikipedia.org/wiki/RISC-V
- https://en.wikipedia.org/wiki/Z/Architecture
- https://en.wikipedia.org/wiki/Quantum_computing

Developer and Research

- https://developer.arm.com/products/architecture (ARM Developer)
- http://infocenter.arm.com/help/index.jsp (ARM Reference Manuals)
- http://www.atmel.com/images/Atmel-8271-8-bit-AVR-Microcontroller-ATmega48A-48PA-88A-88PA-168A-168PA-328-328P_datasheet_Complete.pdf (ATmega Datasheet)
- https://riscv.org/specifications/ (RISC-V Specification)
- https://github.com/riscv (RISC-V GitHub)
- https://www.kernel.org/doc/Documentation/s390/Debugging390.txt (s/ and z/Architecture)
- http://www.ibm.com/developerworks/library/l-basics-inline-assembly/index.html (z/Arch Assembly)
- http://www.cs.ucsb.edu/~chong/QC/ (Quantum Computing Overview)

Introduction

Throughout this text we have used the x86 and x86_64 architectures to teach Assembly programming and architecture concepts. The desired outcome is not only learning about architecture, but also learning an architecture that dominates the personal computer market. However, many other architectures exist and processor design will continue to change. In this chapter, we discuss CISC and RISC in more detail, introduce examples of other architectures, and present evolving modifications and future directions of computer architecture.

CISC versus RISC

In **Chapter 1**, we briefly mentioned CISC and RISC while discussing instruction set architectures. As a reminder, instruction set architectures are generally complex or reduced. **Complex instruction set computing (CISC)** architectures have instructions that vary in length and are complex in the sense that a single instruction may perform more than one task (e.g., access a memory location and perform arithmetic). In **reduced instruction set computing (RISC)** architecture, typically all instructions are the same length and perform one task (e.g., access a memory location, add two registers).

The characteristic of whether instructions access memory as part of another operation (such as ADD) is known as **load/store design**. RISC architectures are load/store, meaning operands are loaded and stored from and to memory with specific instructions. To perform an ADD, first each operand is retrieved from memory and placed in registers; next the two registers are added; and then the result is stored in memory. The practical result of load/store design is that RISC systems typically have more registers than CISC systems. More static (S)RAM and less dynamic (D)RAM means more efficient operation in terms of space and power, hence RISC's popularity in the mobile and embedded markets.

CISC is non-load/store since memory access can happen as part of an operation. In the ADD example, a CISC instruction can add two values, with one operand being a register and the other being a memory location. Since CISC processors more frequently access dynamic memory, high-speed cache becomes an increasingly important key to speed and efficiency. In modern architecture design, both RISC and CISC have plenty of transistors for decoders, logic, and **microcode**. A quickly blurring line in manufacturing is the emphasis on using transistor space for registers or cache. Both designs offer parallelism via split instruction and data caches along with multiple cores and logical units.

Table 11.1 CISC and RISC architecture examples

CISC	RISC	Enhanced RISC
x86, x86_64, IBM 360 – Z, Motorola 68k, PDP	ARM, RISC-V, MIPS, SPARC	PowerPC, ATmega AVR, PIC

 ATTENTION: Microcode is processor-specific logic that usually resides in reserved high-speed memory. Microcode translates machine instructions and system operations into sequences of circuit-level operations. Think of microcode as a programmed layer that defines how a specific instruction is executed on the hardware.

If we take pipelining out of the equation, instruction length differences and memory access differences become more evident. In a RISC system, the instructions are usually fixed at the same length, and most execute in one clock cycle. In a CISC system, instruction length is variable, and many instructions can take multiple clock cycles to complete due to their complexity. However, due to other processor enhancements, the reality is that both designs can achieve execution of multiple instructions in a single clock cycle.

Reduced does not mean fewer instructions and complex does not mean more instructions. For example, one of the Programmable Data Processor (PDP) systems produced by Digital Equipment Corporation (DEC) in the 1960s was the PDP-8: a 12-bit CISC computer with eight instructions. Most of the complexity was in two instructions: IOT (input/output transfer) and OPR (micro-coded operations). As an example, the OPR instruction used 9 of the 12 bits to achieve grouping and sequencing of multi-step operations. On the flip side, the PowerPC RISC architecture developed by Apple, IBM, and Motorola has about 230 instructions.

> ⚠ **ATTENTION:** In the computing market, the x86 CISC architecture has dominated the personal computer space for decades, and IBM CISC designs have held strong in the mainframe market. RISC processors such as ARM have found a stronghold in the mobile market, and most other embedded and specialty devices have also leaned toward RISC design.

RISC systems also tend to reduce datatype-specific instructions. RISC system datatypes and counterpart instructions are fairly primitive: integers, floating-point, really just a sequence of bits. CISC systems usually have instruction support for more complex datatypes such as strings. We have seen this in x86 with instructions like MOVS (move string) and CMPS (compare string).

The comparison of CISC versus RISC is not about which architecture design is better, but rather about which is best suited for a particular device or application. Up to this point in the book, we have used a CISC architecture. The next section introduces several RISC designs along with one other CISC design.

More Architectures

The goal of this section is to briefly introduce you to several other architectures that are popular in various computing markets. For each architecture we provide a short history, an overview of the instruction set architecture (ISA) and registers, and a code example. Throughout the text we provide resource links for further reading. We also draw comparisons between the architectures and x86.

ARM

ARM originally stood for Acorn RISC Machines but is now the name for ARM Holdings, which as a company develops numerous RISC architectures for processors. ARM mainly develops architectures and core designs, then licenses the designs to other companies for production. As mentioned earlier, RISC designs are generally more efficient due to less instruction complexity and thus fewer transistors are used for logic and memory accesses. The result is that ARM's RISC designs have come to dominate the mobile industry. Some examples of devices that use ARM processors are Microsoft Surface, Apple iPhones/iPads, Canon digital cameras, Nintendo DS, and various GPS navigation systems.

ARM has had many evolutions in design, but we focus on two major areas: the ARM 32-bit architecture (**AArch32**) and the ARM 64-bit architecture (**AArch64**). ARM's architectures have three distinct profiles: Application (A), Real-time (R), and Microcontroller (M). The A-series is the most prevalent profile as it comes in both 32-bit and 64-bit variations and is used in devices running user applications. The R-series is 32-bit and is for real-time and safety-critical systems like vehicles and medical devices. The M-series is 32-bit, and it is intended for microcontrollers and is usually found on microcontroller boards from manufacturers such as Arduino and NXP.

Just as the x86 architecture has processor modes such as Protected and Long, ARM processors have various modes. User Mode is the primary mode for non-privileged processing, while up to 10 different privileged modes exist for tasks such as interrupts and exceptions. Most ARM processors have a traditional three-stage pipeline for fetch, decode, and execute, while more recent versions such as ARM8 and ARM9 have more complex pipelines.

The ARM ISA is load/store, has a uniform register set, typically uses a fixed instruction width, and most instructions execute in one clock cycle. Design differences from x86 that enhance speed include not altering the condition codes after arithmetic unless desired, a dedicated register for the return address for function calls, and most instructions are implicitly conditional, meaning no branching overhead. The latter is very different from other architectures. Most instructions in AAarch32 use four bits as a predicate (condition code selector) that indicates the circumstances for which the instruction should be executed, such as unconditional. So instead of a branching mechanism along with its overhead, some ARM architectures sacrifice a clock cycle for a non-executing instruction. ARM did change the use of predication for AArch64, which uses it much less. Branch prediction does vary by profile and core.

Registers available depends on whether the core is 32-bit or 64-bit, whether the core supports the **Thumb** instruction set (a 16-bit encoding of the ARM instruction set), the processor mode, and which variant of the **vector floating-point unit (VFP)** is present. Here we just present common configurations in user mode.

- **AArch32**: 16 32-bit registers *r0–r15* where *r13* serves as the Stack Pointer (*SP*), *r14* serves as the Link Register (*LR*) to hold the return address for function calls, and *r15* is the Program Counter (*PC*). A separate 32-bit register serves as the Current Program Status Register (*CPSR*), which contains processor management bits and arithmetic flags. Many of the 32-bit ARM cores use a variant of the VFP that has 16 or 32 64-bit floating-point registers that can hold single- or double-precision values.

- **AArch64**: 31 64-bit general purpose registers *x0–x30* with 32-bit forms *w0–w30* where *x29* is used as the Frame Pointer (*FP*) and *x30* is the *LR*; a dedicated *SP* register; a dedicated *PC* register; 32 128-bit FPU registers; and with the *Advanced SIMD extension (NEON)* support for 8, 16, 32, and 64-bit integers along with single- and double-precision SIMD operations.

The memory space and addresses in AArch64 are 64 bits, but instructions are still 32 bits. Operands in instructions can usually be either 32 or 64 bits. Many other design variations and enhancements exist, depending on the specific ARM core.

Program 11.1 *Arduino Due Blink program in ARM Assembly*

```
                                    ARM
// written in Arduino 1.6.10

void setup() {
  asm volatile(                     // same as pinMode(13, OUTPUT)
    "mov r0, %[led] \n\t"           // move I/O address to r0
    "mov r1, #1     \n\t"           // store 1 in r1
    "lsl r1, #27    \n\t"           // shift left 27 bits, mask for pin 13
    "str r1, [r0]   \n\t"           // store contents of r1 into address in r0
    : : [led] "r" (&REG_PIOB_OER)   // I/O Port B enable output register
  );
}


void loop() {
    asm volatile(
      "push {r0-r3, lr}   \n\t"     // save registers
      "mov r0, %[ledOn]   \n\t"
      "mov r1, #1         \n\t"
      "lsl r1, #27        \n\t"
      "str r1, [r0]       \n\t"     // turn LED on
      "mov r0, #1000      \n\t"     // constant parameter for delay(n)
      "bl delay           \n\t"     // branch to ARM delay(n) function
      "mov r0, %[ledOff]  \n\t"
      "mov r1, #1         \n\t"
      "lsl r1, #27        \n\t"
      "str r1, [r0]       \n\t"     // turn LED off
      "mov r0, #1000      \n\t"
      "bl delay           \n\t"
      "pop {r0-r3, lr}    \n\t"     // restore register values
      "bx lr              \n\t"     // branch to address in link register
      : : [ledOn] "r" (&REG_PIOB_SODR), [ledOff] "r" (&REG_PIOB_CODR)
    );  // SODR: set output data register; CODR: clear output data register
}
```

To illustrate the ARM architecture, we present Program 11.1 written for the *Arduino Due* microcontroller, which features an ARM Cortex-M3 32-bit processor running at 84MHz. Arduinos use a C-variant language and the AVR-GCC compiler, so Program 11.1 shows the code written as inline ARM Assembly, which is very similar to the GCC inline examples in **Chapter 9**. Although Program 11.1 is a working example of the Arduino Blink program, our purpose is to visualize similarities and differences in instruction mnemonics, registers, and syntax as compared to other architectures. Program 11.1 makes the onboard LED blink.

Instruction mnemonics similar to x86 are MOV, PUSH, and POP, while different mnemonics are LSL (logical shift left), STR (store register), and BL (branch with link). Register names follow the *r#* convention discussed earlier in this section, and numeric immediates start with #. Since AVR-GCC is a variant of GCC, the same inline Assembly template is used, including inputs, outputs, and clobbers. The comments explain more program specifics.

Example 11.1 Disassembly of program 11.1 `setup()`

ARM
| ```
80148: 4b03          ldr    r3, [pc, #12]    ; (80158 <setup+0x10>)
8014a: 4618          mov    r0, r3
8014c: f04f 0101     mov.w  r1, #1
80150: ea4f 61c1     mov.w  r1, r1, lsl #27
80154: 6001          str    r1, [r0, #0]
80156: 4770          bx     lr
80158: 400e1010      .word  0x400e1010
``` |

If we look at the disassembly of the Program 11.1 `setup()` function in Example 11.1, we notice ARM AArch32 attributes. The instruction length is consistent at 32 bits (e.g., `f04f 0101`), with some abbreviated 16-bit Thumb instructions (e.g., `4b03`) for code density. Word length is 32 bits. The compiler placed prologue and epilogue code using the *PC* and *LR* registers and rewrote the LSL instruction to a version of the MOV instruction that performs a shift as part of the move (a feature of ARM that still executes in one clock cycle). To disassemble the Arduino ARM code, we ran the contents of the temporary `.elf` file created during compilation through a version of `objdump` for ARM included with the Arduino hardware tools.

 LEARNING: Information about the Arduinos used for Programs 11.1 and 11.2 can be found via the links:
- https://www.arduino.cc/en/Main/ArduinoBoardDue
- https://www.arduino.cc/en/Main/ArduinoBoardUno

AVR

AVR is an advanced (enhanced) RISC 8-bit architecture developed by Atmel. We have chosen to introduce AVR architecture because of its simplistic 8-bit design, simple instruction set, and popularity on microcontroller boards such as the *Arduino Uno*. The AVR design is a modification of another architecture known as the **Harvard** architecture. Harvard architecture physically separates instruction and data storage. AVR's modification is that although the program and data are stored in separate memory spaces (albeit on the same chip), special instructions allow program memory to be accessed as if it were data.

As with many architectures, several classifications of AVR exist. We focus on the very popular 8-bit **ATmega AVR** design. A 32-bit version known as **AVR32** does exist and is used on some microcontroller boards to compete with ARM, and is similar to more sophisticated cores, including SIMD support. However, the ATmega series has found a high-volume niche in the microcontroller market and is especially suited for prototyping. As an example, we describe the features of the ATmega328p, which as of this writing is the most current design. All versions of the ATmega series are generally the same, just the memory sizes vary.

 LEARNING: The Harvard architecture was introduced with the Harvard Mark I computer in the early 1940s for making war-related computations. Being one of the first major computer systems, the Mark I is often discussed in introductory computer science courses as part of computer history. But remnants of the design remain in modern architectures.

As mentioned, AVR designs have separate program and data memory. All memory spaces are linear (flat). The program memory on the ATmega328p is 32k of flash memory, with 0.5k reserved for the bootloader. Although the ATmega is 8-bit, program instructions are 16 or 32 bits, so the memory space is 16-bit with addresses ranging from `0x0000` to `0x3FFF`. The data memory is 2k of static RAM (SRAM), which is composed of the general purpose register file, I/O registers, extended I/O space, and main data memory that serves as stack space for the program. Data memory accesses happen in two clock cycles, but the 32 general purpose registers are directly connected to the ALU, so register-only operations happen in one clock cycle. An additional 1k of EEPROM is also available for data uses.
```

Table 11.2 ATmega328p SRAM data memory layout

SRAM components	Address range
32 general purpose registers	0x0000 – 0x001F
64 I/O registers	0x0020 – 0x005F
160 extended I/O registers	0x0060 – 0x00FF
Data memory	0x0100 – 0x08FF

The registers are 8 bits and can be used for 8-bit input and output operands. They can also be used in combination for 16-bit operands. The general purpose registers are denoted as *r0–r31*. AVR features an 8-bit status register (*SREG*) and two 8-bit registers—*SPL* (stack pointer low) and *SPH* (stack pointer high)—that comprise the Stack Pointer for addressing the 16-bit address space. *SREG* (Table 11.3) is similar to the *flags* register in x86.

Table 11.3 AVR status register (*SREG*)

Bit	7	6	5	4	3	2	1	0
Purpose	interrupt (I)	bit copy (T)	half carry (H)	sign (S)	overflow (V)	negative (N)	zero (Z)	carry (C)

Since registers are implemented as 16-bit memory locations in SRAM, registers *r26–r31* can be doubled up to serve as register pointers (registers that point to other registers). The register pointer registers are denoted as *X*, *Y*, and *Z*.

Table 11.4 AVR *X, Y*, and *Z* registers

Register pointer	X		Y		Z	
Registers used	R27 (XH)	R26 (XL)	R29 (YH)	R28 (YL)	R31 (ZH)	R30 (ZL)

To illustrate the AVR architecture, we present Program 11.2 written for the Arduino Uno microcontroller, which features an ATmega328p 8-bit processor running at 16MHz. Similar to Program 11.1, Program 11.2 shows the code written as inline AVR Assembly. Again, the purpose of Program 11.2 is to visualize similarities and differences in instruction mnemonics, registers, and syntax as compared to other architectures. Program 11.2 makes the onboard LED blink.

In Program 11.2 we chose to define several constants to showcase some AVR features. One is that C code easily mixes with inline Assembly (as it does with ARM and x86). The setup() function shows the use of system constants, which is the same approach in Program 11.1. The loop() function shows use of programmer-defined constants that give the system constants more explanatory names. Program 11.2 could be rewritten to be more efficient, but our implementation and expanded steps are focused on features and clarity.

ATmega registers are 8-bit, but notice that the DelayTime variable is a 32-bit integer. Even though the Delay-Time value we provided only requires 24 bits, we have a 32-bit operand at our disposal if we want to increase the delay time of blinks. We can operate on the 32-bit integer in an 8-bit environment by chopping the integer into 8-bit chunks and using the appropriate subtraction instructions. Recall from **Chapter 9** that in GCC inline Assembly, the I/O parameters are referred to as %0, %1, %2 … if no symbolic names are defined. AVR allows movement of 16-bit and 32-bit parameters by using the letters A, B, C, and D to refer 8-bit chucks of a 32-bit value. So for example, %D2 is the least significant byte (LSB) of %2, which is DelayTime in the input variable list. In the mainLoop, we use the DelayTime constant twice and set up two distinct timers (*r16–r19* and *r20–r23*) and for on and off.

The use of input parameters and clobbers shows similar syntax to x86 inline Assembly, although the constraint letters vary from architecture to architecture (e.g., I, n, and d). We can use symbolic names for parameters instead of numeric values (e.g., %[port] instead of %0). AVR shares some mnemonics with x86 and ARM, such as MOV, but subtraction, branching, and I/O instructions are different. The comments in Program 11.2 explain more program specifics.

Program 11.2 *Arduino Uno Blink program in AVR assembly*

```
                                      AVR
// written in Arduino 1.6.10
#define LEDPort PORTB             // Arduino pin 13 is bit 5 of port B
#define LEDPort_Direction DDRB    // DDRB is the port B direction register
#define LEDBit 5                  // Constant for bit 5
#define Clock_MHz 16
#define MilliSec 1000000
#define DelayTime (uint32_t)((Clock_MHz * MilliSec / 5)) // set to any rate

void setup() {          // same as pinMode(13, OUTPUT)
  asm volatile (        // shows default parameter use instead of defines
    "sbi %0, %1 \n\t"   // sets port and bit direction
    : : "I" (_SFR_IO_ADDR(DDRB)), "I" (DDB5  // I: 6-bit positive const int
  );}

void loop() {
  asm volatile (
    " mainLoop: "                           // move DelayTime to registers
    "    mov r16, %D2  \n\t"                 // LSB of DelayTime
    "    mov r17, %C2  \n\t"                 // A2, B2, C2, D2 each is 8 bits
    "    mov r18, %B2  \n\t"
    "    mov r19, %A2  \n\t"                 // MSB of DelayTime
    "    mov r20, %D2  \n\t"
    "    mov r21, %C2  \n\t"
    "    mov r22, %B2  \n\t"
    "    mov r23, %A2  \n\t"
    "    sbi %[port], %[ledbit] \n\t"        // set I/O bit (turn LED on)
    " onLoop: "
    "    subi r23, 1  \n\t"                  // subtract constant from register
    "    sbci r22, 0  \n\t"                  // subtract w/carry const from reg
    "    sbci r21, 0  \n\t"
    "    sbci r20, 0  \n\t"
    "    brcc onLoop  \n\t"                  // branch if carry cleared
    "    cbi  %[port], %[ledbit] \n\t"       // clear I/O bit (turn LED off)
    " offLoop:"
    "    subi r19, 1  \n\t"
    "    sbci r18, 0  \n\t"
    "    sbci r17, 0  \n\t"
    "    sbci r16, 0  \n\t"
    "    brcc offLoop \n\t"
    :                                        // no output variables
    : [port] "n" (_SFR_IO_ADDR(LEDPort)),   // input variables
      [ledbit] "n" (LEDBit),                // n: integer with known value
      "d" (DelayTime)                       // d: greater than r15
    : "r16","r17","r18","r19","r20","r21","r22","r23"  // clobbers
  );}
```

RISC-V

Though a large portion of software is proprietary, the software industry continues to experience significant movement toward open software. In similar fashion, throughout computing history most ISAs have been proprietary, but the concepts of open hardware design and instruction set architecture are becoming more prevalent. For example, Arduino microcontrollers are an open-source hardware design. In the ISA space, **RISC-V** (risk-five) is an example of a modern and leading-edge open-source RISC architecture.

The RISC-V architecture was born out of research and educational activities led primarily at the University of California at Berkeley. RISC-V mostly remains in research and specialty environments, but the RISC-V Foundation (organization) and the offering of an open-source architecture are catalysts for future growth in the computing industry. Processor designs that implement RISC-V can be open source or proprietary.

 LEARNING: The design features, specification, news, and information about RISC-V can be found at the following links:
- https://riscv.org/
- https://riscv.org/risc-v-foundation/

As with the other architectures presented in this chapter, our goal is to merely whet your appetite and encourage you to look into RISC-V. The ISA features a scalable address space (e.g., 32, 64, 128-bit) and scalable variable instruction-length encoding. The base RISC-V instruction format (**RV32I**) is 32 bits, but it can be encoded in any number of 16-bit chunks (16, 32, 48, 64-bit, etc.). The 32 general purpose registers are denoted as *x0–x31*, with *x0* hardwired to contain zero. Each thread has its own register state and Program Counter (*PC*) register. A control and status register (*CSR*) also exists. Since each program thread executes independently and sequentially, specific instructions like FENCE help with synchronizing operations given the flexible memory model.

The general purpose registers serve in various roles when it comes to the RISC-V calling convention (**RVG**). Uses include *x1* serving as the link register that holds the return address (*RA*), *x2* is the stack pointer (*SP*), *x10–x17* serve as parameter registers (*a0–a7*), among other specific uses for other registers.

 LEARNING: Why might we want a register to always contain a constant zero? Answer: doing so facilitates implementing operations with fewer instructions and thus fewer logic gates. For example, an add instruction can be used in place of a MOV instruction. In RISC-V, a register-to-register move is actually the `addi` instruction expressed as `addi rd, rs, r0`. A move is accomplished by adding zero to the source register and saving the result in the destination register.

The base RISC-V implementation is only basic integer operations. Extensions can be implemented for more sophisticated operations. To do multiplication and division, the "M" extension must be implemented. **Atomic operations** require the "A" extension. Manufacturers can choose to implement the "F" extension for single-precision floating-point operations, which adds 32 floating-point registers *f0–f31* and a control and status register (*FCSR*). The "D" extension adds double-precision support by expanding the *f#* registers to 64 bits. Other extensions exist or are planned for RISC-V (e.g., "Q" for quad precision, "C" for compressed 16-bit format, etc.).

Program 11.3 provides a copy of a RISC-V unit test program found on the RISC-V GitHub account (https://github.com/riscv) with modified comments. You should notice the similarities with x86 GAS code since the RISC-V toolchain is a standard GNU cross compiler for RISC-V. RISC-V code can be compiled, assembled, and linked using the `riscv-{gcc, as, ld}` tools. So directives such as `.data`, `.align`, and `.dword` are familiar, as is the label syntax (e.g., `fail:`). The in-code comments explain what the specific RISC-V instructions do. Remember the word length is 32 bits.

ARM, AVR, and RISC-V are all examples of RISC architectures. They provide relevant examples and insight into the competitive architecture design to CISC. Another popular RISC architecture we have chosen not to cover, but encourage you to look into, is the **Power Architecture** family of RISC designs (https://www.power.org). Variants of the Power Architecture are used in a significant portion of high-end systems, including game systems, servers, and supercomputers.

Program 11.3 *RISC-V unit test*

RISC-V

```
# Modified from https://github.com/riscv/riscv-tests
.include "riscv_test.h"      # defines the macros (in all-caps)


RVTEST_RV64U                 # define TVM used by program


# Test code
RVTEST_CODE_BEGIN            # Start of test code
        lw      x2, testdata  # load word into x2 (41)
        addi    x2, 1         # add 1 to x2 (our result)
        sw      x2, result    # store word into memory overwriting -1s.
        li      x3, 42        # load immediate into x3 (desired result)
        bne     x2, x3, fail  # branch if not equal: Fail if no match
        RVTEST_PASS           # else success
fail:
        RVTEST_FAIL
RVTEST_CODE_END             # End of test code


# Input data section
# This section is optional, the data is NOT saved in the output
.data
        .align 3
testdata:
        .dword 41


# Output data section
RVTEST_DATA_BEGIN    # Start of test output data region
        .align 3
result:
        .dword -1
RVTEST_DATA_END      # End of test output data region
```

System – z/Architecture

If we were to directly compare the number of RISC versus CISC ISA designs, many more are RISC. But the x86 ISA has dominated the computer market, and IBM's System – z/Architecture has dominated the mainframe market. IBM's powerful 32-bit mainframe System/ architecture was introduced in 1964 with the **System/360**, which was followed by the **System/370** that evolved over twenty years from 1970 to 1990. **System/390** and its variations held the market from about 1990 to 2000, when the zSeries was introduced. The **z/Architecture** is a modern branding of IBM's 64-bit ISA that is backward compatible all the way to the System/360. IBM develops specific operating systems, such as *z/OS*, to take advantage of their CISC design, and alternatives such as *Linux on System z* are also available.

Almost everything in the z/Architecture is 64-bit, although supporting both 32-bit and 64-bit operations for backward compatibility required implementing 64-bit versions of most 32-bit instructions present in the earlier System/ architectures. The move to 64-bit doubled the instructions to more than 300. The address space is 64-bit, so up to 16 exabytes of address space is available. As of this writing, register sizes vary in the z/Architecture: 16 general purpose registers (*r0–r15* or *gpr0–gpr15*) at 64 bits, 16 control registers (*cr0–cr15*) at 64-bits, 16 access registers (*ar0–ar15*) at 32 bits, 16 floating-point registers (*fp0–fp15*) at 64 bits, a Floating-Point Control register (*FPC*) that is 32 bits, and the program status word register (*PSW*) that is 128 bits wide. The *PSW* serves as the program counter, among other things.

To illustrate z/Architecture, we derived Examples 11.2 and 11.3 from a debugging example retrieved from www.kernel.org. Assume we have a simple C++ test program that looks something like Example 11.2.

PROGRAMMING: *Debugging on Linux for s/390 & z/Architecture* by Denis Barrow provides useful information on memory layout, stack frames, and register usage.
Link: https://www.kernel.org/doc/Documentation/s390/Debugging390.txt

Example 11.2 C++ test

C++
```int test (int b) {   return (b + 5); } int main(int argc,char *argv[]) {   return (test(5)); }```

Example 11.3 illustrates characteristics of the z/Architecture with the disassembly of Example 11.2. First, note the AT&T syntax style. Second, notice the variable instruction length found in CISC design, particularly in the disassembly of `main()`. Parameters are passed in registers when possible. Function prologue and epilogue code saves and restores registers as appropriate. Registers are serving special purposes related to the calling convention, such as *r11* as the frame pointer, *r14* as the return address, *r15* as the stack pointer, *r2* as the return value, and *r7* as a pointer to arguments. If successful, the test would return the integer 10.

System/ and z/Architecture provide a point of comparison for the x86 CISC design. We encourage you to examine the z/Architecture further if you have interest in exploring software development on 64-bit mainframes.

Example 11.3 Disassembly of Example 11.2

```
                                z/Architecture
00000000800005b0 <test>:
int test(int b)
{ return(b+5);
  800005b0:    a7 2a 00 05       ahi    %r2,5      # add 5 to r2
  800005b4:    b9 14 00 22       lgfr   %r2,%r2    # downcast to integer (long)
  800005b8:    07 fe             br     %r14       # branch to address in r14
  800005ba:    07 07             bcr    0,%r7      # conditional branch
}


00000000800005bc <main>:
main(int argc,char *argv[])
{
  800005bc:    eb bf f0 58 00 24 stmg   %r11,%r15,88(%r15)   # save registers
  800005c2:    b9 04 00 1f       lgr    %r1,%r15             # load stack pointer
  800005c6:    a7 fb ff 60       aghi   %r15,-160            # point to mem pool
  800005ca:    e3 10 f0 00 00 24 stg    %r1,0(%r15)          # save location
return(test(5));
  800005d0:    a7 29 00 05       lghi   %r2,5                #load 5 into r2
  800005d4:    c0 e5 ff ff ff ee brasl  %r14,800005b0 <test> #branch to test
  800005da:    e3 40 f1 10 00 04 lg     %r4,272(%r15)        #r4 <- ret address
  800005e0:    eb bf f0 f8 00 04 lmg    %r11,%r15,248(%r15)  #restore registers
  800005e6:    07 f4             br     %r4                  #branch, return
}
```

Quantum Architecture

Quantum architecture has been making waves (pun intended) as advances continue in science and technology. Harnessing energy has always been necessary for computing. Classical systems use energy forms such as electricity and magnetism. Quantum systems use more elementary energy sources such as photons, which are discrete quantities (a **quantum**) of light. Thus, a **quantum architecture** is one where the unit of information and/or communication is built upon elementary particles.

In classical architecture, a **bit** is the unit of information. A bit is a binary digit representing 0 or 1 and is in a given state until switched. In other words, a bit is always either 0 or 1. In **Chapter 1** we discussed physical properties used to represent a binary digit. A couple of quick examples are a memory cell being charged or not charged, and a transistor allowing current or not.

In quantum architecture, a **qubit** is the unit of information. A qubit is a quantum digit that is in a given state when observed, but exists in a **superposition** of both states. In other words, when measured, a qubit will represent either 0 or 1, but otherwise it is in both states simultaneously. Physical particles (along with their properties) that can be used as qubits include the polarization of photons (horizontal or vertical) and the spin of an atom (up or down).

As an example, a classic byte (8 bits) has 2^8 possible states. The byte of information is in one of 256 unique combinations (a state) until switched. Like the classical byte, a quantum byte or **qubyte** is 2^n, but with 8 qubits the qubyte exists in all 256 states simultaneously. When observed, the qubyte will collapse into a classical state and one of 256 possibilities.

! ATTENTION: The difference between classical and quantum bits can be expressed in probabilistic terms. Say we have two states, *a* and *b*. In a classical system, the probability that a bit is in a given state sums to 1 (*a + b = 1*). In a quantum system, the probability that a qubit is in a given state is the sum of the squares of the coefficients' magnitudes (the coefficients are complex and a squared magnitude is the probability of a given state), which is also 1 ($|a|^2 + |b|^2 = 1$), but the phase difference between two states is meaningful.

Quantum particles have a beneficial property that can be exploited for computation. **Entanglement** is an unusual correlation between quantum particles where particles maintain a connection no matter the distance. For example, when two qubits are entangled, they are always in opposite states when observed. If two photons A and B are entangled, when A is measured as horizontal, B will always be vertical, and vice versa. If A is 0, B is 1. Due to the inter-correlation, multiple states can be acted on simultaneously.

What is the computational benefit of quantum computing? The key is in considering how classic computers solve problems and the circumstance that superposition and entanglement provide. The process of problem solving in computing is algorithmic—a step-by-step process. For example, if we wanted to test the output of an algorithm given 2^8 (256) possible inputs, we would have to step through the algorithm 256 times, once for each unique input. But in a quantum computer, we could process all 256 possibilities simultaneously with a single logic gate, which is an exponential increase in computation speed.

However, quantum computation is not without its challenges. First and foremost, quantum properties such as entanglement are not fully understood. Second, qubits are susceptible to environmental interactions and can easily lose their state, which is known as **decoherence**. Quantum computing requires qubits to be initialized to states that represent a specific problem (e.g., Shor's algorithm) and then a fixed series of **quantum logic gates** manipulate the qubits, which produces a classic result. Other challenges are initializing qubits to a known state, measuring states, communication between qubits, qubit lifespans, and fault tolerance.

Such challenges leave many questions about large-scale manufacturing of quantum computers, and they are currently out of reach. Very few quantum computers exist; they are confined to research organizations and large corporations, and they average just a few qubits. In the meantime, classical systems can still be improved by harnessing the power of light in other ways. One example is using photonic interconnects in classical systems to speed up intra-chip and inter-chip communication (see following LEARNING note). Fiber optics are faster and more energy efficient than electrical buses, and marrying the two methods on the same chip is becoming a reality. Researchers are figuring out ways to integrate photonics without changing the manufacturing process, which means low cost and easily scalable production.

> 📖 LEARNING: Photonic interconnect example. The processor is based on the RISC-V architecture.
> Citation: Sun, C. et al. Single-chip microprocessor that communicates directly using light. *Nature* 528, 534–538 (2015). doi:10.1038/nature16454.
> Link: http://www.nature.com/nature/journal/v528/n7583/full/nature16454.html

Summary

In this chapter, we diverged from our exploration of x86/x86_64 architecture and introduced several popular ISAs of both RISC and CISC design. As with learning programming languages, learning one architecture very well is better than learning many architectures only slightly. If you have a very good understanding of an ISA such as x86, the transition to learning other ISAs, such as those presented in this chapter, is less difficult. Computer architectures will continue to evolve and markets will shift, but the principles of architecture design are firmly grounded and are mostly transferable from design to design. Yet, what the future holds remains to be seen.

Key Terms

AArch32
AArch64
ARM
ATmega AVR
atomic operations
AVR
AVR32
bit
complex instruction set computing (CISC)
decoherence
entanglement
Harvard
load/store design
microcode
Power Architecture
quantum

quantum architecture
quantum logic gates
qubit
qubyte
reduced enstruction set computing (RISC)
RISC-V
RV32I
RVG
superposition
System/360
System/370
System/390
Thumb
vector floating-point unit (VFP)
z/Architecture

Questions

Short Answer

1. x86_64 is a type of _____ architecture.
2. _____ architecture has found a dominant place in the mobile computing market.
3. Condition code selectors in AArch32 instructions are known as a _____.
4. The ARM Cortex-M3 is based on the _____ profile.
5. In the ARM architecture, the _____ register holds the return address of a function call.
6. Instruction length on RISC ARM processors can vary due to the _____ instruction set.
7. AVR architecture is based on the _____ architecture.
8. AVR is an _____-bit architecture with a _____-bit address space.
9. _____ is an example of an open-source ISA.
10. Uninterruptible sequences of instructions are said to be _____.
11. RISC-V uses the _____ calling convention for function calls.
12. Elementary particles serve as units of information in a _____ architecture.
13. The ability for a photon to exist in multiple states simultaneously is known as _____.
14. Quantum _____ is when environmental factors cause qubits to lose state.
15. If two qubits are entangled, when one is measured, the other will always be the _____.

True/False

1. CISC architecture is said to be load/store design. (T/F)
2. The number of instructions in an ISA has little to do with whether it is RISC or CISC. (T/F)
3. Machine constraints are the same across all architectures. (T/F)
4. Register sizes must all be 64 bits in a 64-bit architecture. (T/F)
5. Classic (n-bit) systems and Quantum (n-qubit) systems are both 2^n when measured. (T/F)

Assignments

11.1   CPU Architecture Report

Write a two- to three-page technical research report on a CPU that implements an ISA other than x86/x86_64 and the four architectures described in this chapter (ARM Cortex-M3, AVR ATmega, RISC-V, and z/Architecture). Some examples are MIPS R4000, Sun UltraSPARC IV, PowerPC G5, MC 68000, Cell, and PIC processors.

   The report should contain information on the following topics:
* Technology introduction/overview (brief), including devices that used or are using the CPU;
* Architecture history and details including an overview of the ISA. (Is it RISC or CISC? How many instructions? For what types of applications and computation is it best suited?) You can follow the general format used for the architecture overviews in this chapter.
* Pipeline Structure (fetch-execution cycle design and/or enhancements);
* Memory specifics (main, cache, registers, virtual);
* Other interesting tidbits ... such as a code example.

11.2   Alternative Assembly

Choose a device or simulator/emulator you have access to that is based on an ISA other than x86/x86_64. Using your preferred or the required development environment for the architecture, write an Assembly program that does a task or tasks of your choosing. The requirements are that the program must have *at least* 20 Assembly *instructions*, all Assembly statements must be commented describing their purpose or operation, and the program must assemble/compile and execute successfully (demonstrate). You may use stand-alone or inline Assembly.

11.3   Alternative Disassembly

Choose a high-level program (e.g., C, C++, Objective-C, Java, a microcontroller variant of a language) that is intended for or portable to an architecture other than x86/x86_64. Using your preferred or the required disassembler for the architecture, disassemble the program, save the contents to a text file, and comment *at least* 30 Assembly statements describing their operation. You can disassemble a program you have written or a program for which you have the source of code. If you use a program that is larger than 30 Assembly statements (which is likely), you can choose any section of the program to comment.

11.4   ISA Design (Challenge Assignment)

If you were to design an ISA, what would it look like? Write an abstracted overview of an ISA that provides the basic need-to-know information. How many bits? Load/store design? Register layout? Floating-point support? Memory design? Pipeline? Instruction format? Calling convention? Sampling of an instruction set? Code examples? What makes your ISA different from other ISAs? For what devices and applications is it best suited and why?

   Assignment 11.4 gives you an opportunity to think of improvements and enhancements, and to tweak things that you find problematic with current ISAs. Or maybe you just want to design something your own way. The best way to approach this assignment is to look at outlines of other ISA specification documents. Most specifications are hundreds of pages, but with just the basic information, brief descriptions, some visualizations, and theoretical code examples you can keep it between 5 and 10 pages.

Hardware and Electrical Components

Objectives

- Identify electrical components
- Describe the function of hardware components
- Solve equations of electrical principles
- Deconstruct electronic devices revealing their base components

Outline

Web Resources

- https://en.wikipedia.org/wiki/Electric_current
- https://en.wikipedia.org/wiki/Voltage
- https://en.wikipedia.org/wiki/Electric_power
- https://en.wikipedia.org/wiki/Electrical_resistance_and_conductance

Introduction

Welcome to the final chapter! Reading this far is quite an accomplishment. We have covered many details of Assembly programming, x86/x86_64 architecture, and taken glimpses at other architectures you may encounter on your journey as a software engineer. Because the primary audience of this book is software engineers, not computer and electrical engineers, we have not discussed electrical design and the components that underpin computer architecture and make programming possible. This chapter dives a little deeper in order to give you a general understanding of electronics. We also intend to provide you with information necessary to build simple hardware devices. This hardware-focused content may help with courses, personal projects, or company projects when prototyping devices, when working with embedded devices, or when working with microcontroller boards and components. Basically, we want to help you avoid burning components or yourself.

Foundations of Electricity

Basic Principles

First, understanding the basic principles of electricity is critical. Electrical principles include current (usually abbreviated with an uppercase I for intensity), voltage (usually abbreviated E or V, though V is usually reserved for the unit of measure), power (usually abbreviated P), and resistance (usually abbreviated R). The principles and their units of measure are shown in Table 12.1.

Table 12.1 Electrical principles

Principle		Unit of measure	
Name	**Abbreviation**	**Name**	**Abbreviation**
Current	I	Ampere	A
Voltage	E or V	Volt	V
Power	P	Watt	W
Resistance	R	Ohm	Ω

Next, we define each of the principles to gain a better understanding of how they are related.

Current can be defined as the rate of electrons flowing past a certain point. In order to better describe the intensity of electron flow, the **Ampere (Amp)** was assigned as the unit of measure. The higher the Amperage, the faster the flow of electrons across a wire. Imagine two pieces of electrical equipment, a desk lamp and a motor that is driving a vacuum cleaner. Relatively speaking, very little electricity is needed to illuminate a light bulb, so light bulbs have a low Amperage. Vacuum cleaners require much more electricity, so vacuums have a high Amperage. Sometimes the flow, or usage, of electricity is called the **draw** (i.e., the amount of current a device needs to draw in order to operate).

 LEARNING: One Ampere is roughly equivalent to 6.24 x 10^{18} or 6,240,000,000,000,000,000 electrons passing a given point per second.

ATTENTION: Using multiple high-Amp devices at the same time in a house can cause a circuit breaker to trip, resulting in loss of power. Breaker trips occur when devices operating at the same time attempt to draw more current than the circuit can provide (e.g., a 10A hair dryer and an 8A vacuum will trip a standard 15A house breaker because the draw exceeds the maximum).

Voltage is electrical pressure, or the difference in charge between two points. As such, voltage is sometimes referred to as *potential*. Electrical pressure is measured in **volts**. You may be confused about the difference between the flow of electricity (current) and electrical pressure (voltage). Comparing electrical pressure to water pressure can help clarify voltage and current.

Imagine a garden hose that has the spigot half way (50%) open. A constant amount of water (current) is now flowing through the hose at any given point. Assume the garden hose has a typical 1-inch opening at the end. Water flows out of the hose with no real force because the 1-inch opening is not creating much pressure (voltage). The stream of water is not very powerful and would not be useful for intense cleaning.

However, if you change one of the variables, such as placing your thumb over most of the 1-inch opening, you can create a more powerful stream of water. Decreasing the opening size creates a higher pressure (voltage) but lowers the current because less water is flowing through the opening. Still, the stream of water would only be slightly more powerful. Were you to keep your thumb mostly over the opening (increasing the voltage) and also open the spigot to 100% (increasing the current), you could create a more powerful stream of water.

The next electrical principle is power. **Power** is the amount of work performed by the electrical current and is measured in **watts**. Going back to the garden hose example, we found that changing one or more of the principles (pressure and current) affects power. The implication is that power is directly related to current and voltage. The relationship can be expressed algebraically with the following formula.

$$P = I * E$$

Using basic algebra, we can determine any one of the principles as long as we know the other two. For example, by knowing the wattage of a device and the voltage of the electrical outlet, you can determine the current to ensure you do not go over the maximum amps of the breaker. Assume you have an air conditioner that is rated at 1560W and a nominal voltage of 120V. Rearranging the equation, we can determine the current necessary to operate the air conditioner.

$P = I * E$	$I = \dfrac{P}{E}$	$E = \dfrac{P}{I}$

$$I = \frac{1560W}{120V} \qquad\qquad 13A = \frac{1560W}{120V}$$

Lastly, we introduce resistance. **Resistance** is the reduction in current due to the material, environment, and components through which current is flowing. Since electrical conductors are not perfect, some electricity is naturally lost in transit. But we can also add resistance in order to ensure electrical energy is at an appropriate level for a component. Resistance is measured in **Ohms**. Resistance and its relationship to other electrical principles is expressed with **Ohm's Law**, which provides equations demonstrating the proportionality of current (I), voltage (E), and resistance (R).

$E = I * R$	$I = \dfrac{E}{R}$	$R = \dfrac{E}{I}$

Given the formulas of Ohm's Law and the formulas relating power, current, and voltage, we can solve electrical equations with only two of the four variables (P, I, E, and R). Here we provide two examples.

Given $P = 1600W$ and $E = 110V$, determine I and R.

$$I = \frac{1600W}{110V} \qquad 14.54A = \frac{1600W}{110V} \qquad\qquad R = \frac{110V}{14.54A} \qquad 7.57\,\Omega = \frac{110V}{14.54A}$$

Given $I = 30A$ and $R = 10\,\Omega$, determine E and P.

$$E = 30A * 10\,\Omega \qquad 300V = 30A * 10\,\Omega \qquad\qquad P = 30A * 300V \qquad 9000W = 30A * 300V$$

AC & DC

With an understanding of the basic electrical principles, we can revisit current and move toward a discussion of components and devices. Electricity is usually delivered in one of two forms, as shown in Figures 12.1 and 12.2: **alternating current (AC)** and **direct current (DC)**.

The form of electricity that comes out of a typical wall outlet is AC. As shown in Figure 12.1, with AC the direction of electrical flow is constantly reversing. The rate of reversing (alternating) is measured in **Hertz (Hz)**. One Hertz is one oscillation per second. Standard AC in the US is 60Hz, which means that electrical flow reverses from +120V to -120V 60 times every second.

The form of electricity that most electronic devices require is DC. DC is usually represented as a positive voltage (e.g., CD-ROM drives that require +5V DC or LED flashlights that require +2.7V DC). With modern electronic devices requiring DC but standard households only providing AC, how do devices such as computers operate when plugged into a wall outlet? Not only is the type of signal incorrect (AC instead of DC), but the voltage is usually high enough (110–120V) to damage the computer and all of its components. The *current* discrepancy leads us to the next section in which we discuss electrical components.

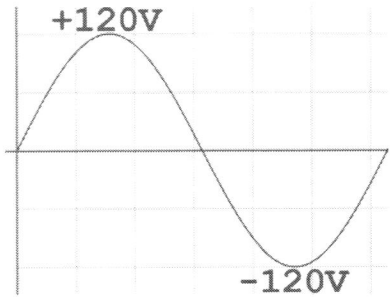

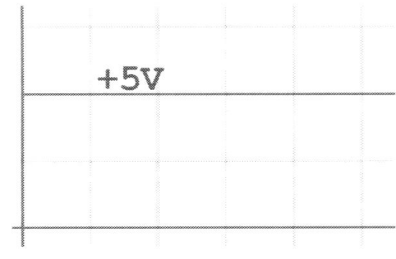

Figure 12.1 Alternating current (AC)   **Figure 12.2** Direct current (DC)

 LEARNING: AC became the standard household electrical current due to its transmission efficiency (3-phase AC power uses a small neutral conductor, reduces generator and motor vibrations, and does not require complex motor designs), lower cost, and political "victory" of Westinghouse over Edison in the late 1800s.

Electrical Components

Powering Devices

As previously mentioned, something needs to alter the electrical current between the time it exits the wall outlet as 120V AC and the time it reaches the computer, where the device needs an appropriate DC voltage (e.g., +3.3V, +5V, etc.). Two electrical components are responsible for handling the current manipulation and both are found in computer power supplies, either built into the case for desktop computers, or in the external power supply ("brick") for laptop computers. The two components are a transformer and a rectifier.

A **transformer** is a component that increases or decreases the voltage of an alternating current via a method known as electromagnetic induction. The transformer lowers the 120V current to a voltage that will not destroy the internal components of a computer. A typical power supply contains two or three transformers that are responsible for lowering the voltages of multiple signals needed to power the many internal components that each get their own supply of electricity.

Once the voltage has been lowered, components responsible for converting AC into DC, known as **rectifiers,** alter the electrical current to only allow flow in one direction. Recall that AC flows in both positive and negative directions. Rectifiers also perform a secondary function: ensuring that the current does not flow backwards. Rectifiers prevent electricity from flowing back through the transformers and, even more dangerous, into the wall outlet should the computer create a surge of electricity due to a malfunction. We discuss the rectifier subcomponent responsible for flow safety control later.

While we are on the topic of powering computers, one more electrical component is worth mentioning. People like having the ability to power devices on the road, perhaps via a cigarette lighter port. The form of electrical current delivered via a lighter port is DC. Even if you had an adapter for the two- or three-prong plug from a laptop's power supply to the DC port, you would still have the issue of the electrical signal. A laptop's power supply expects AC and the vehicle is delivering DC. In such a situation, you need a power **inverter**, shown in Figure 12.3. A power inverter does the exact opposite of a rectifier: it converts DC to AC. An inverter can convert the DC signal from a vehicle to AC, then the laptop power supply converts the AC back to DC at the proper voltage (via the transformer) to properly power the laptop.

 ATTENTION: Power inverters differ in the wattage and voltage they provide. If you are in the market for a power inverter, be sure to find one that provides enough wattage and voltage to power your computer.

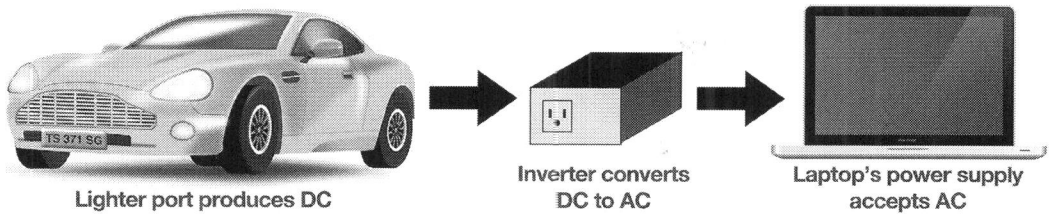

Figure 12.3 Power inverter usage

While some electronic devices such as computers require ample power that is usually provided by a wall outlet, many electronic devices, such as phones, MP3 players, and flashlights, are smaller and are powered by much less electricity. Smaller devices usually contain batteries that provide power. A **battery** is a component with a **cathode** (positive terminal) and an **anode** (negative terminal) with external connections for delivering power to devices. The electricity comes from reactions in the electrochemical cells contained within the battery.

Because of a battery's typically small size, a single battery usually does not provide the voltage required to power certain devices. Some devices can be powered by a single battery, but only for a short amount of time due to the draw rate. Both problems can be remedied by using multiple batteries combined in different ways. In a situation where the electronic device needs more voltage than a single battery can provide, multiple batteries can be connected in series. When batteries are wired in **series** (the anode of one battery is connected to the cathode of the next battery), the voltage calculation is additive while the current is constant.

Figure 12.4 depicts how a remote control for a standard television is powered that requires +6V DC and pulls 1800mA of current. Each battery is rated at 1800mA and +1.5V DC; therefore, wiring batteries in series adds the voltages together and maintains the current.

 ATTENTION: mA is the common abbreviation for milliamps. We use more unit abbreviations in this chapter, and we generally follow the metric system for prefixes (e.g., milli, mega, giga, etc.).

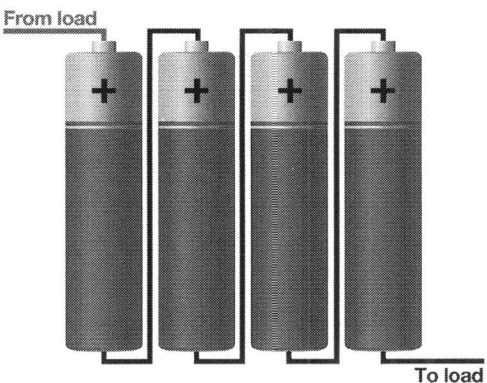

Figure 12.4 – AA batteries wired in series

 ATTENTION: If you have ever wondered why you must reverse batteries from one direction to the other in some devices, the alternating configuration reveals batteries wired in series in such a way that the least amount of connecting wire is necessary. Such is not the case in Figure 12.4, where a battery's positive terminal is distanced away from the next battery's negative terminal.

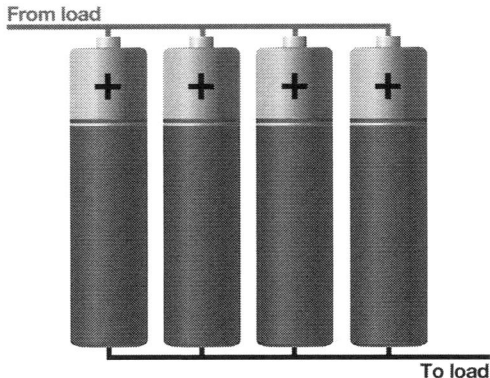

Figure 12.5 AA batteries wired in parallel

In some cases, you might have a device that can be powered by a single AA battery, but only for a short amount of time. If the size of the device permits, the designers could allow for multiple batteries to be present but wired in **parallel** so that the voltage is constant while the current is additive (the opposite of being wired in series). When batteries are wired in parallel, the electricity flows through all batteries at the same time instead of one at a time as illustrated in Figure 12.5.

The remainder of this section focuses on foundational electrical components found in electronic devices.

Resistors

Previously, we introduced resistance with Ohm's Law. Some amount of resistance is always present in any circuit due to the imperfections of conductive and capacitive materials. Still, some circuits need to further reduce the flow of electricity. The electrical component that slows the flow of electrons is called a **resistor**. An example is shown in Figure 12.6.

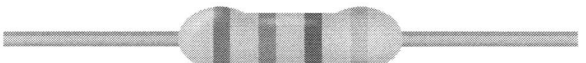

Colored bands left to right: brown, green, red, gold

Figure 12.6 Resistor

Resistors come in many different ratings, measured in Ohms. Resistor ratings are identified by colored bands on the resistor. A typical resistor has four bands to be read left to right (toward the gold or silver band) in order to determine how many Ohms of resistance the resistor provides. The first two bands represent the base digits, the third band is the multiplier in powers of 10, and the fourth band is the accuracy/tolerance. Table 12.2 lists the values for the color bands.

Consider two resistor examples. First, the resistor in Figure 12.6 has four bands: BROWN-GREEN-RED-GOLD. Brown and Green make the whole number 15, and when multiplied by the Red multiplier 10^2 we get $1,500\Omega$ as the resistor's value. The fourth band is gold, so the resistor has an accuracy of ±5%.

Assume a second example has three bands in the following configuration: RED-BLACK-ORANGE. The first two bands represent the digits of the whole number (Red = 2 and Black = 0), so the number is 20. The third band, the multiplier, is Orange (10^3), making the value of the resistor $20 \times 10^3 = 20,000\Omega$. With no fourth band, the $20,000\Omega$ resistor has an accuracy of ±20%.

LEARNING: As with the battery examples, when resistors or other components are attached in serial the voltage is additive, while in parallel the current is additive. So a resistance total R_T of four resistors in series would be $R_T = R_1 + R_2 + R_3 + R_4$. A resistance total R_T of four resistors in parallel would be the inverse $1/R_t = 1/R_1 + 1/R_2 + 1/R_3 + 1/R_4$.

Table 12.2 Resistor values

Color	Band 1	Band 2	Band 3
Black	0	0	10^0
Brown	1	1	10^1
Red	2	2	10^2
Orange	3	3	10^3
Yellow	4	4	10^4
Green	5	5	10^5
Blue	6	6	10^6
Violet	7	7	10^7
Gray	8	8	10^8
White	9	9	-

Color	Band 4
Gold	±5%
Silver	±10%
None	±20%

Resistors also come in a form known as variable resistors, commonly called potentiometers, which can provide a variable amount of resistance. Potentiometers can be thought of as linear as you slide or turn the resistance up or down to the desired rate. A simple example of a variable resistor is a radial volume control on a car radio.

Diodes

Recalling our discussion on rectifiers, we mentioned that in addition to performing current conversion, a rectifier also has an additional component that prevents electricity from flowing backwards. The component that controls current direction is the **diode**, shown in Figure 12.7.

A diode accomplishes its purpose by having low or zero conductance in one direction, while having high or infinite conductance in the opposite direction. Another

Figure 12.7 Diode

way of describing a diode is in terms of resistance: it has high or infinite resistance in one direction while low or zero resistance in the opposite direction. The grey band on a diode shows the direction of electrical flow, with current flowing left to right in Figure 12.7. Diodes most people are familiar with that can also emit light when they are attached in the proper direction are **light-emitting diodes (LEDs)**.

Capacitors

Moving on, **capacitors** are electrical components that temporarily store an electrical charge, two types of which are shown in Figure 12.8.

Capacitors are typically used in circuits as a way to filter the electrical current or ensure that the next component in the circuit always receives the proper voltage, even if the power source is unstable (e.g., drops or surges). Because many electronic components are sensitive to power fluctuations, capacitors help to lengthen component lifespans. A capacitor can provide stability as long as it has a charge (i.e., it has not been depleted of electrons). Think of capacitors as rechargeable batteries; once they are depleted they do not work until they have been charged again. The battery analogy is not perfect since capacitors still allow electricity to flow even when they are depleted (whereas batteries cease to function), but current may not be as stable as when the capacitor is operating at full charge.

Figure 12.8 Capacitors

Because different electrical components require different voltages, different ratings of capacitors exist. Capacitors are rated in terms of their ability to store electrons, also called **capacitance**. Capacitance is measured in **Farads (F)**. A 1F capacitor stores a large amount of electrons, 6.24×10^{18} to be exact. One Farad is much more than most computing components need, so typical capacitors you will encounter when building circuits are measured in picofarads (pF), nanofarads (nF), or microfarads (μF).

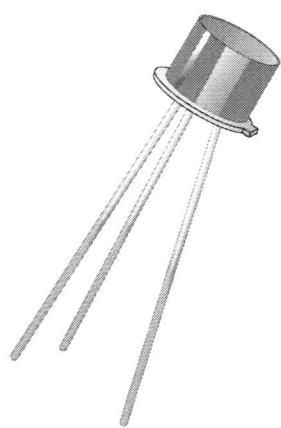

Transistors

The last fundamental electrical component is the foundation of the next section and modern computing: the **transistor**. A transistor is used as a signal amplifier or switch and is a building block of all modern electronics. Modern computer transistors are made of silicon as opposed to the Germanium used in early transistors. Still, different types of transistors can be purchased for use in circuit design. Transistors have three terminals, as depicted in Figure 12.9: the base, the emitter, and the collector.

Applying a current to the base opens the channel between the emitter and the collector, allowing electricity to flow. The amount of flow amplification is proportional to the voltage applied to the base terminal. A common use of transistors that should be recognizable to software engineers is as an electronic switch to represent binary information, off or on. Transistors, serving as switches, are combined together in various configurations to produce logic gates, which give software engineers the ability to execute arithmetic and Boolean expressions discussed in **CHAPTERS 1 AND 2**, such as AND, OR, and NOT.

Figure 12.9 Transistor

 ATTENTION: The transistor's ability to either conduct or not conduct electricity across the emitter and collector terminals is where the term **semiconductor** originated. Silicon (and previously, Germanium) has the ability to partially conduct electricity or to act as a switch that can turn on or off (*semi*-conduct).

Integrated Circuits

All of the previously discussed electrical components come together to create a circuit that performs a specific task. The first step is to design a circuit. Circuit design is typically done with software that produces a **schematic**, an example of which is shown in Figure 12.10. Notice the resistors (R1, R2, and R3), capacitors (open bars; C1 and C2), and transistor (orange in color; Q1). The resistors are labeled with Ohms, the capacitors are labeled with Farads, and the transistor is labeled with an identifier that specifies its function.

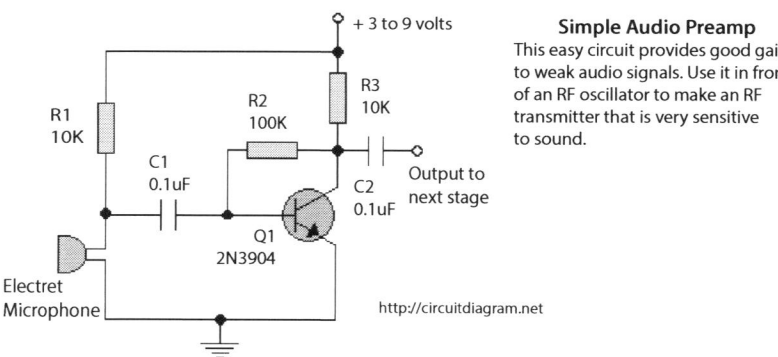

Figure 12.10 Preamp schematic

Figure 12.11 Breadboard

After a schematic is created, engineers might build a bare-bones version using a **breadboard**, shown in Figure 12.11. This is a board containing an array of terminals such that electrical components can be connected together with wires (buses) in the desired configuration without the use of solder. Breadboard circuits are purposefully temporary so components can be easily added, removed, and moved until the circuit functions as desired.

Once a circuit has been built and tested, a more permanent version can be produced. Many years ago, circuits were not too different from the one seen in Figure 12.11. Circuits still had exposed wires and components even though they were soldered together. Although components became smaller over time, their exposure was a challenge. Jack Kilby, while working at Texas Instruments in 1958, created a solution to the problem at the same time as Robert Noyce from Fairchild Semiconductor (later a founder of Intel). Kilby built a complete circuit out of a single block of material rather than using individual components connected together manually. Who created today's interpretation of the **integrated circuit**, Kilby or Noyce, is still hotly debated. The Kilby integrated circuit is shown in Figure 12.12.

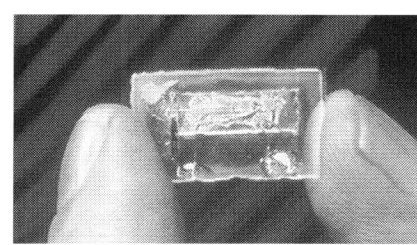

Figure 12.12 Kilby Integrated Circuit (used with permission by Texas Instruments Incorporated)

Though a milestone, the first attempt at a monolithic circuit still had issues, such as protruding wires and fragility. Such issues would soon be solved by Jean Hoerni at Fairchild Semiconductor in 1959, with the invention of the **planar process**. The idea was to view the circuit as a two-dimensional plane with insulated areas and doped areas where the conductive material would reside. The process allowed the entire circuit to be built in layers, by machines, without protruding wires or components. Circuits created with the planar process are the circuits we see in today's electronics. An example of a **printed circuit board** is shown in Figure 12.13.

Figure 12.13 Printed circuit board

The achievements we have mentioned plus many others have led to the powerful, small, and reliable electronics we use every day.

Popular Implementations

Every day, more devices are making use of the amazing technologies we have discussed. Some devices are merely for hobbyists, some are embedded in our daily lives, some are luxuries, and some are modern necessities. In this final section, we briefly discuss a few popular devices that only exist because of the foundational and electrical developments discussed in this chapter.

Figure 12.14 Intel Core i7

Figure 12.15 Raspberry Pi

Figure 12.16 Apple iPhone and watch

Computer Processors

The earliest processors created by Intel, short for Integrated Electronics, could only operate on 4 bits at a time with a clock rate of 740 kHz (kilohertz). At the time of this book's publication, consumer processors such as the Intel Core i7, shown in Figure 12.14, can operate on 64 bits (or more) at a time with clock rates above 4 GHz (gigahertz) at an instruction execution rate of over four billion instructions per second.

Raspberry Pi

The Raspberry Pi, shown in Figure 12.15, is a compact but complete computer. The size of a deck of cards, the Pi is a complete system with HDMI, USB, Ethernet, WiFi, Bluetooth, audio, and General Purpose Input/Output (GPIO) pins for connecting external devices. While the Pi might not be powerful enough for movie studios to render 3D animations, it is powerful enough to act as a retro gaming device, a controller for a home's "smart" devices, or even a network penetration device used by information security engineers. The Raspberry Pi is a hobbyist's dream computer due to its low cost and expandability.

Apple iPhone & Watch

If you have not already realized, the authors of this book prefer Apple products as their daily-use devices. So what better smartphone and other "smart device" examples to present than the Apple iPhone and Watch, shown in Figure 12.16.

The fact that personal computing devices have more processing power than the computers that put men on the moon is nothing short of amazing. For posterity, and because this is a book on Assembly programming, Figure 12.17 shows Margaret Hamilton, the lead software engineer for the Apollo project, standing next to the Assembly listing printout for the Apollo Guidance Computer (NASA).

Between smartphones, such as Apple's iPhone or various Android phones; smart watches, such as Apple's Watch, Samsung's Gear, or Motorola's Moto 360; and other miscellaneous smart devices, such as FitBits and Google Glass, we have computers that can fit in our pockets or be worn on our bodies. Such devices exist thanks to the creation of the integrated circuit and the continued miniaturization and increased efficiency of electrical components.

Figure 12.17 Assembly source code for the Apollo guidance computer (NASA)

Summary

In this last chapter, we discussed fundamentals of electronics at a low level and then built upon each section from the basic principles to modern devices. You should now be familiar with the characteristics of electricity and electrical components that manipulate and harness its power. In addition to presenting electrical principle definitions and formulas, we discussed electrical components at a tangible level. When electrical components come together to make a circuit, the possibilities are endless, as we illustrated with some popular implementations. You made it! May the bits be ever in your favor.

Key Terms

alternating current (AC)
ampere
anode
battery
breadboard
capacitance
capacitor
cathode
current
diode
direct current (DC)
draw

farads (F)
Hertz (Hz)
integrated circuit
inverter
light-emitting diode (LED)
Ohm's Law
ohms
parallel
planar process
potentiometer
power
printed circuit board

rectifier
resistance
resistor
schematic
semiconductor
series
transformer
transistor
voltage
volts
watts

Questions

Short Answer

1. When representing Ohms, use the Greek _____ character.
2. The difference in the charge between two points is known as _____.
3. Computers typically draw _____ current than flashlights.
4. The watt is the unit of measurement for electrical _____.
5. _____ can be calculated if you have both the wattage and the voltage.
6. Because conducting materials are not perfect, they increase _____ on an electrical circuit.
7. Using Ohm's Law and the equation to calculate power, _____ and _____ can be calculated as long as you have resistance and current.
8. Typical wall outlets provide _____ current.
9. Unlike DC, AC constantly reverses its flow at a rate that is measured in _____.
10. A secondary function of a _____ ensures that electricity does not flow backwards.
11. Batteries provide _____ current.
12. The _____ is an electrical component that slows the flow of electrons.
13. Capacitance is measured in _____, although most capacitors are rated much lower than the standard unit.
14. Originally made of Germanium, _____ are now made of silicon.
15. Printed circuit boards are only possible because of the invention of the _____.

True/False

1. Transformers change current from AC to DC for usage in electronic devices.
2. Diodes only allow current to flow in one direction.
3. Wiring batteries in series is used when a device requires more voltage rather than more amperage.
4. A resistor with three colored bands has a tolerance of ±5%.
5. Integrated circuits are devices that an engineer can plug electrical components into to test a circuit.

Assignments

12.1 Don't blow the breaker!

Assume that in your home office you wish to use the devices listed below. Will a 15A breaker trip when you turn on all of the devices at the same time? List all combinations you can use at the same time without blowing the breaker and the total amperage for each combination.

- Air conditioner (1000W)
- Computer (500W)
- Desk lamp (5W)
- Cross-cut shredder (5A)

12.2 Speed Limit

Assume you are building a small electrical circuit. Your power source supplies +5V DC at 500mA, but your electrical components can only handle a max of +5V DC at 200mA. Because the components are extremely sensitive, you must ensure that the resistor's Ohms are appropriate and that the tolerance is as small as possible. What resistor size should you use to accomplish the current drop? (Specify the resistor in terms of the colored bands.)

12.3 Mini-computers

Using the Web and other resources, select a small form factor computer or microcontroller such as the Raspberry Pi or an Arduino board and research some creative uses of the device. Write a two- or three-page paper that 1) describes three of the most interesting implementations you found, and then 2) describes a custom implementation of your own design. You may use a combination of text and visuals.

Introduction to the Appendices

Welcome and Objective

Hello and welcome to the Appendices for *Assembly Programming and Computer Architecture for Software Engineers*. The objective of the Appendices is to provide some practical guidance for various topics related to the main text.

Appendix Outline

- Appendix A: Assembly Syntax Translation
- Appendix B: Environment Setup
- Appendix C: Disassembly
- Appendix D: Command-Line Debugging Assembly with GDB
- Appendix E: Linking Assembly and C++
- Appendix F: Functions and Stack
- Appendix G: Using CPUID
- Appendix H: ASCII and Decimal Arithmetic
- Appendix I: Intrinsics

We decided to take a very practical approach to the Appendices, so you will find very helpful guides, such as Appendix B, D, and E. Appendix A is a lifesaver for an Assembly programmer, and we have found ourselves using it regularly. The other Appendices not only contain supplemental information, but they will help you understand the book content and "how-to" scenarios in more detail. The Appendices also contain additional resources and links that will help with exploring specific topics.

Lost and Found

What you will *not* find in the Appendices is information that is readily found elsewhere. The x86, x86_64, x87, SIMD, AVX, and so on instruction sets are already well documented in the formal Intel and AMD specifications and online resources. ASCII maps can easily be found with a Web search and so on. What we *do* provide is links and references to where important and already well-documented information can be found. Many resources are available via the WEB RESOURCES at the beginning of every chapter.

For the instruction sets, the best resource by far is the **Intel 64 and IA-32 Software Developer's Manual, Volume 1, Chapter 5**. Other information about instructions is scattered throughout the manuals, but Volume 1 Chapter 5 is a great starting point. We recommend downloading the manuals from the Intel website.

- http://www.intel.com/content/www/us/en/processors/architectures-software-developer-manuals.html

AMD manuals can be found on the AMD developer site.

- http://developer.amd.com/resources/developer-guides-manuals/

Agner Fog has some amazing technical documentation about instructions, calling conventions, and optimization.

- http://www.agner.org/optimize/#manuals

If PDFs are not your thing and you prefer an online exploration of instruction details, the following **instruction indexes** are quite useful.

- http://www.felixcloutier.com/x86/
- http://x86.renejeschke.de
- https://en.wikipedia.org/wiki/X86_instruction_listings
- http://www.nasm.us/doc/nasmdocb.html

Application Binary Interface specifications are also particularly helpful. Some good ones are as follows.

- http://refspecs.linuxfoundation.org/elf/x86-64-abi-0.99.pdf
- https://developer.apple.com/library/mac/documentation/DeveloperTools/Conceptual/LowLevelABI/000-Introduction/introduction.html

Assembler References are the go-to place for information related to a specific Assembler, such as supported directives and syntax.

- https://sourceware.org/binutils/docs/as/ (GAS)
- http://www.nasm.us/doc/ (NASM)
- http://www.nasm.us/docs.php (NASM)
- https://msdn.microsoft.com/en-us/library/afzk3475.aspx (MASM)
- https://developer.apple.com/library/mac/documentation/DeveloperTools/Reference/Assembler/000-Introduction/introduction.html (outdated but still informational)

We hope you find the Appendices helpful and if you have an idea for an Appendix let us know!

Assembly Syntax Translation

Objective

Appendix A provides some general rules and a table for translating code between Assemblers and syntaxes.

Rules

- GAS prefixes registers with %
- GAS prefixes immediate values with $
- GAS also uses the $ prefix to indicate an address of a variable
- MASM and NASM use $ as the *current location counter*, while GAS uses the dot (.)
- GAS operands are source first, destination second
- MASM and NASM operands are destination first, source second
- GAS denotes operand sizes with *b*, *w*, *l*, and *q* suffixes on the instruction
- GAS and NASM identifiers are case-sensitive
- MASM identifiers are not case-sensitive by default, but can be by adding `option casemap:none` (usually after the .MODEL directive)
- NASM writes FPU stack registers as *ST0*, *ST1*, etc…without parentheses
- GAS/MASM usually write FPU stack registers as *%st(1)/ST(1)*, *%st(2)/ST(2)*, etc…with parentheses
- GAS uses .equ to set a symbol to an expression, NASM uses EQU, and MASM uses = or EQU
- All three Assemblers can use single or double quotes for strings
- MASM relies more on assumptions (e.g., data sizes), so sometimes interpreting what an instruction does can be difficult
- NASM usually does not require a size directive for source operands, but a size directive can be used. A size directive is required for destination operands.

```
mov eax, [test]          ; source size is not required
mov eax, DWORD [test]    ; but can be used
mov DWORD [test], eax    ; required for destination
```

Operation	GAS	NASM	MASM
Clear a register (*eax*)	xorl %eax, %eax	xor eax, eax	
Move contents of *eax* to *esi*	movl %eax, %esi	mov esi, eax	
Move contents of *ax* to *si*	movw %ax, %si	mov si, ax	
Move immediate byte value 4 to *al*	movb $4, %al	mov al, 4	
Move contents of address 0xf into *eax*	movl 0x0f, %eax	mov eax, [0x0f]	mov eax, ds:[0fh]

Operation	GAS	NASM	MASM
Move contents of variable `temp` into *eax*	`movl temp, %eax`	`mov eax, DWORD [temp]`	`mov eax, temp`
Move address of variable `temp` into *eax* using MOV	`movl $temp, %eax`	`mov eax, temp`	`mov eax, OFFSET temp`
Load address of variable `temp` into *eax* using LEA (32-bit)	`leal temp, %eax`	`lea eax, [temp]`	`lea eax, temp`
Load address of variable `temp` into *rax* using LEA (64-bit)	`leaq temp(%rip), %rax`	`lea rax, [rel temp]`	`lea rax, temp`
Move contents of *eax* into variable `temp`	`movl %eax, temp`	`mov DWORD [temp], eax`	`mov temp, eax`
Move immediate byte value 2 into `temp`	`movl $2, temp`	`mov BYTE [temp], 2`	`mov temp, 2`
Move immediate byte value 2 into memory pointed to by *eax*	`movb $2, (%eax)`	`mov BYTE [eax], 2`	`mov BYTE PTR [eax], 2`
Move immediate word value 4 into memory pointed to by *eax*	`movw $4, (%eax)`	`mov WORD [eax], 4`	`mov WORD PTR [eax], 4`
Move immediate doubleword value 6 into memory pointed to by *eax*	`movl $6, (%eax)`	`mov DWORD [eax], 6`	`mov DWORD PTR [eax], 6`
Include file syntax	`.include "file.ext"`	`%include "file.ext"`	`INCLUDE file.ext`
Identifier syntax	`identifier: type value`		`identifier type value`
Get size of array in bytes using *current location counter* (code directly after array declaration)	`aSize: .long (. - array)`	`aSize: EQU ($ - array)`	`aSize = ($ - array)`
Create and use a symbol with EQU	`.equ temp, (2 * 6 / 3)` `mov $temp, %eax`	`temp: EQU (2 * 6 / 3)` `mov eax, temp`	`temp EQU (2 * 6 / 3)` `mov eax, temp`
Reserve 64 bytes of memory	`.space 64`	`resb 64`	`db 64 DUP (?)`
Create uninitialized 32-bit variable `temp`	`.lcomm temp, 4`	`temp: resd 1`	`temp DWORD ?`
Create initialized 32-bit variable `temp` with value 5	`temp: .long 5`	`temp: dd 5`	`temp DWORD 5`
Create an array w/ 32-bit values	`temp: .long 5, 10, 15`	`temp: dd, 5, 10, 15`	`temp DWORD 5, 10, 15`
Create "Hello, World" string (code on one line)	`identifier: .ascii "Hello, World"`	`identifier: db 'Hello, World'`	`identifier BYTE "Hello, World"`
Create "Hello, World" w/ newline and null (code on one line)	`identifier: .asciz "Hello, World\n"`	`identifier: db 'Hello, World', 10, 0`	`identifier BYTE "Hello, World", 10, 0`

Function structure	`identifier:`
	`...`
	`ret`
			`identifier PROC`
			`...`
			`ret`
			`identifier ENDP`

Operation	GAS	NASM	MASM

Program segments (sections)	```.data```
	 ```.bss```
	 ```.text```
		```SECTION .data```
		 ```SECTION .bss```
		 ```SECTION .text```
			```.data```
			 ```.code```

Data types	```.byte```
	 ```.word```
	 ```.long```
	 ```.quad```
		```db```
		 ```dw```
		 ```dd```
		 ```dq```
			```BYTE```
			 ```WORD```
			 ```DWORD```
			 ```QWORD```

Repetition (code on one line)	```identifier: .fill count,``` ```size, value```	```identifier: TIMES count``` ```type value```	```identifier type count``` ```DUP (value)```

Macro definition	```.macro identifier arg1, arg2…```
	 ```args referenced as \arg1```
	 ```.endm```
		```%macro identifier argcount```
		 ```args referenced as [%1]```
		 ```%endmacro```
			```identifier MACRO arg1, arg2…```
			 ```args referenced as arg1```
			 ```ENDM```

Macro usage	```identifier param1, param2, etc...```		
Comment (single-line)	```# this is a comment```	```; this is a comment```	

32-bit _main exit routine	```# for GAS/Clang on Mac```
	 ```pushl $0```
	 ```subl $4, %esp```
	 ```movl $1, %eax```
	 ```int $0x80```
	
	 ```# for GAS/Clang on Linux```
	 ```mov $1, %eax```
	 ```mov $0, %ebx```
	 ```int $0x80```
		```; for NASM on Linux```
		 ```mov eax, 1```
		 ```mov ebx, 0```
		 ```int 80h```
		
		 ```; for NASM on Mac```
		 ```push DWORD 0```
		 ```sub esp, 4```
		 ```mov eax, 1```
		 ```int 80h```
			```; before .data segment```
			 ```ExitProcess PROTO, dwEx-```
			 ```itCode:DWORD```
			
			 ```; before _main ENDP```
			 ```INVOKE ExitProcess, 0```

64-bit _main exit routine	```# for GAS/Clang on Mac```
	 ```movq $0x2000001, %rax```
	 ```movq $0, %rdi```
	 ```syscall```
	
	 ```# for GAS/Clang on Linux```
	 ```mov $60, %rax```
	 ```xor %rdi, %rdi```
	 ```syscall```
		```; for NASM on Linux```
		 ```mov rax, 60```
		 ```xor rdi, rdi```
		 ```syscall```
		
		 ```; for NASM on Mac```
		 ```mov rax, 2000001h```
		 ```mov rdi, 0```
		 ```syscall```
			```; before .data segment```
			 ```extrn ExitProcess:proc```
			
			 ```; before _main ENDP```
			 ```mov rcx, 0```
			 ```call ExitProcess```

APPENDIX B

Environment Setup for Assembly Programming

Objective

Appendix B describes how to prepare your Development Environment for programming in Assembly. Examples are provided for Windows using Visual Studio and MASM, for macOS using Xcode (Clang/LLVM, GAS compatible), and for Linux using NASM and ld. We offer some basic setup configurations and you can explore other options if desired. The code examples we use are 32-bit.

Windows – Visual Studio (2017) – MASM

1. Install Visual Studio if needed.

2. Open Visual Studio and create a new empty C++ project, giving the project an appropriate name.

3. Once the project has been created and is open, right-click on the project in the Solution Explorer and select "Build Dependencies" → "Build Customizations"

4. Check the "masm" box.

5. In the Solution Explorer, right-click "Source Files" then select "Add" → "New item..."

6. Under "Visual C++" click "Utility" then choose "Text File." When you name the file also type the *.asm* extension.

7. In the Solution Explorer, right-click on the newly created *.asm* file, select "Properties," and under "General" change "Item Type" to "Microsoft Macro Assembler" if not already set.

8. In the Solution Explorer, right-click on the project, select "Properties" and within the Properties you should see a drop-down menu called "Microsoft Macro Assembler." If the menu is missing, return to Step 2. If the menu exists, continue to Step 9.

9. In the project Properties drop-down menu, navigate to "Linker" → "System" and in the "SubSystem" drop-down box select "Windows (/SUBSYSTEM:WINDOWS)"

10. In the project Properties drop-down menu, navigate to "Linker" → "Advanced" and in the "Entry Point" box type either "main" or "_main" depending on your preference for identifying the main function in your Assembly code. We use "_main" throughout the book.

11. Write a sample Assembly program in the *.asm* file.

```
; First Program for MASM

.386
.MODEL FLAT, stdcall
.STACK 4096

ExitProcess PROTO, dwExitCode:DWORD

.DATA
num DWORD 80
sum DWORD ?

.CODE
_main PROC
    mov eax, num
    add eax, 20
    mov sum, eax

    INVOKE ExitProcess, 0
_main ENDP
END
```

12. Set a breakpoint at a suitable location (e.g., `mov eax, num`).

13. Build and Run the program.

14. When the program halts at the breakpoint, arrange the window frames to your preference. We recommend opening the following windows in the "Debug" → "Windows" menu.

    • Registers
    • Memory (choose at least Memory 1, others are optional)
    • Disassembly
    • Autos

15. Another useful option is to right-click anywhere in the Registers window and select "Flags," which enables viewing of the *flags* register. Select any other registers you have interest in watching.

16. To make Visual Studio create a listing file when assembling your code, in the project Properties navigate to "Microsoft Macro Assembler" → "Listing File" and set the following options.

    • "Generate Preprocessed Source Listing" to "Yes"
    • "List All Available Information" to "Yes"
    • "Assembled Code Listing File" to "$(ProjectName).lst" or any desired file path

    After re-running the program to create a listing file, you may need to set the "Generate Preprocessed Source Listing" back to "No" so debugging works correctly.

17. If you re-run the program you will find the listing file created in:

    ProjectFolder\ProjectName\ProjectName.lst (file type is shown as "MASM Listing"). Example file path: C:\Documents\Visual Studio 2017\Projects\masm_testing\ masm_testing\ masm_testing.lst

18. Optional: In the project Properties drop-down menu, navigate to "Linker" → "Advanced" and in the "Image Has Safe Exception Handlers" drop-down box select "No."

macOS – Xcode (8.2) – Clang/LLVM (GAS compatible)

1. Install Xcode from the AppStore if needed.

2. Open Xcode and create a new project.

3. The template for the new project should be a "macOS" → "Application" and select "Command Line Tool"

4. Give the project an appropriate "Product Name," for example "asm_testing"

5. Language should be set to C++.

6. Create the project in an appropriate folder.

7. In the Project Navigator, select "main.cpp," press the "Delete" key, then select "Move to Trash."

8. In the Project Navigator, right-click on the project folder and select "New File…" then under "macOS" → "Other" (scroll down) chose "Assembly File" (the icon has a large "S"). Click "Next."

9. Name the file, then click "Create."

10. Write a sample Assembly program in the .s file.

```
# First Program for GAS, Clang/LLVM

.data
num: .long 80

.bss
.lcomm sum, 4

.text
.globl _main
_main:
    movl num, %eax
    addl $20, %eax
    movl %eax, sum

    pushl $0
    subl $4, %esp
    movl $1, %eax
    int $0x80
.end
```

11. In the Project Navigator, click on the project (top level) and under the "Architectures" drop-down menu and select "32-bit Intel (i386)."

12. Set a breakpoint at a suitable location (e.g., movl num, %eax).

13. Build and Run the program.

14. Arrange the windows to your preference, but we recommend the following setup (selections in blue).

15. Registers are viewable in the lower left "Debug Area" and output is in the lower right.

16. To view disassembly, in the "Assistants Area" window (the overlapping circles in the above figure), click on "Counterparts" (see above figure) and select "Disassembly" (at the bottom of the menu).

17. To create a separate listing file, we recommend using otool.
    • In Terminal.app, navigate to the folder where the object file for the Xcode project was created (an easy approach is to type "cd " in Terminal then navigate to the object file in Finder and drag the folder location into Terminal)
    • Example path:
    • asm_testing/DerivedData/asm_testing/Build/Intermediates/asm_testing.build/Debug/asm_testing. build/Objects-normal/i386/asm_testing.o
    • Run otool in Terminal: otool -dtvj asm_testing.o > disassembly.txt

- To see flag options to get the output you desire simply type `otool` and press return
- We use `d` = print data section, `t` = print text section, `v` = print verbosely, and `j` = print opcode bytes

Linux – NASM

For the Linux configuration we use Ubuntu. You can adjust the steps for your chosen distribution.

1. Ensure that gcc and g++ are installed by issuing the following commands in the Terminal.
   - `~$ gcc -v`
   - `~$ g++ -v`

2. To ensure you can run both 32-bit and 64-bit programs, you need to install the latest "multilib" files.
   - `~$ sudo apt-get install gcc-5-multilib`
   - `~$ sudo apt-get install g++-5-multilib`

3. Install NASM and verify version (2.11 or higher).
   - `~$ sudo apt-get install nasm`
   - `~$ nasm -v`

4. Use your preferred editor such as *gedit*, *vim*, or *vi* to create a *.s* or *.asm* file in an appropriate folder location and write a sample program.

```
; First Program for NASM

SECTION .data
num: dd 80

SECTION .bss
sum: resd 1

SECTION .text
global _main
_main:
    mov eax, DWORD [num]
    add eax, 20
    mov DWORD [sum], eax

mov eax, 1
mov ebx, 0
int 80h
```

5. Assemble the file using `nasm` and then link using `ld`.
   - `~$ nasm -f elf32 -o testing.o testing.asm`
   - `~$ ld -e _main -melf_i386 -o testing testing.o`

6. Run the program: `~$ ./testing`

7. To debug using the command-line, refer to **APPENDIX D: COMMAND-LINE DEBUGGING ASSEMBLY WITH GDB**.

8. To create listing files and perform other tasks with the object file, you can use utilities such as `objdump` or `otool`, but the simplest way is to use the `-l` flag when assembling.
   - `~$ nasm -f elf32 -o testing.o -l testing.lst testing.asm`

Disassembly

Objective

In **APPENDIX B**, we mentioned how to create a listing file for each OS platform that contains the disassembly for a given program. Appendix C identifies elements of disassembly files and also demonstrates how to view Assembly and Disassembly while working in Visual Studio, Xcode, and GDB.

Program

Consider Program C.1, which has one initialized variable (num) and one uninitialized variable (sum). In _main, we move num to *eax*, add 20, then store the result in sum, which equals 100. Then the program exits.

Program C.1 Template

GAS	MASM	NASM
| ```
.data
num: .long 80

.bss
.lcomm sum, 4

.text
.globl _main

_main:
movl num, %eax
addl $20, %eax
movl %eax, sum

pushl $0
subl $4, %esp
movl $1, %eax
int $0x80
.end
``` | ```
.386
.MODEL FLAT, stdcall
.STACK 4096

ExitProcess PROTO, dwExit-
Code:DWORD

.DATA
num DWORD 80
sum DWORD ?

.CODE
_main PROC
mov eax, num
add eax, 20
mov sum, eax

INVOKE ExitProcess, 0
_main ENDP
END
``` | ```
SECTION .data
num: dd 80

SECTION .bss
sum: resd 1

SECTION .text
global _main
_main:
mov eax, [num]
add eax, 20
mov [sum], eax

mov eax, 1
mov ebx, 0
int 80h
``` |

Windows

Using the method for creating a disassembly (listing) file in **APPENDIX B**, the output is shown in Example C.1. We present an abbreviated version: we removed the "Procedures, parameters, and locals" and "Symbols" sections toward the end of the default MASM listing output.
```

Example C.1 Disassembly with MASM

memory offset	machine instruction	assembly instruction

```
Microsoft (R) Macro Assembler Version 14.10.25017.0        03/15/17 16:45:40
testing.asm                                            Page 1 - 1
                              .386
                              .MODEL FLAT, stdcall
                              .STACK 4096

                              ExitProcess PROTO, dwExitCode:DWORD

 00000000                     .DATA
 00000000 00000050                num DWORD 80
 00000004 00000000                sum DWORD ?

 00000000                     .CODE
 00000000                     _main PROC
 00000000  A1 00000000 R          mov eax, num
 00000005  83 C0 14               add eax, 20
 00000008  A3 00000004 R          mov sum, eax

                                  INVOKE ExitProcess, 0
 0000000D  6A 00            *      push    +000000000h
 0000000F  E8 00000000 E    *      call    ExitProcess
 00000014                     _main ENDP
                              END

Microsoft (R) Macro Assembler Version 14.10.25017.0        03/15/17 16:45:40
testing.asm                                            Symbols 2 - 1

Segments and Groups:

N a m e                    Size      Length    Align    Combine Class

FLAT . . . . . . . . . .   GROUP
STACK  . . . . . . . . .   32 Bit    00001000  DWord    Stack   'STACK'
_DATA  . . . . . . . . .   32 Bit    00000008  DWord    Public  'DATA'
_TEXT  . . . . . . . . .   32 Bit    00000014  DWord    Public  'CODE'
```

The memory offsets start at 0h since the object file just contains *relocatable machine language*. The machine instructions are the numeric (hexadecimal) counterparts to the Assembly instructions. The initialized data (num DWORD 80) appears as the raw hexadecimal value (00000050). Note the instructions in _main when comparing the Assembly code and the Disassembly.

Toward the end of the file, you will see the "Segments and Groups" area, which lists segment sizes. The _DATA segment is the combined byte size of all initialized and uninitialized variables. The _TEXT segment (written as .CODE in MASM, but translated to _TEXT behind the scenes and written at .text in the other Assemblers) is the byte-length of the machine instructions. With every two hexadecimal digits equaling a byte, the _main code is 00000014 bytes in length, or 20 bytes in decimal. As an aside, also notice we allocated 4,096 bytes of stack space, which is 00001000.

If you want to view Disassembly while you are debugging in Visual Studio, set a breakpoint and run the program. Click on the "Debug" menu and under "Windows" you will find "Disassembly" (Figure C.1).

Once you have opened the Disassembly window, you will have something that looks like Figure C.2.

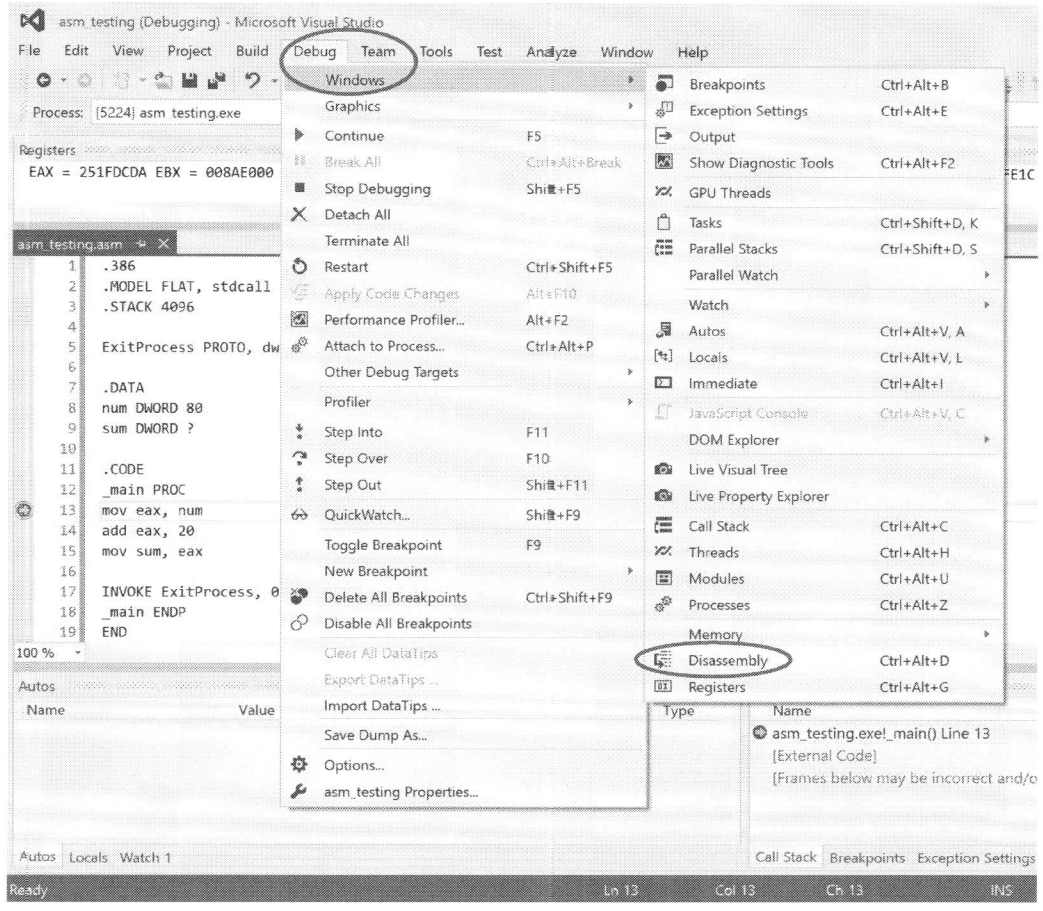

Figure C.1 Disassembly in Visual Studio

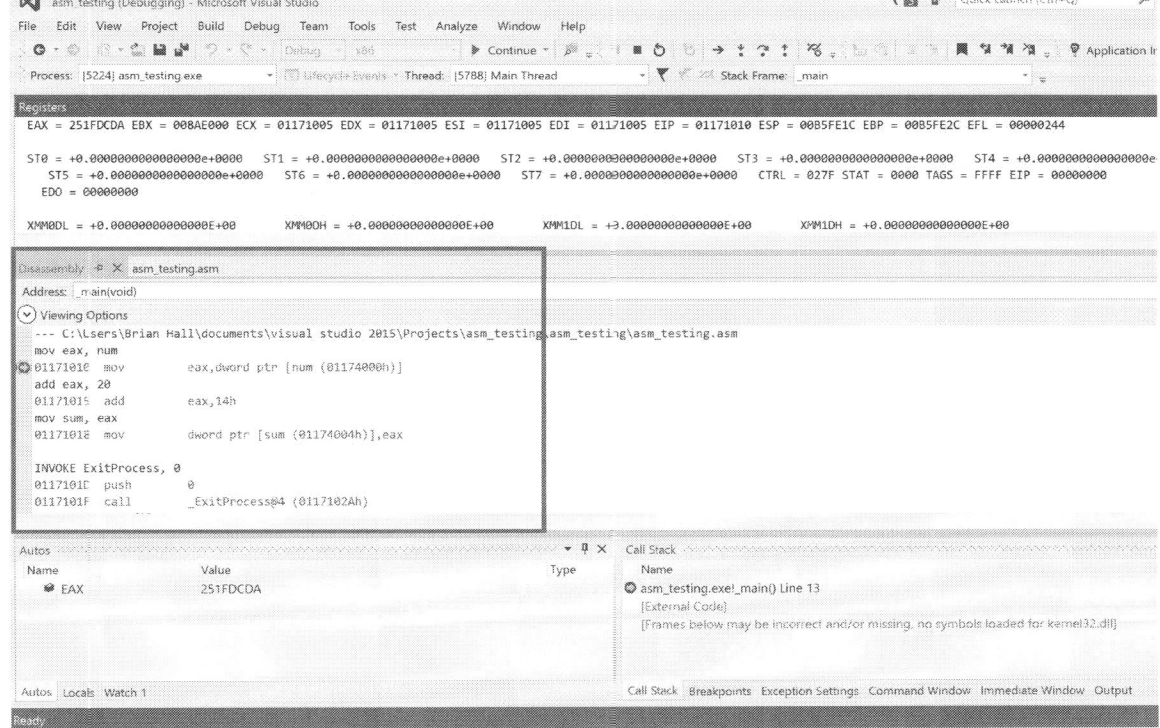

Figure C.2 Visual Studio Disassembly Window

macOS

Using the method for creating a disassembly (listing) file in **APPENDIX B**, the output is shown in Example C.2.

Example C.2 Disassembly with `otool`

memory offset	machine instruction	assembly instruction

```
main.o:
(__TEXT,__text) section
_main:
00000000        a119000000             movl    num, %eax
00000005        83c014                 addl    $0x14, %eax
00000008        a333020000             movl    %eax, sum
0000000d        6a00                   pushl   $0x0
0000000f        83ec04                 subl    $0x4, %esp
00000012        b801000000             movl    $0x1, %eax
00000017        cd80                   int     $-0x80
(__DATA,__data) section
00000019        50 00 00 00
```

The memory offsets start at `0x0` since the object file just contains *relocatable machine language*. The machine instructions are the numeric (hexadecimal) counterparts to the Assembly instructions. The initialized data (num: `.long 80`) appears as the raw value in Little-Endian hexadecimal form (`50 00 00 00`). Note that `_main` has seven instructions and the same is true in the Disassembly.

You might be wondering where the uninitialized data is (`.lcomm sum, 4`), which we declared in the `.bss` section. Since the `.bss` section includes variables that do not have initial values, the system does not need to store them until the program is loaded and running. All that needs to be saved in the object file (`.o`) for `.bss` variables is the *total* amount of storage needed at runtime for uninitialized variables.

An easy way to see how much space is being reserved for `.bss`, other sections, and the program generally is to run the `size` utility on the object file in Terminal. For example, if the object file was named `test.o`, the `size` command provides the information we seek.

```
$ size -m test.o
Segment : 567
        Section (__TEXT, __text): 25
        Section (__DATA, __data): 4
        Section (__DATA, __bss): 4
        Section (__DWARF, __debug_info): 298
        Section (__DWARF, __debug_abbrev): 40
        Section (__DWARF, __debug_aranges): 32
        Section (__DWARF, __debug_line): 164
total 567
```

The `size` utility has several flags for output formatting, but our example shows the sections printed along with the number of bytes, in decimal, that each section requires in memory. Notice that the `.bss` section requires four bytes, which is enough space for one `.long`, the uninitialized variable sum. Since we assembled the program in *Debug* mode in Xcode, the `__debug` sections appear in the output as well.

To clarify, the byte count needed for the executable part of the program is the length of all the instructions combined. The key is to not forget the last instruction, which begins at the last offset.

```
Section (__TEXT, __text): 25
0x17 (beginning of last instruction) + 0x02 (cd08) = 0x19h = 25d
```

If you want to view Disassembly while you are debugging in Xcode, set a breakpoint and run the program.

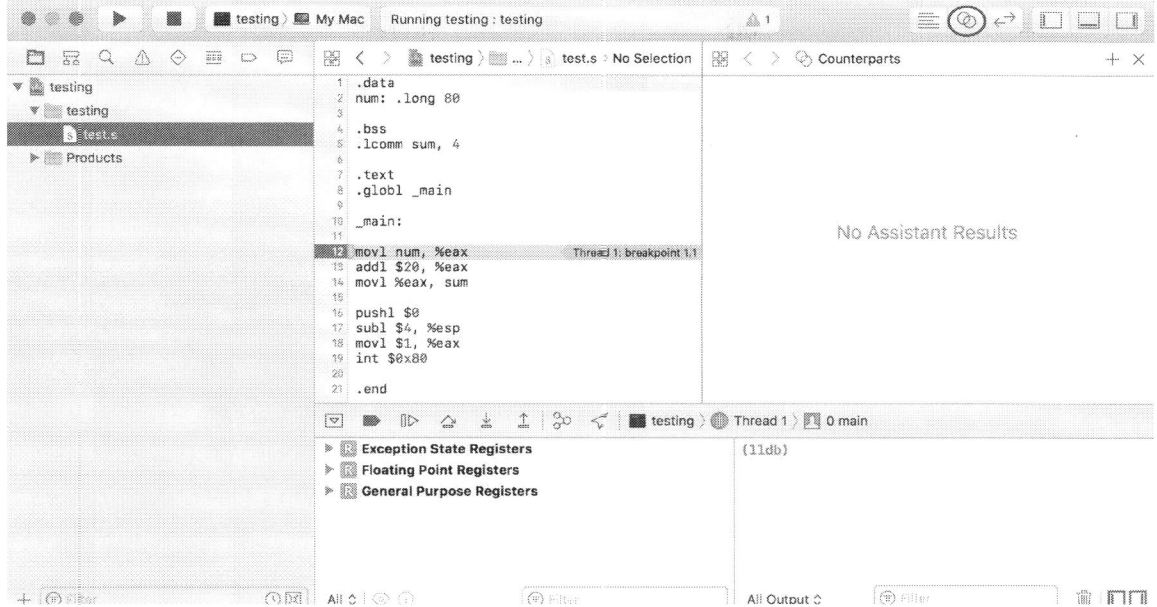

Figure C.3 Opening disassembly in Xcode

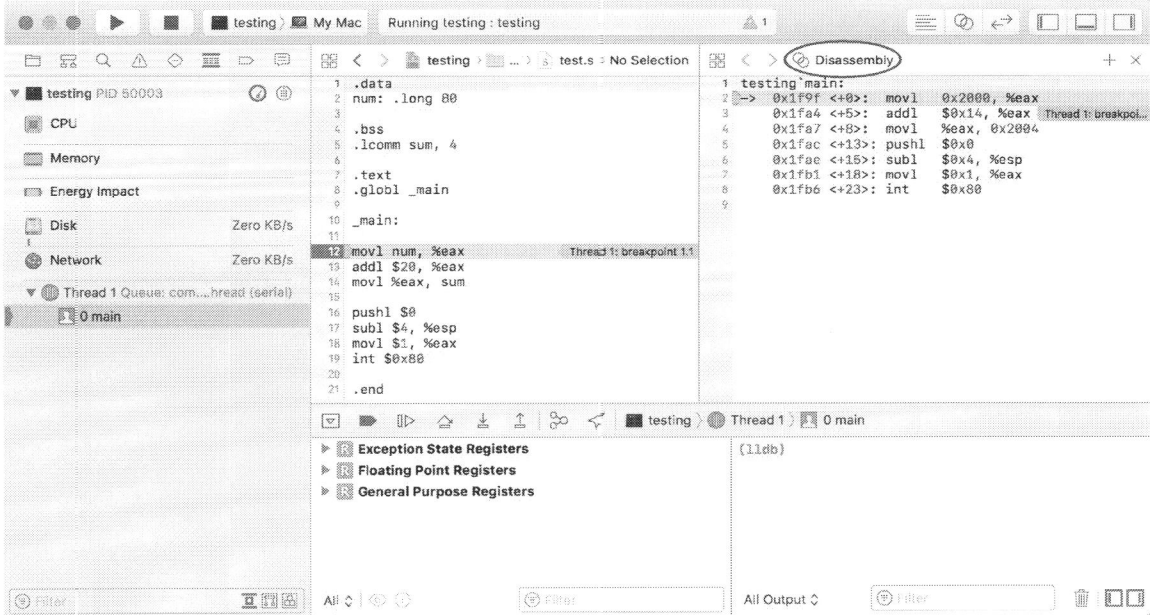

Figure C.4 Disassembly window in Xcode

Click the the "Assistant Editor" button, click on the "Counterparts" text, and in the dropdown box choose "Disassembly." If you were using a language like C++, you can choose "Assembly" when debugging to get a more granular view of your code as it executes.

Linux

Using the method for creating a disassembly (listing) file in **APPENDIX B**, the output is shown in Example C.3.

Example C.3 Disassembly with NASM

memory offset	machine instruction	assembly instruction
1		section .data
2 00000000	50000000	num: dd 80
3		
4		section .bss
5 00000000	<res 00000004>	sum: resd 1
6		
7		section .text
8		global _main
9		_main:
10 00000000	A1[00000000]	mov eax, [num]
11 00000005	83C014	add eax, 20
12 00000008	A3[00000000]	mov [sum], eax
13		
14 0000000D	B801000000	mov eax, 1
15 00000012	BB00000000	mov ebx, 0
16 00000017	CD80	int 80h

In Linux, the `size` utility will likely offer different options for output than in macOS/BSD, so we just show the default output.

```
$ size test.o
text    data    bss     dec     hex     filename
  25       4      4      33      21     test.o
```

As with the macOS version, the `text`, `data`, and `bss` sections are 25, 4, and 4 bytes in size, respectively. The `bss` section includes variables that do not have initial values, so the system does not need to store them until the program is loaded and running. All that needs to be saved in the object file (`.o`) for `bss` variables is the *total* amount of storage needed at runtime for uninitialized variables.

Here we show several options for viewing Disassembly in the GNU Debugger (GDB). One quick way is to use the `layout asm` command. Run the program with GDB (look at **APPENDIX D** if necessary), set a breakpoint at `_main`, and then issue the command.

```
(gdb) layout asm
```

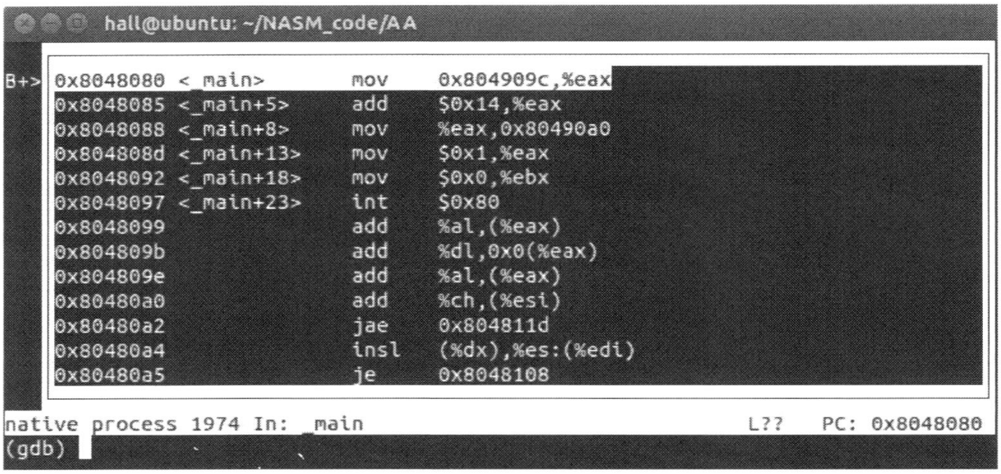

Figure C.5 ASM Layout in GDB

To view the Disassembly of the current instruction, you can use the Program Counter (PC), which is wherever the *ip/eip/rip* register is pointing. Again, look at **Appendix D** if needed, but in the following GDB command, x means examine, i means instruction, and we use the program counter register.

```
Breakpoint 1, 0x08048080 in _main ()
(gdb) x/i $pc
=> 0x8048080 <_main>:            mov     0x804909c,%eax
```

To view multiple instructions, just put a number before the ⸏ as we do in the next example.

```
(gdb) x/6i $pc
=> 0x8048080 <_main>:            mov     0x804909c,%eax
   0x8048085 <_main+5>:          add     $0x14,%eax
   0x8048088 <_main+8>:          mov     %eax,0x80490a0
   0x804808d <_main+13>:         mov     $0x1,%eax
   0x8048092 <_main+18>:         mov     $0x0,%ebx
   0x8048097 <_main+23>:         int     $0x80
```

APPENDIX D

Command-Line Debugging Assembly with GDB

Objective

Appendix D describes how to assemble, link, and then debug a NASM Assembly program with the GNU Debugger (GDB). Being able to examine the flow and behavior of low-level instructions is a useful skill, but it can be tricky for Unix/Linux programmers using a command-line environment. This Appendix assumes installs of NASM, GCC or Clang, and GDB.

Program D.1 Sum

NASM (32-bit) on macOS	NASM (32-bit) on Linux

```section .data```
```num1: dd 2```
```num2: dd 4```
 	
```section .text```
```global _main, _sum```
```_main:```
 	
```mov eax, 10```
```dec eax```
```mov ebx, 5```
 	
```push DWORD[num2]```
```push DWORD[num1]```
```call _sum```
```add esp, 8```
 	
```push DWORD 0```
```sub esp, 4```
```mov eax, 1```
```int 80h```
 	
```_sum:```
```push ebp```
```mov ebp, esp```
```push ebx```
```mov ebx, [ebp + 8]```
```mov eax, [ebp + 12]```
```add eax, ebx```
```pop ebx```
```pop ebp```
```ret```
	```section .data```
	```num1: dd 2```
	```num2: dd 4```
	
	```section .text```
	```global _main, _sum```
	```_main:```
	
	```mov eax, 10```
	```dec eax```
	```mov ebx, 5```
	
	```push DWORD[num2]```
	```push DWORD[num1]```
	```call _sum```
	```add esp, 8```
	
	```mov eax, 1```
	```mov ebx, 0```
	```int 80h```
	
	```_sum:```
	```push ebp```
	```mov ebp, esp```
	```push ebx```
	```mov ebx, [ebp + 8]```
	```mov eax, [ebp + 12]```
	```add eax, ebx```
	```pop ebx```
	```pop ebp```
	```ret```

Code

We use a 32-bit NASM Assembly program to illustrate GDB commands. Program D.1 should be written and saved in a file, we use *sum.asm* as the filename. You can use the *.asm* or *.s* extension.

Assembling and Linking

Assembling takes an Assembly *.asm* or *.s* file and produces an object *.o* file. Object file formats vary by OS platform. The standard object file formats are **ELF** for Linux, **MACH-O** for macOS, and **COFF** for Windows.

- For a Linux system (using the *.asm* extension), the command to assemble the *sum.asm* file might look as follows.

    ```
    nasm -f elf -o sum.o sum.asm
    ```

- For a Mac system (using the *.s* extension), the command to assemble the *sum.s* file might look as follows.

    ```
    nasm -f macho -o sum.o -l sum.lst sum.s
    ```

Notice the use of options. The `-f` (format) flag precedes the desired file format of the object file. The `-o` (output) flag precedes the desired name of the object file. Last is the filename of the Assembly file. In the macOS example, we also wanted a listing file, so we use the `-l` (listing file) flag followed by the desired name of the listing file. The listing file is handy if you wish to verify the instructions and memory offsets of an assembled program.

The formats `elf` and `macho` default to 32-bit. To assemble for 64-bit, use `elf64` and `macho64`.

Linking takes object *.o* files and produces a Unix executable file. Linking can be achieved using the linker (ld) or by using a compiler (e.g., gcc, clang).

- For a Linux system, the command to link using `ld` might look as follows.

    ```
    ld -e _main -melf_i386 -o sum sum.o
    ```

The `-e` (entry point) flag allows you to specify the entry point of the program, in this case `_main`. The `-melf_i386` (emulation) indicates the file format of the object file, in this case `elf`, and specifies the linker emulation, in this case `i386`. In simple terms, we are specifying the target architecture. The `-o` (output) flag precedes the name of the desired executable file. Last is the name of the object file.

- Using a compiler as opposed to directly using the linker is another option. For a Linux or Mac system, the command to link using a compiler might look as follows.

    ```
    clang -o sum -m32 sum.o
    gcc -o sum -m32 sum.o
    ```

First is the compiler used. The `-o` (output) flag precedes the name of the desired executable file. The `-m32` specifies 32-bit architecture. Last is the name of the object file. For 64-bit you would use `-m64`.

Debugging with GDB

After assembling and linking the code, you should have an executable file. To run the *sum* program with GDB, use the following Terminal command.

gdb sum

If you are using macOS and have installed GDB via MacPorts, you must use the alternative name `ggdb`.

ggdb sum

The command will launch the debugger and state the program under examination. Our `gdb` command assumes you are at the same file path level as the executable. You can enter the full file path as well.

Though GDB has many debugging commands, we highlight some basics to get you started. In order to debug, you must set a breakpoint. In this case, we will set a breakpoint upon entry into `_main`.

`(gdb)` **break _main**

Notice in the `break` command that we prefix `main` with an underscore. The underscore is explicitly necessary on some systems (most Linux distributions), but may be implicitly assumed on others (e.g., macOS, FreeBSD).

```
(gdb) break main
```

GDB will report back the memory location where the breakpoint was placed.

```
Breakpoint 1 at 0x1fce
```

We could also set a breakpoint at _sum if we wanted, to which GDB will respond.

```
(gdb) break sum
Breakpoint 2 at 0x1ff5
```

Now we can begin executing the program with the run command. GDB will respond that the program has started and halts at our first breakpoint.

```
(gdb) run
Starting program: /pathToSumProgram/sum
Breakpoint 1, 0x00001fce in main ()
```

Next, we take a moment to examine the current state of the program. Specifically, we want to look at registers and memory. To examine all of the registers, issue the info registers command.

```
(gdb) info registers
eax            0x1fce      8142
ecx            0x0         0
edx            0x984f16d9      -1739647271
ebx            0xbffffb54      -1073743020
esp            0xbffffabc      0xbffffabc
ebp            0xbffffae4      0xbffffae4
esi            0x0         0
edi            0x0         0
eip            0x1fce      0x1fce <main>
eflags         0x246       [ PF ZF IF ]
cs             0x1b        27
ss             0x23        35
ds             0x23        35
es             0x23        35
fs             0x0         0
gs             0xf         15
```

To examine the contents (in decimal) of a specific register, you can use the print command.

```
(gdb) print $eax
$1 = 8142
```

To examine the register in a different format, include the format desired, such as hexadecimal (x).

```
(gdb) print/x $eax
$2 = 0x1fce
```

To examine memory, use the examine (x) command along with the count, display format, unit size, and starting address. For example, to examine (x) eight units (8) in hexadecimal (x) with words being the unit size (w), starting where *esp* is pointing, use the following command.

```
(gdb) x/8xw $esp
0xbffffabc: 0x984f16d9   0x00000001   0xbffffaec   0xbffffaf4
0xbffffacc: 0xbffffb54   0x8fe00000   0xbffffadc   0x00000000
```

To examine memory based on the address where a function begins, use a command like the following.

```
(gdb) x/16xw main
0x1fce <main>:       0x00000ab8   0x05b4800    0xff000000   0x00200435
0x1fde <main+16>: 0x0035ff00   0xe800020    0x00000007   0x0108c483
0x1fee <main+32>: 0x55c348d8   0x8b53e589   0x458b085d   0x5bd8010c
0x1ffe <sum+13>:  0x0002c35d   0x0040000    0x00000000   0x00000000
```

The above examples are prior to executing any instructions in our code. Next, we step through some instructions and re-examine registers and memory along the way. The first instruction in our program is

```
mov eax, 10.
```

To execute the instruction and move to the next, we use the next instruction command (nexti, ni), to which GDB will respond with the address of the next instruction.

```
(gdb) nexti
0x00001fd3 in main ()
```

Now we can re-examine the *eax* register.

```
(gdb) print $eax
$3 = 10
(gdb) print/x $eax
$4 = 0xa
```

Moving on, go ahead and execute the next three instructions, which will take us through the execution of push DWORD[num2], with push DWORD[num1] next in line.

```
(gdb) nexti 3
0x00001fdf in main ()
```

Since we pushed num2 to the stack, we can look at how memory has changed.

```
(gdb) x/8xw $esp
0xbffffab8: 0x00000004  0x984f16d9  0x00000001  0xbffffaec
0xbffffac8: 0xbffffaf4  0xbffffb54  0x8fe00000  0xbffffadc
```

Notice that the item on the top of the stack is 0x00000004, which is the num2 value just pushed. Execute one more instruction and then re-run the examine command.

```
(gdb) nexti
0x00001fe5 in main ()
(gdb) x/8xw $esp
0xbffffab4: 0x00000002  0x00000004  0x984f16d9  0x00000001
0xbffffac4: 0xbffffaec  0xbffffaf4  0xbffffb54  0x8fe00000
```

Now both parameters are on the stack. Next, is call _sum. If we run nexti, then we will *step over* the call to _sum and move along to add esp, 8. If we want to *step into* the _sum function, we would either need a breakpoint in _sum or we can use the step into command (stepi).

```
(gdb) stepi
0x00001ff1 in sum ()
```

We could now step through the _sum function examining registers and memory along the way, ensuring that our code is doing what we expect. If we want to execute until the end of the program or the next breakpoint, we can use the continue command (continue, c).

```
(gdb) continue
[Inferior 1 (process 78292) exited normally]
```

An **inferior** is just GDB's way of managing the state of program execution and is typically tied to a process. If you were to type the quit command (quit) while executing, GDB will output something similar to the following.

```
Inferior 1 [process 78868] will be killed.
Quit anyway? (y or n)
```

After issuing the continue, you can quit GDB.

```
(gdb) quit
```

As shown in **APPENDIX C: DISASSEMBLY**, a way to view instructions and memory as you debug is to use layout asm.

```
(gdb) layout asm
```

Resources

The following resources detail the commands and options of nasm, ld, and gdb.

- NASM manual (Chapter 2): http://www.nasm.us/doc/nasmdoc2.html
- ld man page: http://linux.die.net/man/1/ld
- GDB manual: https://sourceware.org/gdb/current/onlinedocs/gdb/
- GDB command index:
  https://sourceware.org/gdb/current/onlinedocs/gdb/Command-and-Variable-Index.html#Command-and-Variable-Index

Linking Assembly and C++

Objective

Appendix E describes how to create a stub and driver for mixing Assembly and C++ code. Examples are provided for Windows using Visual Studio and MASM, for macOS using Xcode and Clang/LLVM (GAS compatible), and for Linux using NASM.

Windows – Visual Studio – MASM

- Open Visual Studio and create a new empty C++ project.
- Add a new file named something such as *main.cpp*.
- Type the following code in *main.cpp*.

```
// main.cpp
extern "C" void asmMain();

int main(){
        asmMain();
        return 0;
}
```

- Add another new file named something like *code.asm*.
- Type the following code in *code.asm*.

MASM (32-bit)	MASM (64-bit)
``; code.asm
.386
.MODEL FLAT, stdcall
.STACK 4096
.CODE
asmMain PROC C
; your code will go here
ret
asmMain ENDP
END```	```; code.asm
.CODE
asmMain PROC
; your code will go here
ret
asmMain ENDP
END```

- The 32-bit code defines the `asmMain` procedure to use the *cdecl* calling convention, which could be set for all procedures by changing the `.MODEL` directive to be `.MODEL FLAT, C`.

The 64-bit code needs no explicit call type because only one exists, the x64 calling convention.

- Open the **Developers Command Prompt**, which can be found by searching for "dev" or "command prompt" in the Start Menu or by navigating to the appropriate location. The path may vary depending on your Visual Studio version and installation location. We have provided an example path and a couple of MSDN links for more information.

  Path: `C:\Program Files (x86)\Microsoft Visual Studio\2017\Community\Common7\Tools`
  Links: https://msdn.microsoft.com/en-us/library/ms229859.aspx
        https://msdn.microsoft.com/en-us/library/f35ctcxw.aspx

- In the Developers Command Prompt, change directory (`cd`) into the folder that contains *code.asm*, and then run the appropriate command to assemble the file and produce an object file.

32-bit	64-bit
`ml /c /Cx /coff code.asm`	`ml64 /c /Cx code.asm`

`ml` = MASM 32-bit Assembler and linker
Example Path: `C:\Program Files(x86)\Microsoft Visual Studio 14.0\VC\bin\ml.exe`

`ml64` = MASM 64-bit Assembler and linker
Example Path: `C:\Program Files(x86)\Microsoft Visual Studio 14.0\VC\bin\x86amd_64\ml64.exe`

`/c` = assemble only, do not link
`/Cx` = preserves case in public and external symbols
`/coff` = object file format (required in 32-bit, not for 64-bit)

`ml` and `ml64` Command-Line Reference: https://msdn.microsoft.com/en-us/library/s0ksfwcf.aspx

Depending on the version of Visual Studio, Windows, and installation settings, you may need to add the paths for `ml` or `ml64` to the system PATH Environment Variable. We provide an example path and some helpful links.

`C:\Program Files (x86)\Microsoft Visual Studio\2017\Community\VC\Tools\MSVC\14.10.25017\bin\HostX64\x64`

Setting the Path and Environment Variables for Command-Line Builds:
https://msdn.microsoft.com/en-us/library/f2ccy3wt.aspx

General instructions for adding a PATH environment variable:
https://msdn.microsoft.com/en-us/library/office/ee537574.aspx

- Back in Visual Studio, add an "Existing item…" to the project and select the *code.obj* file created in the previous step.
- Build and run the program to verify that it works.
- You can now add code in *code.asm* that calls C/C++ functions defined or included in *main.cpp* and vice versa.
- If you create your own functions, do not forget to add the prototype in the *.asm* file *before* the `.DATA` segment.

  Example: `inputInteger PROTO C`

- Reminder: You *must* re-assemble the *.asm* file after any code changes via the Developers Command Prompt for the changes to take effect when rebuilding and running the program.
- Debugging breakpoints will work on the C++ side, but will not work on the Assembly side. If you want to set a debugging breakpoint on the Assembly side, use the `int 3` instruction where breaks are desired.

macOS – Xcode – Clang/LLVM (GAS compatible)

- Open Xcode and create a new empty C++ project.
- Add a new file named something such as *main.cpp*.
- Type the following code in *main.cpp*.

```cpp
// main.cpp
extern "C" void asmMain();

int main(){
      asmMain();
      return 0;
}
```

- Add another new file named something such as *code.s*.
- Type the following code in *code.s*.

```
# code.s
.data

.bss

.text
.globl _asmMain
_asmMain:
        # your code will go here
ret
.end
```

- Click on the project in the Project Navigator. Scroll down to "Apple LLVM 8.0 – Custom Compiler Flags" and in "Other C Flags" add `"-mstackrealign"`. The flag realigns the stack for function calls, which allows for mixing legacy (4-byte aligned) and modern (16-byte aligned) code. Both 32-bit and 64-bit code on macOS must be 16-byte aligned.
- Build and run the program to verify that it works (the program works for both 32-bit and 64-bit).
- You can now add code in *code.s* that calls C/C++ functions defined or included in *main.cpp* and vice versa.
- Prefix function calls in *code.s* with an *underscore*, even if a function does not begin with an underscore in the *.cpp* file.

Linux – NASM

Using your preferred development environment or editor,

- Create a new file named something such as *main.cpp*.
- Type the following code in *main.cpp*.

```cpp
// main.cpp
extern "C" void asmMain();

int main(){
      asmMain();
      return 0;
}
```

- Create another new file named something such as *code.asm*.
- Type the following code in *code.asm*.

```
; code.asm
SECTION .data


SECTION .bss


SECTION .text
global asmMain
asmMain:
        ; your code will go here
ret
```

- Build and run the program to verify that it works. The following assumes *gcc* and *g++ multilib* are installed on a 64-bit Linux system.
    - ○ 32-bit
        - ▪ Assemble: `nasm -f elf32 code.asm` (just using `elf` also implies 32-bit)
        - ▪ Compile and link `g++ -m32 main.cpp code.o -o test`
        - ▪ Run: `./test`
    - ○ 64-bit
        - ▪ Assemble: `nasm -f elf64 code.asm`
        - ▪ Compile and link: `g++ main.cpp code.o -o test`
        - ▪ Alternative: `g++ -m64 main.cpp code.o -o test`
        - ▪ Run: `./test`
- You can now add code in *code.asm* that calls C/C++ functions defined or included in *main.cpp* and vice versa.

What is `extern "C"`?

Prefixing a C++ function with `extern "C"` turns off **name mangling**. Unlike the C language, C++ allows for *function overloading*: naming multiple functions the same name, assuming the parameter lists are different. Overloading works in C++ because the compiler will "mangle" function names so the system can distinguish between function calls. Mangling involves pre-fixing and post-fixing a function name with symbols that indicate information about the function. Almost every compiler mangles names differently.

Looking at the Disassembly in **EXAMPLE 6.4 – STACK ALIGNMENT USING NOP** in **CHAPTER 6** on line 24, notice that the name of the `sum` function has been modified to be `__Z3sumii`. For the Clang/LLVM compiler, `__Z` indicates a mangled symbol, `3` indicates the number of characters in the function name, `sum` is the original function name, and `ii` signifies that the function receives two integer parameters. Again, the mangling scheme varies from compiler to compiler. You can find mangling schemes online, and a suitable starting point is https://en.wikipedia.org/wiki/Name_mangling.

In order to call a C++ function from Assembly, you need to know the name of the function post-compilation. So unless you want to memorize mangling conventions, turn off name mangling so you can use the name of the function as declared by the programmer (you). Any C++ functions you create for calling from within Assembly and vice versa should be marked as `extern "C"`.

APPENDIX F

Functions and Stack

Objective

Appendix F describes attributes of functions and stack manipulation, and is a useful reference for **CHAPTER 6**. As a primary note, general stack manipulation is achieved with PUSH and POP instructions, and also with ADD and SUB of the stack pointer register (*esp/rsp*).

Registers

ebp/rbp	base frame pointer: points to beginning of currently executing stack frame and is used to reference parameters
esp/rsp	stack pointer: should always point to top of stack (most recently pushed value)
eax/rax	accumulator: used for function return value in most cases, but not all cases
eip/rip	instruction pointer: points to next instruction to be executed; also used for rip-relative addressing in 64-bit programs (see **CHAPTER 6 SUPPLEMENT, PROGRAM 6.3**)
st(0)/stmm0	x87 Floating Point Unit (FPU) stack register used for returning floating point values
xmm0/zmm0	Streaming SIMD Extensions (SSE) register used for returning floating point values

Stack Frames

Stack frames are established in the following steps:

1. Parameters (pass-by-value) or addresses of parameters (pass-by-reference) being passed are placed in registers or pushed to the stack.
2. The function is called, which pushes the return address on the stack.
3. Upon entering the function, *ebp/rbp* is pushed to the stack.
4. Any callee-saved registers needing to be saved are pushed to the stack (typical of 64-bit).
5. *ebp/rbp* is set equal to *esp/rsp*.
6. Bytes may be subtracted from *esp/rsp* to setup space for local values that are subsequently copied, or local values are pushed to the stack (typical of 32-bit); values may be copied from registers into scratch stack space (typical of 64-bit).

Usually, *ebp/rbp* is used to reference parameters within a stack frame. In 64-bit, if no further PUSH, POP, or CALL instructions are used, then *rsp* can be used to reference parameters. However, more commonly *rip*-relative addressing is used to refer to parameters in 64-bit mode, which is the default method in x86_64.

rip-relative addressing is a method that is position-independent and uses memory offsets from the current instruction pointer (where *rip* is pointing) to refer to parameters. Relative addressing using *rip* is available in some 64-bit Assemblers (e.g., GAS, NASM), but is not available in MASM x64 (`ml64.exe`). In MASM 64-bit, variable and address access is similar to 32-bit mode; the conversion to *rip*-relative addressing is done automatically by the linker. For a comparison, see the 64-bit programs in the **CHAPTER 6 SUPPLEMENT**.

Example F.1 illustrates Step #6 in the STACK FRAMES section: creating space for local variables. Notice that to dereference the local variables, you can either add the bytes back to *esp* (GAS) or realign *esp* to *ebp* (MASM and NASM).

Example F.1 Local variables (32-bit)

GAS	MASM	NASM

_Example:
push %ebp
movl %esp, %ebp
subl $8, %rsp
movl $10, -4(%ebp)
movl $20, -8(%ebp)
addl $8, %esp
popl %ebp
retl
	_Example PROC
	push ebp
	mov ebp, esp
	sub esp, 8
	mov DWORD PTR[ebp-4], 10
	mov DWORD PTR[ebp-8], 20
	mov esp, ebp
	pop ebp
	ret
	_Example ENDP
		_Example:
		push ebp
		mov ebp, esp
		sub esp, 8
		mov DWORD [ebp-4], 10
		mov DWORD [ebp-8], 20
		mov esp, ebp
		pop ebp
		ret

Any time you want to get the address of a stack parameter, you must use the LEA instruction because the parameter's exact location is not known until run-time (e.g., `lea esi, variable1`).

Passing Parameters

- In 32-bit, parameters are passed on the call stack.
- In 64-bit, parameters are passed in registers (up to 4 in Windows, up to 14 in Mac/Linux), then the stack is used for additional parameters.
- Using registers to pass parameters requires attention to detail in terms of temporarily saving the contents so the register values can be restored after the function ends.
- *Pass-by-value*: a copy of the value is pushed on the stack. Directly refer to the variable per the Assembler syntax (e.g., `push num`, `push DWORD [num]`).
- *Pass-by-reference*: the address where a value is stored is pushed to the stack. Make use of the Load Effective Address (LEA) instruction for clarity.
- Passing arrays: the address of the first location is pushed to the stack. Arrays are always pass-by-reference.
- If stack space was used for passing parameters, remember to clean up stack after returning from a function.
- When using the C declaration (*cdecl*) calling convention, parameters are passed in reverse order and the calling function cleans up the stack (ADD `constant, esp` instruction after the CALL instruction).
- When using the STDCALL convention, parameters are passed in reverse order and the called function cleans up the stack (`ret constant`).

Referring to Parameters

Referring to parameters on the stack can be achieved a number of ways, as noted in the STACK FRAMES section. Example F.2 shows a couple of methods for explicitly referring to stack parameters.

Example F.2 Referring to stack parameters

Mode	GAS	MASM	NASM
32-bit	movl 4(%ebp), %eax	mov eax, [ebp + 4]	mov eax, [ebp + 4]
64-bit	movl -0x4(%rbp), %rsi	mov rsi, [rbp - 4]	mov rsi, [rbp - 4]

Returning Values

In 32-bit:

- Integer values 32 bits or smaller are returned in *eax*.
- Integer values between 33 and 64 bits (e.g., `long long int` in C++) are returned in *eax:edx*.
- Floating point values are returned in *st(0)* on the FPU stack **and** in *xmm0* (if supported).

In 64-bit:
- Integer values 64 bits or smaller are returned in *rax*.
- Floating point values are returned in *xmm0/zmm0*.

In both 32-bit and 64-bit: structs, object data, and values larger than 64 bits are passed by:
- The calling function allocates enough stack space for the data.
- Pass the stack address (i.e., pointers to object/members) into the called function.
- The called function writes the return data to the address (via the pointers).
- For pass-by-value, use general purpose registers (e.g., *eax/rax*, *edx/rdx*, *edi/rdi*) to copy data/object to new stack location, and the copied data/object is passed to and manipulated in the called function.

  32-bit specifics:
  - For pass-by-value, upon returning, the *ecx* register points to the stack location of the data/object.
  - For pass-by-reference, the calling function uses *eax* to point to the data/object, then *eax* can be used in the called function to manipulate the data/object.

  64-bit specifics:
  - For pass-by-value, upon returning, general purpose registers (e.g., *rax*, *dl*) are used to point to stack locations of the data/object.
  - For pass-by-reference, the calling function uses *rdi* to point to the data/object, then *rdi* can be used in the called function to manipulate the data/object.

More x86_64 Considerations

- Parameters can be up to 8 bytes.
- Parameters placed in registers or memory that are less than 64 bits are not zero extended automatically.
- In Microsoft x64, reserve shadow space as necessary per platform requirements (see **x86_64** in **Chapter 6**).
- Functions must be 16-byte aligned.
- Calling functions are responsible for cleaning up the stack.

MASM Specifics

- PROC directive is used to declare a procedure (function), its attributes, and parameters.
- PROTO (preferred), EXTERNDEF, and EXTERN directives are used to identify *external* functions used in a program.
- ENTER and LEAVE directives automatically create and dereference a stack frame for a called function.
- LOCAL directive can be used to declare a local variable by name and assign sizes.
- INVOKE (32-bit only) can be used instead of CALL, which allows for passing multiple parameters on a single line of code (see **Program 10.4** in **Chapter 10**).

```
INVOKE displayArray, OFFSET array, LENGTHOF array, TYPE array
```

- ADDR (32-bit only) can be used to pass a pointer when using INVOKE.

```
INVOKE displayArray, ADDR array
```

Using CPUID

Objective

Appendix G demonstrates how to use the CPUID instruction to test for processor features. Appendix G assumes you have read through **CHAPTER 9**. As examples, we test for x87 FPU, MMX, SSE (variants), AVX (variants), SYSEN-TER/SYSEXIT, SYSCALL/SYSRET, FMA (fused multiply-add), F16C (half-precision), RDRAND and RDSEED (random number generators). The examples include standard features and extended features.

Developer Resources

- Intel 64 and IA-32 Software Developer's Manual, Volume 1, Chapter 18
- Intel 64 and IA-32 Software Developer's Manual, Volume 2A, Chapter 3
- AMD Architecture Programmer's Manual: http://developer.amd.com/resources/developer-guides-manuals/
- AMD CPUID Specification: http://amd-dev.wpengine.netdna-cdn.com/wordpress/media/2012/10/25481.pdf
- Microsoft __cpuid(): https://msdn.microsoft.com/en-us/library/hskdteyh.aspx

Web Resources

- https://en.wikipedia.org/wiki/CPUID (the best resource for a quick visual of feature bits)
- http://wiki.osdev.org/CPUID

Testing for Features

In Program G.1, we use C++ in combination with inline Assembly to indicate supported features. The primary examples herein show Xcode/GCC inline Assembly, but the Visual C++ equivalent is shown in Table G.2 at the end of Appendix G. For Microsoft systems, keep in mind that Microsoft x64 does not support inline Assembly; so either use x86, an Assembly-only program/module, or use the __cpuid() function. Program G.1 should work for most platforms with no or very little tweaking.

You can also test to make sure the CPUID instruction is supported on your system (which is very likely), but that task is reserved as **ASSIGNMENT 10.3** in **CHAPTER 10**.

The basic process of testing a processor for feature support is to load the appropriate register(s) with a value that indicates the information desired, such as standard features, extended features, cache information, or core topology. In most cases, load the *eax* register with the information value, execute CPUID, and then the information is returned in various general purpose registers (*eax*, *ebx*, *ecx*, *edx*). Each feature has a corresponding bit that is set (1) if supported, or clear (0) if not supported. For example, if the processor has an Onboard x87 FPU, the first bit in *edx* (bit 0) will be set.

Here we show snippets from Program G.1 along with the features and corresponding bit locations. We use **bitsets** to hold the feature bits and we have only selected a subset of the features. You can modify the program to include all features or select the features you wish to test. The full program and example output is included at the end of Appendix G.

Standard Features

To get *standard* processor feature bits, load *eax* with 1, execute CPUID, and the feature bits are returned in *edx* and *ecx*. The code snippet to test for standard features is shown in Example G.1.

Example G.1 Standard features

```
"movl $1, %%eax \n\t"              // EAX = 1
"cpuid \n\t"                       // execute CPUID
"movl %%edx, %[features1] \n\t"
"movl %%ecx, %[features2] \n\t"
```

EDX	ECX
Bit 0 – FPU Bit 11 – SEP (SYSENTER/SYSEXIT) Bit 23 – MMX Bit 25 – SSE Bit 26 – SSE2	Bit 0 – SSE3 Bit 9 – SSSE3 Bit 12 – FMA3 Bit 19 – SSE4.1 Bit 20 – SSE4.2 Bit 28 – AVX Bit 29 – F16C (half-precision) Bit 30 – RDRAND (random number generator)

Extended Features

To get extended processor feature bits, load *eax* with 7, load *ecx* with 0, execute CPUID, and the feature bits are returned in *ebx* and *ecx*. The code snippet to test for extended features is shown in Example G.2.

Example G.2 Extended features

```
"movl $7, %%eax \n\t"             // EAX = 7
"xorl %%ecx, %%ecx \n\t"          // ECX = 0
"cpuid \n\t"
"movl %%ebx, %[eFeatures1] \n\t"
```

EBX
Bit 5 – AVX2 Bit 16 – AVX512f Bit 17 – AVX512dq Bit 18 – RDSEED Bit 21 – AVX512ifma

More Extended Features

To test more extended processor feature bits (assuming the processor supports function parameters over 8000000h), load *eax* with 80000001h, execute CPUID, and the feature bits are returned in *edx* and *ecx*. The code snippet to test for more extended features is shown in Example G.3.

Example G.3 More extended features

```
"movl $80000001h, %%eax \n\t"          // EAX = 80000001h
"cpuid \n\t"
"movl %%edx, %[eFeatures2] \n\t"
```

EDX
Bit 11 – SYSCALL/SYSRET

The reason for including the SYSCALL example is because in 32-bit mode the instruction is not supported, but in 64-bit mode the instruction is supported, so SYSCALL provides a predictable 64-bit feature example.

Output Examples

For brevity, we do not show the CPUID bits for all three examples in Table G.1, but Program G.1 will output the CPUID bits returned in the general purpose registers. Examples G.4 and G.5 show the CPUID bits for an Intel Core i7 (mid 2012) in 32-bit mode and an Intel Core i7 (mid 2015) in 64-bit mode, respectively.

Example G.4 CPUID bits for Intel Core i7 (mid-2012), 32-bit mode

```
CPUID bits (right-to-left)
----------
10111111111010111111101111111111 - EDX bits, EAX=1
01111111101110101110001111111111 - ECX bits, EAX=1
00000000000000000000001010000001 - EBX bits, EAX=7 & ECX=0
00101000000100000000000000000000 - EDX bits, EAX=80000001h
```

Example G.5 CPUID bits for Intel Core i7 (mid-2015), 64-bit mode

```
CPUID bits (right-to-left)
----------
10111111111010111111101111111111 - EDX bits, EAX=1
01111111111111010111110111111111 - ECX bits, EAX=1
00000000000000000010011110101011 - EBX bits, EAX=7 & ECX=0
00101100000100000000100000000000 - EDX bits, EAX=80000001h
```

Table G.1 Program G.1 output

Intel Core 2 Duo (early 2009) 2.93 GHz, 2 core, 32-bit mode	Intel Core i7 (mid 2012) 2.6 GHz, 4 core, 32-bit mode	Intel Core i7 (mid 2015) 2.5 GHz, 4 core, 64-bit mode
CPU Features ------------ x87 FPU: Yes SYSENTER/SYSEXIT: Yes MMX: Yes SSE: Yes SSE2: Yes SSE3: Yes SSSE3: Yes FMA3: No SSE4.1: Yes SSE4.2: No AVX: No F16C: No RDRAND: No Extended Features ----------------- AVX2: No AVX512f: No AVX512dq: No RDSEED: No AVX512ifma: No More Extended Features ---------------------- SYSCALL/SYSRET: No	CPU Features ------------ x87 FPU: Yes SYSENTER/SYSEXIT: Yes MMX: Yes SSE: Yes SSE2: Yes SSE3: Yes SSSE3: Yes FMA3: No SSE4.1: Yes SSE4.2: Yes AVX: Yes F16C: Yes RDRAND: Yes Extended Features ----------------- AVX2: No AVX512f: No AVX512dq: No RDSEED: No AVX512ifma: No More Extended Features ---------------------- SYSCALL/SYSRET: No	CPU Features ------------ x87 FPU: Yes SYSENTER/SYSEXIT: Yes MMX: Yes SSE: Yes SSE2: Yes SSE3: Yes SSSE3: Yes FMA3: Yes SSE4.1: Yes SSE4.2: Yes AVX: Yes F16C: Yes RDRAND: Yes Extended Features ----------------- AVX2: Yes AVX512f: No AVX512dq: No RDSEED: No AVX512ifma: No More Extended Features ---------------------- SYSCALL/SYSRET: Yes

CPUID Program

Program G.1 CPUID features

C++ with GAS inline Assembly

```cpp
// CPUID Features - macOS (Clang/LLVM), Linux (GCC) - 32-bit
// Copyright (c) 2017 Hall & Slonka

#include <iostream>
#include <bitset>
using namespace std;

int main()
{
   bitset<32> features1;     // standard features in EDX
   bitset<32> features2;     // standard features in ECX
   bitset<32> eFeatures1;    // extended features in EBX
   bitset<32> eFeatures2;    // extended features in EDX

   asm ("movl $1, %%eax \n\t"                  // EAX = 1
        "cpuid \n\t"                           // execute CPUID
        "movl %%edx, %[features1] \n\t"
        "movl %%ecx, %[features2] \n\t"
        "movl $7, %%eax \n\t"                  // EAX = 7
        "xorl %%ecx, %%ecx \n\t"               // ECX = 0
        "cpuid \n\t"
        "movl %%ebx, %[eFeatures1] \n\t"
        "movl $80000001h, %%eax \n\t"          // EAX = 80000001h
        "cpuid \n\t"
        "movl %%edx, %[eFeatures2] \n\t"
        :[features1]  "=m"(features1),         // outputs
         [features2]  "=m"(features2),
         [eFeatures1] "=m"(eFeatures1),
         [eFeatures2] "=m"(eFeatures2)
        :                                      // inputs
        :"eax","%ebx","%ecx","%edx"            // clobbered registers
       );

   // binary output of features
   // output in reverse due to little-endian

   cout << "CPUID bits (right-to-left)\n";
   cout << "----------\n";
   cout << features1 << " - EDX bits, EAX=1\n";
   cout << features2 << " - ECX bits, EAX=1\n";
   cout << eFeatures1 << " - EBX bits, EAX=7 & ECX=0\n";
   cout << eFeatures2 << " - EDX bits, EAX=80000001h\n\n";

   cout << "CPU Features\n";
   cout << "------------\n";

   // FPU
   if (features1[0] == 1) {
      cout << "x87 FPU: Yes\n";
   }
   else {cout << "x87 FPU: No\n";}

   // SEP (SYSENTER/SYSEXIT)
   if (features1[11] == 1) {
```

```cpp
  cout << "SYSENTER/SYSEXIT: Yes\n";
}
else {cout << "SYSENTER/SYSEXIT: No\n";}

// MMX
if (features1[23] == 1) {
   cout << "MMX: Yes\n";
}
else {cout << "MMX: No\n";}

// SSE
if (features1[25] == 1) {
   cout << "SSE: Yes\n";
}
else {cout << "SSE: No\n";}

// SSE2
if (features1[26] == 1) {
   cout << "SSE2: Yes\n";
}
else {cout << "SSE2: No\n";}

// SSE3
if (features2[0] == 1) {
   cout << "SSE3: Yes\n";
}
else {cout << "SSE3: No\n";}

// SSSE3
if (features2[9] == 1) {
   cout << "SSSE3: Yes\n";
}
else {cout << "SSSE3: No\n";}

// FMA3
if (features2[12] == 1) {
   cout << "FMA3: Yes\n";
}
else {cout << "FMA3: No\n";}

// SSE4.1
if (features2[19] == 1) {
   cout << "SSE4.1: Yes\n";
}
else {cout << "SSE4.1: No\n";}

// SSE4.2
if (features2[20] == 1) {
   cout << "SSE4.2: Yes\n";
}
else {cout << "SSE4.2: No\n";}

// AVX
if (features2[28] == 1) {
   cout << "AVX: Yes\n";
}
else {cout << "AVX: No\n";}

// F16C (half-precision)
if (features2[29] == 1) {
   cout << "F16C: Yes\n";
}
else {cout << "F16C: No\n";}
```

```
   // RDRAND (random number generator)
   if (features2[30] == 1) {
      cout << "RDRAND: Yes\n";
   }
   else {cout << "RDRAND: No\n";}

   cout << "\n";

   cout << "Extended Features\n";
   cout << "-----------------\n";

   // AVX2
   if (eFeatures1[5] == 1) {
      cout << "AVX2: Yes\n";
   }
   else {cout << "AVX2: No\n";}

   // AVX512f
   if (eFeatures1[16] == 1) {
      cout << "AVX512f: Yes\n";
   }
   else {cout << "AVX512f: No\n";}

   // AVX512dq
   if (eFeatures1[17] == 1) {
      cout << "AVX512dq: Yes\n";
   }
   else {cout << "AVX512dq: No\n";}

   // RDSEED
   if (eFeatures1[18] == 1) {
      cout << "RDSEED: Yes\n";
   }
   else {cout << "RDSEED: No\n";}

   // AVX512ifma
   if (eFeatures1[21] == 1) {
      cout << "AVX512ifma: Yes\n";
   }
   else {cout << "AVX512ifma: No\n";}

   cout << "\n";

   cout << "More Extended Features\n";
   cout << "----------------------\n";

   // SYSCALL/SYSRET
   if (eFeatures2[11] == 1) {
      cout << "SYSCALL/SYSRET: Yes\n";
   }
   else {cout << "SYSCALL/SYSRET: No\n";}

   return 0;
}
```

Inline Assembly CPUID Testing Code

Table G.2 provides the CPUID inline Assembly statement in Program G.1 for both compiler formats.

Table G.2 Inline Assembly CPUID testing code

Xcode/GCC (32 or 64-bit)	Visual C++ (32-bit)
```asm ("movl $1, %%eax \n\t" "cpuid \n\t" "movl %%edx, %[features1] \n\t" "movl %%ecx, %[features2] \n\t" "movl $7, %%eax \n\t" "xorl %%ecx, %%ecx \n\t" "cpuid \n\t" "movl %%ebx, %[eFeatures1] \n\t" "movl $80000001h, %%eax \n\t" "cpuid \n\t" "movl %%edx, %[eFeatures2] \n\t" :[features1] "=m"(features1), [features2] "=m"(features2), [eFeatures1] "=m"(eFeatures1), [eFeatures2] "=m"(eFeatures2) : :"eax","%ebx","%ecx","%edx");```	```__asm {mov eax, 1 cpuid mov features1, edx mov features2, ecx mov eax, 7 xor ecx, ecx cpuid mov eFeatures1, ebx mov eax, 80000001h cpuid mov eFeatures2, edx };```

ASCII and Decimal Arithmetic

Objective

Appendix H presents information and examples for ASCII and Decimal Arithmetic using **Binary-Coded Decimal (BCD)**. BCD is supported in x86 (32-bit), but is not supported in x86_64 (64-bit), although it still has uses.

ASCII Arithmetic

When we receive input from a user via a keyboard or perhaps information from the system via a system call, numeric values are usually in the **ASCII** format, which is a character set for mapping logical symbols to a numeric counterpart (**Chapter 1**). High-level languages have mechanisms that take care of converting character Decimal input entered on a keyboard to a true integer equivalent. Assume we have the following C++ code snippet shown in Example H.1.

Example H.1 Integer input

```
int num1;
cout << "Enter num1: ";
cin >> num1;
num1++;
cout << "num1: " << num1;
```

If we entered "2," the input is initially the character-based ASCII value 32h, which will then be converted to an integer form so the true value of 2 can be used in arithmetic (like incrementing), instead of the raw ASCII value. For output to console, the integer value 3 must be converted back to its ASCII equivalent 33h, which again is handled for us without any extra effort. Table H.1 shows the ASCII equivalents of Decimal values.

Table H.1 ASCII equivalents of decimal integers

Decimal Value	ASCII Value (hex)
0	30
1	31
2	32
3	33
4	34
5	35
6	36
7	37
8	38
9	39

When working with values at a low-level, a programmer must handle ASCII conversions for numeric input and output. A good example is PROGRAM 10.3 in CHAPTER 10 where we output a Process ID to console.

Getting integers from a user, performing arithmetic (such as addition) and displaying the result can generally be achieved in two ways: 1) get input, convert the whole operands from ASCII to decimal, add the values, convert back to ASCII for output; or 2) add by using the ASCII values a pair at a time. In the following exchange, the second option would be like ASCII 2 + ASCII 6 = ASCII 8, display ASCII 8, move to next pair.

```
Enter num1: 3402
Enter num2: 1256
The sum is: 4658
```

Binary-Coded Decimal (BCD) is an approach sometimes used when displaying numeric values. BCD is simply a system where each decimal digit is represented by a fixed number of bits. In a **packed BCD** system (mostly older systems), a decimal digit is stored in a nibble (4 bits) since four bits is enough to represent integers 0–9. In an **unpacked BCD** system (more modern systems), a decimal digit is stored in one byte (8 bits), which means 4 digits can be stored in 32 bits. BCD can be helpful when dealing with decimal values.

As a point of comparison, the char data type in C++ stores one byte. Look at Example H.2, which is a modified version of Example H.1.

Example H.2 Character input

```
char num1;
cout << "Enter num1: ";
cin >> num1;
num1++;
cout << "num1: " << num1;
```

Assume we enter "1" at the prompt in Example H.2. If we were to set a breakpoint and look at the actual stored value, it would be 31h. The statement num1++; does not increment an integer from 1 to 2, but rather increments the ASCII value 31h to 32h, which when output to console will print "2".

Unpacked BCD and ASCII Arithmetic

The high four bits of unpacked BCD integers are always zeros, whereas the same bits in ASCII decimal numbers are 3 (0011b). Both forms store one digit per byte. Assuming the number 3402, the formats would be as follows.

Unpacked BCD: 03 04 00 02
ASCII format: 33 34 30 32

The x86 instruction set contains special instructions to assist in ASCII arithmetic, if you happen to be working with ASCII at a low level. The ASCII instructions adjust unpacked BCD arithmetic results so the value can be easily converted to the appropriate ASCII value by ORing each byte with 30h. The ASCII Adjust instructions take carry and borrow situations into account as well.

Table H.2 ASCII instructions

ASCII Instruction	Description
AAA	ASCII adjust after addition
AAS	ASCII adjust after subtraction
AAM	ASCII adjust after multiplication
AAD	ASCII adjust after division

Program H.1 presents an example of how to use AAA.

Program H.1 *ASCII Adjust after addition (32-bit)*

GAS	MASM	NASM

```.data```
 ```num1: .byte '8'```
 ```num2: .byte '2'```
 	
 ```.text```
 ```.globl _main```
 ```_main:```
 	
 ```xorw %ax, %ax   # must clear```
 ```movb num1, %al```
 ```addb num2, %al```
 ```aaa   # ascii adjust```
 ```orw $0x3030, %ax # convert to ascii```
 	
 ```pushl $0```
 ```subl $4, %esp```
 ```movl $1, %eax```
 ```int $0x80```
 ```.end```
	```.386```
	 ```.MODEL FLAT, stdcall```
	 ```.STACK 4096```
	 ```ExitProcess PROTO,```
	 ```dwExitCode:DWORD```
	 ```.DATA```
	 ```num1 BYTE '8'```
	 ```num2 BYTE '2'```
	
	 ```.CODE```
	 ```_main PROC```
	
	 ```xor ax, ax```
	 ```mov al, num1```
	 ```add al, num2```
	 ```aaa```
	 ```or ax, 3030h```
	
	 ```INVOKE ExitProcess, 0```
	 ```_main ENDP```
	 ```END```
		```section .data```
		 ```num1: DB '8'```
		 ```num2: DB '2'```
		
		 ```section .text```
		 ```global _main```
		 ```_main:```
		
		 ```xor ax, ax```
		 ```mov al, [num1]```
		 ```add al, [num2]```
		 ```aaa```
		 ```or ax, 3030h```
		
		 ```mov eax, 1```
		 ```mov ebx, 0```
		 ```int 80h```

Packed Decimal Arithmetic

The x86 instruction set also contains special instructions to assist with packed decimal arithmetic. As previously stated, packed BCD uses four bits for each digit instead of eight bits, meaning two decimal digits per byte. Visually, packed BCD values use each hexadecimal digit as a literal decimal value. Look at the data declarations in Example H.3.

Example H.3 Packed decimals (GAS)

```
bcd1: .byte 0x42         # 42 decimal
bcd2: .word 0x2001       # 2,001 decimal
bcd3: .long 0x12345678   # 12,345,678 decimal
```

Packed decimal instructions are only for addition and subtraction.

Table H.3 Decimal instructions

Decimal Instruction	Description
DAA	Decimal adjust after addition
DAS	Decimal adjust after subtraction

Program H.2 presents an example of how to use DAA.

Program H.2 *Decimal adjust after addition (32-bit)*

GAS	MASM	NASM

```.data```
 ```.text```
 ```.globl _main```
 ```_main:```
	```.386```
	 ```.MODEL FLAT, stdcall```
	 ```.STACK 4096```
	 ```ExitProcess PROTO,```
	 ```dwExitCode:DWORD```
	 ```.DATA```
	 ```.CODE```
		```SECTION .data```
		 ```SECTION .text```
		 ```global _main```
		 ```_main:```

```
GAS                                    MASM                NASM

.data                                  .386                SECTION .data
.text                                  .MODEL FLAT, stdcall SECTION .text
.globl _main                           .STACK 4096         global _main
_main:                                 ExitProcess PROTO,  _main:
                                       dwExitCode:DWORD
                                       .DATA
                                       .CODE
xor %ax, %ax      # clear AX           _main PROC          xor ax, ax
xor %bx, %bx      # clear BX                               xor bx, bx
mov $0x42, %al    # 42 decimal = 2A hex xor ax, ax         mov al, 42h
add $0x68, %al    # 68 decimal = 44 hex xor bx, bx         add al, 68h
daa               # 110 decimal = 6E hex mov al, 42h       daa
                  # CF = 1, AL = 10    add al, 68h
adc $0, %bx       # BX = 0 + BX(0) + CF daa                adc bx, 0
cmp $0, %bx       # if CF set(1)                           cmp bx, 0
jz done                                adc bx, 0           jz done
carry:                                 cmp bx, 0           carry:
add $1, %ah       # set next byte to 1  jz done            add ah, 1
                                       carry:
done:                                  add ah, 1           done:
pushl $0                                                   mov eax, 1
subl $4, %esp                          done:               mov ebx, 0
movl $1, %eax                          INVOKE ExitProcess, 0 int 80h
int $0x80                              _main ENDP
.end                                   END
```

Resources

Intel 64 and IA-32 Software Developer's Manual, Volume 1, Chapter 4, Section 4.7
Intel 64 and IA-32 Software Developer's Manual, Volume 1, Chapter 7, Section 7.3.3
https://en.wikipedia.org/wiki/Binary-coded_decimal

APPENDIX I

Intrinsics

Objective

Appendix I introduces **intrinsics**, which are functions that are usually not implemented as part of a package or library for a programming language, but instead are implemented and handled by a compiler. Intrinsics work much like inline functions: intrinsics are replaced with a sequence of instructions that represent the desired action at every instance. Intrinsics are highly-optimized since they are built in to the compiler. The optimizations are usually regarding parallelization, such as SIMD operations.

The C-+ compilers we have referenced throughout the book (Clang, GCC, Visual C++) implement intrinsics for x86/x86_64 SIMD instructions. Also as mentioned in Chapter 9, Microsoft x64 does not allow inline Assembly statements, which means to achieve similar low-level operations, programmers *must* use intrinsics. Some compilers use platform-specific intrinsics, while some compiler frameworks provide more portability across platforms. Always keep in mind that intrinsic support will vary by compiler and version.

Resources

- https://software.intel.com/sites/landingpage/IntrinsicsGuide/ (an amazing interactive site by Intel)
- https://software.intel.com/en-us/node/523351 (Intel Intrinsics Reference)
- https://msdn.microsoft.com/en-us/library/26td21ds.aspx (Microsoft Compiler Intrinsics)
- Intel 64 and IA-32 Software Developer's Manual, Volume 2A, Chapter 3, Section 3.1.1.10 "Intel C/C++ Compiler Intrinsics Equivalents Section"
- Intel 64 and IA-32 Software Developer's Manual, Volume 2C, Appendix C "Intel C/C++ Compiler Intrinsics and Functions Equivalents"

Intrinsic Datatypes

Just as with SSE data in raw Assembly, data for SSE intrinsics must be aligned on 16-byte boundaries. Table I.1 presents MMX and SSE intrinsic datatypes.

Table I.1 MMX and SSE intrinsic datatypes

Datatype	Description
__m64	contents of an MMX register (8-bit, 16-bit, 32-bit, and 64-bit values)
__m128	contents of an XMM register used by an SSE intrinsic (one scalar or four 32-bit packed single-precision floating-point values)
__m128d	contents of an XMM register used by an SSE intrinsic (one scalar or two 64-bit packed double-precision floating-point values)
__m128i	contents of an XMM register used by an SSE intrinsic (sixteen 8-bit, eight 16-bit, four 32-bit, or two 64-bit integers)

Table I.2 presents AVX and AVX2 datatypes, which must be aligned on 32-byte boundaries. Most AVX intrinsics can also use SSE datatypes since AVX and AVX-512 are backward compatible.

Table I.2 AVX Intrinsic datatypes

Datatype	Description
__m256	contents of an YMM register used by an AVX intrinsic (eight 32-bit packed single-precision floating-point values)
__m256d	contents of an YMM register used by an AVX intrinsic (four 64-bit packed double-precision floating-point values)
__m256i	contents of an YMM register used by an AVX intrinsic (thirty-two 8-bit, sixteen 16-bit, eight 32-bit, or four 64-bit integers)

Table I.3 presents AVX-512 datatypes, which must be aligned on 64-byte boundaries.

Table I.3 AVX-512 Datatypes

Datatype	Description
__m512	contents of an ZMM register used by an AVX-512 intrinsic (sixteen 32-bit packed single-precision floating-point values)
__m512d	contents of an ZMM register used by an AVX-512 intrinsic (eight 64-bit packed double-precision floating-point values)
__m512i	contents of an ZMM register used by an AVX-512 intrinsic (sixty-four 8-bit, thirty-two 16-bit, sixteen 32-bit, or eight 64-bit integers)

The use of intrinsic datatypes has some restrictions that are covered in the Intel manual. To use intrinsic datatypes, you must include the header file with the datatype definitions. For example, the SSE header file is <xmmintrin. h> and the AVX header file is <immintrin.h>. With Clang and GCC, you can include <x86intrin.h>, which includes all extension headers. The file is <intrin.h> for Visual C++.

Table I.4 Intrinsic header files

Extension	Header file
MMX	<mmintrin.h>
SSE	<xmmintrin.h>
SSE2	<emmintrin.h>
SSE3	<pmmintrin.h>
SSSE3	<tmmintrin.h>
SSE4.1	<smmintrin.h>
SSE4.2	<nmmintrin.h>
SSE4a, XOP	<ammintrin.h>
AES	<wmmintrin.h>
AVX, FMA	<immintrin.h>
AVX512	<zmmintrin.h>

Intrinsics

Most intrinsics are **simple**, meaning only one intrinsic is needed to achieve the desired operation. Some intrinsics are **composite**, which means more than one statement is necessary for implementation.

Intrinsic template

```
__mm_<operation>_<suffix>
```

Referring to the intrinsic template, operations are usually equivalent or similar to some form of Assembly instruction, such as ADD or SUB. The suffix denotes the datatype used in the operation. The suffix begins with p (packed), ep (extended packed), or s (scalar). Additional letters further describe the data. For example, ps indicates packed single precision, while ss indicates scalar single precision. Table I.5 presents examples of additional suffix letters.

Table I.5 Intrinsic suffix examples

Additional suffix letters	Description
s	Single-precision floating point
d	Double-precision floating point
i8	signed 8-bit integer
u8	unsigned 8-bit integer
i16	signed 16-bit integer
u16	unsigned 16-bit integer
i32	signed 32-bit integer
u32	unsigned 32-bit integer
i64	signed 64-bit integer
u64	unsigned 64-bit integer
i128	signed 128-bit integer
i256	signed 256-bit integer
i512	signed 512-bit integer

Based on the intrinsic template, an intrinsic function in code has the following form.

Intrinsic function

```
datatype intrinsic_name(parameters);
```

The datatype is the return datatype, which can be void, int, or one of the supported intrinsic datatypes (e.g., __m64, __m128i). The intrinsic_name is the function-like operation you wish to perform, which is based on the intrinsic template. The parameters are the data on which the intrinsic operates.

Table I.6 presents three intrinsic examples. First is an SSE intrinsic to add packed single-precision values. Second is an AVX intrinsic to move (load) a YMM register with aligned packed double-precision values. Third is an AVX-512 intrinsic to calculate the sine value of packed single-precision floats. Notice that the AVX-512 intrinsic has no Assembly instruction counterpart.

Table I.6 Intrinsic examples

Assembly Mnemonic (ext)	Description	Intrinsic
ADDPS (SSE)	Add packed single precision	`__m128 _mm_add_ps(__m128 a, __m128 b)`
VMOVAPD (AVX)	Move aligned packed double precision	`__m256d _mm256_load_pd(double const *a)`
N/A (AVX-512)	Calculate sine value of packed 32-bit floats	`__m512 _mm512_sin_ps(__m512 v)`

Programs

Here we provide programs to illustrate the behavior and use of intrinsics. We encourage you to work through the examples presented and then explore other intrinsics. The programs include snippets of Disassembly, so this section assumes you have reviewed **APPENDIX C: DISASSEMBLY**. With your preferred development environment and compiler, write Program I.1 and set a breakpoint at `return 0;` so you can examine the local variables and register state.

Program I.1 Intrinsic load packed single precision

C++
| ```
#include <xmmintrin.h>
int main()
{
    float array[4] = { 1.0, 2.0, 3.0, 4.0 };
    __m128 result = _mm_load_ps(array);      // MOVAPS

    return 0;  // set breakpoint here
}
``` |

Program I.1 simply creates an `array` of 32-bit floats, creates a `result` that is of type `__m128`, and uses the `_mm_load_ps` intrinsic to load the array comprised of packed single-precision floating-point values into an SSE register. Note that the intrinsic parameter is the address of `array`.

Example I.1 shows the Disassembly of Program I.1, of which most is the process of setting up the stack frame for `main` and storing local variables. The first arrow (->) in the Disassembly indicates where the data pointed to by the address in *rcx* (the address of `array`) is moved to *xmm0* using the MOVAPS instruction. The second arrow is where the values are copied to `result`.

Keep in mind that the compiler will choose the register(s) to use for operations. For Program I.1, *xmm0* is likely to be chosen.
```

Example I.1 Disassembly of Program I.1

Xcode (Clang/LLVM) – AT&T syntax
| ```
cpp_testing`main:
    0x100000f10 <+0>:   pushq  %rbp
    0x100000f11 <+1>:   movq   %rsp, %rbp
    0x100000f14 <+4>:   subq   $0x40, %rsp
    0x100000f18 <+8>:   movq   0xe1(%rip), %rax
    0x100000f1f <+15>:  leaq   -0x20(%rbp), %rcx
    0x100000f23 <+19>:  movq   (%rax), %rdx
    0x100000f26 <+22>:  movq   %rdx, -0x8(%rbp)
    0x100000f2a <+26>:  movl   $0x0, -0x2c(%rbp)
    0x100000f31 <+33>:  movq   0x68(%rip), %rdx
    0x100000f38 <+40>:  movq   %rdx, -0x20(%rbp)
    0x100000f3c <+44>:  movq   0x65(%rip), %rdx
    0x100000f43 <+51>:  movq   %rdx, -0x18(%rbp)
    0x100000f47 <+55>:  movq   %rcx, -0x28(%rbp)
    0x100000f4b <+59>:  movq   -0x28(%rbp), %rcx
 -> 0x100000f4f <+63>:  movaps (%rcx), %xmm0
 -> 0x100000f52 <+66>:  movaps %xmm0, -0x40(%rbp)
    0x100000f56 <+70>:  movq   (%rax), %rax
    0x100000f59 <+73>:  cmpq   -0x8(%rbp), %rax
    0x100000f5d <+77>:  jne    0x100000f6b
    0x100000f63 <+83>:  xorl   %eax, %eax
    0x100000f65 <+85>:  addq   $0x40, %rsp          ; breakpoint
    0x100000f69 <+89>:  popq   %rbp
    0x100000f6a <+90>:  retq
    0x100000f6b <+91>:  callq  0x100000f70
``` |

If you set the breakpoint and examine *xmm0*, you will find the float values 1.0, 2.0, 3.0, 4.0. Packed floats are stored in reverse order with the lowest element used in scalar operations. Consider the following additional line in Program I.2 (i.e., float element = result[0];).

Program I.2 Accessing the first element in result

```
#include <xmmintrin.h>
int main()
{
    float array[4] = { 1.0, 2.0, 3.0, 4.0 };
    __m128 result = _mm_load_ps(array);

    float element = result[0];

    return 0;
}
```

The float value element will contain 1.0 after the assign statement. So 1.0 is in result[0], 2.0 is in result[1], and so on. A different intrinsic could be used to set the floats in the same way they visually appear in C++ (think Little-Endian versus Big-Endian).

Example I.2 Set packed single precision

```
__m128 result = _mm_set_ps(1.0, 2.0, 3.0, 4.0);
float element = result[0];
```

If executing the code in Example I.2, element would hold 4.0 because we use the _mm_set_ps intrinsic instead of the _mm_load_ps intrinsic.
```

By having SSE registers loaded with values and intrinsic datatype variables, we can achieve low-level operations quite easily. Program I.3 shows another modification to Program I.1, an easy way to square the contents of `result`.

Program I.3 *Square elements in* `result`

```
#include <xmmintrin.h>
int main()
{
    float array[4] = { 1.0, 2.0, 3.0, 4.0 };
    __m128 result = _mm_load_ps(array);

    result = result * result;

    return 0;
}
```

The Disassembly of the `result` multiplication in Program I.3 will look something like Example I.3, which shows the Assembly instructions the compiler uses to achieve the operation.

Example I.3 Partial disassembly of Program I.3

```
0x100000f3b <+59>: movaps %xmm0, -0x40(%rbp)
0x100000f3f <+63>: mulps  -0x40(%rbp), %xmm0
0x100000f43 <+67>: movaps %xmm0, -0x40(%rbp)
```

In Example I.3, we see the values in *xmm0* are copied to memory, the elements in memory are multiplied by their counterparts in *xmm0* using the MULPS instruction with the result stored in *xmm0*, which is then copied back to memory (`result`). We could have used a multiplication intrinsic if desired, as shown in Example I.4.

Example I.4 Multiply packed single precision

```
result = _mm_mul_ps(result, result);
```

Program I.4 shows another way in which intrinsics can be used. Intrinsic datatypes can be used in aggregates such as **unions** so the elements of a vector can be manipulated easily. For example, the address of a vector and addresses of elements can be taken, and brackets [] can be used to access elements.

Program I.4 also illustrates the use of AVX2 intrinsics. AVX introduced the 256-bit YMM registers with floating-point instructions; and AVX2 introduced integer operations with YMM registers. If using Clang or GCC, the -mavx2 complier flag is necessary to enable the AVX2 instruction set for a target. Specific flags can be used for each extension (e.g., -msse, -msse4, -msse4.2). Another approach is to enable all available extensions supported by the processor using -march=native. **APPENDIX G: USING CPUID** explains how CPUID can be used to test for extensions supported by a processor.

Program I.4 Add thirty-two packed 8-bit integers

C++

```cpp
#include <immintrin.h>
// also set -mavx2 compiler flag

union U32i
{
    __m256i v;
    int8_t a[32];
};

int main()
{
    U32i testing;

    for(int i = 0; i < 32; i++){
        testing.a[i] = i;
    }

    __m256i v2 = _mm256_add_epi8(testing.v, testing.v);  // VPADDB

    _mm256_load_si256(&v2);  // VMOVDQA

    return 0;  // set breakpoint here
}
```

The U32i union contains an __m256i 256-bit integer vector (v), and sharing the same memory space is an array of thirty-two int8_t 8-bit integers (a). Using a *union* allows us to access all elements of the vector via the array. We use a for loop to fill the vector with integers in ascending order from 0 to 31. Then, the instance of the union in Program I.4, testing, serves as a parameter for two intrinsics.

First, we create another vector (v2) that stores the result of the intrinsic addition. We just add the vector to itself, effectively doubling all the values simultaneously. Note that the _epi8 suffix indicates extended packed 8-bit integers (extended meaning AVX and YMM as opposed to SSE and XMM). Second, we load the signed integers in the 256-bit vector into a YMM register. The Disassembly of the intrinsics is shown in Example I.5.

Example I.5 Partial disassembly of Program I.4

```
0x100000f6f <+79>:   vmovaps 0x40(%rsp), %ymm0
0x100000f75 <+85>:   vmovaps %ymm0, 0xa0(%rsp)
0x100000f7e <+94>:   vmovaps %ymm0, 0x80(%rsp)
0x100000f87 <+103>:  vmovaps 0xa0(%rsp), %ymm1
0x100000f90 <+112>:  vpaddb %ymm0, %ymm1, %ymm0
0x100000f94 <+116>:  vmovaps %ymm0, (%rsp)
```

Breaking down the Disassembly: (1) the vector values are moved to *ymm0*, (2) the vector values are copied to two memory locations (a copy of each parameter) by using the VMOVAPS instruction, (3) the vector is copied to *ymm1*, (4) the VPADDB instruction adds *ymm0* and *ymm1*, saving the result to *ymm0*, and (5) the result is saved back to memory.

Notice that even though intrinsics are in the form of functions, with return values and parameters, no actual *call* takes place, similar to inline functions. Yet, some behaviors are similar, which is why the vector is copied to memory locations in pass-by-value fashion; a local copy is made for each parameter. Also, even if an intrinsic is used that has an SSE or AVX equivalent, such as our second intrinsic in Program I.4, the compiler may not use the equivalent. A more optimal instruction or combination of instructions may be used to accomplish the task. In Program I.4, the *ymm0* register already holds the vector values after the addition, so the load intrinsic is optimized away.

Index

Made in the USA
San Bernardino, CA
29 November 2019